SCHOOL COUNSELING IN THE 21ST CENTURY

School Counseling in the 21st Century brings the theoretical aspects of school counseling to life. As they move through the book, school counselors in training will begin to identify and develop the significant pieces of a comprehensive school counseling program. They will also experience, through real and relevant case studies, how school counselors are using technology, assessment data, and leadership skills to implement effective programs aimed at serving their students. Each chapter reflects on how the national model for school counseling, standards of practice, multicultural skills, and ethical guidelines are the foundation of building comprehensive programs. *School Counseling in the 21st Century* comprehensively addresses the 2016 CACREP Standards: the beginning of each chapter outlines which core and school counseling standards are addressed, and chapters support CACREP's requirement for material on multicultural counseling, ultimately enhancing readers' knowledge and effectiveness in working with diverse populations.

Sejal Parikh Foxx, PhD, is an associate professor of counselor education and the director of the school counseling program at the University of North Carolina at Charlotte.

Stanley B. Baker, PhD, NCC, LPC, is professor of counselor education at North Carolina State University. He is the founding editor of *Professional School Counseling*.

Edwin R. Gerler, Jr., EdD, is professor of counselor education at North Carolina State University and the founding editor of the *Journal of School Violence*.

SCHOOL COUNSELING IN THE 21ST CENTURY

Sixth Edition

Sejal Parikh Foxx, Stanley B. Baker,
and Edwin R. Gerler, Jr.

Routledge
Taylor & Francis Group

NEW YORK AND LONDON

This edition published 2017
by Routledge
711 Third Avenue, New York, NY 10017

and by Routledge
2 Park Square, Milton Park, Abingdon, Oxon, OX14 4RN

Routledge is an imprint of the Taylor & Francis Group, an informa business

First edition published in 1992 by Macmillan Publishing Company
Fifth edition published in 2007 by Pearson

Library of Congress Cataloging-in-Publication Data
Names: Foxx, Sejal Parikh.
Title: School counseling in the 21st century / Sejal Parikh Foxx, Stanley B. Baker, and Edwin R. Gerler, Jr.
Description: New York : Routledge, 2016.
Identifiers: LCCN 2016001143 | ISBN 9781138838284 (hardback : alk. paper) | ISBN 9781138838291 (pbk. : alk. paper) | ISBN 9781315734477 (ebook)
Subjects: LCSH: Educational counseling—Encyclopedias.
Classification: LCC LB1027.5 .F668 2017 | DDC 371.4—dc23
LC record available at http://lccn.loc.gov/2016001143

ISBN: 978-1-138-83828-4 (hbk)
ISBN: 978-1-138-83829-1 (pbk)
ISBN: 978-1-315-73447-7 (ebk)

Typeset in Simoncini Garamond
by Apex CoVantage, LLC

Visit the companion website: www.routledge.com/cw/foxx

Printed and bound in the United States of America by
Edwards Brothers Malloy on sustainably sourced paper

To my number one cheerleader, my rock, and my husband, Shawn. You are the epitome of what it means to be a partner. To my family, I would not be where I am today without your love and support.

Sejal Parikh Foxx

To my wife, partner, and best friend, Mary Esther, and our family team members: Susan, David, Edwin, Elizabeth, John, Mary Tiffany, Amanda, Jonathan, Colin, Stephen, and Sailor

Stanley B. Baker

To my wife and best friend, Muffin Padgett Gerler.

Edwin R. Gerler, Jr.

CONTENTS

1 THE SCHOOL COUNSELING PROFESSION   1

2 TOWARD A COMPREHENSIVE MODEL FOR PROFESSIONAL SCHOOL COUNSELING   21

3 ACCOUNTABILITY AND ASSESSMENT IN SCHOOL COUNSELING   51

11 PARTNERS IN BUILDING A POSTSECONDARY EDUCATION–GOING CULTURE   311

12 BEYOND THE TRAINING PROGRAM: A SCHOOL COUNSELING CAREER   327

PREFACE

This book is a compilation of each author's efforts to contribute to the training and development of school counselors who are well prepared to support students in the 21st century. We each bring unique insights and experiences to contribute to the writings in this book. These insights are based on diverse experiences from our work as school counselors, counselor educators, and researchers. Although we are currently employed in graduate training programs, we are firmly grounded in the current practices in the field. We also wrote this book from our own experiences as school counselors that live with each of us daily. Some of these experiences are advocating for our role with administrators, working with families who have lost their possessions because of house fires, referring students out to community health agencies for mental services, and helping seniors apply for financial aid and scholarships. Given we each value and believe in the importance of multicultural counseling, it is our hope that you read this book through that lens. For it is that lens that will help you develop into a professional school counselor who is determined, willing, and able to work with students and families from all different backgrounds and walks of life.

From the moment you open this textbook, you will see a table of contents with the titles of 12 chapters. We thought very carefully about these chapters, as we wanted to give you as much insight about current status of the profession as we could. For many of you, this is your first school counseling course and, therefore, we wanted to walk you through this dynamic profession by providing details about U.S. models, standards, roles, and skills. Although these are simple terms when reading, they hold weight in meaning and action. As such, we have provided the human side of this work by providing real case studies throughout and opportunities for reflection in each chapter. Each chapter of this book also gives you an opportunity to develop the components of a comprehensive school counseling program and integrate technology into those practices. These are the skills of a 21st-century school counselor, and we hope that the work you begin here will continue and evolve as you move through your training program and beyond.

We are so excited that you have chosen to join the profession of school counseling. It is you who will continue to lead this profession so that students are served in the way they deserve. When you read the final chapter and close this book, we hope to have further sparked your desire and commitment to join this profession. Remember, your decision to join this profession is a personal and professional calling. Keep intact the reasons you chose to enter, as we know the work will be challenging yet rewarding.

Finally, some of you may still have copies of the previous editions of this textbook. You may notice that the first author is a new contributor. As first author, I want you to know that I was invited by the previous authors of the first five editions to join them on this journey. I took this invitation as an honor and, thereafter, quickly committed to give my best work. Stan and Ed, thank you for leading, teaching me the ropes, and being patient every step of the way. As readers of this textbook, I hope you sense and appreciate the balance of tradition with innovation.

ACKNOWLEDGMENTS

There are several individuals who have contributed to the development of this textbook. First, we would like to thank graduate assistant Merry Leigh Dameron, who proofread each of the chapters and references, assisted with permissions, and supported with the development of the accompanying materials. We would also like to acknowledge Karen Arrington, Bradley Demmin, Carlyn Joseph, Zachary Massey, and Jacob Olsen for contributing their stories and helping bringing our chapters to life.

THE SCHOOL COUNSELING PROFESSION

1

RELATED STANDARDS OF PRACTICE

CACREP CORE	F.1.a, d, f, g
CACREP SCHOOL COUNSELING	G.1.a, G.2.l, G.2.m

Goal: To introduce the school counseling profession and present our ideas for building a comprehensive school counseling program.

As the authors of this textbook, we have together more than 17 years of experience as school counselors and educators in elementary, middle, and high school settings and 72 years of experience as counselor educators. We have informed our teaching practices through our own experiences in the field, continued partnerships with school districts, and ongoing professional development and research. Over this span of 72 years, we have also heard countless stories from our students about their decision to join this dynamic profession. Here are some of their reasons:

> School counseling is a field that I am truly passionate about. I always knew I wanted to help youth navigate through all of life's overwhelming challenges. Not only does this profession require having the compassion for young people but having the willingness and heart to work with others that have the ability to create impactful changes in their lives. I also think another important component of this work is being able to be an advocate for children. I strongly believe I have been called to work on behalf of children in order to help them become productive, successful individuals.
>
> Karen Arrington, UNC Charlotte

The reason that I have chosen the path as a future school counselor is because I want to make a larger impact with students. Not only will I be able to reach a larger number of students, but I will also be able to emphasize many more areas other than the academic. In my current role as a special education teacher, it is my job in the classroom to push primarily academic success; I want more than that. I understand that development of individuals comes from many different factors. Even though I will not have access to a lot of those factors, it makes me feel good knowing that I can still help students proceed with their lives as more well-rounded people.

Bradley Demmin, UNC Charlotte

The calling to be a school counselor is both rewarding and daunting because it challenges you to serve one of the most oppressed populations. Children have so much to say but a lot of the times lack the platform to voice their opinions, thoughts, and concerns. I feel like I was led to school counseling so that I could advocate for adolescents, one of the most misunderstood populations (in my opinion), and help create a safe place where they can feel cared for and heard. The relationships created with these students is incredibly therapeutic and one that can positively impact them and their decisions throughout adolescences and into adulthood. My role is not to judge or discipline them but to allow them to be vulnerable and feel safe with whatever they bring to the table.

Carlyn Joseph, UNC Charlotte

Growing up I was very fortunate to have many different positive adult role models in my life, but some of the most impactful for me were my school counselors. My school counselors were very motivational and always advocated for myself and other classmates not only in our academic development, but our growth towards our social and career development as well. I am very passionate towards giving back to a profession that molded me into the individual that I have become today. My love for therapeutic and positive communication or connection amongst students is something that I strive to continuously implement in my practice going forward in being a school counselor.

Zachary Massey, UNC Charlotte

We imagine that you have your own reasons for joining the ranks of this profession. One assumption is what brought you here is a commitment and passion to help others. It is our hope that the thoughts and feelings during this time are carried with you long after you graduate from your training program. Therefore, in this chapter, we help aspiring counselors understand the school counseling profession and the challenges they face in preparing to become outstanding school counseling professionals. This textbook is unique in that it offers a place to not only acquire knowledge but also develop skills that will bring the graduate classroom and the practice of school counseling into closer harmony.

In addition, the end of every chapter in this book offers you the opportunity to:

- Develop a portion of a comprehensive school counseling program,
- Share your voice on the material we presented using reflection points, and
- Incorporate the use of technology, thereby helping you develop your technology skills.

INTRODUCTION

"HISTORY IN THE MAKING"

In July 2014, First Lady Michelle Obama was the general session keynote speaker at the annual American School Counselor Association (ASCA) conference in Orlando, Florida. This moment was historic for a number of reasons. First, Mrs. Obama announced that, for the first time in history, the ASCA School Counselor of the Year would be honored at the White House. Second, she shared her Reach Higher Initiative, which aligns with President Barack Obama's 2020 College Completion Goal (U.S. Department of Education, 2011) to expand postsecondary access for all students. In her speech, Mrs. Obama noted that school counselors were central to this mission. Although we now have a national stage to highlight the important work of our profession, this moment has not arrived in isolation. In fact, this moment has come to fruition from years of evolution.

The profession known today as school counseling began as individual manifestations of the Progressive Reform Movement in the late 19th and early 20th centuries and is perhaps most clearly depicted today by the ASCA's National Model for School Counseling Programs (ASCA, 2012). Gysbers and Henderson (2000) refer to this century-long transition as "positions to programs" (p. 3). Just who determines what school counselors do has not been clear over the past century. School boards and administrators, state departments of education or public instruction, counselor educators, textbook authors, parents and students, and school counselors themselves have had their say while not speaking with a unified voice. Consequently, the role of professional school counselors still lacks clarity. We applaud the efforts of the ASCA to achieve clarity through the development and presentation of National Standards for School Counseling Programs (Campbell & Dahir, 1997) and subsequently of the National Model for School Counseling Programs (ASCA, 2001).

School Counseling in the 21st Century is designed for an introductory course in school counseling to help build the groundwork for a strong professional identity. It is evident that virtually all higher education programs for training school counselors must meet the standards established by respective state departments of education/public instruction in order for their graduates to receive school counseling licenses or certificates. These minimum standards vary from state to state. Among the virtually universal requirements these standards present is coursework designed to socialize the students to the school counseling profession. Enhancing that socialization process is the general goal of this textbook.

STANDARDS OF THE COUNCIL FOR ACCREDITATION OF COUNSELING AND RELATED EDUCATIONAL PROGRAMS

Although license/certification standards vary from state to state, the Council for Accreditation of Counseling and Related Educational Programs (CACREP, 2016) provides that most universal set of standards for training school counselors as well as those preparing for such fields a community/agency, college, and mental health counseling. The CACREP Standards for school counseling are equal to or more comprehensive than those established by the state departments of education/public instruction.

Table 1.1 presents the eight common core areas of the 2016 CACREP Standards. The present text is designed to highlight the eight standards in the Professional Identity core area so that students have the desired curricular experience and acquire "demonstrated knowledge."

The 2016 CACREP Standards also present a section devoted to the standards for school counseling programs (www.cacrep.org/section-5-entry-level-specialty-areas-school-counseling/). The three primary standards are as follows:

1. Foundation for School Counseling
2. Contextual Dimensions of School Counseling
3. Practice.

Appendix A presents the CACREP Standards for School Counseling Programs. This text addresses many of these standards, either in depth or via an overview. Some state departments of education/public instruction use the CACREP Standards completely or as an option in the school counselor licensure/certification process. Those individuals who have completed CACREP-accredited programs or state-approved programs not accredited by CACREP (who have acquired 2 years of postgraduate experience) and have received acceptable scores on the National Counselor Examination (NCE) can become National Certified Counselors by the National Board for Certified Counselors. In some states, successful completion of the NCE is one of the criteria for becoming a licensed professional counselor. We view the present text as a vehicle for providing

TABLE 1.1 *CACREP Core Areas for Entry-Level Programs*

Core	Areas for Entry-Level Programs
1.	Professional Counseling Orientation and Ethical Practice
2.	Social and Cultural Diversity
3.	Human Growth and Development
4.	Career Development
5.	Counseling and Helping Relationships
6.	Group Counseling and Group Work
7.	Assessment and Testing
8.	Research and Program Evaluation

Note: CACREP = Council for Accreditation of Counseling and Related Educational Programs

information and exercises in support of instruction in courses designed to meet the professional identity goals established by CACREP and state departments of education/public instruction. As well, the text will help individuals prepare for the NCE and for the Educational Testing Service's Professional School Counselor (#5421) PRAXIS II test that is required in some states as part of the licensure/certification process.

OUR BACKGROUND

Although we attempted to be evenhandedly objective on our treatment of ideas and information, the content covered and the point of view presented in this text is influenced by the experiences and philosophy of the authors. Each of us has been associated with the school counseling profession for a number of years, and this text has a history of five previous editions dating back to 1992. The first author (SPF) is the newest contributor and began her entry-level program at the University of North Florida. She began working as an elementary school counselor in Jacksonville, Florida, and, after 3 years, she made the transition into a high school counseling position in Orange Park, Florida. Her experience in academia comprises the University of North Florida (3 years), North Carolina State University (2 years) and the University of North Carolina at Charlotte (present). The second author (SBB) began his entry-level program at the University of Minnesota, Minneapolis, in 1960 and opened his career as a high school counselor in 1964 at Janesville, Wisconsin, senior high school. His higher education career as a counselor educator spans over 3 decades from 1971 (doctoral degree from SUNY at Buffalo) to the present at both Penn State and North Carolina State universities. The third author (ERG) completed his entry-level program at Bucknell University in Louisburg, Pennsylvania in 1969 and opened his career as an elementary/middle school counselor in Millville, Pennsylvania, in 1972. His higher education career spans 3 decades from 1975 (doctorate from Penn State) to the present at both the University of Wisconsin–Whitewater and North Carolina

State University. In the remainder of this opening chapter, we present topics presenting information that students enrolled in an introductory course should be aware of at the beginning of the course and the training program so they can carefully process the meaning of that information for them during the remainder of the course and the training program.

PROFESSIONAL SCHOOL COUNSELORS

Are school counselors professionals? If they are professionals, what defines them as such? *Professional* is a term used frequently and somewhat loosely in U.S. society because it seems to create an aura of respectability. Some individuals do not deserve that respectability, whereas others truly do. Some professionals assume the respectability and accompanying status without giving much thought to the real meaning of the word *professional* and to the responsibilities it implies. Others know full well the responsibilities associated with being a professional. Ideally, all professionals would fit into the latter category.

A *profession* is a vocation requiring special knowledge or education in some department of learning or science; a *professional* is one belonging to a learned or skilled profession; and *professionalism* is the character, spirit, or methods of a professional or the standing, practice, or methods of a professional as distinguished from an amateur, according to the *American College Dictionary*. If school counselors are professionals, then school counseling is a vocation requiring special knowledge or education in some department of learning or science. What is the department of learning or science from which school counselors receive their special knowledge? This is a somewhat difficult question to answer. The historical information presented in Chapter 2 reveals the guidance field from which school counseling evolved had several influences, including vocational guidance, psychometrics, mental health, and clinical psychology. Further, with the added emergence of social networking (Boyd, 2014; Casas, Del Rey, & Ortega-Ruiz, 2013) there are more complexities as to how school counselors can respond. Thus, the evolution of school counseling as a profession has not been clear-cut.

School counseling is a part of two larger applied professions: counseling and education. These broader fields draw from the behavioral sciences such as anthropology, political science, psychology, and sociology. They have developed their own knowledge bases. Both have influenced school counseling. School counseling has been developing its own knowledge base over the years, which also influences practicing and emerging school counseling professionals. Consequently, school counseling is a profession with the behavioral sciences and the applied fields of counseling and education as its foundational departments of learning, and a profession in the process of developing its own knowledge base.

Drawing on the work of Barber (1965) and Greenwood (1957), Herr and Cramer (1987) suggest additional criteria for attributing professional status to a vocation. In summary, those criteria are as follows:

- The members have a service orientation (they are educated to serve community rather than self-interests);

- The degree of self-control is high (practitioner behaviors are regulated via community sanctions, ethical codes, and the like);
- Systems of rewards (monetary and honorary) are included that are not only symbols of work-related achievements but also ends in themselves;
- A professional culture is perpetuated via consistent training programs.

It is our contention that school counselors have a service orientation, are regulated by community sanctions and ethical codes, derive their monetary and honorary rewards from work-related achievements, and have consistent training programs. Therefore, the evidence indicates that school counseling is a profession and that school counselors are professionals who should be expected to behave in a professional manner.

COUNSELING IN THE CONTEXT OF EDUCATION

According to Holland (1997), persons and environments interact, and both individuals and working environments may have personality types or structures. Of the six Holland personality types, school counselors tend to be primarily social. Social types value helping others and tend to be friendly, enthusiastic, understanding, receptive, warm, and generous. They function best in predominantly social environments. In many schools, the predominant environment is not social. Unfortunately, the dominant environment in many schools is conventional, and conventional environments tend to be conservative and dogmatic. Preferred traits in conventional environments are conformity, conscientiousness, practical-mindedness, neatness, obedience, and docility.

The primary actors in creating and maintaining the school's environment are the administrators and teachers, in that order. Principals clearly influence the environment in their schools. What they value most will influence their own behavior and what they reinforce positively or negatively in the values and behaviors of their subordinates, in the school rules, and in the assignment of responsibilities within their purview. Teachers will influence the environment because they are the largest single group of professionals in a school. Depending on the circumstances, the teachers may or may not reflect the environmental preferences of the principal, especially if the principal was not involved in hiring them. Although teachers and counselors may differ from their principal(s) with respect to personality type, Holland (1997) believes that the most powerful individual in the environment will have the greatest influence. A principal can influence the environment as a model or by force of personality and will.

What does this mean for school counselors in training? Most prospective school counselors look forward enthusiastically to a career of applying the values, knowledge, and competencies acquired from their training in an environment that is conducive to achieving their goals. Unfortunately, many school administrators and teachers have other ideas about what counselors should do. Fitch, Newby, Ballestero, and Marshall (2001) found that, although many of the future school administrators they surveyed were aware of and appreciated roles and duties for school counselors that were commensurate with their training, some of them also rated noncounseling functions such as discipline, record keeping, and registration as important.

Two factors about school administrators and their training have been and will continue to be challenges for school counselors. First, many individuals who become school administrators are more conventional than social types of people. Second, programs that train school administrators rarely attempt to inform trainees about the roles and functions of school counselors according to either the content of the counselor education training programs or the content of the standards for training school counselors of the respective states. Although counselor educators have attempted to address the second challenge both individually and collectively, their efforts have not been very successful, and we do not envision a breakthrough in that domain in the near future. Therefore, the brunt of trying to do something constructive about this challenge seems to fall upon the shoulders of individual school counselors at the grassroots level—each trying to make an impact on his or her own environment in order to make it more congruent. We conclude that the availability of the ASCA National Model for School Counseling Programs may be the resource school counselors can use to meet this challenge.

Some beginning school counselors experience the challenge of incongruent environments as interns and others do so in their first jobs. Not all school counselors will experience this incongruence. Some will find themselves in a school environment that is congruent with their type and goals. Others will not, and we do not know the exact probabilities. Regarding this challenge, Fitch et al. (2001) highlight the importance of the job interview. They recommend using the first interview to present a summary of one's programmatic plans and goals to the chief school administrator. The administrator's response to this introduction is an important indicator of what the environment is and will be like for the prospective counselor. It is recommended that you take advantage of the opportunities to build a portion of a comprehensive school counseling program as outlined in each chapter. Ideally you can share this portfolio with your future employer in efforts to demonstrate your how your training has provided you with the knowledge and skills to make a positive impact in your school building.

THE PROFESSIONAL IDENTITY OF SCHOOL COUNSELORS

YOU NEVER TOLD US ABOUT . . .

Occasionally, interns and former students challenge us about not preparing them for the often onerous noncounseling functions they encounter on the job as school counselors. The implicit message is that, somehow, we should have included preparation for those functions in the training program. Should we write chapters about and teach units on how to build and monitor master schedules; coordinate testing programs; discipline misbehaving students; set up filing systems; and conduct lunchroom, hall, and bus duty? We think not! These are not functions that are included in role statements by the ASCA, CACREP, and state departments of education or public instruction. We view our role as ensuring that the training program meets the standards of the relevant professional and educational oversight organizations. We must prepare school counselors to be proficient at what they are supposed to do. On the other hand, we are very aware that many school counselors are assigned noncounseling tasks. Therefore, we do feel responsible for preparing school counseling students to cope with the noncounseling challenges. Our formula for meeting the challenges is as follows.

First, school counselors must know what they should be doing and be proficient at the requisite competencies. Proficiency leads to demonstrated competence that garners support from significant others, such as parents, students, teachers, and administrators. Second, school counselors will be challenged to advocate for themselves and their profession, as are counselor educators. Third, school counselors, as advocates, are challenged to provide leadership in helping colleagues and administrators discover better ways to get things done and use counselor time and talents wisely.

Our role as counselor educators then is to make students aware of the noncounseling challenges and prepare them to cope successfully—not train them to be proficient at noncounseling tasks. The remainder of this section of the chapter addresses some of the most prevalent noncounseling functions that school counselors may be requested to perform.

DEALING WITH RESPONSIBILITY FOR NONCOUNSELING FUNCTIONS

Because of its diverse origins, school counseling has experienced greater identity problems than other professions in the field of education. On the one hand, most laypeople and professional educators have clear and relatively similar ideas about the roles of teachers and administrators. On the other hand, those same people have widely differing opinions about the role of school counselors. Counselor education and training programs for school counselors have gradually reached the point where they have more similarities than differences; the differences often reflect the experiences and preferences of the counselor educators more than radical differences in the training programs. Professional organizations dedicated to promoting the counseling professions (the American Counseling Association [ACA], Association for Counselor Education and Supervision [ACES], and ASCA) have developed and promoted role statements such as "Role Statement: The School Counselor" (ASCA, 1990) and developed training standards. In addition, CACREP is an accrediting agency whose attention is focused on counselor training programs. A relatively new accrediting agency, CACREP may have considerable influence in the 21st century. Although counselor education and ASCA have gradually developed a somewhat uniform identity for school counselors through its training programs and professional literature, the message has not reached the decision makers in the schools; many school counselors still find themselves engaging in functions such as scheduling, registering, test coordination, and preparing individual education plans that are unrelated or only remotely related to their training. These noncounseling functions, often highly regarded by individual principals and teachers, receive priority over counseling functions, leaving counselors to attend to noncounseling duties first and to engage in counseling functions in the remaining time. These conditions discourage some from entering the school counseling field; cause others to leave early, defeated and disappointed; cause some to adjust and become pseudocounselors; confuse students, parents, and colleagues about the roles and functions of counselors; and leave many counselors disappointed in their training and trainers because they were not properly prepared for the noncounseling responsibilities and because their mentors cannot relieve them of the onerous responsibilities.

Fortunately, there are actions school counselors can take to combat many of these challenges. Clark and Amatea (2004) offer recommendations for school counselors and counselor educators that may help them address these challenges. Teachers in elementary, middle, and secondary school settings were interviewed, and the themes derived from those interviews suggest that school counselors can be most effective and accepted if they communicate and collaborate in the process of helping students achieve success academically. Being visible and involved in the total school were additional themes.

Scheduling

School counselors have acquired some noncounseling functions. One of the most onerous and time-consuming is the gatekeeping and custodial tasks associated with scheduling. This administrative function has become the traditional responsibility of counselors in most secondary schools. Secondary school counselors, responding to a survey from Tennyson, Miller, Skovholt, and Williams (1989), reported that as a group they are involved more frequently in scheduling than in any other activity. Although it is a lesser task in middle and elementary schools, scheduling may still be among the responsibilities of middle and elementary school counselors. Gatekeeping occurs when counselors must determine which students will be allowed to enroll in specific classes and which students will be allowed to change classes. These responsibilities place counselors in potentially adversarial relationships with students and teachers, groups who should view counselors in more positive ways for counseling services to be received favorably. Students, and sometimes their parents, view counselors as adversaries whom they must cajole or entreat in order to receive limited resources (e.g., oversubscribed courses) or exceptions to the rules (e.g., making a course change after a course-drop deadline has passed). These encounters are hardly conducive to healthy helping relationships outside the scheduling domain. For some students, these are the only or initial encounters, and their impressions are colored unfavorably thereafter.

Teachers may view counselors as adversaries because, as gatekeepers, the counselors are directly responsible for fluctuating class enrollments. All teachers want class enrollments that are both consistent and sufficient. Receipt of additional students after the term has started creates stress for teachers, as does having students leave classes suddenly. Not having enough students in an elective course is threatening to teachers whose jobs are vulnerable. The number of students in their classes and the amount of student traffic into and out of their classes are annoyances that teachers attribute to the scheduling gatekeepers. When they are unhappy with the results of gatekeeping efforts, they blame the gatekeepers. Our experiences as school counselors, counselor educators, and consultants have led to the conclusion that the opinions of most secondary school teachers about the value and competence of their counselors are heavily influenced by the way counselors are perceived to deal with scheduling gatekeeping chores. Not being able to please teachers as scheduling gatekeepers may condemn many school counselors to eternal disfavor, negating all their counseling accomplishments in the minds of these important colleagues.

Custodial tasks associated with scheduling include correcting mistakes on individual students' schedules and on master schedules; organizing, filing, and distributing student schedules; and screening individual student schedule requests for mistakes. These are tasks that can be performed by clerical personnel or mechanically (via computer) but are often done manually by school counselors. When the schools begin their academic years, they are captive to the activities and abilities of a handful of counselors who are trying to fit all students into the master schedule. Doing such work on a large scale is a demeaning and wasteful misuse of professionals trained to deliver much different services. Students and teaching colleagues, observing counselors performing these custodial functions, conclude that counselors are essentially professional clerks. Therefore, they, too, often dismiss counselors as having few worthy services to offer or as being too busy with clerical tasks to be bothered with higher order needs of students and colleagues.

Scheduling is an administrative function, but principals, usually fewer in number than counselors, do not have the time or the inclination for most gatekeeping or custodial tasks. Interestingly, however, they usually control scheduling policies tightly. If scheduling is an administrative function and if the role of administrators is making policy, then they do need help with such gatekeeping and custodial responsibilities. Our position is that using counselors as gatekeepers and custodians is a mistake. If counselors are not the appropriate choice, who is? Even though scheduling is an administrative function, it serves teachers as well, providing them with a system that controls enrollments, assigns students to appropriate courses, and indicates where the participants are to meet. Therefore, because teachers benefit so greatly from the scheduling function, one can argue that they should be involved in the process. They should be involved in scheduling but not in the gatekeeping and custodial tasks any more than counselors should. Placing these responsibilities on teachers will have the same negative effects on them as it has on counselors.

Because the master schedule is an essential component of basic education and touches the lives of everyone in the schools, a team approach to making it work seems appropriate and fair. Baker (1982) offers an idea for implementing the team approach that provides basic responsibilities and leaves the details to those who might adapt the idea to specific settings. Specific task categories are identified. Adapted from that idea, five task categories are recommended here:

1. *Instruction* consists of administrators' informing counselors, teachers, students, parents and guardians, and other interested persons about the purposes, procedures, and content of the schedule and the scheduling process.

2. *Direction and control,* or gatekeeping, is an administrative function, so this can be the responsibility of administrators with the assistance of teachers, counselors, and clerical and paraprofessional personnel as consultants.

3. *Consultation* involves teachers, counselors, and students in the process of advising administrators about the strengths and weaknesses of the scheduling process and about the needs of individuals and of the system. For example, teachers can suggest that students be assigned to certain classes, counselors can provide information about student problems associated with scheduling, and students can make their own needs and opinions known. Administrators can serve as clearinghouses for this information with the assistance of clerical and paraprofessional personnel.

4. *Counseling* occurs when counselors, administrators, and teachers help students make decisions that affect their choices and schedules. In a system managed by administrators who make the policies, it stands to reason that they should also be the gatekeepers, setting rules about entering and leaving courses and making decisions when the rules are appealed or challenged. Teachers and counselors may provide counsel when asked.

5. *Custodial tasks* (e.g., processing and filing documents) are to be performed by clerical and paraprofessional personnel responsible to administrators.

This plan places the gatekeeping responsibilities in the administrative domain where they should be, recommends that clerical and paraprofessional personnel perform the custodial tasks they have been trained to do, and places teachers and counselors in the active and professional roles of fulfilling the consultation and counseling functions they have been trained to provide. If implemented, plans of this nature will free counselors from some undesirable noncounseling responsibilities and offer enhanced opportunities to provide professional services more attuned to their training.

Discipline

Many counselors find that students they have requested to come to their office for service-oriented reasons often arrive displaying symptoms of tension and anxiety. The more assertive students want to know what they did wrong, and others behave reticently until put at ease by a quieting explanation or simply by an opportunity to experience a friendly, empathic atmosphere. Why do so many children and adolescents approach appointments with school counselors with tension and anxiety? Why do they think they must be in trouble if a counselor has asked to see them? To attribute these reactions to one cause would be an oversimplification of what is probably a complex set of reasons. Two very real and important reasons are that some counselors have disciplinary responsibilities and that others are assumed to have them. In either case, school counselors are viewed as disciplinarians by many students.

Discipline and guidance may have been linked through the concept of deans of men and women that was popular in student services before the influence of client-centered counseling ideas and before the counseling professions developed clear statements of roles and functions. Early, simpler models of guidance viewed student services workers (e.g., deans) as wise, caring, and authoritarian individuals who were parent figures, providing support, advice, and discipline as needed. Currently, discipline is an administrative function in elementary, middle, and secondary schools. All disciplinary actions are subject to the scrutiny of school administrators. The schools that have assistant principals recognize them as having student discipline among their responsibilities. Discipline and counseling are antithetical when students are to be lectured, scolded, punished, interrogated, or accused. If counselors engage in such negative interactions with students, no matter how deserving, it will be very difficult to also establish empathic, unconditional helping relationships with them. Students will then view going to the counselor's office as an aversive experience—one to be avoided if at all possible.

One of the best solutions to this dilemma will be recognition by the school administrators' profession, trainers of school administrators, and individual administrators that school counselors are professionals with their own definite and valuable programs to offer (e.g., the ASCA National Model for School Counseling Programs); they are not administrative assistants. Although individual counselors may contribute to this change, most are too isolated and powerless to do so; those who are successful may have only local or regional influence. A solution to this problem and to all the other noncounseling responsibilities that interfere with counseling services will probably have to come at a national level, through the efforts of professional organizations like the National Education Association, ACA, ACES, and ASCA. These organizations may influence members of other professional organizations such as the National Association of Secondary School Principals and perhaps legislators and the public. In the meantime, counselors are left with the challenge to devise solutions at the local and area levels.

School counselors who balk at the assignment of disciplinary responsibilities will probably have to determine ways to change the thinking of those who assign them such responsibilities. Successful attention-getting approaches may range from diplomacy to confrontation. Whatever approach is used, it will probably have to be accompanied by efforts to educate those who make the decisions. In short, school counselors need to be advocates for themselves and their profession. Professional counseling associations have helpful resources, primarily publications and media, and counselor educators may also be willing to offer consultation services.

Overcoming the image of being a disciplinarian requires more subtle efforts. Proactive strategies seem in order. The best way to change an undesirable image is to create a desired one. For example, elementary school counselors can engage in programmatic activities in the classroom that help them achieve counseling and developmental goals while introducing them to students as the kinds of professionals they want to be known as—caring, empathic, helpful, nonthreatening, and knowledgeable. Middle school and secondary school counselors can engage in similar activities. All school counselors may also be able to use individual counseling contacts to introduce themselves appropriately. Get-acquainted interviews allow counselors to reach out to prospective student clients proactively and to establish a preferred agenda. Included in topics for get-acquainted interviews can be open-ended questions about interests and hobbies, future plans, progress in school, recreational activities, and perceptions of the counseling services. Responses to open-ended questions may lead to specific topics on which students wish to work once they accept the counselor as someone to trust who may be helpful (e.g., "What things interest you?" "What else would you like to talk about today?"). Personal topics (e.g., "Tell me about your family") and questions that focus the response on other individuals (e.g., "Who is your favorite teacher?") may be too threatening for students to handle in get-acquainted interviews.

The way invitations to students are made may prevent students from assuming the worst before learning the truth. Students who are invited with an advance explanation of the purpose of the interview, oral or printed, are less likely to think they have been summoned to the office for a threatening purpose. The purpose of get-acquainted interviews is to provide students with accurate perceptions of the kinds of people counselors are and the reasons why students might visit them again, either by appointment or self-referral. Additional proactive activities include newsletters for adults and older students, in-service programs for adults, and presentations for children—all designed to communicate accurate and understandable information about counselors and their services. A proactive approach to image management requires advance planning and assertiveness in gaining opportunities to meet with those whose favorable impressions are desired.

Secretarial and Clerical Tasks

Secretaries and clerks perform noble and useful work. They choose to do so and prepare themselves accordingly before beginning their careers. School counselors, in contrast, receive specialized training at the graduate level to perform tasks other than secretarial and clerical work. School counselors need secretarial and clerical support because of the nature of their work. They must request or provide college transcripts, letters of recommendation to prospective employers, cumulative records, lesson plans and handouts for prevention programming activities, individualized educational plans, newsletters, informational fliers and memos, drop-in requests for appointments, incoming telephone calls, media and materials for the information service, tests and testing reports, and various other items. These tasks are all reasons why school counselors need clerical and secretarial support to carry out their professional responsibilities successfully. Noncounseling responsibilities such as scheduling create additional needs for clerical and secretarial support.

Despite these legitimate reasons, many school counselors have either no or little secretarial and clerical support. One result is that counselor time and energy that should be devoted to legitimate professional activities are spent on such support tasks. Another result is that the tasks are not done at all, or not done well, because there is too little time, interest, or talent for them. The first situation leads to making counselors into undertrained, part-time clerk-secretaries, and the second leads to diminished effectiveness and negative impressions by students, colleagues, and administrators. All these people are influenced by their first impressions of the obvious components of sional's services—neatness, punctuality, availability, responsiveness, dependability, anu organization.

Fair Share Duties

Fair share duties are those tasks in which all members of the school staff take some sort part. Responsibilities include monitoring bus schedules, determining whether students have met graduation requirements, organizing and monitoring student fund-raising activities, monitoring prom and banquet planning, planning and conducting award ceremonies, and monitoring the distribution of diplomas at graduation ceremonies. All these are time-consuming noncounseling functions, administrative in nature, that have been assigned to counselors, teachers, and other staff by their administrators. Few can argue that these tasks are unimportant in the life of the school, but the counseling profession argues that they are not appropriate assignments for school counselors (ASCA, 1990).

A widely held assumption in educational administration is that school counselors are supposed to serve primarily as administrative assistants to principals. How else can one explain the widespread assignment of so many noncounseling duties to school counselors? This mistaken assumption must be altered if school counseling is to achieve its necessary professional identity. In our opinion, the only way this assumption and the actions it inspires will be changed is through a concerted effort by school counselors to use data that demonstrates how the school counseling program is making a difference in the academic achievement, attendance, and positive discipline within the school.

Changes may require assertive and provocative actions by school counselors and their colleagues to get the attention of consumers, who may offer sympathetic support, and in educating administrators, who may respond in an adversarial fashion to proposals that threaten their assumptions about the role of school counselors. To do little or nothing about this will support the status quo; counselors in the 21st century, though possibly better prepared than their predecessors, will still be administrative assistants performing many noncounseling tasks unless they advocate for themselves and their role.

Substitute Teaching

Administrators sometimes find it convenient and cost-effective to call on school counselors to substitute for missing teachers and school nurses. The false assumptions and negative outcomes stated earlier apply in these instances as well. In addition, students are likely to receive lower quality instruction than from a qualified substitute teacher, and counselors engaging in substitute teaching or nursing are more vulnerable to accusations of negligence or malpractice than are qualified substitutes or than the counselors would be if they were engaging in responsibilities for which they have been trained and certified/licensed. Perhaps counselors will serve themselves and the profession better by being more the devil's advocate than the good guy or gal when asked to help out in this manner.

Challenges From Individuals and Groups Outside the School System

In the 1990s, school counseling experienced challenges to elements of and entire school counseling programs. For example, a disagreement over materials and methods led to the cancellation of an entire school counseling program in Clackamas, Oregon, and self-esteem programs in the Capistrano, California, school district were challenged as unlawful (McCullough, 1994). Although it is difficult to predict exactly what might be challenged in the future, previous challenges seem to have focused on materials, programs, and practices that are viewed by some individuals and groups as invasions of privacy, religious in nature; as unlawful psychotherapeutic interventions, sacrilegious in nature; and as in opposition to the values of the dissenting groups or individuals. The issues become emotional and tend to polarize communities, leading to nastiness, attempts at censorship, political pressuring, and bad publicity for professionals and communities.

McCullough (1994) cites prevention advice from Greg Brigman, a counselor educator who recommends the following responses:

- Contact the ASCA for information on resources and procedures,
- Have district policies for reviewing curriculum materials and follow them,
- Keep the educational community informed about programs and materials, and
- Have a clear idea of what the national and local communities want children to learn in schools.

McCullough's article provides additional specific advice to counselors. Although it is tempting to view the challengers as reactionaries, these events contain an important message for all school counselors. A careful examination of the teaching/instruction domain of the schools will usually lead one to discover that the content of courses taught in English, social studies, mathematics, science, kindergarten, third grade, and the like is the result of a curriculum development process and that the content is based on foundational principles and guidelines, studied, and approved by committees, administrators, and school boards before it is implemented. Sometimes prevention programming by school counselors has gone through much less rigorous planning and scrutiny, leaving the programs and the counselors more vulnerable when challenged. Therefore, an important message the challenges seem to provide for school counselors is that their prevention programming should be developed with as much care and scrutiny as are the academic curricula in their schools. Doing so will help make school counselors less vulnerable to outside challenges.

We hope that this introduction to school counseling provided you with a realistic perspective of working conditions and challenges. Our aim was not to present only the challenges but simply to offer perspectives that you will no doubt see, hear about, or experience yourselves. The challenge will be to use what you will learn from this textbook and your graduate program to educate others about your role and how you can use your training to support the needs of all students.

PROFESSIONAL ADVOCACY

Now that we have shared some of the challenges related to our profession, it is also important for us to highlight that we can use our knowledge, training, and skills to engage in professional advocacy. In Chapter 5, you will learn about advocating for your students, but it is important for you to be able to first advocate for your profession and your position. Given that the world of education is driven by accountability, we must also be accountable for our time and our practices. We must prove that the services we provide are necessary and effective. Therefore, in the following chapters you will learn about accountability, action research, and building comprehensive programs. These knowledge and skill domains will assist you with engaging in your own professional advocacy should the need arise.

Another form of engaging in professional advocacy is by keeping abreast about the current state of education at the federal, state, and local levels. By understanding the current climate, we can ensure that we continue to meet the standards and expectations set forth by policymakers. For example, No Child Left Behind (U.S. Department of Education, 2002) set in motion the need for accountability in schools. This mandate did not leave out school counselors. In fact, we are central to this legislation as principals are forced to make decisions about and justify the resources that exist in any school building. School counselors must now answer the question, "How are students different as a result of what we do?" (ASCA, 2012). Therefore, it is one of the aims of this textbook to assist you in developing the knowledge and skills to answer this question.

COMPREHENSIVE SCHOOL COUNSELING PROGRAM COMPONENT

1. Develop a professional mission statement that includes your philosophy about your role as a school counselor.

REFLECTION POINT

1. What are your reasons for becoming a professional school counselor?
2. Survey a sample of school counselors and ask them how they educate their principal, teachers, staff, and parents about their role.

3.   Interview two school counselors about their daily tasks and how they manage their time. Ask if they engage in any noncounseling duties and how they navigate those situations with the principal.

APPLICATION TO TECHNOLOGY

1.   Create a professional website and add pieces of your comprehensive school counseling program components as they are developed.
2.   Add your professional mission statement to your website.

REFERENCES

American School Counselor Association. (1990). *Role statement: The school counselor. ASCA guide to membership resources.* Alexandria, VA: Author.

American School Counselor Association. (2012). *The ASCA National Model: A framework for school counseling programs* (3rd ed.). Alexandria, VA: Author.

Baker, S. B. (1982). Free school counselors from gatekeeping and custodial tasks. *NASSP Bulletin, 66*(457), 110–112.

Barber, B. (1965). Some problems in the sociology of a profession. In K. S. Lynn (Ed.), *The Professions in America* (pp. 15–34). Boston, MA: Houghton Mifflin.

Boyd, D. (2014). *It's complicated: The social lives of networked teens.* New Haven, CT: Yale University Press.

Campbell, C. A., & Dahir, C. A. (1997). *Sharing the vision: The national standards for school counseling programs.* Alexandria, VA: American School Counselor Association.

Casas, J. A., Del Rey, R., & Ortega-Ruiz, R. (2013). Bullying and cyberbullying: Convergent and divergent predictor variables. *Computers in Human Behavior, 29,* 580–587.

Clark, M. A., & Amatea, E. (2004). Teacher perceptions of expectations of school counselor contributions: Implications for program planning and training. *Professional School Counseling, 8,* 132–140.

Council for Accreditation of Counseling and Related Educational Programs. (2016). 2016 *CACREP standards.* Retrieved from http://www.cacrep.org/for-programs/2016-cacrep-standards/

Fitch, T., Newby, E., Ballestero, V., & Marshall, J. L. (2001). Counselor preparation: Future school administrators' perceptions of the school counselor's role. *Counselor Education and Supervision, 41*(2), 89–99.

Greenwood, E. (1957). Attributes of a profession. *Social Work, 2,* 45–55.

Gysbers, N. C., & Henderson, P. (2000). *Developing and managing your school guidance program* (3rd ed.). Alexandria, VA: American Association for Counseling and Development.

Herr, E. L., & Cramer, S. G. (1987). *Controversies in the mental health professions.* Muncie, IN: Accelerated Development.

Holland, J. L. (1997). *Making vocational choices: A theory of vocational personalities and work environments* (3rd ed.). Odessa, FL: Professional Assessment Resources.

McCullough, L. (1994). Challenges to guidance programs: How to prevent and handle them. *Guidepost, 36*(8), 1–12.

Tennyson, W. W., Miller, C. D., Skovholt, T. G., & Williams, R. G. (1989). Secondary school counselors: What do they do? Why is it important? *School Counselor, 36,* 253–259.

United States Department of Education. (2002). *Executive summary: The No Child Left Behind Act of 2001.* Washington, DC: U.S. Department of Education.

U.S. Department of Education. (2011). *Meeting the nation's 2020 goal: State targets for increasing the number and percentage of college graduates with degrees.* Retrieved from https://www.whitehouse.gov/sites/default/files/completion_state_by_state.pdf

TOWARD A COMPREHENSIVE MODEL FOR PROFESSIONAL SCHOOL COUNSELING

2

RELATED STANDARDS OF PRACTICE

CACREP CORE	F.1.a, b
CACREP SCHOOL COUNSELING	G. 1. a, b; G.2.a; G.3.a

Goal: To promote comprehensive, balanced K–12 school counseling programs conducted by professional school counselors capable of meeting both remedial and developmental goals for children and adolescents living in a pluralistic society.

School counselors often reflect on the large responsibilities they encounter daily and over the course of a school year. Here are samples of what they say:

> The children who are leaving elementary school for middle school have no idea what they are about to face. We try our best to help them prepare, but we have neither the time nor the resources to reach all the children. I think effective, transition-to-middle-school programs should be a top priority for all school counselors.
>
> What am I going to do if a natural disaster hits my school—like a tornado, or heaven forbid, a disaster like Hurricane Katrina in New Orleans? How can I prepare myself and the teachers at my school to deal with the horrendous psychological consequences of disasters? I've read lots of good ideas in counseling articles but, somehow, I just don't think these articles provide a realistic flavor for what happens in these events. How can I help children through a disaster when, in all likelihood, I'm try to survive the event myself—perhaps, even the destruction of my own house?

I had a father tell me that I had no business running groups for parents since I'm not a parent and have no idea what its really like to raise a child and, in his words, "am hardly more than a child myself." I am defensive about his comments but don't want to alienate him and hurt my chances to work with other parents who are more accepting of me. Unfortunately, he is a prominent citizen and may turn others against me. How can I work with him and win him over?

Some of the migrant workers in my community, who have children at my school, have asked me to help them stay in the United States. I think they've come to me because I speak Spanish, and no one else at my school understands any Spanish. I am really conflicted over their request. I hardly have enough time to do what I need to do at school, much less spend spare time in the evenings wrestling with their problems—which seem so insurmountable.

A few days ago one my favorite students, who has already been accepted to an Ivy League school, was accused of date rape by his former girlfriend. She made this accusation during our meeting to prepare her for spending her junior year abroad in France. She wanted to talk about nothing about her plans for France. She doesn't think it's fair for her ex-boyfriend to receive all the glory for his admission to an Ivy League institution while she spends all her time in guilt and anger resulting from the way he treated her. I can't even sleep; I'm so worried about what I need to do.

I have all these ideas about how we can use computer technology to improve the counseling services we offer our students. But no one seems to want to listen to me; they are all too busy with their own work, and they have no time to learn the technology necessary for planning and implementing new programs that integrate technology.

School counseling offers professionals a wide choice of options for improving life at school among students, parents, teachers, and school administrators. Counselors need to explore a balanced approach to their work and to consider how to establish priorities. A comprehensive approach means that we ensure that all students are receiving the services they need. Further, given the myriad of student concerns and that current school counselor-to-student ratio is 471 to 1 (The College Board, 2011), a balanced approach will also require systemic thinking and action. Therefore, this chapter is devoted to presenting some history of the profession and our thoughts on a comprehensive, balanced model for school counseling programs and what the implications for practice might be.

THE IMPORTANCE OF HISTORY

Prior to discussing comprehensive school counseling, is important to understand the evolution of the school counseling profession. Numerous pioneers have responded to meeting the needs and challenges of an ever-changing society.

PIONEERS

Seen as a "series of learning experiences complementing the existing curriculum" (Aubrey, 1977, p. 289), guidance first appeared in the schools like any other subject. Guidance had a curriculum, the goals of which evolved from the social reform movements of the late 19th and early 20th centuries. Guidance teachers also sought to have a positive impact on the moral development of their charges. One such program was established by Jesse B. Davis, a high school principal in Grand Rapids, Michigan who, in 1907, had one period per week set aside in English composition classes for vocational and moral guidance. The goals for this early guidance curriculum were to help high school students better understand their own characters, emulate good role models, and develop into socially responsible workers.

What we think of currently as school counseling did not begin with a formal design consisting of established goals, assumptions, and functions. It evolved to what it is today. Davis and other pioneers were responding to local needs. His ideas led to a school guidance curriculum. Others, like David S. Hill, Anna Y. Reed, and Eli W. Weaver, founded their guidance services on different ideas, such as making students employable, helping them find suitable employment, and responding to their individual differences (Rockwell & Rothney, 1961). Additional influences outside education were integrated into the structure of guidance and gradually reshaped its features. For example, those involved in the vocational guidance movement created an interest in assessing individual differences and making personal, educational, and vocational decisions based on the resulting data. What have become known as the psychometric and mental health movements also had an impact on the guidance movement.

VOCATIONAL GUIDANCE MOVEMENT

Near the end of a long career as a social reformer, Frank Parsons (1909) in 1908 established a Vocation Bureau in Boston, the purpose of which was to provide vocational guidance for out-of-school youths. Parsons believed that individuals must have dependable information about occupations and about themselves in order to make good occupational choices. He also believed that the role of the vocational counselor was to make such information available and to help individuals comprehend and use it.

At about the same time, programs that would later be categorized together as representing vocational guidance were being introduced in a few metropolitan school districts. For example, selected elementary and secondary teachers in Boston were appointed to *positions* as vocational counselors (Gysbers & Henderson, 2000). Some universities offered courses in vocations, and the federal government passed legislation that subsidized vocational education and teacher training (e.g., the Smith-Hughes Act of 1917; the George-Reed Act of 1919). Yet in the first quarter of the 20th century, the influence of vocational guidance on school guidance was minimal, there were no accredited training programs, and there were no widely accepted theoretical underpinnings (Aubrey, 1977).

PSYCHOMETRIC MOVEMENT

A series of events in the first quarter of the 20th century led to the use of psychometric principles and techniques in applied settings. Psychometric principles, such as reliability theory and test validity, as well as techniques for standardizing psychometric instruments and making them precise, had previously been used by academicians and researchers to enhance their scholarly efforts. In 1905, Alfred Binet and his colleague T. Simon developed a scale to measure mental ability in order to help the school system in Paris, France, classify students for educational instruction. Binet's scale popularized the idea of using psychometrics to solve practical problems and was the forerunner of modern intelligence testing.

In response to the federal government's need to classify millions of young men eligible for the military when the United States entered World War I in 1917, several eminent psychologists produced a group-administered intelligence test. The success of the military use of the tests, known as Army Alpha (paper-and-pencil administration) and Beta (performance administration), popularized the idea of using group testing in education. In addition, vocational guidance workers found testing attractive as an apparently scientific means of determining a person's interests, strengths, and limitations.

Psychometrics offered school guidance not only the tools for assessment but also corresponding respectability because the tools seemed so precise and scientific. Psychometrics emphasized objectivity, individual differences, prediction, classification, and placement. With these emphases came tendencies for some school guidance workers to engage in testing and telling—relying on testing and information giving as the basis for guidance. As was the case with vocational guidance, because no uniform national guidance program existed, some were more influenced than others by the psychometric movement.

MENTAL HEALTH MOVEMENT

Several parallel movements in the early part of the 20th century ushered in what has been called the mental health movement. In 1908, Clifford Beers, a former mental patient, published a book called *A Mind That Found Itself,* which brought about reforms in the treatment of mental illness and fostered widespread interest in mental hygiene and the early identification and treatment of mental illness. Sigmund Freud's psychoanalytic ideas focusing on the importance of individual development and the influence of the mind on one's mental health became popular in the treatment of mental health problems and in mental health studies. These activities led to a newfound interest in the importance of the formative years as the foundation of personality and development. This interest in the promotion of healthy individual adjustment eventually influenced early school guidance workers.

EMERGENCE OF A SCHOOL GUIDANCE PROFESSION

In the 1920s and 1930s, the number of guidance specialists in the schools increased, although no widely accepted standards for training or practice existed. School administrators, circumstances, and the training and beliefs of the specialists combined to influence the philosophies and practices in those early school guidance programs. Often, the secondary school guidance programs that emerged in the 1920s were imitations of college student personnel programs that emphasized discipline and attendance (Gibson & Mitchell, 1981). Like college and university deans of students, high school guidance counselors acquired some administrative responsibilities and often concerned themselves with remedial goals. One outcome was that guidance counselors became responsive to the day-to-day wishes of their school administrators and were more and more likely to be identified with them (Shaw, 1973).

The advent of compulsory school attendance and the influence of the vocational guidance and mental health movements helped shape school guidance in the direction of a specialty. Compulsory school attendance increased the number of students who were unsure about their future plans and who had difficulty adjusting to the school environment. Proctor (1925) advocated guidance as a means of helping students cope with life forces by providing help in the selection of school subjects, extracurricular activities, colleges, and vocational schools. Through the end of World War II in 1945, school guidance was characterized by a relatively narrow focus on vocational guidance, adjustment to one's environment, and accompanying administrative duties. Between 1924 and 1946, four states required guidance counselors to have special certificates (Smith, 1955), indicating that school guidance was largely a function of local influences. In the few instances where guidance was offered at the elementary school level, it was most often a transplanted version of the secondary school program (Zaccaria, 1969).

What emerged as the dominant school guidance model in the 1930s and early 1940s has been labeled *trait and factor,* or directive guidance (Aubrey, 1977). Publications by E. G. Williamson (1950; Williamson & Darley, 1937) had considerable influence at this time. Williamson promoted enhancing normal adjustment, helping individuals set goals and overcome obstacles to those goals, and assisting individuals to achieve satisfying lifestyles. Influenced by the medical model for treating individuals, Williamson recommended that counseling competencies comprise analysis, synthesis, diagnosis, prognosis, counseling, and follow-up (Ewing, 1975; Smith, 1955). Techniques were suggested for forcing conformity, changing the environment, selecting the appropriate environment, teaching needed skills, and changing attitudes (Williamson, 1950). The descriptor *trait and factor* was applied to these techniques because diagnostic data derived from standardized tests and case studies emphasizing individual differences were used to advise students about vocational and adjustment issues.

The directive approach to guidance eventually proved to be too narrow in the changing times following World War II. Aubrey (1977) thought the changes were influenced by an increasing desire for personal freedom and autonomy. Into this setting came Carl Rogers (1942, 1951, 1961), whose nonmedical approach to counseling had an impact on the field unlike the work of any person before him. His ideas transferred the focus of counseling away from problems and onto the individuals receiving counseling. Rogers emphasized the counseling relationship and climate. His general goal was to help individuals grow so that they might resolve their own problems and have the strength to function effectively.

Individual counseling had gradually emerged as the dominant guidance function in the 1930s and 1940s. The changing social environment after World War II and the addition of Rogers's ideas led Smith (1955) to conclude a decade later that counseling had become the central secondary school guidance function, with all other functions in supplementary roles. Smith observed that the nondirective and directive approaches each had proponents, as did an eclectic approach that occupied the middle of the road but was more directive in practice. Rogers's influence had moved school counselors away from being highly directive toward being eclectic. In addition, group counseling was emerging as a relatively new idea with some merit for school counseling (Smith, 1955).

The creation of the American Personnel and Guidance Association in 1952 (APGA), the passage of the George-Barden Act of 1946 National Defense Education Act in 1958, and the increased school enrollments caused by the baby boomers born after World War II all caused the training of school counselors to become more standardized and increased their number in the 1960s. This was the boom era in school counseling, and Rogers's theory and techniques dominated the training programs and practices of school counselors. Reflecting back on these times, authors of the ASCA National Model for School Counseling Programs (ASCA, 2005) seemed to regret the infusion of psychological and clinical paradigms into training programs once rooted in education paradigms because it caused role confusion for school counselors and their constituents.

Two divisions of the APGA—the American School Counselor Association (ASCA) and the Association for Counselor Education and Supervision (ACES)—led the way to developing and promoting standards for the training of school counselors that strongly emphasized counseling theory and practicum training. Practicum training often focused on the development of skills for one-to-one counseling relationships and occurred at the end of the training program, leaving the impression that the counseling function was very important. Although the standards tended to fortify the importance of counseling, other functions, such as record keeping, information dissemination, placement, follow-up, and evaluation, were also identified as important. In addition, uniformity was introduced to collegiate training programs and state certification standards. In the years after World War II and into the 1960s, the remaining states adopted certification standards for school counselors. In 1957, the ASCA, recognizing a need, initiated a study on elementary school counseling.

The George-Barden Act of 1946 (PL 586) ruled that federal funds could be used to support such activities as (a) state supervision programs, (b) salaries for counselor-trainees, (c) research in the guidance field, and (d) salaries for local counselors and supervisors (Gysbers & Henderson, 2000). The National Defense Education Act of 1958 (NDEA) was passed after the Soviets successfully launched the space satellite *Sputnik* in 1957. On the basis of this perceived threat of Soviet educational superiority and the subsequent desire to identify academically talented students and guide them into careers in strategic fields, the NDEA provided federal funds to the states for the enhancement of school counseling programs and to colleges and universities to update working school counselors and train new ones. Even though the primary purpose of the funding was rather narrow, the funding was used to achieve goals of a much broader scope. New and improved counselor education programs proliferated. The demand for graduates was immense because of the need for counselors to serve the growing number of students in the schools as a result of the bulge in the birth rate after World War II.

In 1959, James B. Conant recommended a ratio of one full-time high school counselor for every 200 to 300 students in his widely read book *The American High School Today*. Conant's focus on the importance of guidance helped create an impression that all high school students should have access to school counselors. The following year, the 1960 White House Conference on Children and Youth emphasized the importance of extending counseling services to preadolescents. Consultants to the U.S. secretary of health, education, and welfare recommended that the NDEA be extended to elementary schools. The 1964 amendments to the NDEA gave impetus to elementary school counseling by providing funds for training to extend the search for talent to elementary schools. This instigated a period of debate over models for elementary school guidance that extended into the 1970s.

In *The Counselor in a Changing World*, 60,000 copies of which were printed between 1962 and 1966, C. Gilbert Wrenn chided secondary school guidance counselors for having allowed themselves to become narrowly focused on the remedial needs of a few students. He recommended that the newly evolving population of elementary school counselors learn from the mistaken decision by secondary school counselors to build crisis-oriented programs and instead emphasize responding to the developmental needs of the total range of students in their programs. Wrenn's advocacy of developmental rather than remedial goals for elementary school and secondary school guidance came at a time when others were voicing similar opinions. Dinkmeyer (1967) advocated helping children to know, understand, and accept themselves. Also emphasizing the importance of promoting positive individual growth and development, Zaccaria (1969) pointed out that the emphasis of developmental guidance should be on preventing problems. Writing that the major emphasis among authorities publishing papers and books about guidance programs seemed to be on a developmental approach, Shaw (1973) concluded that the term *developmental guidance* was being used so globally that it had yet to be defined precisely. As the 1970s approached, the number of school counseling professionals being trained and employed had grown significantly, elementary school counseling was emerging and seeking an identity, and the traditional service delivery model was being challenged.

AFTER THE BOOM

An era of declining enrollments in the schools and economic problems across the United States led to reductions in personnel in numerous school districts during the 1970s and into the 1980s. Many school counseling positions were eliminated, significantly fewer jobs were available for newly trained school counselors, and the thrust for elementary school guidance programs initiated in the 1960s was muted. At the same time, several themes about the appropriate roles for school counselors were championed. Influenced by the turbulent 1960s and the problems of the inner-city schools, Menacker (1974, 1976) called for counselors working in metropolitan areas to become more active in the schools and communities and to rely more on the fields of sociology, political science, and economics than on psychology for helping models. The developmental guidance approach was also gaining momentum at this time. One reason for this momentum was the compatibility of the idea with elementary school guidance. The enhancement of self-understanding and adjustment and the importance of consulting and collaboration for elementary school counselors were already emphasized. A second reason for the momentum was ideas generated by career education proponents. Emphasizing the importance of work and careers to healthy human adjustment, career education advocates recommended integrating general and vocational education, instruction, and guidance around a career development theme from kindergarten through the 12th grade (Hoyt, Evans, Mackin, & Mangum, 1974). Some federal funds were made available for career education programming in basic education during the 1970s. A third reason was the attention given to psychological education after Mosher and Sprinthall (1970) introduced psychologically based curriculum interventions for counselors to offer students in an effort to persuade guidance programs to help the schools focus more on personal development.

Shaw (1973) advocated what Zaccaria (1969) classified as a *services approach* to guidance. Shaw believed that guidance programs should be founded on clearly stated goals and objectives. He also believed that guidance workers should be able to provide a set of functions as needed, depending on where guidance goals belonged on a continuum ranging from primary prevention to diagnosis and therapy. The functions, or services, comprised counseling, consultation, testing, curriculum development, provision of information, in-service training, use of records, articulation, referral, and evaluation and research. Others, like Keat (1974), advocated eclectic models. Keat's eclecticism, designed for elementary school counselors, was summarized in a blended set of roles. Group and individual counseling, collaboration and consultation with teachers, and coordination with school district and community resources were taken from the recommendations of professional organizations (APGA, 1969); communication with children and adults and offering an effective curriculum were borrowed from Stamm and Nissman (1971); and fostering child growth and development and teaching coping behaviors were added to the set by Keat.

In an increasing number of states, counseling students who had no teaching experience were trained and certified, creating greater diversity among the new generation of school counselors. At this time, school counseling was still a field without a central unifying theme. It was, in fact, experiencing an increasing number of themes, all having varying degrees of influence across training programs and among counselors. The newer activist, developmental, service-oriented, and eclectic themes mixed with remnants of the trait and factor, adjustment, administrative, and counseling themes that were still very much alive. In times of job shortages and threats to existing jobs, school counseling was at a loss to define itself uniformly. The winds of change led the APGA to rename itself the American Association for Counseling and Development (AACD) in the mid-1980s and to the American Counseling Association (ACA) in the early 1990s. Divisions and state organizations followed suit or had already initiated similar changes (Herr, 1985). Officially, the words *guidance* and then *development* had become archaic. The term *counseling* now represented the goals of the organized members of the profession more accurately. Table 2.1 presents a summary of many of these important events in chronological order.

TABLE 2.1   *Highlights of the Evolution of School Counseling in the 20th Century*

Date	Event
1905	Binet and Simon develop mental ability scale
1908	Frank Parsons establishes Vocation Bureau in Boston
1920	Sigmund Freud's ideas begin to influence mental health professionals
1920–1930	Number of school guidance specialists increases in this decade—no widely accepted training or practice standards
1924	State certification of guidance counselors begins
1925	Proctor advocates guidance program to help students make educational and vocational choices
1937	Williamson and Darley publish *Student Personnel Work: An Outline of Clinical Procedures* and begin *trait and factor* approach
1942	Carl Rogers publishes *Counseling* and *Psychotherapy* and begins the era of individual counseling
1945	Changing social environment after World War II and influence of Rogers's writings cause counseling to become the dominant school guidance service
1946	George-Barden Act (PL 586) passed
1952	American Personnel and Guidance Association (APGA) created
1953	American School Counselors Association (ASCA) joins the APGA
1958	National Defense Education Act (NDEA) passed
1960	Beginning of a boom decade in school guidance and counseling and in counselor education

(Continued)

TABLE 2.1   (Continued)

Date	Event
1964	NDEA amended to provide funds for enhancing elementary school guidance
1985	APGA changes its name to the American Association for Counseling and Development (AACD)
1987	AACD task force on school counseling as a profession at risk publishes its report
1988	Gysbers and Henderson publish *Developing and Managing Your School Guidance Program*
1990	Interdivisional task force (AACD, Association for Counselor Education and Supervision, ASCA) begins working on plans to improve school counseling
1991	"Multiculturalism as a Fourth Force in Counseling" is introduced in a special issue of the AACD journal
1992	AACD changes its name to the American Counseling Association (ACA)
1993	ASCA, ACA, and others reintroduce the Elementary School Counseling Demonstration Act
1997	ASCA proposes *The National Standards for School Counseling Programs*
1997	DeWitt Wallace Reader's Digest Fund provides the Education Trust with funding to initiate a transformation of school counseling
1999–2000	Funding achieved for the Elementary and Secondary School Counseling Demonstration Program under the Elementary and Secondary Education Act
2000	Application of school-community collaboration model selected by U.S. Department of Education as one of 22 outstanding model schools are encouraged to support
2001	No Child Left Behind initiative becomes legislation (PL 107–110)
2002	ASCA presents the National Model for School Counseling Programs
2002	The Education Trust receives funds from Met Life for the Transforming School Counseling Initiative
2003	*ASCA National Model Workbook* published
2004	ASCA announces that five schools had met the criteria for becoming Recognized ASCA Model Programs (RAMP)
2005	*ASCA National Model,* second edition is published
2012	*ASCA National Model,* third edition is published
2014	First Lady Michelle Obama is the Featured Speaker at the ASCA National Conference in Orlando, Florida
2015	First School Counselor of the Year White House Ceremony
2015	ASCA continues to offer important webinar series
2015	President Obama signs the Every Student Succeeds Act

Generally, basic education and school counseling have been bombarded by a range of challenges that, when evaluated closely, seem to place increasing responsibility on elementary, middle, and secondary school educators to respond to the nation's problems and to prepare future generations of students to cope with economic competitors. These challenges include demands that the school curriculum be made more rigorous, drug abuse be prevented, drug users be treated and rehabilitated, exceptional students and culturally different populations be integrated and their differences appreciated, dropout rates be reduced, children of working parents be cared for, students be prepared for more complex and challenging jobs, gender equity be promoted, and local and state taxes for supporting the schools be reduced or maintained at existing levels.

LATE 20TH AND EARLY 21ST CENTURIES

Multicultural Competence

From within the general field of counseling came a call for multicultural competence (American Association for Counseling and Development, 1991). Professional counselors are challenged to (a) know about and be able to establish relationships with individuals in all cultural groups (Westbrook & Sedlacek, 1991), (b) be able to conceptualize client concerns from their perspective or worldview (Ibrahim, 1991), and (c) provide proactive programming that is culturally sensitive (Dobbins & Skillings, 1991). Knowledge of differing worldviews is incomplete unless accompanied by corresponding knowledge of one's own feelings, thoughts, and experiences, according to Speight, Myers, Cox, and Highlen (1991).

Educational Reform

President George W. Bush's No Child Left Behind initiative was, according to Herr (2002), the latest national educational reform movement at the beginning of the 21st century, and the school counseling profession found itself assessing its role—collectively and individually:

> Each time there is a change of national presidential administrations, there is likely to be a proposed shift in the emphasis that national policy and practice should address, creating a constant process of "starting over," looking for new solutions to enduring problems.
>
> (Herr, 2002, p. 220)

Herr's paper was among several articles published in the April 2002 issue of *Professional School Counseling,* the goal of which was to address the role of school counseling in the latest school reform movement. Herr carefully addressed school reform from a historical perspective and presented viewpoints on why previous reform movements had limited success. One was left with the belief that school counselors need to be careful not to become caught up in reform efforts that focus only on restructuring schools via increased academic rigor. That school counselors and school reform should also focus on alleviating the circumstances that prevent some children and youths from being successful in school seems clear.

Increasing Enrollments

Information from the U.S. Department of Education indicated that school enrollment would increase dramatically at some levels of education and in some regions of the nation over the decade of approximately 1996–1997 through 2006–2007. The impact of this *baby boom echo* or *millennial generation* would be felt the most in high schools (15% enrollment increases) and in the southern and western parts of the country (Goetz, 1997; Morrissey, 1996). These demographics indicated that the decade of transition from one century to the next would present opportunities and challenges ranging from increased employment for school counselors to larger caseloads than were previously experienced. Four possible causes of the rising enrollment were (1) many baby boomers delayed marriage and childbearing, (2) more children enrolled in preschools and were remaining in school to get diplomas, (3) birth rates were high among ethnic minority populations, and (4) immigration to the United States increased.

Emerging Themes

Several themes seem to emerge from these challenges. First, external circumstances such as growing enrollments and decreasing revenues indicate that school counselors will be challenged to demonstrate their worth and cost-effectiveness in the schools. Second, national, state, and local governments recognize the importance of education in the future health of the nation and are concerned about viable outcomes and accountability. Third, these circumstances lead to national school reform efforts, such as President George W. Bush's No Child Left Behind initiative. Fourth, as was the case in early school reform efforts, school counseling has not been included as an important participant in the reform's response. Fifth, there is widespread belief that many school counseling programs have been and remain marginalized ancillary services that are endangered in economic hard times (ASCA, 1996; Baker, 2001; Campbell & Dahir, 1997; House & Hayes, 2002). Sixth, without a designed program, a clear mission, and an identified role or vision, counselors will continue to function at the discretion of others (Borders & Drury, 1992; Gysbers & Henderson, 2000; House & Hayes, 2002; Paisley & Borders, 1995). Seventh, a well-conceived effort by school counselors to address the needs of all students seems to be essential for the future good health of individual school counselors, school counseling programs, and the school counseling profession (Hatch & Bowers, 2002).

Federal Funding

The ASCA, ACA, and other sister professional organizations reintroduced the Elementary School Counseling Demonstration Act (ESCDA) in 1993. Their activity had potential for responding constructively to the challenges just listed. The prospective legislation called for funding to schools proposing promising and innovative approaches to expanding elementary school counseling programs. Included among the criteria for funding programs under the legislation were recommendations that school counselors work cooperatively with school psychologists and social workers in integrated teams, that student-to-counselor ratios be not more than 250 to 1, that 85% of the team members' time be devoted to providing direct services with no more than 15% devoted to administrative tasks, and that the program be developmental and preventive.

Working cooperatively, ACA, ASCA, the National Association of School Psychologists, the National Association of Social Workers, the American Psychological Association, and the School Social Work Association of America convinced Congress to reauthorize/rewrite the ESCDA as part of a larger Elementary and Secondary Education Act (ESEA) bill and to fund it as part of an appropriations bill in 1998 (Urbaniak, 2000). Funding victories were accomplished in 1999 and 2000 (Urbaniak, 2000). Since 2000, school counselors, school psychologists, school social workers, and other interested professionals have worked independently and through respective professional organizations to enhance the ESCDA/ESEA legislation (e.g., provide for counseling programs in secondary schools), get ESEA authorized, and acquire funding.

Comprehensive Guidance Programs

Reports by Lapan, Gysbers, and Sun (1997), Neukrug, Barr, Hoffman, and Kaplan (1993), and Sink and MacDonald (1998) indicated that the number of states adopting comprehensive guidance programs had been increasing steadily. This development suggested a growing awareness of, and appreciation for, the concept of guidance for everyone and corresponding emphases on planned, sequential, and flexible guidance curricula integrated into the general curriculum. In turn, de-emphasis of the importance of administrative and clerical-centered response modes is suggested.

National Standards for School Counseling

In an attempt to respond to Goals 2000: The Educate America Act (EAA) of 1994, the ASCA adopted *School Counseling 2000,* a set of goals for school counseling derived from the six broad goals for achieving success in U.S. education in the EAA. The general theme of the school counseling goals is to work directly and collaboratively with students, parents, teachers, community members, and employers to develop policies and programs that address the challenging problems that have been widely identified.

The ASCA governing board was committed to developing national standards for school counseling programs (Dahir, 2001). The National Standards for School Counseling Programs (Campbell & Dahir, 1997) were completed in 1997. The standards are designed to (a) shift the focus from counselors to school counseling programs, (b) create a framework for a national school counseling program model, (c) establish school counseling as an integral part of the academic mission of the schools, (d) lead to equal access to school counseling services for all students, (e) highlight the key ingredients of developmental school counseling, (f) identify the knowledge and skills to which all students should have access from comprehensive school counseling programs, and (g) ensure that comprehensive school counseling programs are delivered in a systematic manner (Dahir, 1997). Emphasis is on the role of counseling in student achievement, on collaboration with teachers and school administrators toward helping students be successful in school, and on program content standards that specify what students should know and be able to do (Dahir, 2001).

Findings from a survey of 1,127 ASCA members indicated strong support for the National Standards (82%) especially that they may help clarify the scope and practice of school counseling (Dahir, 2004). They appreciated the goal of having school counseling programs become integral components of the academic missions of their respective schools. There also seemed to be a preference for basing standards on envisioned practice rather than either theory or current practice. Dahir (2004) concluded, "The school counseling community has never been in a better situation to position itself at the forefront of school improvement and educational change" (p. 352).

The Transforming School Counseling Initiative

Supported by a 1996 grant from the DeWitt Wallace Reader's Digest Fund, the National Education Trust set out to bring about dramatic changes in the training of school counselors in order to transform school counseling by causing school counselors to become more responsive to student needs (Guerra, 1998). Six counselor education programs were selected to receive funding for developing model school counseling training programs. Advocates of the Trust's initiative believe that the programs for training school counselors must change if there are to be constructive changes in school counseling (Sears & Granello, 2002). New funding from the Met Life Foundation allowed the Education Trust to initiate the National School Counselor Training Initiative (Stone & House, 2002). An underlying theme of this initiative is that school counselors need to be integral participants in closing the gap between poor students and students of color and their more advantaged peers (House & Hayes, 2002). Therefore, school counselors must believe that all students can achieve at a high level and act accordingly.

House and Hayes believe school counselors are in the best position to assess their schools for barriers to academic success for all students and to use that information to be advocates for equity and entitlement. While not negating the importance of traditional school counselor roles such as counselor, coordinator, and consultant, this initiative emphasizes the roles of leader, advocate, and collaborator. According to Sears and Granello (2002), the traditional roles, and their corresponding skills, remain necessary yet are no longer sufficient for school counselors to be effective in today's schools. Instead, school counselors attempting to achieve the goals of this initiative will develop, coordinate, and implement well-articulated developmental counseling programs with attention to equity, access, and support services (House & Hayes, 2002). These programs will be designed to improve the learning success of all students, especially those who experience difficulty in rigorous academic programs. School counselors will provide leadership and collaborate in building teams of students, professional and support staff members, parents, and individuals in the community in order to accomplish a community-wide effort to achieve the goals of educational reform.

If school counselors proactively emphasize and implement the educational leader, advocate, and collaborator roles and are successful, then they will move school counseling from the periphery to a central position in the schools (Education Trust, 1997; House & Hayes, 2002). In so doing, they will make a significant contribution to closing the achievement gap between poor students and students of color and their more advantaged peers.

THE CURRENT STATUS OF PROFESSIONAL SCHOOL COUNSELING

Clearly, many historical events have shaped the profession of school counseling. From the economy and legislation, to professional organizations, each has been influential in how we educate and train future school counselors. Since the No Child Left Behind Act (NCLB) of 2001, educators were mandated to demonstrate accountability in closing the achievement gap between minorities and their more advantaged peers. This task has not been easy given significant budget cuts. School counselors were central to this piece of legislation as the profession had to demonstrate how students are different as a result of the school counseling program. On December 10, 2015, President Obama signed into law, the Every Student Succeeds Act (ESSA). This law gives power back to state and local administrators, which is significantly departs from the one-size-fits-all mandates of NCLB.

Bemak, Williams, and Chung (2014) remind us that ASCA revised the National Model (ASCA, 2012) in efforts to provide directions for the use of data in promoting school counselor accountability. School counselors are expected to collect and analyze data to determine program effectiveness. These programs include small groups, large group guidance, and school-wide programs. Individual counseling sessions can also be monitored through progress monitoring, which is based on the implementation of multitiered systems of supports such as Response to Intervention.

As the ASCA National Model (ASCA, 2012) has increased in significance and reach, it is important to note another major focus that has garnered national attention regarding college and career readiness. This national attention has stemmed from

President Barack Obama's "North Star" goal that by 2020 the United States will return to having the largest proportion of college graduates in the world. To support this effort, First Lady Michelle Obama established the Reach Higher initiative (The White House, 2015). In the summer of 2014, First Lady Michelle Obama's keynote at the ASCA national conference was instrumental in bringing to light how school counselors are central to the mission of increasing postsecondary access for all students. In alignment with this initiative, ASCA (2014) released the next generation ASCA Mindsets & Behaviors for Student Success: K-12 College- and Career-Readiness Standards for Every Student. These standards now replace the former National Standards for Students that were published in 1997 and can be viewed in Appendix B. Although society and policies are ever-changing, the ASCA National Model (ASCA, 2012) continues to provide a foundation and framework from which school counselors can operate.

THE ASCA NATIONAL MODEL FOR SCHOOL COUNSELING PROGRAMS

The ASCA National Model (ASCA, 2012) is sponsored by the ASCA and includes School Counselor Competencies. The general goal is that comprehensive school counseling must be integral to student academic achievement and must help set high standards for student achievement. It is believed that school counselors must be trained to inform administrators of the contributions they plan to make rather than asking them what to do.

It is also believed that the National Model maximizes the full potential of the National Standards and reflects the current education reform movements. In so doing, the National Model incorporates school counseling standards and competencies for all students. The School Counselor Competencies are results based and serve as a foundation for the National Model and lead to an organized, planned, sequential, and flexible school counseling program. Interventions will be intentional and designed to meet the needs of all students. A primary objective of intentional planning will be to close the gap between academically disadvantaged students and their advantaged peers.

The National Model is perceived as a flexible template that individual school districts can use to create programs that reflect their own needs and accountability expectations. The components of the model include, but are not limited to, (a) the ASCA National Standards; (b) implementation of a district-wide delivery system that includes a guidance curriculum, individual planning, responsive services, and system support; (c) a management system that ensures that programs are based on student needs; (d) a data-driven evaluation system; (e) intentional services for academically underperforming students; and (f) infusion of systemic change, leadership, and advocacy throughout all components. The National Model was tested by seven school districts in Riverside, California, in 2001 and reviewed by school counseling leaders. In 2004, five schools in California, Oregon, and Arizona were declared Recognized ASCA Model Programs (RAMP) (ASCA, 2004). Further recognition of the increased implementation of the ASCA National Model is that the current number of RAMP recognized programs across the nation is 545 as of summer 2015 (ASCA, 2015).

The ASCA School Counselor Competencies are viewed as complementing the comprehensive school guidance and counseling program concept, and the ASCA National Model is strongly influenced by that concept as well. Sink and MacDonald (1998) reported that 35 state departments of education or school counseling associations have promoted the implementation of comprehensive school counseling models. Herr (2001) believes the concept, originally depicted as comprehensive guidance programs, has its roots in the 1960s when a systems approach in guidance was being advocated. The concept of planned, comprehensive, systematic guidance programs emerged in the 1980s and has received support from national professional associations, such as the ASCA, and from federal legislation, such as the Carl D. Perkins Vocational Education Act of 1984 and the School to Work Opportunities Act of 1994 (Herr, 2001).

Many advocates were supporting this concept in the professional literature, and we have selected Gysbers and Henderson (2012) to represent them here. According to Gysbers and Henderson (2001), a comprehensive guidance and counseling program consists of three elements: content, organizational framework, and resources. Content refers to the competencies students achieve through participation in components of a comprehensive guidance and counseling program. The organizational framework consists of a K–12 curriculum of guidance activities designed to help students achieve the competencies. For example, the curriculum might include a classroom guidance program designed to help students investigate the world of work, acquire a better understanding of themselves in the world of work, and eventually make wise career decisions.

Furthermore, the organizational framework includes delivery modes for the organized curriculum such as classroom and school-wide activities and individual planning. Individual planning is a comprehensive process designed to help students learn about themselves and plan accordingly, and it calls upon counselors to possess appraisal, advisement, placement, and follow-up competencies. The organizational framework also includes services needed to respond to student problems that deter academic, career, and personal-social development. These services are identified as personal counseling, diagnostic and remediation activities, consultation, and referral. Finally, it is important not to overlook the necessity for an ongoing support system consisting of (a) program evaluation leading to continued program development, (b) continuous professional development of school counselors, (c) public relations thrusts to keep all stakeholders informed, (d) service on advisory boards, (e) community outreach, and (f) continuous program planning and management.

The resource element of a comprehensive program refers to the importance of human, financial, and political resources. School counselors, teachers, administrators, parents, students, community members, and business and labor representatives all have important contributions to make in a comprehensive guidance and counseling program. Adequate financial support is needed as well. Political resources need to be mobilized appropriately in order to achieve full endorsement by school district boards of education. Gysbers and Henderson (2001) believe

> The program's organizational structure not only provides the means and a common language for ensuring guidance for all students and counseling for students that need it, it also provides a foundation for the accountable use of an ever-broadening spectrum of resources.
>
> (p. 256)

Finally, Gysbers and Henderson (2001) view the comprehensive school guidance and counseling program approach as the best vehicle for achieving the convergence of the currently incongruent goals of providing an academically rigorous education while including all students.

According to Rowley, Stroh, and Sink (2005), variations of the comprehensive guidance and counseling programs are being implemented throughout the United States. Rowley et al. (2005) surveyed a national sample of school counselors working within comprehensive guidance and counseling programs and found that, although implementation methods were varied, the guidance curriculum component of the model was viewed as fruitful. That is, many counselors thought their implementation of the curriculum was helping students attain developmental competence, and they were using a wide range of curriculum materials in support of achieving their program goals. Hatch and Chen-Hayes (2008) also surveyed a sample of 3,000 school counselors regarding their beliefs about the ASCA National Model program components. The study revealed participants reported the Mission, Goals, Competencies, and Administrator support was more important than the use of data and accountability. The authors noted the results were not surprising, as some counselors may be intimidated by the use of data or may not be adequately trained.

GOALS OF A BALANCED APPROACH TO SCHOOL COUNSELING

Here we state specifically the goals of our balanced approach to professional school counseling. In the remainder of this chapter, we elaborate on the goals, using that information to set the stage for the remainder of the textbook. We believe that school counseling is best viewed as a program within a school system and that professional school counselors should be trained for competence and motivation to achieve the following goals.

- Attend to the affective and cognitive development of all students;
- Be an advocate for all students;

- Be an integral part of the academic mission and total education program of the schools;
- Collaborate with families, other human services providers, and communities;
- Provide both prevention programming and responsive services;
- Conform with applicable laws, regulations, and guidelines and the appropriate professional ethical standards;
- Achieve accountability;
- Be an advocate for the school counseling profession.

ATTEND TO THE AFFECTIVE AND COGNITIVE DEVELOPMENT OF ALL STUDENTS

Most school counselors believe that human learning is the product of development in a variety of areas. Carl Rogers, Rudolph Dreikurs, and William Glasser are among the counseling theorists whose writing has helped school counselors and others in education to understand that learning involves more than cognitive activity, that education involves emotional, social, and other factors as well.

The affective domain of human existence encompasses the whole range of human feelings and emotions, including feelings about self, fear, anxiety, joy, and many others. This domain is important in the learning process. No one more clearly spelled out the relationships between emotions and learning than did Brown (1971) in his book *Human Teaching for Human Learning: An Introduction to Confluent Education*. He noted that "the relationship between intellect and affect is indestructibly symbiotic . . . it is the passion of the scholar that makes for truly great scholarship" (p. 11). Brown's view about the coming together of the affective and cognitive domains, however, is only one of many attempts at explaining the role of emotions and feelings in learning. The whole notion of affective education, which gained popularity in the late 1960s and early 1970s, reflects the importance with which many educators regard the affective domain.

The most studied and discussed aspect of the affective domain is self-concept (i.e., how students view themselves). Many other affective variables such as anxiety, motivation, and interest also influence learning. As is the case with self-concept, the degree to which these factors affect learning is uncertain. Factors of this kind cannot be neglected in the classroom if learning opportunities are to be maximized.

BE AN ADVOCATE FOR ALL STUDENTS

The ASCA National Model for School Counseling Programs (ASCA, 2012) recommends that the majority of a school counselor's time should be spent in direct service to all students. This ensures that through comprehensive school counseling services, every student receives the necessary interventions and support services needed to be academically successful. Further evidence regarding the importance of advocacy is highlighted in the *Ethical Standards for School Counselors* (ASCA, 2012), which state "Professional school counselors are advocates, leaders, collaborators and consultants who create opportunities for equity in access and success in educational opportunities by connecting their programs to the mission of schools and subscribing to the following tenets of professional responsibility" (Preamble).

As advocates, school counselors are committed to helping all students achieve their goals. Helping students achieve their goals may require active responses to those conditions that may impede goal achievement (e.g., coordinating community mental health services for students who need them). Advocacy requires a sense of social responsibility (Lee & Sirch, 1994) and suggests collaboration and leadership competencies. We elaborate more on advocacy, collaboration, and leadership in Chapters 5 and 6.

BE AN INTEGRAL PART OF THE ACADEMIC MISSION AND TOTAL EDUCATION PROGRAM OF THE SCHOOL

The ASCA National Model for School Counseling Programs (ASCA, 2012) highlights this goal succinctly, stating that professional school counselors support the academic mission of the schools by "promoting and enhancing the learning process for all students through an integration of academic, career, and personal/social development" (p. 15). Requisite competencies for achieving these objectives include (a) having specialized knowledge in child and adolescent development, (b) coordinating a developmental school counseling program, (c) calling attention to conditions in the schools that prevent academic success, and (d) providing leadership and collaboration in the process of resolving the conditions preventing academic success.

According to Gysbers and Henderson (2012), school counseling becomes a part of the total education program when it is has its own content base and is viewed as an integral component of the educational process. The ASCA National Model is structured to achieve the goals established by the proponents of developmental guidance (aka developmental school counseling). Ways to achieve this goal are integrated into many of the remaining chapters of this textbook.

COLLABORATE WITH FAMILIES, OTHER HUMAN SERVICE PROVIDERS, AND COMMUNITIES

The importance of this goal was introduced in the earlier supporting material for the student advocacy and academic mission goals. That is, professional school counselors are uniquely positioned to identify impediments that prevent students from achieving academic success and are also strategically positioned to serve as coordinators of community and human service resources that may help students overcome the impediments (e.g., substance abuse, homelessness, dysfunctional families, and poverty). Luongo (2000) points to overwhelming evidence indicating that core social institutions (including schools) have a constant need for behavioral health services. He emphasizes, "If partnerships at the service delivery level are to make the best use of existing resources, they need to reflect not only collaboration among service institutions and providers, but also an actual integration of basic services" (p. 308). Luongo cites data that indicate a 30%–40% overlap in services to children by core social institutions. That is, many children, while receiving special services in schools, are also receiving special services in the community. In addition to partnering multiple social institutions, he states that the home must be involved as a "critical partner." Luongo concludes,

> The execution of the function of schools, however, must change. . . . schools will take on an even greater collaborative and integrative relationship to other core social institutions. . . . Onsite collaboratives within schools. . . . have rapidly spread throughout the country. . . . Schools redefining school counselors as school-community counselors is a critical component. . . . professional practice does not end at the school house door. . . . Effective practice requires familiarity and expertise in the workings and methods of other disciplines.
>
> (p. 313)

PROVIDE BOTH PREVENTION PROGRAMMING AND RESPONSIVE SERVICES

The ASCA National Model (ASCA, 2012) and the comprehensive guidance program (Gysbers & Henderson, 2012) highlight the importance of a school counseling program founded on proactive planning. Such planning requires (a) goals based on knowledge of basic developmental needs of children and adolescents and academic expectations of schools, (b) measurable objectives for achieving those goals, (c) deliverable programs designed to achieve the goals and objectives, (d) requisite competencies needed to achieve those goals, (e) a place in the school's curriculum to provide the programs, and (f) evaluation of the effects of delivering the programs in order to achieve accountability.

Because the programs are based on knowledge of the developmental needs of children and adolescents, they are preventive in nature. That is, they are designed to prevent recipients from encountering negative experiences such as floundering and indecisiveness in career development and choice and anxiety that prevents achievement of academic success. These programs are developmental and preventative. We agree that prevention programming is an important component of a school counseling program.

Of equal importance is responding to and providing intervention for students who are already experiencing many of the challenges that prevention programming is designed to address. Through student self-referrals, referrals from others such as teachers and parents, and initiation of contacts by counselors based on observation of documents, school counselors find themselves expected to address the needs of students who are at risk in some way. The list of reasons to be responsive is quite long. A short list, for example, includes divorce, grief, abuse, school phobia, depression, sexuality, and peer relationships. These issues demand responsive rather than proactive programming. School counselors are confronted with these issues and challenged to respond in a helpful way.

A balanced school counseling program is designed to provide both proactive prevention programming and responsive counseling interventions. The different nature of these two approaches, that is, proactive versus responsive, present unique challenges. Demands for responsive intervention services happen. They do not have to be planned, developed, and delivered systematically as is the case with prevention programming. Therefore, it is highly likely that many school counselors and school counseling programs are overwhelmed by responsive service demands and find themselves pressed for time to engage in prevention programming or else opt out of it voluntarily. Consequently, many current school counseling programs are not balanced because of an overemphasis on responsive services.

CONFORM WITH APPLICABLE LAWS, REGULATIONS, GUIDELINES, AND THE APPROPRIATE PROFESSIONAL ETHICAL STANDARDS

In Chapter 1, we ascribed professional status to school counselors. One of the criteria for ascribing professional status to professions is that they practice a degree of self-control via community sanctions, ethical codes, and the like. Both the ACA and ASCA have had codes of ethics in place for quite some time. This topic is covered in detail in Chapter 4.

School counselors are employed in positions of public trust. Parents in particular and communities in general entrust counselors and their professional colleagues with the education and care of their children. The general expectations of that trust are that counselors and their colleagues will obey the laws and regulations that relate to their activities and abide by the ethical guidelines of their professions. State departments of education/public instruction establish standards that determine the minimum competencies that counselors and their professional colleagues must meet to be eligible for employment in the schools. The standards usually include expectations that counselors and their professional colleagues be familiar with pertinent legal codes and concepts, governmental regulations, and ethical standards. Therefore, at the level of basic counseling training, school counselors are challenged to become grounded in these important competencies and to adopt the appropriate frame of mind toward legal and ethical responsibilities. "Appropriate frame of mind" means simply that school counselors recognize the responsibilities they have assumed, strive to acquire the requisite knowledge, and endeavor to act responsibly and in good faith. These concerns are important in all facets of a balanced approach to school counseling.

Herlihy and Remley (2001) depict laws as the "musts" components in our professional behavior. Laws "dictate the minimum standards of behavior that society will tolerate" (p. 71). On the other hand, Herlihy and Remley depict ethics as the "shoulds" of our professional behavior. Ethics "represent the ideals or aspirations of the counseling profession" (p. 71).

ACHIEVE ACCOUNTABILITY

Achieving accountability is a systematic process that incorporates evaluation of one's programmatic efforts. As presented in this textbook, the words *evaluation* and *accountability* are neither interchangeable nor synonymous. Each represents an important ingredient of the accountability domain, and both functions are important. Each complements the other. *Evaluation* is the act of gathering information about the attributes of one's program; *accountability* is the act of sharing the results of the evaluation. Evaluation precedes accountability. Translating evaluative data into accountability information completes the process and leads to accomplishing the goals of the accountability process.

The ASCA National Model (ASCA, 2012) is especially adamant about the importance of accountability: "To demonstrate the effectiveness of the school counseling program in measurable terms, school counselors analyze school and school counseling program data to determine how students are different as a result of a school counseling program" (p. xiv). The Model emphasizes the importance of evaluating and immediate, intermediate, and long-range impact of school counselor programming and using the information to inform stakeholders and to improve the programs.

Although evaluation and accountability are relatively easy concepts to understand and champion, they require competencies that are especially challenging to master and use successfully. The competencies associated with evaluation and accountability are challenging for most individuals with master's degrees in counseling. With that challenge in mind, the chapter in this textbook on accountability and assessment will follow this one (Chapter 3), and we will provide recommendations for applying the information throughout the remaining chapters where it seems appropriate.

BE AN ADVOCATE FOR THE SCHOOL COUNSELING PROFESSION

Confusion about the role of school counselors was referred to as an "old ghost" more than four decades ago (Shertzer & Stone, 1963). In many schools, counselors find themselves outside the mainstream looking inward for direction from various stakeholders such as administrators, teachers, students, parents, and other interested citizens/taxpayers. These stakeholders often send messages to counselors about their roles and the program goals that are deemed important. These messages are sometimes inconsistent with the training counselors received and the standards established by accrediting agencies and professional associations (e.g., expecting counselors to perform clerical and administrative functions and be responsible for disciplining students). In order to counter these misperceptions and corresponding inappropriate expectations, professional counselors are challenged to advocate for themselves and for balanced school counseling programs both as individuals and collectively through participation in and support of their respective professional associations. We present more on this topic in Chapters 5 and 6.

DIRECT AND INDIRECT PROGRAMMING

In most instances, the demands on, and expectations of, school counselors challenge or exceed their ability to respond in a manner that results in all their clientele receiving desired responses all the time. The somewhat open-ended nature of the school counselor's role and the relatively small size of counseling staffs create settings in which a systematic and careful approach is necessary both for effective programming and for protecting the mental health of the counselors themselves.

This textbook is designed to help counselors become systematic and organized. An important step in that direction is to understand that all programming need not be direct to be effective. Direct programming is provided when counselors interact with the people they are helping; indirect programming is provided when counselors influence or serve third parties such as teachers, parents, and principals who, in turn, interact with the persons to be helped. A balanced counseling program may include both direct and indirect programming.

Prevention offers a vehicle for both direct and indirect programming. On the one hand, counselors may offer prevention programs directly by designing the programs and leading the groups. On the other hand, counselors may offer prevention programs indirectly by helping classroom teachers design and/or deliver prevention programs.

Direct and indirect options are available in responsive counseling interventions, too. The traditional one-to-one counseling relationship is a common example of direct intervention: Counselors meet directly with students to help them in making decisions, resolving problems, changing their behaviors, or changing environmental circumstances. Consultation relationships, in contrast, are indirect interventions: Counselors help students through others who have responsible relationships directly with the students (e.g., a counselor helps a teacher design and implement a plan for helping a child interact more successfully with classmates).

Realizing the importance of direct and indirect helping leads school counselors to more efficient programming than would occur with an overreliance on one type. Balanced programs require balanced counselors who envision a place for both direct and indirect helping in their plans and who possess the competencies to provide both kinds.

BENEFICIARIES OF A BALANCED PROGRAM

School counseling programs exist to help a clientele ranging from kindergarten through senior high school students (K–12). Although not all school systems have K–12 counseling programs, professional counseling associations, the Council for Accreditation of

Counseling and Related Educational Programs, and state departments of education/public instruction recognize the importance of continuous, developmental programming and have designed training programs and developed certification criteria accordingly. In balanced, comprehensive programming, K–12 counseling programs will be designed around developmental concepts and organized so that all activities are coordinated across administrative levels (elementary, middle, and secondary). Conversely, allowing elementary, middle, and secondary school units to develop their own programs independently may lead to duplicated and disjointed programs, lost opportunities, elitism, and estrangement among counselors in the different units, as well as negative opinions by parents, teachers, and administrators.

Much has been discovered and written about human development, but there is still much to learn. Generally, writers view human development as a somewhat linear process. For the sake of clarity, categories or stages of development across what is essentially a continuous life span are identified. Age groupings or ranges, often called *stages,* are the most common categories. Scholarly studies reveal common variables shared by those within a particular developmental stage (e.g., physical changes, cognitive changes, societal expectations). Finding that differences exist among individuals within any stage (e.g., adolescence), developmentalists assume that those differences are distributed normally. Thus, characteristics of the average members of a developmental stage are depicted as typical, although experts fully realize that variation occurs within the group. For example, if hypothetically the available data about the height of 12-year-old boys indicate that the average height is 5 ft, boys around that height will be considered normal for 12-year-olds even though some are as short as 4 ft and some as tall as 6ft. Not all 12-year-old boys will be at the average or "normal" height, nor should they be expected to be. The range of heights for 12-year-old boys provides information about the distribution of their heights and indicates that most of them are around 5 ft tall.

Counselors who understand the attributes of developmental stages and the concepts of normality and variability can have a better sense of what to expect of children or adolescents in any particular age-group. Powers, Hauser, and Kilner (1989) suggest that individual differences may vary dramatically, not only within a developmental sphere but also across spheres. For example, a child may have average height, above-average intelligence, and below-average social skills, compared with others in his or her age group. Therefore, practitioners are encouraged to assess the performances and experiences of individuals within each developmental sphere, rather than try to impose global developmental expectations.

People of color may be dealing with issues related to their racial status that influence their development differently. Helms (1995) believes that people of color in the United States have acquired and internalized racism that may cause them to have to cope with such issues as devaluing their own race, being confused about their racial identity, and learning to embrace their own culture while attempting to achieve a positive racial identity. These issues, coupled with the general issues offered by Erikson's model, indicate that children and youths of color may have additional developmental challenges. School counselors are challenged to be aware of the values and assumptions that influence development differentially across the various worldviews that are represented in our multicultural society. Failing to do so may lead to what Sue (1992) describes as cultural oppression, that is, imposing one's values on culturally different student clients.

Acknowledging developmental changes and stages while recognizing the existence of individual and worldview differences within stages and across spheres enhances the balanced counseling program concept. In a comprehensive counseling program, counselors work cooperatively across grade levels to provide direct and indirect prevention and intervention programming appropriate for the developmental needs of average students while remaining cognizant of the possibility of developmental and cultural variations among individuals.

COMPREHENSIVE SCHOOL COUNSELING PROGRAM COMPONENT

1. Develop a hypothetical school counseling program mission statement that includes the goals of a balanced approach to school counseling.

REFLECTION POINT

1. What do you consider the most important historical events that have shaped the current status of professional school counseling?

2. One of our busy graduate students (who is taking one class per semester toward a master's degree) commented that "balanced equals overwhelmed." And, "I'm not good at all that is included in a balanced approach." She asked, "How in the world can school counselors balance their own professional and personal lives and try to manage a balanced approach to school counseling?"

   How would you answer this student's question?

APPLICATION TO TECHNOLOGY

1. Add your school mission statement to your website.

2. Conduct an Internet search for school counseling program websites. Identify the major components that related to comprehensive school counseling services. Use those sites as examples of what to include on your professional website and begin to imbed placeholders or tabs for you to add to later. Examples include academic, college and career, and social/emotional.

REFERENCES

American Association for Counseling and Development. (1991). *Special issue: Multiculturalism as a fourth force in counseling.* Alexandria, VA: Author.

American Personnel and Guidance Association. (1969). *The elementary school counselor in today's schools.* Washington, DC: Author.

American School Counselor Association. (1996). *School counseling legislation: Elementary and Secondary Act (ESEA).* Alexandria, VA: Author.

American School Counselor Association. (2004). 2004 ASCA RAMP schools announced! *ASCA School Counselor, 41*(6), 32–33.

American School Counselor Association. (2005). *The ASCA national model: A framework for school counseling programs* (2nd ed.). Alexandria, VA: Author.

American School Counselor Association. (2012). *The ASCA National Model: A framework for school counseling programs* (3rd ed.). Alexandria, VA: Author.

American School Counselor Association. (2014). *Mindsets and behaviors for student success: K-12 college- and career-readiness standards for every student.* Alexandria, VA: Author.

American School Counselor Association. (2015). *Past RAMP recipients.* Retrieved from http://www.ascanationalmodel.org/learn-about-ramp/past-ramp-recipients

Aubrey, R. F. (1977). Historical development of guidance and counseling and implications for the future. *Personnel and Guidance Journal, 55,* 288–295.

Baker, S. B. (2001). Reflections on forty years in the school counseling profession: Is the glass half full or half empty? *Professional School Counseling, 54,* 75–83.

Bemak, F., Williams, J. M., & Chung, R. C.-Y. (2014). Four critical domains of accountability for school counselors. *Professional School Counseling, 18,* 100–110.

Borders, L. D., & Drury, R. D. (1992). Comprehensive school counseling programs: A review for policy makers and practitioners. *Journal of Counseling and Development, 70,* 487–498.

Brown, G. I. (1971). *Human teaching for human learning: An introduction to confluent education.* New York: Viking.

Campbell, C. A., & Dahir, C. A. (1997). *Sharing the vision: The national standards for school counseling programs.* Alexandria, VA: American School Counselor Association.

The College Board. (2011). *School counselors literature and landscape review.* Retrieved from http://media.collegeboard.com/digitalServices/pdf/advocacy/nosca/counselors-literature-landscape-review.pdf

Conant, J. B. (1959). *The American high school today.* New York: McGraw-Hill.

Dahir, C. (1997). National standards for school counseling programs: A pathway to excellence. *ASCA Counselor, 35*(2), 11.

Dahir, C. (2001). The national standards for school counseling programs: Development and implementation. *Professional School Counseling, 4,* 320–327.

Dahir, C. (2004). Supporting a nation of learners: The role of school counseling in educational reform. *Journal of Counseling and Development, 82,* 344–353.

Dinkmeyer, D. (1967). Elementary school guidance and the classroom teacher. *Elementary School Guidance and Counseling, 1,* 15–26.

Dobbins, J. E., & Skillings, J. H. (1991). The utility of race labeling in understanding cultural identity: A conceptual tool for the social science practitioner. *Journal of Counseling & Development, 70,* 37–44.

Education Trust. (1997). *Working definition of school counseling.* Washington, DC: Author.

Ewing, D. B. (1975). Direct from Minnesota—E. G. Williamson. *Personnel and Guidance Journal, 54,* 78–87.

Gibson, R. L., & Mitchell, M. H. (1981). *Introduction to guidance.* New York: Macmillan.

Goetz, B. (1997). School enrollment to hit all time high. *Counseling Today, 40*(4), 12.

Guerra, P. (1998). Revamping school counselor education: The DeWitt Wallace Reader's Digest Fund. *Counseling Today, 40*(8), 19–36.

Gysbers, N. C., & Henderson, P. (2000). *Developing and managing your school guidance program.* Alexandria, VA: American Counseling Association.

Gysbers, N. C., & Henderson, P. (2001). Comprehensive guidance and counseling programs: A rich history and a bright future. *Professional School Counseling, 4,* 246–256.

Gysbers, N. C., & Henderson, P. (2012). *Developing and managing your school guidance program* (5th ed.). Alexandria, VA: American Counseling Association.

Hatch, T., & Bowers, J. (2002). The block to build on. *ASCA School Counselor, 39*(5), 12–17.

Hatch, T., & Chen-Hayes, S. F. (2008). School counselor beliefs about ASCA National Model School Counseling Program components using the SCPCS. *Professional School Counseling, 12,* 34–42.

Helms, J. E. (1995). An update of Helms's white and people of color racial identity models. In J. G. Ponteroto, J. M. Casas, L. A. Suzuki, & C. M. Alexander (Eds.), *Handbook of multicultural counseling* (pp. 181–198). Thousand Oaks, CA: Sage.

Herlihy, B., & Remley, T. P. (2001). Legal and ethical challenges. In D. C. Locke, J. E. Myers, & E. L. Herr (Eds.), *The handbook of counseling* (pp. 69–89). Thousand Oaks, CA: Sage.

Herr, E. L. (1985). AACD: An association committed to unity through diversity. *Journal of Counseling & Development, 63,* 395–404. doi: 10.1002/j.1556-6676.1985.tb02819.x

Herr, E. L. (2001). The impact of national policies, economics, and school reform on comprehensive guidance programs. *Professional School Counseling, 4,* 236–245.

Herr, E. L. (2002). School reform and perspectives on the role of school counselors: A century of proposals for change. *Professional School Counseling, 5,* 220–234.

House, R. M., & Hayes, R. L. (2002). School counselors: Becoming key players in school reform. *Professional School Counseling, 5,* 249–256.

Hoyt, K. B., Evans, R. N., Mackin, E. F., & Mangum, G. L. (1974). *Career education: What is it and how to do it* (2nd ed.). Salt Lake City, UT: Olympus.

Ibrahim, F. A. (1991). Contribution of cultural worldview to generic counseling and development. *Journal of Counseling & Development, 70,* 13–19.

Keat, D. B. (1974). *Fundamentals of child counseling.* Boston: Houghton Mifflin.

Lapan, R. T., Gysbers, N. C., & Sun, Y. (1997). The impact of more fully implemented guidance programs on the school experiences of high school students: A statewide evaluation study. *Journal of Counseling & Development, 75,* 292–302.

Lee, C. C., & Sirch, M. L. (1994). Counseling in an enlightened society: Values for a new millennium. *Counseling and Values, 38,* 90–97.

Luongo, P. F. (2000). Partnering child welfare, juvenile justice, and behavioral health with schools. *Professional School Counseling, 3,* 308–313.

Menacker, J. (1974). *Vitalizing guidance in urban schools.* New York: Dodd, Mead.

Menacker, J. (1976). Toward a theory of activist guidance. *Personnel and Guidance Journal, 54,* 318–321.

Morrissey, M. (1996). The baby boom echo generation: Ready or not, here it comes. *Counseling Today, 39*(6), 1, 6, 8.

Mosher, R. L., & Sprinthall, N. A. (1970). Psychological education in secondary schools: A program to promote individual and human development. *American Psychologist, 25,* 911–924.

Neukrug, E. S., Barr, C. G., Hoffman, L. R., & Kaplan, L. S. (1993). Developmental counseling and guidance: A model for use in your school. *School Counselor, 40,* 356–362.

Paisley, P. O., & Borders, L. D. (1995). School counseling: An evolving specialty. *Journal of Counseling and Development, 74,* 150–153.

Parsons, F. (1909). *Choosing a vocation.* Boston: Houghton Mifflin.

Powers, S. I., Hauser, S. T., & Kilner, L. A. (1989). Adolescent mental health. *American Psychologist, 44,* 200–208.

Proctor, W. (1925). *Educational and vocational guidance: A consideration of guidance as it relates to all of the essential activities of life.* Boston: Houghton Mifflin.

Rockwell, P. J., & Rothney, J.W.M. (1961). Some ideas of pioneers in the guidance movement. *Personnel and Guidance Journal, 11,* 34–39.

Rogers, C. R. (1942). *Counseling and psychotherapy.* Boston: Houghton Mifflin.

Rogers, C. R. (1951). *Client-centered therapy.* Boston: Houghton Mifflin.

Rogers, C. R. (1961). *On becoming a person.* Boston: Houghton Mifflin.

Rowley, W. J., Stroh, H. R., & Sink, C. A. (2005). Comprehensive guidance and counseling program's use of guidance curricula materials: A survey of national trends. *Professional School Counseling, 8,* 296–304.

Sears, S. J., & Granello, D. H. (2002). School counseling now and in the future: A reaction. *Professional School Counseling, 5,* 164–171.

Shaw, M. C. (1973). *School guidance systems.* Boston: Houghton Mifflin.

Shertzer, B., & Stone, S. (1963). The school counselor and his [sic] publics: A problem in role definitions. *Personnel and Guidance Journal, 41,* 687–693.

Sink, C. A., & MacDonald, G. (1998). The status of comprehensive guidance and counseling in the United States. *Professional School Counseling, 2,* 88–89.

Smith, G. E. (1955). *Counseling in the secondary school.* New York: Macmillan.

Speight, S. L., Myers, L. J., Cox, C. I., & Highlen, P. S. (1991). A redefinition of multicultural counseling. *Journal of Counseling & Development, 70,* 29–36.

Stamm, M. L., & Nissman, D. (1971). *New dimensions in elementary guidance.* New York: Richards Rosen Press.

Stone, C., & House, R. (2002, May–June). Train the trainers program transform school counselors. *ASCA Counselor, 39,* 20–21.

Sue, D. W. (1992). The challenge of multiculturalism: The road less traveled. *American Counselor, 1,* 6–14.

Urbaniak, J. (2000, September). The ESCDA battle. *Counseling Today,* 18.

Westbrook, S. D., & Sedlacek, W. E. (1991). Forty years of using labels to communicate about nontraditional students: Does it help or hurt? *Journal of Counseling & Development, 70,* 20–28.

The White House. (2015). *Reach higher.* Retrieved from https://www.whitehouse.gov/reach-higher

Williamson, E. G. (1950). *Counseling adolescents.* New York: McGraw-Hill.

Williamson, E. G., & Darley, J. G. (1937). *Student personnel work: An outline of clinical procedures.* New York: McGraw-Hill.

Wrenn, C. G. (1962). *The counselor in a changing world.* Washington, DC: American Personnel and Guidance Association.

Zaccaria, J. (1969). *Approaches to guidance in contemporary education.* Scranton, PA: International Textbook.

ACCOUNTABILITY AND ASSESSMENT IN SCHOOL COUNSELING

3

RELATED STANDARDS OF PRACTICE

CACREP CORE	2.F.1.k., 2.F.4.e., 2.F.5.i.j., 2.F.7.a.e.f.g.j.i.m., 2.F.8.b.c.e.i.j.
CACREP SCHOOL COUNSELING	5.G.1.e, 5.G.3.b.e.n.o.

Goal: To promote comprehensive evaluation strategies, understandable informative accountability information, evidence-based practice, and reasonable assessment expectations for school counselors.

I have been at Greenstone High School for 15 years. I have spent most of my time helping kids with taking the right classes and getting our seniors into the right colleges. I have occasionally helped a pregnant girl break the news to her parents and have sometimes helped kids who are drinking too much—or abusing drugs. I've enjoyed work and have experienced the rewards of being a counselor.

Yesterday, my principal asked me to justify my job. I asked him what that meant. He said, "How does your work improve our dropout rate and influence the academic success of our students?" He added, "I need you to quantify your contribution to our school." When I reminded him of what I do and told him that I didn't have any numbers, he said, "Get the numbers, Eric. We are living in a new world of education. Numbers are the name of the game."

I'm so tired of trying to satisfy higher-ups. Wouldn't it be just as easy to sell insurance? I might even make more money. How can I show what I do in a spreadsheet? My work just doesn't lend itself to numbers, tables, and graphs.

DATA DRIVEN YET SERVICE ORIENTED

How can Eric solve his dilemma and translate the impact of his dedicated services to students to meaningful data without losing his sense of delivering human services to students and their families? Accountability and assessment in school counseling share common goals related to collecting data to better serve students and society. Evaluation data are collected and used to achieve accountability and establish evidence-based practices. Assessment data are collected to help students engage in individual planning successfully. Collecting accurate and meaningful data and using it appropriately are common features of the school counseling accountability and assessment functions.

DEFINITIONS

School counselors are challenged to understand the meaning of several important terms in order to engage in the accountability and assessment functions successfully. Although presented separately, in reality the requisite behaviors for school counselors are interactive rather than independent. For example, school counselors will have to evaluate their work in order to produce evidence of accountability.

Evaluation

We define evaluation as gathering information or data about the effectiveness of one's work as a school counselor. The American School Counselor Association (ASCA, 2012) recommends that school counselors "self-evaluate" their programs in comparison with the ASCA National Model. The following evaluation data components are recommended: (a) use-of-time, (b) process, (c) perception, and (d) outcome.

Use-of-Time Data

Use-of-time data are derived from recording how much time is spent when engaged in providing professional services as a school counselor and how the time is distributed across the various school counselor role categories (e.g., individual counseling, testing, and consultation).

Process Data

Process data are derived from collecting evidence about specific events or activities that occurred that were services provided by school counselors to students or others who received something of value. Examples suggested by ASCA (2012) are "Eight fourth grade students participated in a study skills group that met six times for 45 minutes" and "38 parents attended the middle school orientation meeting" (p. 51). Note the inclusion of use-of-time data in conjunction with the process data in the examples.

Perception Data

Perception data are derived from surveys distributed to various stakeholders (e.g., students, teacher, administrators, and parents). The content of the surveys can be varied (e.g., attitudes, opinions, needs, and informed knowledge). The range of potential perception data survey items can be quite broad.

Outcome Data

Outcome data provide information about the impact of various activities and programs that are delivered by school counselors. There are two potential forms of outcome data. One form is known as *distal data.* Examples of distal data are as follows: "graduation rate improved from 79 percent to 86 percent"; "average attendance improved from 88 percent to 91"; "discipline referrals decreased by 30 percent for students with four our more referrals" (ASCA, 2012, p. 52). These data are considered distal because they are about schools or school systems rather than individual counselors, and the outcomes could be attributed to others as well as school counselors (e.g., teachers and administrators). *Proximal* outcome data are directly attributable to the efforts of school counselors. One example would be when school counselors deliver classroom guidance programs and measure the effects of their efforts via data collected from the students who participated in the program (e.g., change in attitudes or increased knowledge about the topic).

Accountability

A basic definition of accountability is analyzing, processing, and sharing the results of the evaluation endeavors. ASCA (2012) promotes data-driven decision making, that is, school counselors using data to inform themselves and others. In the accountability process, evaluation data are analyzed to (a) better understand how time was used, (b) document the processes involved, (c) capture the perceptions of stakeholders, and (d) provide evidence of effects of goal-driven interventions. The analyses lead to processing the findings in order to improve the school counseling program and specific components therein *(internal accountability)* or sharing the findings with stakeholders *(external accountability)*.

Evidence-Based Practice

Evidence-based practice means that behaviors of school counselors when providing professional services to others are based on and supported by empirical evidence. The American Counseling Association (ACA, 2014) *Code of Ethics* states, "When providing services, counselors use techniques/procedures/modalities that are grounded in theory and/or have and empirical or scientific foundation" (C.7.a. Scientific Basis for Treatment). There are two sources of evidence for school counselors. One source is published reports in the professional literature that provide a scientific, empirical foundation for the interventions and programs delivered by school counselors and the theories they are based upon. Finding and collecting reports that are directly related to the daily efforts of school counselors can be time-consuming and unproductive in some cases. Nevertheless, school counselors are expected to seek and find as much evidence as is possible. A useful resource for information about related research findings that may be useful for school counselors is the Ronald H. Fredrickson Center for School Counseling Outcome Research and Evaluation (www.CSCOR.org).

A second source of evidence is evaluation data produced by professional school counselors themselves. Therefore, the evaluation data identified earlier that are acquired for accountability purposes are also potentially rich depositories of local evidence for one's evidence-based practice. This manner of evaluation is also referred to as *practitioner research*, that is, research conducted by school counselors for school counselors in order to inform the practice of school counseling. Consequently, the data that school counselors collect via the evaluation function also serves as evidence to justify the professional behaviors in which they engage when attempting to serve their stakeholders. We elaborate upon and promote *evidence-based practice for school counselors* later in this chapter.

Assessment

Assessment is a term used quite broadly in the counseling profession, and we are focusing on those aspects of assessment in which school counselors are attempting to help students engage in individual planning successfully. Individual student planning "consists of ongoing systemic activities designed to help students establish goals and develop future plans" (ASCA, 2012, p. 85). The primary sources of assessment data available for the individual planning process are either quantitative or qualitative in nature. Standardized tests and inventories provide quantitative data for helping students learn about their abilities and interests (e.g., *Preliminary Scholastic Aptitude Test; Career Key*). There is a broad range of qualitative assessment data that can be valuable resources in the individual student planning process. Examples are observations from significant others, narrative self-assessments, retrospective recollections of previous experiences, and hypothetical role-playing opportunities. They become assessment data used in the individual student planning process when students are able to use the information for immediate and long-range academic, career, and personal/social planning.

BUILDING A CONVENIENT AND COMPREHENSIVE ACCOUNTABILITY FRAMEWORK

Given the busy environment in which school counselors find themselves, evaluation activities need to be convenient and efficient. Also, given the press of external demands for accountability, supporting data need to be comprehensive, informative, and understandable to stakeholders. Finally accountability data are most helpful when used constructively.

CONVENIENT AND EFFICIENT EVALUATION

Accountability activities will be less burdensome and aversive if fitted in with all other counseling activities. One important factor to be controlled is the amount of time devoted to evaluation and accountability activities; it would be ridiculously cost-inefficient to spend an inordinate amount of time collecting and reporting information about one's own performances. It would also be cost-inefficient and demoralizing for counselors to have to engage in antiquated, burdensome, and time-consuming data-collecting behaviors. Time can be better managed and convenience enhanced if data collection and reporting are streamlined and systematic.

A second important factor to be controlled is the procedure for collecting data. To avoid demoralization and increase efficiency, the procedures can be made convenient by streamlining the process and using systems that are not overly sophisticated and confusing. The systems and procedures should be commensurate with the training that school counselors at the master's degree level have received.

COMPREHENSIVE ACCOUNTABILITY DATA

Comprehensiveness is a desirable characteristic of the evaluation/accountability function because the programs provided by school counselors have many facets, and school counselors have a varied set of stakeholders to serve. Therefore, no one approach to evaluation is broad enough to be all encompassing. Indeed, to rely on a narrow repertoire of evaluation approaches is to risk missing important information, underserving one's stakeholders, and being judged unfairly. Following is an inventory of recommended categories of evaluation/accountability data that together represent a comprehensive set of approaches. We believe our emphasis on comprehensiveness conforms to the position taken by the ASCA (2012). A listing of important evaluation/accountability data components is presented in Table 3.1. In the following section of this chapter, we elaborate on important competencies associated with each of the data components.

TABLE 3.1 *Important Evaluation/Accountability Data Components*   5 Types of Data

| Needs assessment data |
| Process data |
| Use-of-time data |
| Perception data |
| Outcome data |
| Disaggregated data |

COMPONENTS OF A COMPREHENSIVE ACCOUNTABILITY FRAMEWORK

Our position is that use-of-time, perception, and outcome data each provide different proximal data information about school counseling programs, and a comprehensive accountability process needs to include all three components because they complement each other. For example, a counseling program goal may be to help all students use effective communication skills (ASCA National Personal/Social Standard A.2.6) (ASCA, 2014). A prevention program is designed to achieve this goal and others. At the end of the program, student performance in a simulated communications skills test provides outcome data, a record of how much counselor time was involved in planning and delivering the program provides use-of-time data, and participant responses to an attitude survey instrument about the program provides perception data. If the evaluators find that the outcome data were favorable, then the outcome based accountability goal would have been met. Yet what if the participants gave the program low perception data ratings (e.g., "It was boring." "It took too much time."), and the amount of time devoted to preparing and delivering the program was not cost-effective? Given the relative importance of each form of proximal data, our presentation in this chapter includes all of the accountability components in Table 3.1, and we consider each of them important enough for counselors to acquire the requisite knowledge and skills. We also include information about needs assessments that preclude program evaluations and disaggregated data, an important source of distal outcome data. This textbook, of course, is introductory and survey in nature and cannot devote sufficient space to the comprehensive training associated with acquiring the required competencies. Comprehensive training is the grist for more domain-specific courses in a training program.

NEEDS ASSESSMENT DATA

Needs Assessment

Needs assessment is a common term referring to activities designed to acquire information about consumer needs. Cook (1989) sums up the needs assessment process as identifying those to be assessed, determining a method for reaching them, devising a measuring plan, and interpreting the results to those stakeholders who will make relevant decisions.

Whose Needs Should Be Assessed?

Needs assessments are best conducted with a broad brush. It is good to know the expectations and perceived needs of a wide range of potential consumers, including minority and special populations. Knowing the needs of all prospective consumers, however, is not synonymous with guaranteeing delivery to all of them or even with agreeing that their expectations are legitimate. Eventually, school counselors learn they cannot be all things to all people. Program delivery is best approached from a realistic perspective. Knowledge of the range of expectations and needs allows counselors to make informed decisions about using limited time and resources.

How Should Needs Be Assessed?

Needs may be assessed in several ways, some of which are more challenging and time-consuming than others. Comprehensiveness is an important guiding principle. Possibilities include the following:

- Publications about child and adolescent development offer suggestions about the common needs that individuals have in various stages of life.

- Key stakeholders in the school and the community can share what they know about the setting. One has to guard against views representing only a particular bias when gathering this kind of information or when receiving unsolicited offerings (Cook, 1989).

- Community forums provide access to groups that have garnered consensus about some needs and expectations. Care must be taken to achieve true representation or to recognize that it has not been achieved (Cook, 1989).

- Stakeholders can be surveyed to learn about their needs and expectations.

A survey is probably the most popular and common approach to assessing needs. It is also probably the most time-consuming, challenging, and expensive approach. The challenge, in addition to time and expense, is in having the requisite skills to design a survey, administer it, and evaluate the results. Fortunately, others have designed needs assessment surveys and published them and consultants are able to assist in the design and conduct of needs assessments or have surveys to share.

Needs assessment surveys can take one of two approaches: Ask respondents what their needs are, or offer them a predetermined list of possibilities from which to choose (Cook, 1989). Each approach has advantages and disadvantages. Open-ended surveys may be easier to design. They also allow respondents to state their own minds, volunteering ideas that surveyors using a predetermined list might not think of asking. Results, however, may be more difficult to understand. Respondents are limited to immediate needs and often cannot forecast needs they will have eventually but whose importance they do not realize at the time. Surveys based on predetermined lists often include topics that counselors know are important but that might not have been thought of by youthful respondents. These surveys are more difficult and time-consuming to develop. Fortunately, once developed, they are easier to interpret than open-ended surveys and can be used repeatedly. They are limited to the range of questions the designers think to ask, however, and the potential range of needs is enormous.

Which Needs Assessment Strategy Should Be Used?

The information presented in the preceding section paints a picture of two incomplete approaches, which may leave the impression that the best approach is to use both the open-ended and predetermined listing methods to get comprehensive coverage of the consumers' needs. Development of surveys representing either approach or a combination begins with goals and objectives. The surveyors then develop survey questions that reflect those goals and objectives. Specifying objectives helps surveyors design questions, open ended or specific, that address the issues. The basic competencies required are stating goals and objectives in measurable terms, designing survey items that measure those objectives appropriately, and conducting surveys systematically. If these skills were not developed adequately in one's counselor training program, they can be learned through continued education efforts. An alternative is to acquire the consultant services of others who already possess the requisite competencies.

Additionally, those who would employ the needs assessment survey approach must keep in mind the differences in students. Plans for surveying children differ from those for surveying adolescents. Goals and objectives may remain similar, but methods are different. Younger respondents will be less able to answer in writing, for example, and oral responses may be necessary in some cases.

How Will the Results Be Interpreted to Stakeholders?

Because the ultimate purpose of assessing consumer needs is to determine the best ways to serve those consumers, stakeholders should be involved in the process at the outset. If this is done, they can become informed of the intentions for the assessments and better able to respond to the results intelligently. Working with stakeholders in this manner helps school counselors know their expectations. Counselors can then plan for those expectations throughout the assessment process. When school counselors are the decision makers themselves, objectivity is of the utmost importance.

Advisory committees may be beneficial in the decision-making process. Said committees, representing various stakeholders (e.g., parents, community members, faculty members, students), can provide useful feedback and be helpful in the needs assessment process. Because of their commitment, advisory committee members are likely to become knowledgeable about the program and supportive of its efforts to respond to consumer needs. All this, in turn, has potential for enhancing public relations.

PROCESS DATA

A sample listing of process data categories for a school counseling program might include the following program services or functions that are represented in the chapters within the present textbook: individual and group counseling, prevention programming, consultation, program evaluation, and referral and coordination. Process data inventories, to be more complete, should include definitions or descriptions of the specific functions or services. The process of listing and defining services or functions will help professional school counselors make their role more clear to stakeholders. The guiding criteria for determining the content and extent of process data is "'What did you do for whom?' and provide evidence if the event occurred" (ASCA, 2012, p. 51).

USE-OF-TIME DATA

Counselors inventory their activities to acquire use-of-time data. Enumerating use-of-time data usually takes the form of keeping records of how individuals use their time. Targeted behaviors are identified, and their frequency and duration are tallied.

Consider the following simulation. The evaluation stage has two parts:

- Counselors in a school district make a list of the activities they engage in when carrying out their responsibilities and trying to achieve program goals. Some activities are general and some are specific to elementary, middle, and high school levels.

- Individual counselors keep records of how often the activities are performed and how much time is devoted to each of them. The use-of-time data are recorded as hours per activity (e.g., for one counselor in 1 week: individual counseling = 5 hours, scheduling = 15 hours).

The accountability stage also has two parts:

- The hours-per-activity data are then multiplied by the hourly pay rate of the respective counselors to acquire evidence of cost-effectiveness. If the hourly pay rate for the counselor is $50, for example, then the amount of money spent on individual counseling services and scheduling is $250 for the 5 hours of counseling and $750 for the 15 hours of scheduling.

- Stakeholders will have use-of-time data indicating how much time and money are devoted to each activity, and that information can be used in making cost-effectiveness decisions. The decisions will be based on the goals and priorities of the stakeholders and those whom they represent.

In the example, the amount of money spent on scheduling is three times that devoted to individual counseling. Determining whether the expenditures of time and money are cost-effective is based on a variety of factors important to those making the cost-effectiveness decisions. Questions they must answer when establishing a foundation for making cost-effectiveness decisions include these:

- What is the relative importance of the individual counseling and scheduling functions? (If one is more important than the other, it seems that more time and money should be spent on it.)

- What is being accomplished during the time devoted to each function?
- Is the money spent on each function worth the results being achieved?

Notice that use-of-time data do not provide qualitative information. Data that answer such questions as "How much?" or "How many?" are quantitative and objective and are not qualitative unless outcome goals have been determined. Therefore, use-of-time data cannot be used to provide qualitative information unless accompanied by outcome data. Using the use-of-time data from this example, outcome data are added to provide an example of the previous point.

Outcome data were reported for each student who received individual counseling and scheduling assistance as follows: In the 5 hours devoted to individual counseling, two students made decisions with which they were satisfied, one received needed support for anxieties associated with enrolling in a new school, and two thought the counselor understood them well enough to make appointments for follow-up interviews. In the 15 hours devoted to scheduling, 10 schedules were changed as requested, 3 could not be changed as requested but alternatives were determined, and 2 remained unchanged.

The combination of use-of-time and outcome data provides information about how much time is used and what goals are accomplished. The addition of perception data may complete the picture when trying to determine the cost-effectiveness of the counselor's activities. In Gibson's (1990) study, teachers ranked individual counseling as the most important activity. Scheduling or administrative duties ranked 10th of 10 activities.

Given all this information, a stakeholder's thoughts might be as follows:

- The amount of time and money devoted to the lowest ranked activity is three times that devoted to the highest ranked activity.
- The results associated with individual counseling seem clearer and more important than those associated with scheduling.
- Therefore, it appears that the counselors' time is not being used in a cost-effective manner.

This is one of many possible responses to the data. Responses differ, depending on the goals and biases of individual stakeholders.

PERCEPTION DATA

Knowledge of stakeholder satisfaction comes directly from stakeholders. Asking for their opinions is a relatively common practice in the business world, where corporations employ experts to find out what customers want and how much they value the services they have received, and in politics where the opinions of prospective voters are valued highly. When school districts evaluate their programs, stakeholder opinions are also important. Because formally assessing consumer satisfaction is not a routine counseling function, the process can be onerously time-consuming and frustrating, especially if the people involved have little experience and expertise with surveys. School counselors are challenged to know how to identify their stakeholders, what to ask them, and how to acquire the desired information.

Identifying Stakeholders

Who are the consumers of the counselor's services? We prefer a broad definition, believing that individuals who are influenced both directly and indirectly should be included. Also, stakeholders with perceptions about the program services, even though they are not students, should be surveyed. Categorically, then, this broad definition of stakeholders includes currently enrolled students, former students, members of the teaching faculty, members of the administration, members of the school board, parents and guardians, and citizens without direct ties with the schools.

Determining What Information Should Be Asked of Stakeholders

A popular saying in the computer sciences is "Garbage in, garbage out." A poorly conceived perception survey generates information that will haunt those who developed it and who depended on that information. The key principles are that surveys must contain questions that elicit relevant information and that the items are constructed and phrased so that the expected information is achieved. Accomplishing these goals requires direct involvement of those who know what the relevant information is. They pay close attention to how the items are worded and constructed.

School counselors are most likely to know what the relevant information is. Therefore, it will be to their advantage to have direct involvement in the construction of perception surveys. Committees can be established to work on developing surveys for specific stakeholders, and representatives of those stakeholder populations can be invited to participate in the survey construction. For example, school counselors working on surveys for teachers and parents may invite representatives of those groups to join their committee.

Item construction requires some sophistication about wording questions so that their intent is clear to the readers, they are easy to score objectively, and they generate information that is constructive while not being unwittingly deceptive. Clarity is enhanced by proper grammar, simple sentence structure, jargon-free terminology, and sequencing of items according to a logical system.

Open-ended questions are useful for finding out what is on the respondents' minds. Therefore, a place is included for a limited number of open-ended questions at the close of the survey. (Be sure to leave enough room on the survey for responses.) Used as the primary item strategy for opinion surveys, open-ended questions create problems that mitigate the initial advantage of generating them more quickly than closed-ended questions. First, open-ended questions are difficult to score collectively and objectively, presenting surveyors with interpretation, tabulation, and presentation difficulties. Second, such questions limit the range of provided information to that which is in the front of the respondents' minds.

Closed-ended questions, though more time-consuming to develop, have advantages that make them preferred for the bulk of perception surveys. One advantage is that they can be scored objectively. There are several common types of objective scoring systems for perception and attitude surveys, all of which are easy to tabulate and generate information easily understood by professionals and laypeople. For instance, questions that can be answered *Yes* or *No* can be tabulated so that the percentages of affirmative and negative responses can be reported. In an example, student responses to the survey item "Do you think that counselors are available to the students?" were Yes = 75%, No = 25%. Another common tactic is to employ some sort of rating system that employs numbers. One example is asking respondents to rate the college counseling efforts on a scale from 1 to 10, with 10 being the most positive. The average of the individual ratings can be reported. For instance, the average rating of the college counseling efforts in the program was 6.76 on such a 10-point scale. A very simple scoring system is to have respondents check or leave blank items according to predetermined instructions. For example: "Check the activities listed below that you knew existed before you received this survey." The total number of students who checked each activity can be reported, as well as the percentage of all students who completed the questionnaire: Crisis Counseling Interventions = 750 students (75% of the student population); Classroom guidance = 375 students (37.5% of the student population); and so forth.

Another advantage to using closed-ended questions is that survey constructors can ensure that they have developed items to represent all the topics they wish to have covered. This forces respondents to think about all the topics the designers deem important, some of which the respondents would not have known prior to the survey. Also, it is easier to report the results of surveys with closed-ended questions. In the previous examples, percentages and totals were cited as tabulating methods that can be used to report the results. These methods and others like them allow perception surveyors to report simply the collective results of surveys given to groups of respondents.

Acquiring Desired Information

After developing the surveys, the next step is to use them in the field. Decision making focuses on whether to survey all the targeted population or to sample it; whether to have the respondents fill in their own answers or to have the questions presented by others who may also have to fill in the answers; whether to mail the surveys, use electronic mail, or use another delivery system; and whether to make responding a requirement or a voluntary act. If a survey program is comprehensive, all the aforementioned decisions are made. Possible decisions are these: when the number of administrators in a school system is small, all will be surveyed; because many adults are in the school district, an arbitrarily determined percentage of them will be surveyed randomly; older children, adolescents, and adults will complete their own survey, but primary-grade teachers will read the questions to their students and fill in the answers for them if necessary; and all administrators will be expected to complete a survey, whereas students and other adults will be allowed to do so voluntarily.

After such decisions have been made, perception-surveying skills have to be employed. For instance, respondent anonymity must be protected, appropriate sample sizes determined, and strategies for getting adequate responses from mailed or electronic surveys developed. Some of these competencies are within the range of professional school counselors and their colleagues, and some may have to be acquired from professional literature or from consultants.

Getting started may seem like a monumental task. Indeed, it is a lot of work. Most of the work is at the beginning, however. Once surveys have been designed, they can be reused with some necessary modifications at other future times. In addition, not all stakeholders need to be surveyed all the time, nor do all members of a targeted group need to be surveyed at any one time. Samples can be selected and surveyed periodically according to a predetermined schedule. Therefore, getting started represents the major time commitment, one that must be made if there is a desire or a need to acquire meaningful perception data.

OUTCOME DATA

Outcome data focus on results from evaluations of programs and interventions. A basic outcome data question is, What was the impact of the program or intervention on the participants? Four important stages for collecting outcome data are available to evaluators. They are (1) preprogram presentation data (Answers the question, What knowledge, skills, or attitudes exist among the participants at the outset of the program?); (2) intermediate data (Answers the questions, How well is the program doing as it progresses and what may need to be changed?); (3) immediate data (Answers the question, What are the effects at the end of the program?); and (4) long-range data (Answers the question, How well have the effects held over time?). An important basic ingredient of outcome data is formulating goals/objectives for programs and interventions that can be measured in order to determine if the desired outcomes were produced. For example, ASCA (2014) National Standards A.1.5 and A.1.6 state that students will learn to make decisions and how to set goals. The minimum outcome to be assessed for a program designed to achieve those objectives would need to include procedures for determining how many participants acquired the competence at the intermediate results-based stage. Long-range results would be even more convincing. Preprogram data would help the evaluators learn how much change may have occurred during the program, and intermediate data would provide helpful data during the program delivery process.

Determining Outcome Goals and Objectives

For the sake of simplicity, the word *goal* is used in the remainder of this chapter as a global term representing goals and objectives because of the tendency for the terms to be used differently in the professional literature. Determining what outcome data to collect and how to collect them depends on the goals one is trying to achieve. Therefore, the collection and reporting of outcome data depends on the identification of outcome goals. Sometimes the goals and the means of assessing them are clear. On other occasions, the goals may be clear but the means of assessing them are difficult to identify. At still other times, both the goals and the means of assessing them are difficult to discern. Two important skills emerge. School counselors are challenged, first, to be able to identify goals for their professional endeavors that can be assessed objectively and, second, to identify outcomes that measure whether those goals were achieved.

Often, counselors engage in activities for which the goals are implied or determined by others. In responding to the demands for such activities, counselors find themselves proceeding without fully realizing what the underlying goals are. Instead, they simply do what they are expected to do. For example, many secondary school counselors find themselves involved in the gatekeeping and clerical chores associated with scheduling, such as determining whether students should be allowed to make schedule changes, recording the changes, and monitoring the master schedule. On the surface, the goals appear to have been imposed by the school's administration. Indeed, some implied administrative goals are measurable: Is the system running smoothly? Has everyone who desired services been served? Is the paperwork in order? Are the class sizes balanced? Additionally, each student who seeks scheduling-related counseling services has his or her own goals. In these individual cases, counselors and students can determine goals cooperatively, giving counselors a foundation for determining the outcomes for which to strive.

On some occasions, counselors can set goals in advance of their activities. For example, an elementary school counselor planned a classroom guidance program that was to be delivered in selected classrooms by basing the activity on predetermined goals. On still other occasions, counselors set goals after engaging in activities. This is often the case when counselors engage in individual counseling. Goal setting usually follows time spent exploring and clarifying the presentation of issues and feelings with student clients.

The underlying principle here is that there are goals for all the programs and interventions that counselors render. Some goals are predetermined by students, administrators, and teachers. Others are negotiated. Realizing that all their activities are goal directed is the first step counselors can take to understand how to assess the final effects of their efforts. The next step is actively interpreting those goals as desired outcomes of their programs. For example, a middle school student was miserable because her friends were shunning her. She did not know what to do. The goal negotiated by the student and her counselor was to help her determine a plan of action. The outcome was a workable plan. Once counselors make the identification of goals a conscious behavior, they are in a position to consider methods for assessing outcomes. Perhaps another way to state this belief in the importance of goals is to put it in terms of job satisfaction. A clear understanding of goals will lead to a clear job description, whereas a lack of goals or unclear goals will, in turn, lead to an unclear job description.

Assessing Outcomes

Having mastered the art of identifying goals and translating them into outcomes, counselors then need outcome measures. Although not limitless, the universe of possible outcome measures is large and impossible to inventory in this textbook. Essentially, the desired outcomes dictate the measures to be used in assessing those outcomes. For example, in the cases cited previously in which counselors helped students make decisions about their schedules, whether a decision was made is an example of outcome data for one client. In the case of the middle school student who was being shunned, whether a plan for responding was developed would be outcome data. Whether the plan worked successfully would be outcome data for another goal: to carry out the plan. In such cases, the outcome data are unique to one student client and do not lend themselves to summarizing and categorizing across student clients.

In the situation of the elementary school counselor planning a classroom guidance program with goals determined in advance, means for measuring the outcomes can also be planned in advance, allowing the counselor to choose one or more measures to be given to student participants at strategic times during the program. For example, if the purpose of the program is to make children aware of nontraditional careers, the counselor might present an inventory of pictures or titles of careers to participants at the outset to determine how many of the nontraditional careers presented in the inventory are familiar to them. The same inventory can be given at the close of the program to determine how much was learned. Another measure the counselor can use in the same manner is to assess whether the attitudes of participants toward the nontraditional careers become more favorable after the program.

Additional information about collecting outcome data is presented in Chapters 7 and 8. Information about evaluating prevention programming via comparing preintervention and postintervention assessments is presented in Chapter 7. A case-by-case approach for individual and small group counseling is presented in Chapter 8. Both presentations provide more detailed suggestions for collecting outcome data that also serves as evidence for one's evidence-based school counseling practice.

DISAGGREGATED DATA

Global school system data can be collected, disaggregated, and used to develop responsive strategies and then reported as possible outcomes that school counselors contributed to broader school improvement and achievement goals. These data are by nature distal because they are school system–wide (e.g., attendance records, standardized test scores, and graduation rates) and can conceivably be influenced by a number of groups and individuals in addition to school counselors who may have targeted some part of a set of solutions to challenges that the data represent.

Stone and Dahir (2007) provided detailed recommendation for collecting these data. They introduced a six-step process for collecting the data and achieving accountability that is represented by the acronym MEASURE. This process provides a mechanism for getting organized, targeting critical data elements to be disaggregated, and reporting the results.

Step 1: Mission (M)

The mission is to align the school counselor's role with the school's mission and goals of the annual school improvement plan. Stone and Dahir (2007) offered a sample school mission statement: "To promote the conditions necessary so that each student experiences academic success. Each student will have the coursework required to choose from a wide array of options after high school" (p. 23).

Steps 2 and 3: Element (E) and Analyze (A)

School counselors are directed to examine critical elements of available data that are important to the school's mission. These data should be found in the school district or building report card and are usually stored in a retrievable format. An important skill for school counselors to acquire in this process is the ability to *disaggregate* data. School districts collect and report student achievement data about attendance, promotion rates, number of suspensions, graduation rates, postsecondary education attendance, and standardized testing results. School counselors are encouraged to collect these *aggregated* data and separate (i.e., disaggregate) them according to important *equity variables* such as ethnicity, gender, socioeconomic status, and teacher assignment. Each equity variable has the potential to become an element in the school counseling program's accountability efforts. At this stage, decision making is based on analyzing the data and determining which indicators (i.e., elements) of school success the school counselors believe that they believe they can have an impact on. Stone and Dahir (2007) provided an example.

> The data revealed (among other important things) that 50% of your students seeking postsecondary education, 34% came from one particular feeder school where all students were assigned to algebra classes in eighth grade and were supported with mentors and tutors, so they would be successful. This feeder middle school placed every student in algebra, a positive practice that could be replicated by other feeder schools.
>
> (p. 25)

Step 4: Stakeholders (S) Unite (U)

At this point, school counselors are encouraged to "identify stakeholders to help and unite to develop an action plan" (Stone & Dahir, 2007, p. 25). This process places school counselors in *leadership* roles because they attempt to identify stakeholders to be involved in teamed efforts to address selected data elements derived from the disaggregation of school achievement reports and develop action plans. *Collaborating* with others rather than working in isolation is advocated. Prospective stakeholders may reside in the schools (e.g., administrators and teachers) or in the community (e.g., parents and business representatives).

Step 5: Results (R)

A reanalysis helps determine whether the goals were met. Reanalysis data can be used to reflect on what worked and what needs to be improved and to determine what goals and activities need to be revised. Stone and Dahir (2007) recommended that, if targeted outcomes are met, set new targets and new strategies, and replicate what was successful. If the targeted outcomes are not met, make changes to remain focused on student success. Either revise or cancel unsuccessful programs in order to be cost efficient.

Step 6: Educate (E)

This is a vital step in the accountability process. Stone and Dahir (2007) recommend that school counselors disseminate data about changes in the targeted elements to both internal and external stakeholders so they can see the positive impact the school counseling program is having on student success. A MEASURE report card can be used to depict the accomplishments.

PRESENTING EVALUATION DATA SUCCESSFULLY AND ACHIEVING ACCOUNTABILITY

The act of collecting evaluation information, though important, is not sufficient in itself. Evaluative information has to be shared with others in a manner that leads to understanding. Making their evaluative data understandable and informative is primarily the responsibility of school counselors. Therefore, school counselors are challenged to be competent in translating evaluative data into meaningful accountability information. This means that school counselors must be able to implement understandable and informative data-reporting systems.

Some data-reporting systems have been described in the professional counseling literature, and many other adequate systems remain to be developed by creative minds. Although reporting systems differ, they share some basic principles that make them understandable and informative:

- The information is summarized and organized systematically;
- The presentation is clear, concise, and understandable to stakeholders;
- Reports are as brief as possible without omitting valuable information.

In 2014, North Carolina instituted a very comprehensive required accountability system for school counselors. Although localized to one state in nature, the plan had considerable input from school counseling professionals and serves as a model for individual school counselors, school counseling programs, and other states to consider.

The central product of the system is a set of standards for professional school counseling and rubrics for evaluating efforts to meet the standards. The mission for the standards is that of the North Carolina State Board of Education for every public school student, that is, "graduate from high school globally competitive for work and postsecondary education and preparation for life in the 21st century" (www.ncpublicschools. org/studentsupport/counseling/standards/). The vision for school counselors cites 16 competency areas that reflect the influence of both the ASCA National Model (ASCA, 2012) and the Council for Accreditation of Counseling and Related Educational Programs (CACREP, 2016) Standards. The purposes of the standards are to "guide professional development of school counselors forward in the twenty-first century and provide the focus for schools and districts as they support, monitor and evaluate their school counselors."

There are five standards that represent broad knowledge and skill categories (e.g., school counselors demonstrate leadership, advocacy, and collaboration). Each standard is accompanied by an explicit description of its content. The system also provides listings of various tasks that may be undertaken to demonstrate having met the standards and suggests criteria for judging how well the standards have been met (i.e., developing, proficient, accomplished, distinguished, and not demonstrated). As well, examples of artifacts that might be presented as evidence of accountability by school counselors are provided (e.g., analysis of program data, advisory council documents, individual growth plans, accountability process documentation).

The comprehensiveness of the system reflects the multifaceted role and functions of professional school counseling. An initial observation might be that it is too complicated and potentially overwhelming to implement. We believe that the system provides school counselors and school counseling programs with an important array of standards and rubrics that can serve them wherever they are employed. In addition, the broad set of recommended artifacts covers varied forms of data that may provide evidence of having achieved something of value. Knowing in advance what artifacts are of value makes data collection a proactive rather than reactive process. The system is designed to provide guidance for evaluating one's practice and is based on constructive accountability principles.

ACCOUNTABILITY AS A MEANS OF ENHANCING PUBLIC RELATIONS

The evaluation/accountability process provides school counselors with ample opportunities to influence public relations. Of the programs offered by the schools, counseling is usually less well understood by the public than teaching and administering. Consequently, misinformation and misperceptions about the counseling program are more likely to occur. This circumstance challenges school counselors to inform the various stakeholders about their goals, programs, and accomplishments. Notice the assumption that programs with goals are in place before public relations activities are undertaken. Failure to do so entertains the risk of advertising one's shortcomings in advance of attempting to recognize and correct them if they exist.

Strategies for influencing public opinion are numerous. For example, *advisory committees* consisting of cross sections of people from one's school and community provide important feedback for counseling programs and educate these influential members about the intricacies of the program (Fairchild & Seeley, 1995). Another strategy is to hold *accountability conferences* with one's administrators. Such conferences encourage administrators to be actively involved in the accountability process, keep them informed, request them to be allies, and enlist their support (Fairchild & Seeley, 1995). Another strategy with promise is to prepare a *formal written report* that brings together all of the program's accountability data into one document that, in turn, can be shared with one's stakeholders. Fairchild and Seeley recommend that, once the report has been prepared and disseminated, a school board presentation and presentations to the teaching faculty be requested. Both meetings provide opportunities to inform important publics and to correct misinformation that has occurred. Fairchild and Seeley cite other opportunities to enhance public relations that can be undertaken as well, including speaking to parent groups, civic organizations, and classrooms of students. Such meetings can focus on accountability data and can be used to share the expertise of the counseling staff through accurate, helpful information-sharing or town meeting formats. Clearly, systematic public-relations activities have an important place in the accountability function, and the evaluation data collected by counselors can be the centerpiece of public relations efforts. All of these suggestions can be accomplished within a comprehensive accountability system similar to the North Carolina program described earlier.

ESTABLISHING AN EVIDENCE-BASED SCHOOL COUNSELING PROGRAM

As presented earlier, evaluation data can be an important and useful source of evidence for school counselors and school counseling programs. School counselors bear the responsibility for evaluating of the effects of their work. We believe that evidence-based practice can be the product of the evaluation and accountability efforts of school counselors who are engaging in practitioner research that is within the range of research competencies that they possess (Baker, 2012). The data produced from engaging in the data collection practices presented earlier in the comprehensive accountability framework and the additional ideas presented in the North Carolina professional school counseling standards provide a comprehensive set of content categories for collecting data that can serve as the evidence upon which local school counseling programs are based. The final step is to believe that the cumulative data collected for local evaluation and accountability purposes also represent the evidence for one's evidence-based school counseling practice. Evidence-based school counseling consists of using local data in a number of constructive ways for making informed decisions, including (a) identifying student needs, (b) deciding how to spend time and use resources, (c) identifying effective interventions, (d) supporting systems changes, and (e) informing stakeholders (Dimmett, 2015). Specific strategies are presented at the close of Chapters 7 and 8.

DESIGNING A COMPREHENSIVE ASSESSMENT STRATEGY TO ENHANCE INDIVIDUAL STUDENT PLANNING

I have little time to do what I really need to do to help students with all the other things going on in their lives. The emphasis on testing has also created new problems for kids. I spent many hours visiting with parents who are concerned about whether their children will pass the required tests at the end of the year. The children also worry. I can hardly believe how many cases of test anxiety I handle. Children feel as if their lives will be total failures if they don't mark on end-of-grade tests. I am at a loss to know how to handle all of this. What can I do?

The broad demand for assessment is wrapped up in the history of standardized testing and the demand for testing in society and education. How can school counselors "handle" the assessment demands confronting them and find a meaningful place for themselves among the assessment expectations found in today's educational enterprises?

As stated earlier, *assessment* is a term used quite broadly in the counseling profession, and we are focusing on those aspects of assessment in which school counselors are attempting to help students engage in individual planning successfully. Individual student planning "consists of ongoing systemic activities designed to help students establish goals and develop future plans" ASCA, 2012, p. 85). A broad range of quantitative and qualitative assessment data can be used for immediate and long-range academic, career, and personal/social planning. What data are available, and how can school counselors use the data effectively?

The ASCA (2012) description of individual student planning serves as a foundation for our assessment recommendations:

> Through individual student planning, school counselors assist students as the students evaluate educational, career, and personal goals. School counselors promote individual student planning by helping students develop individual learning plans, make the transition from elementary to middle, middle to high or make the transition from school to higher education or work. Activities may be delivered on an individual basis, in small groups or classroom settings. Parents or guardians and other school personnel are often included in the activities.
>
> (p. 86)

The vocational guidance and psychometric movements in the early 20th century influenced the assessment domain that is of interest in school counseling today. The former movement popularized the importance of helping young people acquire useful information about occupations and find a place for themselves in the increasingly complex world of work, and the latter introduced standardized tests that could serve as tools for helping young people find meaningful work. School counselors have used aptitude test and vocational interest inventory data to help students make educational and career decisions over the intervening decades. For example, school counselors may arrange for students making the transition from middle to high school to take the Armed Services Vocational Aptitude Battery and the Kuder Career Planning System in order to provide standardized information about their abilities and interests that, in turn, might make their future planning decisions better informed than they would have been without the information.

Standardized tests have a broad appeal because of the objective numerical scoring systems that appear to indicate that the scores are accurate. On the other hand, how many people do you know who believe that their SAT or GRE scores do not accurately depict their abilities or state that they do not perform well on the objective, multiple-choice type questions found in these tests? As well, how convincing are the arguments for the high-stakes achievement testing that is common in basic education today? Are you convinced that schools should be graded on the performance of their students on end-of-grade or end-of-course examinations, or are there other important factors to consider as well?

Based on evidence that counselors were not using standardized test data appropriately in the mid-20th century, Goldman (1972) referred to the situation metaphorically as the marriage that failed. His evidence was convincing and helped to pave the way for challenging counselors to focus on using the data to help students learn more about themselves, rather than attempting to predict whether they would succeed in the future. As Goldman pointed out, the data derived from standardized testing were not accurate enough for counselors to engage in predictions about whether their students would succeed in the future or what jobs/careers were best for them. The changed focus on using standardized test data to encourage students to explore rather than predict also opened the way for seeking and using qualitative assessment data to achieve the same goals.

Although school counselors currently use standardized test data to help students acquire information that will assist in their individual planning via an exploratory rather than predictive process, understanding the basic principles of measurement remains important for school counselors. Consequently, the 2016 CACREP Standards for counselor education training programs include the following assessment and testing standards: (a) basic concepts of standardized and nonstandardized testing, norm-referenced and criterion-referenced assessment, and group and individual assessments; (b) statistical concepts, including scales of measurement, measures of central tendency, indexes of variability, shapes and types of distributions, and correlations; (c) reliability and validity in the use of assessments; (d) use of assessments relevant to academic/educational, career, personal, and social development; and (e) ethically, culturally, and developmentally relevant strategies for selecting, administering, and interpreting assessment and test results. These topics should be covered in required courses in entry-level training programs devoted to assessment and tests and measurement.

KNOWLEDGE ABOUT PRINCIPLES OF MEASUREMENT

Lacking basic knowledge of measurement principles, test users are navigating without compasses. They know they are going somewhere, but they don't know where or how to get there. Test users who lack basic knowledge about measurement may harm the individuals they are trying to serve. Those individuals would have best received no service at all. Unfortunately, most people whose use of tests is coupled with misinformation about measurement are not aware of that shortcoming or do not realize how crucial their behavior can be.

What should school counselors know about measurement? This is a difficult domain to master and, unfortunately, it often ranks low in the minds of many counseling students. In addition, quantitative psychological measurement can appear complex if taught in a manner that befuddles counseling students and/or if taught by instructors who cannot apply it to using tests in counseling. Beginning school counselors are not expected to know all the intricacies of measurement at the outset of their careers. They are encouraged to increase their knowledge beyond their graduate-level training. Following is an attempt to identify a set of important assessment competencies. This information cannot replace the knowledge acquired from courses in descriptive statistics, measurement, and assessment. A goal of these subsections is to give relevance to the large body of information presented in such courses.

Scales and Scoring Systems

All standardized and some nonstandardized assessment instruments have scales and scoring systems that report individual and group results. School counselors are challenged to be familiar with these systems in order to understand the results correctly and to help others understand and use the results appropriately. The following simulation supports the contention that counselors serve students better if they understand the scales and scoring systems of various assessment instruments:

> *Simulation:* All students in the elementary schools of a school district participate in an annual achievement-testing program. Standardized achievement tests are given in each grade to compare the average scores of the school district with national norms to evaluate teachers, locate content areas that need to be improved, and identify students who need remedial or advanced work. One of the scales used by the test publisher is known as *grade equivalents*. Individual scores on specific content area subtests are reported as grade levels with corresponding months above and below the first month in that grade level. For instance, Jafar, a fourth-grade student, received scores of Second Grade–Third Month, Second Grade–Fifth Month, Second Grade–Tenth Month, and Third Grade–First Month on the language, reading, arithmetic,

and social studies subtests, respectively. Jamilah, also a fourth-grade student, received scores of Sixth Grade–Seventh Month, Sixth Grade–Eighth Month, Sixth Grade–Tenth Month, and Seventh Grade–First Month on the same subtests. In addition, approximately half of the fourth-grade class had average scores below Fourth Grade–First Month.

The following false conclusions were made about this information by otherwise intelligent and well-meaning persons. Jafar's teacher entertained thoughts of recommending that he be given second-grade materials to study as part of a remedial program. Jamilah's parents considered requesting that she be advanced to sixth grade. The principal was upset to learn that half of the fourth grade was below grade level on the tests. Why were these false conclusions made, and what were the reasons for making them?

Jafar's teacher, Jamilah's parents, and the school principal, not knowing the scoring system on which grade-equivalent scales are based, interpreted the words (i.e., grade levels) literally and came to apparently logical conclusions. Counselors are challenged not to make such conclusions. Their job is to understand the scales and scoring systems used in various assessment programs and, therefore, to be able to help others avoid such errors. Detailed information about grade equivalents can be presented as part of well-designed and comprehensive courses on assessment, including information about measurement systems.

Briefly, Jafar's teacher and Jamilah's parents made conclusions without knowing that Jafar's and Jamilah's test results had been compared only with those of other fourth graders. They had not been compared with second, third, sixth, or seventh graders. The grade equivalents in Jafar's case indicated that he is well below average fourth graders. Jamilah is well above average. On grade-equivalent scales, test publishers use grade levels higher and lower than the one of interest—in this case, fourth grade—for scores outside the 10 months of the school year. Therefore, Fifth Grade–First Month follows Fourth Grade–Tenth Month, and Third Grade–Tenth Month precedes Fourth Grade–First Month even though the scale is used exclusively for fourth graders.

The school principal did not realize that the average score for fourth graders should identify them as being where they were when they took the test—which was the Fourth Grade–First Month. If they achieve average performance on the tests, they will be at that point. Those who score below the middle will have third-grade or lower grade equivalents. If the class has a normally distributed group of fourth-grade students, about half of them will have scores below the average or middle of the distribution of scores. Therefore, it is to be expected that a substantial number of students have grade equivalents below Fourth Grade–First Month. The fact that half of the students are below grade level merely means that half of them are below the middle or average score.

This example shows only a few of the many problems that can occur when assessment data are misunderstood. Scales and scoring systems represent an important technology about which school counselors are challenged to be sophisticated. It appears as if minimum competence should include knowledge about the following:

- The different kinds of scales (nominal, ordinal, interval, and ratio) and their properties;

- The scoring systems derived from the basic scales used in psychological and educational assessment (e.g., standard scores, percentile ranks);

- The standard normal distribution and its properties—leading to an understanding of the role of norms in assessment;

- Sampling theory for selecting test items and establishing norms or reference groups;

- Basic descriptive statistics (e.g., measures of central tendency, such as means, medians, and modes; measures of dispersion from the center of a distribution, such as standard deviations and ranges).

Reliability and Validity

Simply stated, *validity* means that assessment tools should achieve the goals they are designed to achieve. Validity also means that tests should be used appropriately. *Reliability* means that the assessment tools perform consistently. The following simulation highlights the importance of counselors being knowledgeable about these measurement principles:

> *Simulation:* Middle school and junior high school students are given a vocational interest inventory as part of a career exploration unit. One purpose of the inventory is to provide food for thought—to suggest careers about which participants might acquire further information because they demonstrated higher interest in them than most other individuals of their age and gender. Jana brought her results home and announced that they indicated she should be an artist. Jarek filed his results and discovered them 3 years later when planning for life after high school. He used the results to begin a search for information about careers appropriate for him to pursue.
>
> Both Jana and Jarek used the results of their interest inventories inappropriately because they knew nothing about validity and reliability. That is to be expected in most instances. Therefore, school counselors are challenged to prevent these situations as often as possible. Jana misinterpreted the purpose of the inventory and ascribed a degree of certainty to

the results that was not intended by the test publisher or by the individuals who designed the career exploration program. She invalidated the results by assuming that they identified a specific career for her when, in fact, the inventory was designed to compare her interests with those of others of her age and sex.

Jarek created a reliability problem when he assumed that the results were useful 3 years later. Because of the dramatic changes that occur in individuals as they mature from childhood through adolescence, it was likely that Jarek's interests had changed in 3 years and that his later responses would be quite different from the earlier ones. The reliability of interest inventories over a period of 3 years is limited—not in every case, but certainly in many cases. Jarek would have been served better by the results of an inventory taken concurrently with his career search activities, and a school counselor who understood reliability principles would have been able to provide Jarek with helpful information in that regard.

Reliability and validity are important concepts; minimally, a school counselor should know the following:

- Classic reliability theory, including the concepts of true scores and observed scores;
- Methods for estimating reliability used by test publishers, such as the test-retest, parallel forms, split halves, and internal consistencies strategies;
- Basic statistical procedures used when reporting most reliability and some validity estimates (correlation analyses and correlation coefficients);
- Methods used by test publishers for estimating validity (content validity, construct validity, predictive validity, and concurrent validity);
- Procedures used to translate reliability and validity data into counseling information (e.g., the standard error of measurement, the standard error of estimate, expectancy tables).

QUALITATIVE OR NONSTANDARDIZED ASSESSMENTS

As shared earlier, the focus of assessment in school counseling has broadened from prediction to exploration goals. Therefore, the range of assessment data that can be useful has also broadened.

Consequently, school counselors are able to use both quantitative and qualitative data when attempting to assist students during the ongoing individual planning process. Perhaps it is easier to define qualitative assessments by what they are not rather than what they are. That is, qualitative assessments are not standardized and quantitative. Therefore, virtually anything else of value in the individual student planning process can qualify as qualitative in nature. Each student's unique circumstances may dictate what qualitative data may contribute to the individual student planning process. Qualitative data that seem to have potential across numerous students are (a) course grades, (b) teacher evaluations and comments, (c) behavior observations, (d) retrospective recollections of personal histories, (e) narrative self-assessments of personal likes and dislikes, (f) health statuses, (g) future goals, (h) family resources, (i) simulation data from role-playing endeavors, and (j) student motivation levels. What are your thoughts about the value of these suggestions and what additional ideas can be generated?

HELPING STUDENTS UNDERSTAND AND PROCESS ASSESSMENT DATA

Assumptions associated with this presentation are that students will benefit from engaging in academic, career, and personal planning, and school counselors can assist these students with the appropriate use of quantitative and qualitative assessment data. How do school counselors achieve this goal? We believe that individual student planning is a form of individual counseling devoted to a specific set of *planning* goals yet requiring the same interpersonal communication skills as other forms of counseling, including crisis counseling. Communicating standardized assessment data accurately is one of the most difficult challenges school counselors face when engaged in individual student planning, and that challenge is the focus of the following presentation.

Test interpretations might be described as efforts by counselors to help test takers make sense out of the results and process the information to use it constructively. Test interpretation, like the test selection process, is best accomplished by making it a part of the individual planning process, rather than an adjunct activity. Therefore, counselors can incorporate test interpretations into the individual planning process. To accomplish this, counselors blend their knowledge of basic measurement principles with their counseling competencies. The following presentation suggests how the blending might occur.

If one is viewing test interpretation as part of the individual planning process, the first step or goal is to establish a mutually acceptable working relationship between the counselor and the student. These attitudes and competencies are described in Chapter 8. Beyond that, the reasons for taking the test are made clear to all involved, and the counselors know what their student's expectations are. Unrealistic or misinformed expectations may need to be challenged immediately, and unmet expectations will need to be addressed eventually. Judicial use of basic communication skills will help counselors learn about students' expectations.

Relationship development and expectation assessment set the stage for disseminating the information if the student is ready and interested. The information is often technical and sometimes comprehensive, leaving counselors with the challenge of keeping it from overwhelming and confusing the student. In meeting this challenge, counselors will share their technical knowledge about tests and measurement while remembering their communication skills. They will translate technical terms into words and phrases understandable to the student and not use those terms directly with the student unless necessary. For example, students seldom need to know what methods were used to estimate the reliability or validity of a test. They can be helped to understand the concept of the standard error of measurement without being introduced to the term *standard error of measurement* or to the formula for estimating it. The developmental stage of students will also serve as a guide to what technical information they can process. Certainly, children need to be treated differently from high school adolescents.

Graphic aids such as test publisher–generated profiles provide visual assistance to counselors and students. Counselors can help students by making sure they are able to see the aids clearly and understand them. Computerized printouts from test publishers or from the Internet can also be very helpful, providing printed and graphic interpretive information. Many students will need help with the computer-generated printouts because such reports often provide more information than students can process successfully and may include information they do not understand.

Because the information dissemination segment of the test interpretation process contains so much that needs to be shared and explained, there is a danger of too much counselor and too little client involvement in the process. Counselor overactivity and student passivity can be avoided through the use of counseling skills. The counselor can draw students into the information dissemination process by asking them to summarize at strategic points, to answer questions that will inform the counselor how well they understand the information, and to explain results in their own words after having observed counselor demonstrations. It may also help to incorporate segments of student data processing into the dissemination process. Getting students involved in the information dissemination process should be primary in counselors' minds and within their range of basic skills.

Student processing of the information leads to a continuation of the individual planning decision-making process, completing the test-interpreting component. Basic counseling skills can be used to invite students to begin processing the information. For example, a counselor might ask, "What are your thoughts about these test results?" after sharing the appropriate information. Student processing can lead the counseling relationship in several directions, such as decision-making counseling and support counseling. Accurate communication of assessment information requires attitudes and skills that are commensurate with good counseling. The ingredient that differentiates these interpretations from other counseling endeavors is the technical information generated by the assessments that begs to be translated clearly in order to be useful.

The following simulation is an abbreviated example of a test interpretation interview. The student, Ned, is an eighth grader who took an aptitude test as an assignment in a career-planning unit led by the counselor, Ms. Bigelow. The purpose of the testing is to use data from the test to help Ned and his classmates think about future plans and, more immediately, make course selections for ninth grade. Ned is having difficulty

...derstanding the information on the profile of scores provided by the test publisher and seeks out Ms. Bigelow for assistance:

Ms. Bigelow (B):   Hello, Ned, what can I do for you?

Ned (N):   Hi! Ms. Bigelow, I'm having trouble understanding these test scores. Can you help me?

B: I certainly will try. Tell me what you think you know about the scores and what you hope to learn from them.

N: Well, I hope to find out what I want to do when I grow up and what courses I should take next year—and I'm not sure what I know about the scores.

B: OK! You would like to use the information to make plans for the future, and it appears as if you are really confused about the scores. Should we begin with them?

N: Yes. I'm really confused about all the numbers and graphs.

B: They can be confusing for many people. In fact, it took me a while as an adult student in graduate school to feel that I understood the information well enough to explain it to others. Let's look at the profile sheet you have together. OK?

N: Yes.

B: Some of the information can be read. For example, the name of the test, the names of the subtests, and descriptions of each of the subtests and what they are supposed to measure. Are you experiencing any difficulty understanding that part of the profile?

N: No. I don't think so. It seems clear right now.

B: OK! Let's look at the graphic and numerical parts. There seem to be two kinds of numerical scores—percentile ranks and standard scores—and there are shaded areas on each graph, about an inch in length, above and below where your scores fall on the scale. Do you see all that?

N: Yes. I see them but am not sure how to use them.

B: Let's choose a place to start because several subtests and different kinds of scores are reported. Do you have a preference?

N: Not especially. Let's start with the numerical section. That seems to be my worst score, and I don't like math very much. Yet my dad says that I'll need to take a lot of math to get along well in the world.

B: OK! Let's look at your math score on the profile. Do you understand percentile ranks?

N: I don't know. Does that mean the percentage of questions I got right?

B: Not exactly, but that is a conclusion many people make when first experiencing percentile ranks because the word *percentile* is used. Actually, your performance on the test is being compared with the performances of a large group of people your age who already took the test, and the percentile rank informs us how you compared with that group. Does that make sense?

N:	I think so.
B:	So on the numerical section, the number of questions you answered correctly was equal to or higher than 40% of the people in that comparison group, which is labeled as a norms group. On the other hand, 60% of the norms group had higher scores on the test than you did. Does that help?
N:	I think so.
B:	Well, let's check you out by looking at the verbal section next. Why don't you explain to me what it means so that I can check out how well you understand that information?
N:	My score on the verbal section is at the 80th percentile, which means my score is higher than 80% of the norms group.
B:	That's pretty good! What percentage of the norms group scored higher than you did?
N:	Twenty percent.
B:	Correct. You seem to understand it quite well now.

Note: At this time, the counselor may decide to explain the nuance about Ned's score actually being equal to or higher than those in the norms group and may also choose to explain the concept of standard error of measurement and how it is applied. Having taken care of these matters, the counselor may also then make sure the student is able to engage in the same process without prompting on the remaining subtest scores on the test. The simulation resumes after these procedures have been completed:

B:	Well, you seem to have a better understanding now. At least, that is the way it appears to me because you are now able to explain to me what the scores mean. Do you have any more questions about the scores?
N:	No. I think I understand them better now. Thanks!
B:	Good! Now, earlier in our interview you mentioned some things that I believe would be important to discuss further. One is that you hope the scores will help you decide what to do when you grow up. Another is that you hope they will tell you what courses to take next year. Yet another comment was that you believe math is your weak academic area and that your father believes you should continue taking math courses because they are important for getting along in the world. Finally, I think we should talk about your reaction to your performance on the test, that is, how do you feel about your scores? Those seem to be some important issues we probably should discuss further. Would you like to do that?
N:	OK. That's something I wanted to talk about too, and I was hoping the test scores would be helpful.
B:	Fine. If it is OK with you, tell me what you think the test scores should be able to do for you. . . .

Ms. Bigelow has helped Ned understand the scoring system of the test further by involving him in the process and providing him with information he can understand. She also has identified issues that need to be addressed further as a part of the individual planning process. Several tracks are possible at this point, all of which may be interwoven: (a) clarifying Ned's too narrow perception about the usefulness of the test scores, (b) processing his thoughts about his father's beliefs and their influence on him, (c) thinking more about career planning, (d) helping Ned plan his course of studies for ninth grade, and (e) processing negative affect derived from his performance on the test.

The simulation presents one of many possible scenarios involving the application of assessment to individual planning. The counselor provided a direct service in response to a request for assistance from the student. Basic counseling and assessment skills were combined to help the student, and the test interpretation opened the door to further steps or interactions in the individual planning process. It appeared as if the counselor was sufficiently competent to explain the technical information associated with standardized testing in a manner that the student could comprehend, and she involved him in the process while doing so. Competent counselors can bridge the gap between assessment data and constructive student use of those data.

DATA AND SCHOOL COUNSELORS: WILL THE MARRIAGE SUCCEED?

As stated earlier, the accountability and assessment functions in the school counselor's role share common goals involving using data to better serve students and society. The importance of locating, collecting, analyzing, understanding, reporting, and sharing data is highlighted throughout this chapter. There are several important roles that data play in the school counseling profession. Consequently, professional school counselors are challenged to accept this relationship intellectually and attitudinally and master the requisite competencies. The ASCA (2012) emphasizes data-driven decision making. The information in this chapter promotes data-driven decisions by school counselors and by students with the assistance and support of their counselors. The goals are developmental in nature, designed to help counselors improve their services and help students make important individual planning decisions. These circumstances seem to represent a metaphorical marriage between professional school counselors and data. Will the marriage be successful?

COMPREHENSIVE SCHOOL COUNSELING PROGRAM COMPONENT

1.   Develop a plan for collecting comprehensive evaluation data and using it in manner that will achieve accountability and evidence for one's practice in a hypothetical school setting.

2.   Develop brief needs assessment forms to be completed by (a) teacher, (b) parents, and (c) students (select a grade level for the students).

3. Develop one prospective goal for each of the following simulations that can be measured with objective, quantitative data: (a) a classroom guidance program designed to provide students with information about financial aid for higher education, and (b) a counseling relationship in which the counselor is working with a student who wants to be more successful academically.

4. Create an inventory of quantitative and qualitative assessments that would be most useful for eighth-grade students engaged in individual planning about their immediate transition to ninth grade and a future potential transition to postsecondary education.

REFLECTION POINT

1. Access the North Carolina Professional School Counseling Standards website and review the content carefully (www.ncpublicschools.org/studentsupport/counseling/standards/). Do you agree with our opinion that the system has merit for school counselors? What about the system seems most useful? What seems least useful or most difficult?

2. Analyze the position Baker (2012) takes in "A New View of Evidence-Based Practice." Some scholars believe the only appropriate evidence is from rigorous empirical studies using control groups and inferential statistics. Baker believes that data from replicated practitioner research studies are equally viable and perhaps more useful. What are your thoughts?

3. The content of this chapter places a heavy emphasis on data-driven decision making. How convinced are you that this is important? What doubts if any do you have? If supportive, what convinced you?

4. What challenges does the emphasis on data-driven decision making create for you in the current counselor education training program (e.g., tests and measurements and statistics courses)? How do you plan to respond to the challenges?

5. How useful was the example of test interpretation counseling for you (i.e., Ned and Ms. Bigelow)? What components were most useful? How would you enhance Ms. Bigelow's performance?

6. How realistic did our data and school counselors metaphor seem to you? If your response was positive, explain why. If negative, please elaborate on your reasons.

APPLICATION TO TECHNOLOGY

1. Use Google docs to create the aforementioned needs assessment surveys.

2. Access the Ronald H. Fredrickson Center for School Counseling Outcome Research and Evaluation website (www.CSCOR.org), select "Our Services" from the "About Us" tab, read synopses of one or more of the "Past Projects" or

read about the "Current Projects" under the "Research" tab, and consider how the Center may be useful in the future.

3.   Find and take a free online career assessment and analyze the face validity of the instrument (i.e., Does it appear to do what it purports to do?).

4.   Compare the free assessment with what you can learn from the *Career Key.*

REFERENCES

American Counseling Association. (2014). *ACA code of ethics.* Alexandria, VA: Author.

American School Counselor Association. (2012). *ASCA National Model: A framework for school counseling programs* (3rd ed.). Alexandria, VA: Author.

American School Counselor Association. (2014). *ASCA national standards for students.* Alexandria, VA: Author.

Baker, S. B. (2012). A new view of evidence-based practice. *Counseling Today, 55*(6), 42–43.

Cook, D. W. (1989). Systematic needs assessment: A primer. *Journal of Counseling & Development, 67,* 462–464.

Council for Accreditation of Counseling and Related Educational Programs. (2016). *2016 CACREP standards.* Alexandria, VA: Author.

Dimmett, C. (2015). Theory into action. *ASCA School Counselor, 52*(4), 34–40.

Fairchild, T. N., & Seeley, T. J. (1995). Accountability strategies for school counselors: A baker's dozen. *School Counselor, 42,* 377–392.

Gibson, R. L. (1990). Teachers' opinions of high school guidance and counseling programs: Then and now. *School Counselor, 37,* 248–255.

Goldman, L. (1972). Tests and counseling: The marriage that failed. *Measurement and Evaluation in Guidance, 4,* 213–220.

Stone, C. B., & Dahir, C. A. (2007). *School counselor accountability: A MEASURE of student success* (2nd ed.). Upper Saddle River, NJ: Pearson, Merrill, Prentice Hall.

LEGAL AND ETHICAL RESPONSIBILITIES IN SCHOOL COUNSELING

4

RELATED STANDARDS OF PRACTICE

CACREP CORE	2.F.1.i.
CACREP SCHOOL COUNSELING	5.G.2.n.

Goal: To establish the importance of legal codes and ethical standards in school counseling.

An elementary school counselor we know asked permission from a parent to do play therapy with a boy in first grade who was having many behavioral and social problems at school. The counselor received permission to conduct the therapy sessions and to videotape the sessions. The student's behavior improved noticeably, and he got along better with other children in his grade.

The child's mother was astounded by her son's progress and complimented the counselor repeatedly for the successful intervention. The mother and the school counselor became good friends as a result of their mutual concerns about this boy. A few weeks after the play therapy sessions ended, the mother said that she was curious about why the sessions had been so effective. She asked to borrow some of the videotapes of her child's therapy sessions; she wanted to see what had transpired in the sessions.

wouldn't they be property of school?

"crossing confidentiality lines".

THE IMPORTANCE OF LEGAL AND ETHICAL RESPONSIBILITIES IN BALANCED SCHOOL COUNSELING PROGRAMS

What should school counselors do ethically and legally in situations such as the one described earlier? What additional legal and ethical challenges do professional school counselors face regularly as part of their professional lives? The responsibility for acting in an ethical, law-abiding manner permeates all of the competencies in a balanced program. That is, school counselors are governed by legal and ethical responsibilities in all of their roles and functions. The codes of ethics provide guidelines for performing the competencies presented in this textbook. In addition, all of the concepts and competencies highlighted in this textbook are influenced by legal and ethical responsibilities. Stone (2005) presents the importance of ethics and law for school counselors well:

> School counseling has an inherent moral dimension because of the nature of student/school counselor relationships. Public education involves the exercise of power by one group, educators, over another group, students, and, therefore, educators' work must meet high ethical standards. Educators, especially school counselors, are involved in a particular kind of interpersonal relationship with students, and by virtue of this relationship we have a deeper moral responsibility to our students.
>
> (p. 45)

Herlihy and Remley (2001) depicted laws as the "musts" components in our professional behavior. Laws "dictate the minimum standards of behavior that society will tolerate" (p. 71). Ethics depict the "shoulds" of our professional behavior. Ethics "represent the ideals or aspirations of the counseling profession" (p. 71).

LEGAL CONCEPTS

Each state has its own laws, and new laws continue to be passed as legislators deem necessary. Some laws have a direct influence on school counselors, and counselors need to be familiar with those laws. For instance, Pennsylvania has a statute stating that no school counselor who has acquired information from students in confidence shall be compelled or allowed to disclose that information in legal or governmental proceedings without the student's consent or the consent of the parent or guardian if the student is under the age of 18. This act does not supersede counselors' responsibility to report evidence of child abuse or neglect. Obviously, all school counselors in Pennsylvania should understand the meaning of these two legislative acts.

Legal concepts are operationalized in specific pieces of legislation. For instance, Pennsylvania's statute operationalized the concept of privileged communication. School counselors can become familiar with some important legal concepts before learning the specific laws that operationalize them. Pertinent examples are negligence, malpractice, libel, and slander. Counselors and their stakeholders are served best if knowledge about such important legal concepts is part of the school counselor's basic education. To assist you, a glossary of the relevant technical terms used in this chapter is presented in Box 4.1.

Box 4.1 Glossary of Terms

Abuse: The infliction by other than accidental means of physical harm upon a body of a child, continued psychological damage, or denial of emotional needs (American School Counselor Association, 1988).

Civil liability: The condition of being available, subject, exposed, or open to legal proceedings connected with the private rights of individuals.

Confidentiality: A situation in which one has been entrusted with the secrets or private affairs of another.

Criminal liability: The condition of being subject, exposed, or open to legal proceedings for which punishment is prescribed by law.

Defamation: An act that injures someone's reputation without foundation.

Duty to warn/protect: When a professional has a special relationship with a client and that individual's conduct needs to be controlled, the professional has a duty to act in a manner that protects the client and/or warns foreseeable victims of the client's actions (Gehring, 1982).

Ethical standards: The rules of practice set forth by a profession. Such standards tend to be general and idealistic, seldom answering specific questions for the practitioner (Remley, 1985).

Laws: The standards of behavior a society demands of its members. Laws set forth the rights of citizens and usually define minimal acceptable behavior rather than idealized expectations (Remley, 1985).

Libel: Words written, printed, or published, in any form other than speech or gestures, that maliciously or damagingly misrepresent.

Malpractice: Improper treatment or action of a client by a professional from neglect, reprehensible ignorance, or with criminal intent.

Mandated reporter: Those required by law (i.e., teachers, counselors, and school administrators) to report suspected child abuse immediately. Suspicions are sufficient grounds. Investigation is the domain of others.

Neglect: The failure to provide necessary food, care, clothing, shelter, supervision, or medical attention for a child.

Negligence: The failure to exercise the degree of care that the law requires, under the circumstances, for the protection of the interests of other persons who may be injuriously affected by the lack of such care.

Privileged communication: If an interaction is designated as privileged communication under the law, a judge may not force the professional involved to disclose what was said by a client in an interview (Remley, 1985).

Reasonableness and good faith: Criteria used by the courts to judge the conduct of professionals. Was the conduct what a reasonably prudent adult might do under similar circumstances, and was the action clearly for the benefit of the child and the employing entity?

Sexual abuse: Any act or acts involving sexual molestation or exploration, including but not limited to rape, carnal knowledge, sodomy, and unnatural sexual practices.

Slander: Spoken statements that are malicious, false, and defamatory.

GOVERNMENTAL REGULATIONS

State and local governing agencies, in their responsibility to care for and educate children and adolescents, may enact regulations to which professionals under their jurisdiction must conform. Such regulations are usually printed and distributed to affected professionals. Some states, for example, have a regulation that all school districts must have a student record-keeping system approved by the state department of education and that the system must have printed guidelines for all staff members to follow. Examples of local school district regulations include requiring professional staff members to sign a form when seeking access to individual students' cumulative records and requiring that all instances of suspected child abuse to be reported to the building principal. Most regulations have merit and provide guidance for professionals.

ETHICAL STANDARDS

Professional groups provide their members codes of ethics that serve as standards for their behavior. The groups have established standards for several reasons (Van Hoose & Kottler, 1978). First, they are supposed to provide autonomy from governmental regulation and interference by serving as a basis for self-regulation. Second, ethical codes provide behavioral standards for members of a professional group. Third, the codes protect members of the public by providing for their welfare, and protect the professionals by providing guidelines that serve as criteria for judging their actions if individuals sue them for malpractice.

    The ethical codes best designed to serve school counselors are the *Code of Ethics* of the American Counseling Association (ACA, 2014) and the *Ethical Standards for School Counselors* of the American School Counselor Association (ASCA, 2010). Although very useful, ethical standards have limitations. One is that some legal and ethical issues are not addressed by the codes because of changing times, recent legal precedents, and the inability of the codes to cover every possible situation. Ethical codes are primarily reactive, evolving from previous practices and problems. Recognizing the limitations of ethical standards, we recommend that counselors supplement them by keeping up with state and local legislation, reading professional journals and newsletters for up-to-date information on legal and ethical issues, and seeking advice from other professionals such as attorneys, counselor educators, supervisors, and colleagues. Although limited in their coverage, ethical codes are the best source of criteria for appropriate professional behaviors.

PERTINENT LEGAL CODES AND CONCEPTS

FEDERAL LEGISLATION

Title IX

Known by its full name as Title IX of the Education Amendment Acts of 1972, this legislation prohibits discrimination on the basis of gender by any institution receiving federal funds in any form. Regulated through the U.S. Department of Education, a specific section (45 C.F.R. 586.36) prohibits discrimination on the basis of gender in counseling or guidance of students. In general, this legislation reminds school counselors not to treat children and adolescents of one gender differently from the other in ways that place them at a disadvantage. It provides legal sanctions that support the gender equity principles.

Several potential manifestations of gender discrimination exist in school counseling. One that has received considerable attention is the way standardized tests and information is used in career and educational planning. For example, older interest inventories that restricted young women to considering only the limited range of careers traditionally occupied by women have been changed. School counselors are challenged to be aware of the issues and of the choices available to all standardized test takers when using interest inventories. Whenever standardized tests or norms are separated by gender, the potential for discrimination exists. Whether discrimination always occurs is less certain. *girls & meath*

The Family Educational Rights and Privacy Act of 1974 (FERPA)(PL 93–380)

Referred to as FERPA or the Buckley Amendment (after the late Senator James Buckley of New York, who sponsored it), the act was designed as a means of restoring parental rights and protecting privacy. FERPA has four major parts. Part I states that federal funds will be denied to any educational institution that prevents authorized access to school records by students who are over 18 years of age or by parents of students who are under 18 years of age. When such a request is made, the authorized student or parents are to be allowed to inspect the student's entire educational record. However, the school is allowed up to 45 days to comply with such a request.

Part II of FERPA states that parental consent, if a student is under 18 years of age, or the student's consent, if the student is over 18 years of age, is required before a student undergoes medical, psychological, or psychiatric examinations, testing, or treatment or participates in any school program designed to affect or change the personal behavior or values of a student. This part of FERPA, of course, has implications for many activities included within the realm of classroom guidance programming described in Chapter 7.

Part III forbids the schools to allow any individuals other than those directly involved in the student's education to have access to the records or to any information from the records without written consent of the student, if over 18 years of age, or the parents, if the student is under 18 years of age. Some exceptions to this section are stated later in the chapter.

Part IV of FERPA states that the U.S. Secretary of Health Education and Welfare is required to develop regulations to ensure the privacy of students with regard to federally sponsored surveys. Because FERPA was developed and passed into law rather quickly, some basic implementation questions about it confronted confused school officials in the mid-1970s. This situation ushered in a series of amendments and guidelines, the intent of which was to clarify the implementation problems. In December 1974, a "Joint Statement in Explanation of the Buckley/Pell Amendment" was published in the *Congressional Record* (1974). This statement remedied certain omissions in the provisions of the existing law and clarified other provisions that were subject to extensive concern. Several important points from this statement are as follows.

- FERPA applies only to those programs delegated for administration to the commissioner of education;
- *Education records* are defined as those records and materials directly related to students that are maintained by a school or one of its agents;
- Private notes or confidential notes are exempt, provided they are not revealed to another qualified person;
- Certain law enforcement records are excluded;
- FERPA does not alter the confidentiality of communications otherwise protected by law;
- Hearing procedures are to be developed by local school districts;
- Wherever possible, actual documents are to be shared. When this is not possible, an accurate summary or interpretation is necessary;
- The federal government will withdraw federal funds from violating or nonconforming schools;
- Exceptions to the need-for-written-consent requirement for allowing access to information are as follows: state and local officials where state laws are more liberal than FERPA, organizations giving entrance or selection examinations, accrediting agencies, parents of students over 18 years of age if the students are still dependent according to the Internal Revenue Service, and in cases of health and safety emergencies.

Another clarification appeared in January 6, 1975. This statement clarified the relationship between the institution's right to destroy records and the individual's right to have access to the records. Eligible students or their parents are to be granted access to information in the records if said information was in the records when the request was made. If a request for information in a student's records is pending, the institution is not allowed to destroy any such information until after the requesting student or parent has had access to it. When no such requests have been made, institutions do have the right to destroy information in student records unless otherwise forbidden to do so by law. The long-range effect of FERPA has been to encourage institutions to keep and use fewer records than in the past.

Connors (1979) surmised that defamation suits can be filed against people whose comments in the records are deemed libelous by students or parents who have gained access to the records. Although the law is not retroactive before January 1, 1975, the statute of limitations starts when a comment is discovered, rather than when it was written. Thus, since passage of the so-called Buckley Amendment, it has become more important to give careful consideration to entries one places in student records. Connors recommends that subjective notations such as "Johnny is a cheat" be avoided. Anything that is entered should be stated objectively—for example, "Johnny has been observed copying answers from his neighbor's test paper on 10 different occasions this year." Even objective statements such as this one may be unwise, in Connors's opinion. Perhaps the best protection against defamation suits is to enter no descriptive statements whatsoever into student records.

LEGAL CONCEPTS

Privileged Communication

A legal responsibility mandated by state codes, privileged communication is a client's right to have prior confidences to certain professionals maintained during legal proceedings. Some states have granted it to school counselors; others have not. For example, Pennsylvania mandates that school counselors maintain student client confidences during legal proceedings unless requested to disclose that information by their students or by the parents of the students who are under 18 years of age. Privileged communication is not extended to instances of suspected child abuse.

Privileged communication legislation mandates that counselors follow the ethical principle of maintaining confidentiality in specific instances, that is, during legal proceedings. Although privileged communication assists school counselors in their efforts to maintain client confidentiality and recognizes their confidences as being as important as those of medical doctors, lawyers, psychologists, and the clergy, the primary purpose of the legislation is to protect student clients.

According to Glosoff, Herlihy, and Spence (2000), it is very difficult to list general exceptions to privileged communication. This difficulty arises because provisions for privileged communications may be buried in state statutes, each state has its own statutes, and statutes are being modified continually. An exhaustive, yet admittedly incomplete, computerized search by Glosoff et al. (2000) led to their presentation of a matrix of exceptions to privileged communication by states and the District of Columbia. Nine categories of exceptions were found across the 50 states and the District of Columbia. The list includes all professional counselor categories and is not restricted to school counselors. Listed in the order of most to least often found, they are (a) when there is a dispute between the student client and a counselor, (b) when the student raises the issue of mental condition in a court proceeding (e.g., insanity defense and claim of emotional damage), (c) when the student's condition poses a danger to self and others, (d) child abuse or neglect, (e) knowledge that a student is contemplating commission of a crime, (f) information from court-ordered psychological examinations provided by counselors, (g) when counselors wish to participate in the involuntary hospitalization of students, (h) knowledge that a student has been a victim of a crime, and (i) harm to vulnerable adults (e.g., disabled or institutionalized).

Most instances that require school counselors to testify in court involve abuse or custody cases (Anderson, n.d.). Being informed and prepared is important. Discussions with parents or lawyers who may want a counselor to testify will help determine whether a court appearance is necessary. Reasons for not testifying include having limited information to offer and having several individuals who can provide similar testimony. School counselors may receive subpoenas, which are official court documents and cannot be ignored. Remley and Herlihy (2005) recommend that school counselors consult with and receive advice from an attorney if they have received subpoenas. A counselor should consider several important guidelines if testifying in court: (a) remember that a school counselor is a licensed or certified educator, and limit comments to facts about what students are doing in school; (b) remember that attributions about the causes of behaviors are in the domain of licensed psychologists and other professionals qualified to assess behavior; (c) review relevant information and check the facts without violating confidentiality; and (d) review and bring pertinent factual data and refer to them as needed when testifying (Anderson, n.d.). It is recommended that counselors withhold their confidential notes unless required to share them. Notes should not be destroyed after a request has been made, and they may be entered into the record if presented. The content of personal notes and how long they should be kept are covered in the record-keeping section of this chapter.

Malpractice and Negligence

Counselors, like others in the helping professions, may be subjected to charges of malpractice or negligence. Malpractice refers to practices that are outside a professional's training or ability and that result in damage to the recipient of those services—for example, a school counselor recommends or gives medicines or drugs to a student, causing deleterious results. Negligence is a breach of legal duty, or a failure, resulting in damage to a student, to perform acts that are part of the professional's obligation—for example, a school counselor fails to report evidence of child abuse.

Stone (2002) reported two instances where school counselors were embroiled in negligence cases. One case was a suit charging negligence in academic advising (*Sain v. Cedar Rapids Community School District,* 2001), and the second involved a suit alleging negligence in abortion counseling (*Arnold v. Board of Education of Escambia County,* 1989). A careful study of both cases indicates that the school counselors involved were attempting to be advocates for their student clients and believed they were acting in good faith. In the first case, the majority of the Iowa Supreme Court ruled in favor of the plaintiff, stating that "negligent misrepresentation may be applied to the school counselor–student relationship when erroneous advice means a student loses a lucrative scholarship" (Stone, 2002, p. 30). The court also cautioned that "the ruling should have limited effect as negligent representation is confined to students whose reliance on information is reasonable" (p. 31).

In the latter case, the ruling was in favor of the defendants. The trial court concluded that the students had not been coerced by the principal and school counselor. Although negligence was not proven in this case, Stone (2002) pointed out that "The question remains: May counselors be held liable for giving abortion advice to pregnant minors?" (p. 33). Stone recommends avoiding referrals to birth control clinics and never taking students to facilities where medical procedures are to occur.

You may be wondering what to do. Our best advice is to be well informed about your legal and ethical responsibilities and to act in good faith. In those rare cases when school counselors are sued for malpractice or negligence, the courts are likely to use the concept of whether the counselor acted in good faith as the criterion for determining guilt or innocence. The concept of *acting in good faith* is based on the principle of using the ethical standards of one's profession as a criterion for making a legal determination. Therefore, school counselors will be judged by the ethical codes of the professional organizations to which they belong or could belong. If, according to the best interpretation of the ethical standards, a counselor acted appropriately, he or she can be judged as having acted in good faith and will likely be cleared of the charges. Knowing whether one is acting in good faith may be a difficult undertaking, however. Accomplishing that goal will be enhanced if school counselors do the following:

- Belong to a professional organization, know its ethical codes, and abide by them;
- Know the relevant state codes and the local board of education regulations and abide by them;
- Know the local school policies and abide by them;
- Develop program policies;
- Develop personal working policies based on knowledge of relevant developmental issues, parental rights, diversity issues, and personal values.

Child Abuse

All states and the federal government have passed legislation to stop child abuse or neglect. The state codes and regulations have several common ingredients, among which are child protective services agencies, procedures for reporting and investigating child abuse, penalties for abuse and for failing to report it, a toll-free telephone system for anonymously reporting suspected abuse, and designations of certain professionals as mandated reporters. School counselors are usually included among those professionals designated as mandated reporters (Bryant & Milsom, 2005). Although it is clear that child abuse is abhorrent, the signs of abuse are much less clear in some instances. Therefore, the mandate to report child abuse becomes less clear when counselors and their professional colleagues attempt to recognize and report it. According to Remley (1985), many states that require disclosing suspected child abuse fail to define clearly what it is. Remley (1992) also pointed out that although some states specifically note that child abuse must be reported no matter how much time has elapsed since it occurred, many states do not make the time frame clear, leaving it to individuals and the courts to determine how much should be reported. To help you respond to this challenge, Box 4.2 presents a suggested set of signs of child abuse, and Box 4.3 offers suggested steps in the reporting process.

Box 4.2 Signs of Child Abuse and Neglect

Examples of Child Abuse

1. Extensive bruises or patterns of bruises
2. Burns or burn patterns
3. Lacerations, welts, or abrasions
4. Injuries inconsistent with information offered
5. Sexual abuse
6. Emotional disturbances caused by continuous friction in the home, marital discord, or mentally ill parents.

Examples of Neglect

1. Malnourished, ill-clad, dirty, without proper shelter or sleeping arrangements, lacking appropriate health care
2. Unattended, lacking appropriate health care
3. Ill and lacking essential medical attention
4. Irregular/illegal absences from school
5. Exploited, overworked
6. Lacking essential psychological/emotional nurturance
7. Abandonment.

Source: Data from "The School Counselor and Child Abuse/Neglect Prevention," by the American School Counselor Association, 1988, *Elementary School Guidance and Counseling, 22,* pp. 261–263.

Box 4.3 Suggested Steps for a School District Employee in Reporting Child Abuse

1. Report suspected cases of child abuse to the building principal immediately, that is, children under age 18 who exhibit evidence of serious physical or mental injury not explained by the available medical history as being accidental; sexual abuse or serious physical neglect, if injury, abuse, or neglect has been caused by the acts or omissions of the child's parents or by a person responsible for the child's welfare.
2. Each building principal will designate a person to act in his or her stead when unavailable.
3. The principal may wish to form a team of consultants with whom to confer (e.g., school nurse, home and school visitor, counselor) before making an oral report to public welfare service representatives. This should be done within 24 hours of the first report.
4. It is not the responsibility of the reporter to prove abuse or neglect. Reports must be made in good faith, however.
5. Any person willfully failing to report suspected abuse may be subjected to school board disciplinary action.

Abuse can include a variety of acts. Included among those acts listed in the professional literature are inadequate supervision that leads to failure of the child to thrive, emotional neglect, abandonment, psychological bullying by classmates, physical abuse (often the easiest to detect), verbal abuse, and sexual abuse or molestation. Sexual abuse encompasses a variety of acts, including using children in pornographic films. Mandated reporters are immune from civil or criminal liability in all 50 states and the District of Columbia if they have reported in good faith (Hinson & Fossey, 2000; Kenny, 2001). They may be fined for knowingly failing to report suspected child abuse. Civil or criminal liability should occur only for knowingly making false accusations (Knapp, 1983). For one reason or another, most cases of child abuse go unreported (Crenshaw, Crenshaw, & Lichtenberg, 1995). From a Kentucky survey of elementary school and middle school counselors, Wilson, Thomas, and Schuette (1983) concluded that the majority of respondents thought that the problem was more serious elsewhere than in their communities and believed that they were aware of the signs of abuse. Overall, the respondents reported a low incidence of actually reporting child abuse. These findings left several questions: Is relatively little abuse going on with children and adolescents in the United States? Are counselors and other mandated reporters missing or overlooking the signs of abuse, or are the signs too subtle or hidden to uncover in many cases? Are school counselors trained sufficiently to discover abuse and report it?

In a more recent survey of school counselors in a midwestern state, Bryant and Milsom (2005) found higher reporting rates than in the Wilson et al. (1983) study. They also found that most cases were reported by mandated reporters, elementary school counselors made more reports that middle and secondary school counselors, and counselors in schools with higher percentages of children qualifying for free and reduced-cost lunch were more likely to report abuse. The primary reason given for not reporting was concern that the Department of Human Services would not investigate.

Concern about doing something in advance of discovering and treating child abuse that has already occurred led to an increase in systematic prevention efforts. Adair (2006) reported that reviewers of sexual abuse prevention program evaluations found it difficult to ascertain effectiveness because of methodological problems in the evaluation studies. Adair's review led to the following observations about programs designed to prevent sexual abuse: (a) Many different program formats are used; (b) such programs are available in almost all school districts; (c) common topics for programs devised for children are saying no and getting away, telling on adults, body ownership, good touch/bad touch, no secrets, and getting help; (d) little has been reported about programs for adolescents; and (e) almost all prevention programming takes place in schools, which overlooks children who are being served by community agencies. Adair recommended that, to be effective, sexual abuse prevention programs should (a) provide information in a manner that will influence behaviors, (b) achieve accurate awareness of one's vulnerability to sexual assault, (c) be of a sufficient length of time to achieve objectives and offer follow-up sessions, (d) be based on up-to-date information about child and adolescent development, (e) be available for children and adolescents, (f) be conducted in collaboration with community organizations that serve children and adolescents, and (g) be carefully evaluated.

Libel, Slander, and Defamation

Libel is a legal term referring to false statements that are published and bring about hatred, disgrace, ridicule, or contempt toward the individual about whom they are written. *Slander,* also a legal term, refers to verbally communicated statements that have the same results. In civil suits, plaintiffs must prove that damages in the form of *defamation*—an injured reputation—resulted. Historically, the number of such civil cases against counselors has been small. Nevertheless, some counseling duties and functions have the potential for making counselors vulnerable. Sharing standardized test scores over the telephone, telling bystanders about students' grades, and relaying information to third parties about students when there is no clear obligation to do so are examples of questionable behaviors that could lead to charges of defamation. Also, parents or students may take action over comments in students' cumulative records they deem to be inflammatory. It is also conceivable that information counselors share with colleges, universities, and prospective employers in confidence via recommendations can find its way back to the subjects of the comments and, if viewed as defamatory, lead to civil suits.

Anyone can sue another person but, in so doing, is not guaranteed recovery of damages. Suits, whether won or lost by the plaintiffs, have the potential for causing counselors considerable stress and mental anguish, public embarrassment, and possible financial losses associated with defending themselves if the individuals and school districts do not have sufficient insurance. It is recommended that school counselors carry professional liability insurance. Regardless of insurance, it behooves counselors to be prudent about what they write and say about their students. This, of course, is also an ethical recommendation.

Several recommendations, if followed, may help counselors minimize the chance of being sued for libel or slander and reduce the probability of the plaintiff recovering damages if a suit does occur. Subjective notations need not be entered in student records, or anywhere else, for that matter. Determine the inquirer's need to know any information before sharing it. For example, in the potentially libelous or slanderous cases cited earlier, the need of the person requesting standardized test scores over the telephone to know the desired data can be assessed by acquiring written permission from the individual whose scores are desired, and bystanders by definition have no responsible need to know information about students.

In some instances, determining the need to know is relatively easy. For example, students who plan to matriculate to post–high school educational institutions usually must submit transcripts and letters of recommendation; in doing so, they grant permission to representatives of their high schools, often counselors, to transmit the information and recommendations. The need to know is clear. When some of the same institutions ask questions about the character of students and request narrative evaluations, the need to know is less clear. Exactly what they need to know is left to the respondents to determine.

What to do? With regard to determining the need to know, it seems logical to question the motives behind the request, to predict what will be done with the information, and to understand how that response will affect the student whose information is being shared. With regard to what to do, one is expected to act in good faith, according to the ethical principles of one's profession. Believing what one is saying or writing is also important. Knowing it is true is even better because truth is an important criterion in civil cases. Report objectively and factually, but some things might best be left unsaid, even objectively (e.g., accusatory statements). Bronner (1998) reports that school counselors are caught between college admissions officers desiring to ensure campus safety and avoid liability for student violence and parents who do not want details of disciplinary problems their children had to ruin their chance of getting into college. Both parties may be more determined than ever to protect their constituencies. A personal guideline of ours has been to say and write only things that are true and favorable about students unless there is a clear and imminent danger to themselves or others. If there is not much true and favorable to write in a recommendation about a student, then the brevity of the recommendation may speak for itself. Another option is to refuse the recommendation request.

Unclear Areas

Desiring to know what to do legally and ethically is a meritorious goal, as is acting responsibly. Yet efforts to understand what to do sometimes lead to mixed messages, leaving one unclear about the definition of responsible behavior. Some areas covered by the concepts of duty to warn and duty to protect are chief among the unclear legal areas with which counselors must grapple. The concepts of duty to warn and duty to protect have been highlighted by prominent court decisions (e.g., *Tarasoff v. Regents of the University of California*, 1976), which focused on concern about warning potential victims of violent behavior. In school settings, the concepts might also be applied to cases of advising minors without parental consent (e.g., providing information about abortions) and cases of suicide (counselors' apparent knowledge of the student's desire to harm himself or herself).

Tarasoff occurred in California during the mid-1970s, and the decision set off a tidal wave of concern and uncertainty across many levels of helping professionals in the United States. In this case, a client informed a psychologist of his intention to kill another individual. Care was taken to commit and confine the client for observation, and the campus police were notified of his stated intentions. He was released after appearing rational and promising to stay away from the individual whose life he had threatened. The psychologist had not warned the intended victim, who was out of the country at the time, or her parents. The client went to her residence and killed her after her arrival home. The courts ruled the therapist and institution in error because there was a foreseeable victim and a duty to warn the victim or her parents. In courts that follow the reasoning of this case, mental health workers will be expected to warn people who have a special relationship with the dangerous person, as well as to warn the intended victim of that person (Gehring, 1982).

Because the *Tarasoff* case occurred in California, its results are not binding elsewhere. Courts in other states, however, may use that case as a precedent for similar decisions, although some states have not adopted the "Tarasoff doctrine" (Herlihy & Remley, 2001). In some decisions in other states, the courts have interpreted similar situations differently. For instance, in North Carolina (*Currie v. United States,* 1986), an employee, while he was in therapy, threatened to kill unspecified coworkers. Subsequently, he did indeed enter the workplace and kill a coworker. The court created what was called the *psychotherapist judgment rule,* in which it refused to allow liability for simple errors in judgment in commitment decisions. The therapist had consulted with several colleagues before deciding not to commit the client ("Therapists Bear a Duty," 1987). Clearly, this case differs from *Tarasoff* in that the intended victim was unspecified, and as it was reported, the client had threatened the therapist. Despite these differences, mental health professionals working with clients who pose a threat to themselves or to others or who indicate a disposition toward child abuse should be prepared to report to the proper authorities and to potential victims ("Legal Considerations," 1983).

Writing from his experience as a lawyer to an audience of clinical psychologists, Monahan (1993) offers guidelines for limiting exposure to duty to warn liability. Although the package of recommendations contains entries that are perhaps more extreme than most school counselors require, they provide food for thought:

- Know how to assess client risk, make a real effort to do so thoroughly, and communicate that information to those responsible for making final decisions.

- Have a risk management plan in place (prepare for the few exceptions in advance with a plan for monitoring and managing individuals who may endanger themselves or others).

- Document information received and actions taken. According to Monahan (1993), "It would be an exaggeration to state that in a tort case what is not in the written record does not exist—but not much of an exaggeration" (p. 246). He recommended noting three things: the source of the information, the content, and the date.

- Written policies or guidelines that have been externally reviewed by experienced clinicians and lawyers should be in place, and the staff should receive training about using the guidelines. Compliance with the guidelines should be audited, and forms developed or revised to "prompt and record the actions contemplated by the policy statement" (Monahan, 1993, p. 247).

- If something goes wrong, one can control the damage by relying on the truth and remaining silent publicly when experiencing doubts about one's decisions from the vantage point of hindsight.

Advising minors without parental consent is a particularly unclear area that each counselor needs to investigate. From an ethical standpoint, adherence to the principle of confidentiality usually leads counselors to keep in confidence what minors say during counseling sessions. An example of a troublesome topic held in confidence is knowledge of pregnancy, including the student's planned responses such as abortion, and the counselor's sharing of information about the possible options, including abortion. This has been and continues to be a legal minefield because statutes vary from state to state, as do decisions in court cases, and the national conflict between right-to-life and prochoice supporters promises to lead to more changes in the future. According to Hopkins and Anderson (1990), "counselors are generally free to inform clients of the availability of birth control methods without fear of legal liability and to refer clients to family planning or health clinics for more information" (p. 33). Hopkins and Anderson went on to point out the distinction between providing information and imposing one's own views on a minor client, particularly one who is already pregnant. Additional important information in this domain is that states may regulate the performance of abortions, parents of unmarried pregnant minors may have some rights to know about and consent to an abortion, and physicians are recognized as qualified to provide pregnant women information and decision-making advice about abortions. Kiselica (1996) offers suggestions for counselors. Helping clarify confusion about legalities and being advocates on behalf of the clients' legal rights are important ways that counselors can help. Beyond the legal issues, counselors may also be able to provide emotional support and decision-making counseling that includes accurate information.

Because the resolutions of issues in this section are unclear, advice is scarce and conflicting. Two suggestions that have merit are to have policy statements for crises and challenging situations that will guide individual counselors and help others determine whether the counselor acted in good faith (Lawrence & Kurpius, 2000; Monahan, 1993) and to keep proper notes about one's actions and decisions in order to support one's claims if ever called into court or some other formal proceeding (Lawrence & Kurpius, 2000; Monahan, 1993; "Therapists Bear a Duty," 1987).

Most Frequently Reported Legal Issues

Hermann (2002) surveyed 273 members of the ASCA who were school counselors, using the Legal Issues in Counseling Survey. The most frequently reported legal issues over the past 12 months, ranked in order of frequency, were as follows: (a) determining whether a student was suicidal (90% of sample; 76% two or more times), (b) determining whether to report suspected child abuse (89% of sample; 74% two or more times), (c) determining whether a student posed a danger to others (73% of sample; 51% two or more times), (d) being pressured to verbally reveal confidential information (51% of sample; 34% two or more times), and (e) students expressing dissatisfaction with counseling services (42% of sample; 19% two or more times).

Hermann (2002) also inquired about the participants' perceptions of how prepared to respond to the respective legal issues they thought they were. The same five legal issues that were presented earlier are presented with the percentage in parentheses of the participants who believed they were well prepared to respond: (a) determining whether a student was suicidal (72%), (b) determining whether to report suspected child abuse (91%), (c) determining whether a student posed a danger to others (63%), (d) being pressured to verbally reveal confidential information (57%), and (e) students expressing dissatisfaction with counseling services (48%).

It is not surprising that reporting child abuse ranks highest given the explicit mandates found in all of the state statutes. The legal issues with lower percentages of perceived preparedness seem to fall into a rank ordering according to the severity of complications that can be encountered. For example, the professional literature is replete with checklists to be used when assessing suicide ideation, and suicide ideation is often clearly recognized. On the other hand, pressure to reveal confidential information can occur in different ways, and there are no common guidelines for dealing with these requests. This issue, as well as discerning danger to others and student client dissatisfaction, may manifest themselves in more subtle, unclear ways.

Two other legal issues that occurred less often in the survey yielded higher percentages of feeling unprepared. Of the sample, 54% felt unprepared to respond to a subpoena to appear as a witness in a legal proceeding, and 22% believed they were not prepared for being asked to turn over confidential records. These two legal issues were encountered less often than the other five. Therefore, participants, having less experience and perhaps less preparation, felt less well prepared.

It appears as if experience is the best way to prepare for responding to legal issues. Actual experience is one way to address this challenge; however, real-life experiences of this nature are few and far between. The challenges can also be addressed proactively by covertly and overtly simulating what one would do if presented with each of these legal challenges and basing the rehearsed simulations on a thorough study of the relevant professional literature.

ETHICAL RESPONSIBILITIES

AMERICAN COUNSELING ASSOCIATION *CODE OF ETHICS*

The ACA published a revised *Code of Ethics* in 2014, which can be accessed on this book's companion website and on www.counseling.org/resources/aca-code-of-ethics. pdf. The *Code* has nine major sections: The Counseling Relationship; Confidentiality and Privacy; Professional Responsibility; Relationships With Other Professionals; Evaluation, Assessment, and Interpretation; Supervision, Training, and Teaching; Research and Publication; Distance Counseling, Technology, and Social Media; and Resolving Ethical Issues. This section of the chapter highlights parts of the code that are most relevant to school counselors.

The ACA Ethics Revision Task Force realized that there had been substantial growth in the counseling profession and they had to bring the code up-to-date with the current professional and social climate (Meyers, 2014). Two particularly challenging issues were confusion over the difference between values and competence when referring clients and the ethical use of technology and social media in counseling: "These areas wound up influencing the ethics code in its entirety" (Meyers, 2014, p. 33). Comments on each of the sections of the *Code* are presented in the following sections, with highlights associated with the new code.

Preamble

The Preamble states,

> The American Counseling Association (ACA) is an educational, scientific, and professional organization whose members work in a variety of settings and serve in multiple capacities. Counseling is a professional relationship that empowers diverse individuals, families, and groups to accomplish mental health, wellness, education, and career goals. Professional values are an important way of living out an ethical commitment. The following are core professional values of the counseling profession: (a) enhancing human development throughout the life span; (b) honoring diversity and embracing a multicultural approach in support of worth, dignity, potential, and uniqueness of people within their social and cultural contexts; and (c) practicing in a competent and ethical manner. These professional values are deemed to provide a conceptual basis for the following ethical principles: autonomy, nonmaleficence, beneficence, justice, fidelity, and veracity.
>
> (ACA, 2014, p. 2)

The focus of the 2014 *Code* is on the entire counseling profession, including all subspecialties, rather than exclusively on ACA members (Kaplan & Martz, 2014a). Because school counselors who are members of the ASCA may also belong to the ACA, school counselors are subject to the codes and standards of both professional organizations.

The Counseling Relationship

Dealing with practices and procedures of individual or group counseling or both, this section focuses on such matters as client welfare, informed consent, clients served by others, avoiding harm and imposing values, prohibited noncounseling roles and relationships, multiple clients, group work, fees and business practices, termination and referral, and abandonment and neglect.

Confidentiality and Privacy

Confidentiality being a key ethical principle for counselors, this section covers respecting client rights, exceptions, information shared with others, groups and families, clients lacking the capacity to give informed consent (e.g., minors), records and documents, and case consultation. The assumption of confidentiality is a foundation for the counseling, consulting, assessment, transition, and record-keeping functions. It is the foundation for the trust that helps individuals share intimate information with counselors truthfully. Although school counselors have an ethical responsibility to their student clients, they also have an ethical and legal responsibility to the parents of minor clients; this can sometimes lead to decision-making dilemmas. As Huey (1986) points out, ethical codes do not recommend violating the law. At the same time, Huey cites advice from Corey, Corey, and Callanan (1984) recommending that counselors not become hamstrung by legal concerns to the point they become ineffective. No one seems to have a definitive answer about this issue. Most counselors will not want to lose the power to help individuals that confidentiality offers. Therefore, it appears that they will have to deal with the legal ramifications on a case-by-case basis, checking applicable state laws in the process. Zingaro (1983) provides an example of a case in which a counselor faces this dilemma:

> A child may ask to talk to you about a problem, such as how to get along with a new stepparent. After discussing the child's concern, you arrange a time to meet at a later date. The following day one of the child's parents calls you to ask about the content of your counseling session. It seems obvious from the questions that the parent is aware of some of the issues that you discussed with the child. Would you disclose information that you received from the child with the parent? What would be the effects on the child, parents, and you if you comply with the parent's request? If the child's self-referral is viewed as a step toward autonomy and independence in solving his or her problems, have you handicapped the child's efforts? Would these questions be answered differently if the parent had asked you to speak with his or her child and then asked about the content of your counseling session?
>
> (p. 262, used with permission)

Professional Responsibility

In this section, matters such as knowledge of and compliance with the ethical standards, professional competence (i.e., practicing only within boundaries of one's professional competence and accepting employment only where qualified), advertising and soliciting clients, professional qualifications, nondiscrimination, public responsibility, treatment modalities (e.g., importance of scientific bases and limits to use of innovative techniques), and responsibility to other professionals are covered. Among the components important to school counselors are the emphases on monitoring one's effectiveness, consulting with other professionals about ethical questions and professional practice, keeping current, and representing one's credentials appropriately.

Relationships With Other Professionals

This section contains important standards about relationships with colleagues, employers, and employees (e.g., confidentiality, personnel selection, and negative conditions) and provision of consultation services.

Evaluation, Assessment, and Interpretation

As the title implies, this section is devoted to concerns about the use of educational, mental health, psychological, and career assessment instruments. Among the specific standards are statements concerning the importance of being competent to use and interpret assessment instruments, providing informed consent to clients, releasing data to qualified professionals, making proper diagnoses of mental disorders, selecting instruments carefully, providing appropriate assessment conditions, recognizing the need for caution in testing because of multicultural and diversity issues, scoring and interpreting assessments appropriately, keeping tests and assessment data secure, avoiding use of obsolete assessments and outdated results, using scientific assessment construction procedures, and engaging in forensic evaluations appropriately. You are challenged to recognize a strong relationship between the standards in this section of the code and the information in Chapter 3 of this book.

Supervision, Training, and Teaching

This section is of more interest to trainers of school counselors than to school counselors yet has considerable influence on the training of counselors. The standards herein focus on counselor supervision and client welfare; counselor supervision competence; supervisory relationships; supervisor responsibilities; student supervisee responsibilities; counseling supervision, evaluation, remediation, and endorsement; responsibilities of counselor educators; student welfare; evaluation and remediation; roles and relationships between counselor educators and students; and multicultural diversity competence in counselor education and training programs. The way the standards influence the training of school counselors may influence the direction of the profession throughout the 21st century.

Research and Publication

Probably of less interest and use to most school counselors than other parts of the code, this section points out that all participants in a research study must be told which information can be shared without affecting the study and that they must be given the opportunity to decide whether to participate. This is referred to as informed consent. In addition, the identity of the participants must be disguised when reporting results or making original data available, results reflecting unfavorably on the schools or other vested interests must not be withheld, and agreements to cooperate in research projects imply a responsibility to do so punctually and completely. Disguising student identity will be a requisite for school counselors when collecting data while engaged in evaluation endeavors and translating said data into accountability information to be shared with stakeholders. These evaluation and accountability strategies are elaborated upon in Chapters 3, 7, and 8.

Distance Counseling, Technology, and Social Media

This is a new section of the *Code* that was influenced by dramatic changes in the uses of technology over the past 10 years. Those who designed the new code attempted to devote a section to technology and also infuse it throughout. In addition to addressing the challenges currently associated with social media and evolving technology, there was an attempt to have guidelines that are broad enough to be relevant when new technologies emerge in the future. Specific subjects covered in this section are knowledge of legal considerations, informed consent and security, client verification, distance counseling relationships, records and Web maintenance, and social media.

Resolving Ethical Issues

The standards in this section admonish counselors to know the *ACA Code of Ethics* thoroughly, to respond to suspected violations appropriately, and to cooperate with ethics committees.

Challenges Addressed in or Created by the 2014 *ACA Code of Ethics*

Some issues preceded the presence of related standards in the new *Code* and others appeared because of the new standards. They are introduced in the following sections.

Values Versus Competence

Earlier versions of the *ACA Code of Ethics* were less clear about whether counselors should refuse to see clients whose values clash with theirs or refer them elsewhere. Consequently, some counselors previously referred clients because they did not believe they possessed the requisite competence or because the values of the clients conflicted with their own. The 2014 *Code* makes it clear that perceived lack of competence is the only legitimate reason for referring clients elsewhere. Standard A.11.b. states,

> Counselors refrain from referring current and prospective clients based solely on the counselor's personally held values, attitudes, beliefs, and behaviors. Counselors respect the diversity of clients and seek training in

areas in which they are at risk of imposing their values onto clients, especially when the counselor's values are inconsistent with the client's goals or are discriminatory in nature.

The content of the standard challenges counselors to accept diverse values and proactively seek consciousness-raising training when challenged to do so. Not doing so is in conflict with the postmodernist multicultural values of the ACA and its members and is viewed as discriminatory in nature. The client's goals, rather than the values of the counselor, are to be the focus of the counseling process, and when counselors allow their personal values to interfere with the counseling process, the client's autonomy is threatened (Wade, 2015).

Two well-documented civil cases involving counselor education students appear to have influenced the task force developing the 2014 *Code* to emphasize the importance of client goals over counselor values. In *Ward v. Wilbanks* (2010), the student refused to counsel a client who had concerns related to same-sex relationships and wanted to make a referral prior to seeing the client because same-sex relationships were viewed as immoral from her religious perspective. In *Keeton v. Anderson-Wiley* (2011), the student was opposed to counseling lesbian, gay, bisexual, and transgender clients and proposed using reparative therapy with members of that community. Both students refused remediation offered by their training programs, were subsequently removed from their training programs, and filed civil suits against the programs.

The values of the two students in the aforementioned cases cited were challenged by members of the faculties in their respective training programs who were serving as gatekeepers for the counseling profession. Who monitors the behavior of graduates of training programs who are employed as professional counselors? Wade (2015) proposes that counselors are responsible for detecting, treating, and correcting their own impairments and those of other counselors who are known to be engaging in potential harm to clients (see Standard C.2.g.). She also posits that counselors who allow their values to trump the goals of clients are displaying signs of impairment.

Counselors are expected to be able to bracket their personal values when serving clients (Kaplan & Martz, 2014b). That is, counselors set aside or suspend their own personal values when engaging with clients. Consequently, counselors are not expected to abandon their values. Instead, they are expected to prevent their values from influencing the counseling process by recognizing them and purposefully preventing them from interfering with serving their clients.

This situation highlights the importance of valuing multiculturalism and diversity that is introduced in Chapter 5. If counselor education students and professional school counselors truly believe in the principles of multiculturalism and diversity, then they will accept the values of all prospective student clients and attempt to help them achieve their goals. Refusing to serve students with different values or attempting to alter their values because of personal beliefs held by counselors is contrary to the foundational beliefs of the counseling profession.

Ethical Challenges Related to Technology

The topics covered in section H of the *Code* include distance counseling, technology, and social media. The middle word, *technology,* indicates how broad the domain of this section might be. In the introduction to the section, counselors are challenged to "strive to become knowledgeable about these resources . . . understand the additional concerns . . . and make every attempt to protect confidentiality and meet any legal and ethical requirements for the use of such resources." Most school counselors will not be involved in distance counseling. On the other hand, forms of social media such as Facebook, Twitter, Instagram, tumblr, and Google engulf the lives of current students. In addition, cell phones (e.g., texting) and computers represent a broader technology widely used in this context. Although most agree that the technology domain presents ethical challenges, there is less agreement about how the challenges will manifest themselves and what to do to be prepared when they do. The following recommendations are based on recent suggestions published in *Counseling Today* by Meyers (2014) and Reinhardt (2014). The former publication includes comments by counselors and counselor educators interviewed by Meyers.

- Think about using and responding to social media from an ethical perspective;
- Don't follow student clients online (e.g., on Facebook, Twitter, or Google), respecting their virtual privacy, unless consent is given;
- Clearly distinguish between one's (i.e., counselors) personal and professional online presence—establish distinct and separate profiles and e-mails;
- If clients request counselors to follow them on social media outlets or to share text messages, the challenges should be discussed and negotiated clearly before agreeing to do so;
- Be sufficiently aware of the workings of the forms of social media that students are using in order to be aware of issues that students may be addressing (e.g., cyberbullying);
- Note that the new code prohibits certain kinds of virtual relationships with former students as well as current ones (see Standard A.5.c.);
- Update one's informed consent to include both face-to-face and technological interactions with students;
- Be aware of the forms of encryption that are feasible, available, or required in one's professional setting and use them accordingly (i.e., school settings).

Required Use of Problem-Solving Model
When Making Ethical Decisions

The counseling literature is replete with recommended stepped models for making ethical decisions, and some are more complex than others. Previous versions of the ACA *Codes* did not specifically require that counselors engage in systematic ethical decision making. Standard I.1.b. of the 2014 *Code* requires an ethical decision-making process and states that counselors are expected to be able to provide evidence of using one:

> When counselors are faced with an ethical dilemma, they use and document, as appropriate, an ethical decision-making model that may include, but is not limited to, consultation; consideration of relevant ethical standards, principles, and laws; generation of potential courses of action; deliberation of risks and benefits; and selection of an objective decision based on the circumstances and welfare of all involved.

The presence of the verbs *use* and *document* in the standard seems to be a clear statement of expected behaviors of professional counselors when engaging in ethical decision making.

The recommended components of the ethical decision-making model in the standard represent what might be considered the simplest and briefest of the published frameworks. It is linear, and the assumption is that it is applicable to all situations. The steps are clear, and they can be remembered easily. Unfortunately, there are important domains that are not addressed in the recommended steps that can make the process more challenging to complete while also causing decision makers to fail to address multicultural nuances. The task force that developed the *Code,* probably realizing this, noted that the recommended model "may include, but not be limited to" the recommendations in the standard. Ethical decision making is covered in greater detail later in this chapter.

You will find that the ASCA (2010) ethical standards also present an expectation that school counselors will use an ethical decision-making model and documentation is expected. Consequently, the ASCA code may have influenced the more recent ACA code in this regard. The standard recommends a potential model (i.e., "such as Solutions to Ethical Problems in Schools [STEPS]"). STEPS is a 9-step decision-making model authored by Stone (2001).

AMERICAN SCHOOL COUNSELOR ASSOCIATION *ETHICAL STANDARDS*

Ethical Standards for School Counselors (ASCA, 2010) in many ways reflects the standards of the ACA code while also presenting issues in a manner recognizing the unique preparation and work settings of school counselors. This can be seen when comparing the ASCA standards with the ACA code and standards. The first section is entitled Responsibilities to Students and includes emphases on providing confidentiality; ensuring academic, career/college postsecondary access and personal-social plans; avoiding dual relationships; making appropriate referrals; engaging in group work appropriately; recognizing and reporting danger to self and others; maintaining and securing student records; following professional assessment standards; engaging technology appropriately; and conducting peer support programs appropriately. The second section, Responsibilities to Parents/Guardians, covers parents' rights and responsibilities and confidentiality issues related to parents/guardians. The third section, Responsibilities to Colleagues and Professional Associates, deals with such matters as relationships with other professionals, sharing information with said professionals, and collaborating with and educating related to the school counselor's. A fourth section, Responsibilities to School, Communities and Families, deals with supporting school missions and policies and advocating equity for all students. The remaining three sections are Responsibilities to Self, Responsibility to the Profession, and Maintenance of Standards.

While the ACA code is designed for a diverse cross-section of professional counselors and is, therefore, more broadband in its scope, the ASCA code is primarily for school counselors and is more narrowband in scope. For example, the ACA code uses the words *counselor* and *client* and the ASCA code *professional school counselor* and *student*. In truth, the primary recipients of the services of school counseling programs are *student clients*. To decide that the ASCA code is the only code of interest for school counselors because of its primary focus on school counseling would be a mistake because the ACA code, being more comprehensive in nature, covers important ethical matters that are not addressed in the ASCA code (e.g., Research and Publication; Supervision, Training, and Teaching) and, being the more recently published code, focuses on issues such as values versus competence in making referrals and the nuances of social media and technology for counselors that are not covered as comprehensively in the older ASCA code.

AVOIDING ETHICAL VIOLATIONS

The most logical recommendation for avoiding ethical violations is that counselors be familiar with the codes and continually aware of their ramifications—always employing an ethical mindset—without being debilitated by reactionary fears of accusations of wrongdoing. Be alert, yet not fearful. DePauw's (1986) classic recommendations offer useful guidance for avoiding ethical violations via a timeline for organizing one's thoughts ethically. Users of DePauw's timeline can recognize ethical considerations that are relevant to phases in the counseling relationship. Four phases are addressed in the timeline: initiation, counseling, crisis, and termination.

Initiation

A major consideration relevant to school counselors in the initiation phase of the counseling relationship is that of assessing the student's needs and determining whether one is qualified to be of service. Related to this appropriateness issue is whether the prospective student client may be seeing another professional helper, such as a psychologist or psychiatrist. If this is the case and if the school counselor has determined himself or herself to be an appropriate helper, the student may have to choose between helpers, negotiate with the school counselor a way to inform the other helper, or seek approval for concurrent counseling. One example is partial referrals, which are described in Chapter 9.

Nevertheless, both the *ACA Code of Ethics* (A.1. Client Welfare; A.2. Informed Consent in the Counseling Relationship; A.8. Multiple Clients; B.5. Clients Lacking Capacity to Give Informed Consent) and the ASCA *Ethical Standards* (A.2. Confidentiality; B.1. Parent Rights and Responsibilities; B.2. Parents/Guardians and Confidentiality) are clear in stating that informed consent is expected for student clients and their parents. Kaplan (1996, p. 3C) offers the following analogy:

> Imagine the following scenario: *a person with whom you've had a slight acquaintance comes up to you and insists that they can help you with your problems. However, they will not tell you how they are going to help you, what will be done with the information you provide, who will be told that you are being helped, or the possibilities of what may go wrong if you allow yourself to be helped.* The next thing you hear this person saying is: "Relax and tell me your deepest, darkest secrets."

To meet the spirit of the informed consent expectation, counselors must provide enough information to ensure an informed choice (Kaplan, 1996). Traditionally, school counselors, because of the nature of their work, have not emphasized informed consent as much as counselors and therapists in other settings. Prospective student clients are often children and adolescents, and it is not always clear when talking with school-age students in a private or semiprivate setting that a request for counseling services has occurred. To launch into an informed consent explanation at this point could be counterproductive, overwhelming students and causing them to back off or possibly not return, not wanting to be labeled as "needing a shrink."

Because verbal statements may be misunderstood and because offering informed consent in the presence of a prospective student client may be problematic, the best approach is probably to have a blanket informed consent form for all parents/guardians and students to sign when students are enrolled in school, keeping the form on file while they are in attendance. What should the informed consent form contain? Kaplan (1996), borrowing from private practitioners, offers a comprehensive approach, suggesting that the consent form might contain (a) the counselor's theoretical framework and treatment approach, (b) a section on confidentiality, (c) the counselor's educational background and training, (d) rules about appointments, (e) session charges and program fees (if appropriate), and (f) an acknowledgment sheet to be signed by the students and parents/guardians.

O'Connor, Plante, and Refvem (1998) offer a less comprehensive approach, a one-page counseling consent form containing (a) the name of the school district and the title of the form, (b) an explanation (e.g., "Counseling services are offered to all students in ____ county. Any parent may withhold consent by checking in front of the specific service and then signing and dating the form. Please return this form to the counseling office by _____. Permission is presumed if this form is not returned."), (c) options to check or not check (e.g., group counseling, individual counseling of more than two sessions, individual nonmandated testing, and referrals—community services or medical), and (d) an acknowledgment section for signatures and dates. Glosoff and Pate (2002) provide additional important advice regarding informed consent. They recommend that school counselors treat informed consent as an ongoing process rather than attempting to address all of it at the beginning of the helping relationship. Stone (2014) reminds us that for professional school counselors

> confidentiality can never be guaranteed . . . informed consent is largely unattainable in schools [and] the reality of working with minors in groups requires school counselors to come from the posture that confidentiality will be breached, and informed consent will be elusive.
>
> (p. 6)

Counseling

Chief among the ethical considerations during ongoing counseling are confidentiality, consultation, and record keeping. Beyond informing student clients about confidentiality, school counselors also consider what is confidential and what is not. Certainly, it would be imprudent and inaccurate to inform students that everything they say is confidential and then not to act accordingly. If counselors are aware of the limitations to confidentiality, such as child abuse, threats to others, and admission of a crime, they will be prepared to respond immediately when those exceptions occur. Being aware and able to respond proactively enhances the chance that making exceptions to the confidentiality principle will not ruin one's relationship with the student and one's reputation among prospective student clients.

An awareness of ethical responsibilities will help school counselors in determining ways to seek consultation without violating confidentiality or placing consultants in an awkward position. One way to accomplish this is to use hypothetical information. This allows counselors to maintain anonymity for student clients while acquiring helpful assistance. As the counseling phases progress, counselors will decide what will be recorded in cumulative files and private case notes. Useful guidelines for record keeping in greater depth appear later in this chapter.

Crises

Prominent among the crises for which ethical guidance can be given are threats to oneself and to others. When students present threats to themselves (e.g., suicide ideation), school counselors must assume responsibility for the student client's welfare after carefully determining how serious the threats are. DePauw (1986) thinks that an open discussion of the counselor's concerns with an accompanying attempt to involve the student in the decision-making process enhances the chance of voluntary cooperation.

The parameters of the school counselor's ethical duty to warn others when student clients threaten others have been presented in the section of this chapter entitled "Unclear Areas." Although it is usually clear that threats are occurring, it is less clear what to do about them. DePauw (1986) recommends having contingency plans derived from consulting with informed specialists such as attorneys, psychiatrists, and law enforcement officials.

The following list of possible ingredients of a contingency plan is taken from Sheeley and Herlihy's (1989) guidelines for counseling practice related to duty-to-warn-and-protect issues associated with counseling suicidal clients:

- Know the privileged communication or confidentiality laws in the state where one is employed,
- Keep abreast of related court decisions,
- Communicate the need for related school board policies,
- Develop policy handbooks and ask parents to confirm that they received the materials,
- Circulate descriptions and explanations of the confidentiality principles,
- Encourage students and parents to sign waivers allowing counselors to disclose certain kinds of specified information that is confided during counseling,
- Keep good notes and records,
- Consult with professional peers when in doubt about student client assessments and treatments,
- Know a lawyer to contact for legal assistance, and
- Know the status of the professional liability insurance coverage plan the school district has and have an additional personal liability insurance policy. The ACA and the ASCA make this coverage available to their members.

Evidence or suspicion of child abuse is a third ethical crisis area, and mandated reporting is also backed by legal statutes. As is true in cases of threats of suicide, counselors must decide how much to explain to student clients in advance of making a report. The challenge here is to conform with the law while also trying to help and protect the student.

Termination

Two ethical concerns associated with termination are the responsibility to determine whether a counseling relationship is still productive and the decision to submit one's work for review and evaluation. Application of the former concern may lead to a decision to refer. Therefore, one is obligated ethically to know referral sources and to make appropriate referral suggestions. More information on this subject is found in Chapter 9.

The concept of submitting one's work for review and evaluation may be interpreted as an ethical responsibility to engage in evaluation associated with one's counseling services. Thus, the advocacy of accountability made in Chapter 3 has an ethical foundation.

ETHICAL MULTICULTURAL COUNSELING

The introduction to Section A (The Counseling Relationship) of the *ACA Code* provides statements about understanding diverse cultural backgrounds of clients and exploring one's own cultural identities and how they affect values and beliefs about the counseling process, and Standard A.2.c. indicates that counselors "communicate information in ways that are both developmentally and culturally appropriate." The ASCA *Ethical Standards* state, "Respect students' values, beliefs and cultural background and do not impose the school counselor's personal values on students or their families" (Standard A.1.c.) and "affirm the multiple cultural and linguistic identities of every student and all stakeholders" (Standard E.2.d.). Thus, both ethical codes seem to indicate that failure to consider a student client's culture(s) may very well be unethical.

Much of what is written about the application of ethics to multicultural counseling is at a somewhat abstract level. For example, Pedersen (1997), believing that the ethical codes are derived from a western cultural perspective that emphasizes relativism and absolutism, recommends an approach that can fit different cultural contexts. In addition, LaFromboise, Foster, and James (1996) encourage consideration of viewing ethical decisions from both a care perspective (emphasis on relationships) and a justice perspective (social contract emphasis).

At a more practical level, LaFromboise et al. (1996) make several recommendations, taken from their review of the professional literature, that may be considered guidelines for ethical multicultural counseling:

- Consider the client's unique frame of reference and personal history. This is consistent with Herring's (1997) synergistic counseling approach.
- Provide the necessary information for informed choices. This includes a treatment plan with alternative intervention methods (e.g., traditional healers) and consideration of potential outcomes with regard to one's family and community.
- Take an activist stance when it appears necessary to protect student clients from pathological systems.

The foregoing thoughts about the importance of ethical multicultural counseling indicate the importance of cultural considerations in the ethical decision-making process. On the other hand, the basic ethical decision-making models offered in the ACA and ASCA codes do not openly invite users to consider cultural implications. The basic models are easier to learn and use and provide a starting platform for students and professional counselors to use when attempting to meet the expectations for using and documenting an ethical decision-making processes. Unfortunately, adding cultural perspectives to the ethical decision-making process makes it more challenging to conduct and document. In the next section, we highlight the basic models recommended in the ACA and ASCA codes and also provide information about more sophisticated models that school counselor may consider when attempting to enhance his or her ethical decision-making sophistication.

MAKING GOOD ETHICAL DECISIONS

Although the codes of ethics are indeed comprehensive, the standards sometimes are in conflict with each other, and they may not be specific enough to give individual counselors definitive answers to ethical dilemmas they may encounter. Consequently, we guarantee that counseling students and professional counselors will eventually face having to make challenging ethical decisions. Both the ACA and ASCA standards indicate that counselors are expected to use and document a recognizable ethical decision-making model. In this section, the two models recommended by the ACA and ASCA codes respectively are reviewed and highlights from more complex models designed to provide recommendations for adding a multicultural context to the ethical decision-making process are presented.

ACA Model

As reported earlier, Standard I.1.b. provides several steps that are deemed acceptable for counselors to use when engaged in the ethical decision-making process while also indicating that there are other models that may suffice. The steps are linear, that is, the first one leads to the second and so forth.

- Generate potential courses of action
- Engage in deliberations about the risks and benefits of the potential courses
- Make a decision based on the circumstances of all involved.

The model consists of three basic steps and reflects what Cottone and Claus (2000) labeled as a "practice-based" model. An example of a well-known practice-based model that is straightforward was published by Forester-Miller and Davis (1996), and the components of the model presented in Standard I.1.b. can be found among the steps of the Forester-Miller and Davis model that follow:

- Identify the problem
- Define the potential issues
- Consult legal and ethical guidelines
- Evaluate the rights, responsibilities, and welfare of all
- Generate alternate decisions
- Enumerate the consequences of each decision

- Estimate probability for outcomes of each decision
- Make the decision.

ASCA Model

The ASCA model is presented at the close of the 2010 code and is taken from a publication by Stone (2001). The components of STEPS follow. They are similar to those found in the ACA and Forester-Miller and Davis (1996) models, and there is an overlay of content specific to school counselors (e.g., apply ASCA standards, consider student characteristics and rights of parents of minors):

- Define the problem emotionally and ethically
- Apply the ASCA ethical standards and the law
- Consider the students' chronological and developmental levels
- Consider the setting, parental rights, and minors' rights
- Apply moral principles
- Determine your potential courses of action and their consequences
- Evaluate the selected action
- Consult
- Implement the course of action.

Multicultural Ethical Decision-Making Models

Two models are presented in this section. Both use a linear model similar to that of Forester-Miller and Davis's (1996) model and provide additional components designed to challenge counselors to attend to the worldviews of culturally diverse clients from a multicultural perspective. The Transcultural Integrative Model for Ethical Decision Making in Counseling (TIM) was developed by Garcia, Cartwright, Winston, and Borzuchowska (2003) and the Multicultural Ethical Decision-Making Model by Frame and Williams (2005). In proposing the TIM, Garcia et al. (2003) considered previous models and evaluated them from a cultural perspective. Frame and Williams (2005) highlight a weakness of basic models such as those presented earlier being an implicit belief that one decision-making model serves all people. They emphasize the importance of knowing about others' cultures, not imposing one's own values, and being able to enter another's world while cognizant of one's own cultural background, that is, *reciprocal empathy*. Components of the two models that challenge counselors to engage in multicultural ethical decision making follow:

- Interpret the situation through awareness and fact finding; enhance sensitivity and awareness (e.g., awareness of attitudes and emotional reactions toward cultural groups, knowledge of client's culture) (Garcia et al., 2003).

- Determine the cultural and historical factors at play; explore the context of power (i.e., Where are the client and the counselor located in related power structures?) (Frame & Williams, 2005).

- Assess acculturation and racial identity development of the client and the counselor (Frame & Williams, 2005).

- Ensure that cultural information gathered is considered when reviewing the dilemma (Garcia et al., 2003).

- Make sure courses of action reflect cultural worldviews of all parties involved (Garcia et al., 2003).

- Consider the positive and negative consequences for each alternative from the cultural worldviews of all parties involved (Garcia et al., 2003).

- Consult with others who are culturally competent (Frame & Williams, 2005; Garcia et al., 2003).

- Select an option that best represents agreement between the worldview of the client and all other parties involved (Garcia et al., 2003).

- Identify culturally relevant resources and strategies for implementing the decision (Garcia et al., 2003).

- Evaluate the decision on the basis of how well the client's cultural values and experiences were considered, how the counselor's values were affirmed or challenged, and how power influenced the outcome (Frame & Williams, 2005).

Obviously, implementation of the aforementioned multicultural ethical decision-making elements will make the process more complicated, arduous, and difficult to document. On the other hand, it is also obvious that the multicultural elements add something of value to the decision-making process. The simpler models presented earlier represent a modernist perspective for ethical decision making, that is, one size fits all. Frame and Williams (2005) advocate a postmodern approach: "A postmodern approach means abandoning assumptions of objectivity, empirical knowledge, and universal truth. Thus, the one (dominant, Western) perspective must give way to the many (multicultural) perspectives" (p. 174).

Should you use the modernist approaches approved by ACA and ASCA or attempt to employ the more inclusive and sophisticated postmodern approaches to ethical decision making? Cottone and Claus (2000) reported that the literature abounded with decision-making models over a decade ago and concluded that many of them lacked foundational premises, theoretical grounding, or empirical support. Which model is the best choice for a specific counselor when attempting to deal with a specific ethical decision is essentially unknown. We recommend that this dilemma be approached from the evidence-based practice perspective presented in Chapter 3. That is, gather evidence of the effects of whatever ethical decision-making model one chooses to use (i.e., expected by ACA and ASCA codes) and use the data to determine how to proceed with ethical decision making in the future.

KEEPING GOOD STUDENT RECORDS: A MERGING OF LEGAL AND ETHICAL CODES

School record keeping in the United States can be traced back to the 1820s and 1830s. The original purposes of record keeping seem to have been to certify student enrollment and attendance and to recognize levels of accomplishment (Fischer & Sorenson, 1996). As the schools became more committed to the "whole child" concept, the cumulative record folder became more than an academic record; it became a humanistic document. The cumulative record files are now repositories for a variety of information about students.

A very significant development in the arena of student record keeping was the passage of FERPA in 1974. Details about FERPA were presented in an earlier section of this chapter. The FERPA legislation provides specific legal guidelines for student record keeping. The ACA and ASCA codes of ethics provide guidelines, too, including clarification of the differences between confidential records and public records, a caveat to share appropriate information with those who have the right to know it, and instruction about appropriate procedures for transmitting and releasing information to third parties.

FERPA AND CODES OF ETHICS

McGuire and Borowy (1978) insist that some confidential information typically included in student records was excluded from coverage under the Buckley Amendment. This exception hinges on the purpose or use of the information, rather than on the nature of its content. In their opinion, information obtained solely for the purpose of providing professional and diagnostic services to children is to remain confidential, on the assumption that the information has not been shared with anyone else, including fellow professionals. If it has been shared with anyone, it is no longer confidential.

Prior to the passage of PL 93–380, counselors had no guidelines other than ethical codes to use when faced with requests for information that challenged the principle of confidentiality. Such requests, for instance, may have been made by school administrators, school boards, or other persons of authority. PL 93–380 supplements the existing codes of ethics. Better definitions of appropriate counselor behaviors are provided through this union of law and ethics.

Getson and Schweid (1976) offer suggestions for alleviating potential conflicts between PL 93–380 and codes of ethics:

- Remove all information that might be misinterpreted by nonprofessionals,

- Initiate a policy that allows parental review of only those records that are not a threat to student welfare,

- Be sure students are aware of the limits of privacy that exist in a counseling relationship because of parental rights to review student records, and

- Make a personal study of the possibility of conflicts between PL 93–380 and the counselor's professional code of ethics.

DEVELOPING A SYSTEMATIC PLAN FOR COLLECTION, MAINTENANCE, AND DISSEMINATION OF SCHOOL RECORDS

Guided by ethical standards to take care in record-keeping matters and mandated to engage in certain record-keeping procedures by PL 93–380, school counselors needed ideas for conducting the collection, maintenance, and dissemination of school records in a systematic manner. Into this setting came the Russell Sage Foundation (1970) guidelines, which became the foremost source of ideas for systematizing school record keeping. For example, in Pennsylvania, detailed school record-keeping systems were mandated by the state's department of education in 1976, and the Russell Sage guidelines were used as the criteria for judging the acceptability of each school district's submitted plan.

Several useful ideas are found in the Russell Sage guidelines. First, they cover the collection of data in which the distinction between individual and representational (parents' legally elected or appointed representatives) consent is discussed. Second, a useful and important system for categorizing data is given. It can be summarized as follows.

Category A Data

In this category are the minimum personal data necessary for operation of the education system. Examples are names, addresses, birth dates, and grades. This information is to be maintained perpetually.

Category B Data

This category includes verified information of clear importance but not absolutely necessary to the school in helping the child or in protecting others. Examples are scores on standardized intelligence tests, aptitude tests, and interest inventories; family background; and systematic teacher ratings. It is recommended that parents be informed periodically of the content of these records and of their right of access to the content. It is also recommended that Category B data be destroyed, or only maintained under conditions of anonymity, after a student leaves school.

Category C Data

Potentially useful data that are primarily time-bound to the immediate present are assigned to this category. Examples are legal or clinical findings, personality test results, and unevaluated reports of teachers or counselors. It is recommended that these data be destroyed as soon as their usefulness is ended, unless it is reasonable to transfer them to Category B.

A survey of elementary and middle school counselors in New Hampshire led Merlone (2005) to conclude that there was "confusion and diverse practices regarding the storage, sharing, and destruction of counselors' notes" (p. 372). Ironically, Merlone recommended that the very same Russell Sage guidelines cited earlier provided the best resource for helping counselors become more competent and consistent in their management of student records.

Confidential Data

Any records or notes that are to be kept confidential should be located in the counselor's personal files, rather than in the cumulative records.

IMPLEMENTING A RECORD-KEEPING SYSTEM

In a position statement on guidance services made at the time Pennsylvania was mandating detailed record-keeping systems, the Pennsylvania Department of Education (1977) made two useful records maintenance suggestions. First, a school district's record-keeping policies should allow for the retention of information necessary to permit full counseling, referral, and placement services in the years following a student's departure from school. This recommendation will have an important influence on what information is maintained in Category A after a student departs from school. Second, a centrally located storage facility should be established in order to allow easy access to records for those who have a legitimate interest in them. At the same time, provisions must be made for security against unauthorized use and accidental dissemination of information in student records.

In the same document, the Pennsylvania Department of Education (1977) offered useful advice (heavily influenced by the Russell Sage guidelines) for administering the record-keeping system:

- The mechanical aspects of record collection, maintenance, security, and dissemination should be handled by the clerical and/or paraprofessional staff under the supervision of the chief school administrator or that administrator's delegate. (In many instances, that authority is delegated to a school counselor.)

- Each school district should have a committee made up of staff members (instructional, pupil personnel, and administrative), parents, and students that is charged with deciding what information is to be collected and maintained for students' school records.

- The counselor's primary concern and involvement in the area of student records should be to participate with the others listed in the preceding paragraph to determine the content of records and to interpret and apply that content in the education of the student.

- The director of guidance should be responsible for establishing procedures for carrying out the school policy on records.

How involved school counselors are in the school's record-keeping system varies across districts. Certainly, they will keep and handle student records. It is assumed that most counselors will have their own confidential file notes and that they will have to conform to legal codes, ethical guidelines, and local policies when using the cumulative files. Some additional options counselors will not control because they are imposed. Those options include being the person to whom responsibility for administering the record-keeping system has been delegated, serving on the committee that determines what information should be collected and maintained, helping others to be better informed through in-service training efforts, and interpreting contents to laypeople when needed. Burky and Childers (1976) offer a good general principle for counselors: Counselors should model behavior displaying their belief in the paramount rights of individuals.

SOURCES OF ETHICS CONSULTATION

American Counseling Association (www.counseling.org)

Members may call either 800-347-6647 or submit an e-mail (ethics@counseling.org) five days a week from 8:30 a.m. to 4:30 p.m. and will be referred for consultation to an ACA specialist. If implication of the issue is beyond ethics, a referral to the ACA-sponsored Risk Management Service affiliate may occur.

American School Counselor Association (www.schoolcounselor.org)

Members may post questions on the ASCA SCENE under the Legal & Ethical category or submit an e-mail to ethics@schoolcounselor.org.

COMPREHENSIVE SCHOOL COUNSELING PROGRAM COMPONENT

1. Review your knowledge of state and local legislation relative to counseling.
2. Develop an informed consent statement, if you do not already have one. Have your statement critiqued by your instructor, colleagues, and prospective clients.
3. Set up two plans for training teachers to use the record-keeping system appropriately. Have one plan in a group in-service format and the other in a programmed format for self-instruction.
4. Develop a plan of action for responding to the following legal/ethical challenge:

    An 18-year-old female high school student has left home. Suspecting that the reasons for her leaving may be explained in the young woman's records, one of her parents calls the school counseling office and asks to see the records. Meanwhile, the young woman has decided to withdraw from school and also requests to see her records. She wants them purged of personal information. Two weeks later, the police call the guidance office for access to the young woman's file during a routine investigation. A prospective employer also calls the guidance office and requests the young woman's IQ score or equivalent information for assistance in making a decision about hiring her.

REFLECTION POINT

*Discuss the following cases, which are taken from "An Ethics Quiz for School Counselors" (Huey, Salo, & Fox, 1995). Determine whether you agree (A) or disagree (D) with the counselor's decision in each case, and place the corresponding letter in the blanks:

a.   ____ A group member became very upset and wanted to leave after several members ganged up on her in a vicious verbal attack. The counselor physically barred the sobbing girl from leaving and told her that she must learn to handle conflicts within the group.

b.   ____ A counselor self-described his dislike of a new technology as "computer phobia." As part of the school's counseling program, all ninth-grade students were required to use a newly purchased computerized interest inventory. The counselor joked that he was "not sure that he could even turn the machine on" and left the students to themselves "because they were better with computers anyway."

c.   ____ As part of an ongoing peer program to assist students in being better able to help their peers with personal concerns, the counselor scheduled regular supervision sessions. Even though the peer helpers were well trained and had not had any problems, the counselor felt an obligation to check in with them.

d.   ____ A male counselor refused to close his door when counseling teenage girls, even when requested by students who were emotionally upset. A female colleague believed the counselor was unnecessarily cautious and unethical in not providing the privacy needed by clients. The colleague decided to speak to the counselor to be sure he was aware of his responsibilities.

e.   ____ A counselor strongly disliked a particular student assigned to his caseload and found himself distracted by negative feelings every time he saw the student. Despite good faith attempts to change his feelings, the counselor still disliked the student and subsequently referred the student to another counselor.

f.   ____ The parents of a sophomore who was having academic problems told the counselor they were going to transfer their son to a private school the next school year. The student loved his current school and was very involved in extracurricular activities. The parents would not reconsider and asked the counselor not to tell their son about the plans. When advising the student about his academic course work for the next year, the counselor was careful not to reveal the parents' plans.

Reflect on your positions on the following recommendations:

- School counselors should not refer student clients for reasons related to their personal values.
- School counselors should not follow students on Facebook and other social media outlets.
- School counselors should use and document ethical decision-making models.
- The best ethical decision-making models contain multicultural overlays.

*Suggested and keyed responses for the aforementioned cases.
Answer key for activity: a = D, b = D, c = A, d = A, e = A, f = D

APPLICATION TO TECHNOLOGY

1. Create an inventory of forms of social media that students currently use that might challenge school counselors from legal and ethical perspectives and develop a list of ways that the challenges might be manifested.
2. Develop a plan for using technology to keep student records in a manner that meets FERPA guidelines and those in the ACA and ASCA codes of ethics.

REFERENCES

Adair, J. (2006). The efficacy of sexual violence prevention programs. *Journal of School Violence, 5,* 87–97.

American Counseling Association. (2014). *ACA code of ethics.* Alexandria, VA: Author.

American School Counselor Association. (1988). The school counselor and child abuse/neglect prevention. *Elementary School Guidance and Counseling, 22,* 216–263.

American School Counselor Association. (2010). *Ethical standards for school counselors.* Alexandria, VA: Author.

Anderson, R. F. (n.d.). *Counselors going to court.* Unpublished paper, Wake County, North Carolina, Public Schools.

Arnold v. Board of Education of Escambia County, 880 F.2d 305 (Alabama 1989).

Bronner, E. (1998, March 14). Guidance counselors fearful of litigation. *The News & Observer,* p. 12A.

Bryant, J., & Milsom, A. (2005). Child abuse reporting by school counselors. *Professional School Counseling, 9,* 63–71.

Burky, W. D., & Childers, J. H., Jr. (1976). Buckley Amendment: Focus on a professional dilemma. *School Counselor, 23,* 162–164.

Congressional Record. (120S21487, daily edition, December 13, 1974). *Joint statement in explanation of the Buckley/Pell Amendment.* Washington, DC: Government Printing Office.

Connors, E. T. (1979). *Student discipline and the law.* Bloomington, IN: Phi Delta Kappa Foundation.

Corey, G., Corey, M. S., & Callanan, P. (1984). *Issues and ethics in the helping professions* (2nd ed.). Monterey, CA: Brooks/Cole.

Cottone, R. R., & Claus, R. E. (2000). Ethical decision-making models: A review of the literature. *Journal of Counseling & Development, 78,* 275–283.

Crenshaw, W., Crenshaw, L., & Lichtenberg, J. (1995). When educators confront child abuse: An analysis of the decision to report. *Child Abuse & Neglect, 19,* 1095–1113.

Currie v. United States, 644 E Supp. 1074 (N.C., 1986).

DePauw, M. E. (1986). Avoiding ethical violations: A timeline perspective for individual counseling. *Journal of Counseling & Development, 64,* 303–305.

Fischer, L., & Sorenson, G. P. (1996). *School law for counselors, psychologists, and social workers* (3rd ed.). New York: Longman.

Forester-Miller, H., & Davis, T. (1996). *A practitioner's guide to ethical decision-making* [Online]. Retrieved from http://www.counseling.org/knowledge-center/ethics

Frame, M. W., & Williams, C. B. (2005). A model of ethical decision making from a Multicultural perspective. *Counseling and Values, 49,* 165–179.

Garcia, J. G., Cartwright, B., Winston, S. M., & Borzuchowska, B. (2003). A transcultural integrative model for ethical decision making counseling. *Journal of Counseling and Development, 81,* 268–277.

Gehring, D. C. (1982). The counselor's "duty to warn." *Personnel and Guidance Journal, 61,* 208–210.

Getson, R., & Schweid, R. (1976). School counselors and the Buckley Amendment—Ethical standards squeeze. *School Counselor, 24,* 56–58.

Glosoff, H. L., Herlihy, B., & Spence, E. B. (2000). Privileged communication and the counselor-client relationship. *Journal of Counseling & Development, 78,* 454–462.

Glosoff, H. L., & Pate, R. H., Jr. (2002). Privacy and confidentiality in school counseling. *Professional School Counseling, 6,* 20–27.

Herlihy, B., & Remley, T. P. (2001). Legal and ethical challenges. In D. C. Locke, J. E. Myers, & E. L. Herr (Eds.), *The handbook of counseling* (pp. 69–89). Thousand Oaks, CA: Sage.

Hermann, M. A. (2002). A study of legal issues encountered by school counselors and perceptions of their preparedness to respond to legal challenges. *Professional School Counseling, 6,* 12–19.

Herring, R. D. (1997). *Multicultural counseling in schools: A synergistic approach.* Alexandria, VA: American Counseling Association.

Hinson, J., & Fossey, R. (2000). Child abuse: What teachers in the 90s know, think, and do. *Journal of Education for Students Placed at Risk, 5,* 251–266.

Hopkins, B. R., & Anderson, B. S. (1990). *The counselor and the law.* Alexandria, VA: American Association for Counseling and Development.

Huey, W. C. (1986). Ethical concerns in school counseling. *Journal of Counseling & Development, 64,* 321–322.

Huey, W., Salo, M. M., & Fox, R. W. (1995). An ethics quiz for school counselors. *School Counselor, 42,* 393–398.

Kaplan, D. M. (1996). *Developing an informed consent brochure for secondary students: All about ASCA membership.* Alexandria, VA: American School Counselor Association.

Kaplan, D. M., & Martz, E. (2014a, July). An overview of the revised *ACA Code of Ethics. Counseling Today, 57*(1), 20–21.

Kaplan, D. M., & Martz, E. (2014b, August). Preamble scramble. *Counseling Today, 57*(2), 20–21.

Keeton v. Anderson-Wiley, 664.F. 3d 865-Court of Appeals, 11th Circuit 2011.

Kenny, M. C. (2001). Child abuse reporting: Teacher's perceived deterrents. *Child Abuse and Neglect, 25,* 81–92.

Kiselica, M. S. (1996). Legal issues in abortion counseling with adolescents. *ASCA Counselor, 33*(4), 1.

Knapp, S. (1983). Counselor liability to report child abuse. *Elementary School Guidance and Counseling, 17,* 177–179.

LaFromboise, T. D., Foster, S., & James, A. (1996). Ethics in multicultural counseling. In P. B. Pedersen, J. G. Draguns, W. J. Lonner, & J. E. Trimble (Eds.), *Counseling across cultures* (4th ed., pp. 47–72). Thousand Oaks, CA: Sage.

Lawrence, G., & Kurpius, S.E.R. (2000). Legal and ethical issues involved when counseling minors in nonschool settings. *Journal of Counseling & Development, 78,* 130–136.

Legal considerations should not shape clinical decisions, seminar told. (1983, July 6). *Mental Health Reports,* 7–8.

McGuire, J. M., & Borowy, T. D. (1978). Confidentiality and the Buckley/Pell Amendment: Ethical and legal considerations for counselors. *Personnel and Guidance Journal, 56,* 554–557.

Merlone, L. (2005). Record keeping and the school counselor. *Professional School Counseling, 8,* 372–376.

Meyers, L. (2014, June). A living document of ethical guidance. *Counseling Today, 56*(1), 32–40.

Monahan, J. (1993). Limiting therapist exposure to *Tarasoff* liability. *American Psychologist, 48,* 242–250.

O'Connor, K., Plante, J., & Refvem, J. (1998, March). *Parental consent and the school counselor.* Poster session presented at the annual meeting of the North Carolina Counseling Association, Chapel Hill.

Pedersen, P. B. (1997). *Culture-centered counseling interventions: Striving for accuracy.* Thousand Oaks, CA: Sage.

Pennsylvania Department of Education. (1977). *Guidance services in Pennsylvania: Position statement.* Harrisburg: Author.

Reinhardt, R. (2014, August). The ethics of technology use. *Counseling Today, 57*(2), 22–24.

Remley, T. P., Jr. (1985). The law and ethical practices in elementary and middle schools. *Elementary School Guidance and Counseling, 19,* 181–189.

Remley, T. P., Jr. (1992). How much record keeping is enough? *American Counselor, 1,* 31–33.

Remley, T. P., Jr., & Herlihy, B. (2005). *Ethical, legal, and professional issues in counseling* (2nd ed.). Upper Saddle River, NJ: Pearson-Merrill-Prentice Hall.

Russell Sage Foundation. (1970). *Guidelines for the collection, maintenance, and dissemination of pupil records.* Hartford, CT: Author.

Sain v. Cedar Rapids Community School District, 626 N.W.2d 115 (Iowa 2001).

Sheeley, V. L., & Herlihy, B. (1989). Counseling suicidal teens: A duty to warn and protect. *School Counselor, 37,* 89–97.

Stone, C. (2001). *School counseling principles: Ethics and law.* Alexandria, VA: American School Counselor Association.

Stone, C. (2002). Negligence in academic advising and abortion counseling: Courts rulings and implications. *Professional School Counseling, 6,* 28–35.

Stone, C. (2005). Ethics and law for school counselors. *ASCA School Counselor, 42*(6), 44–49.

Stone, C. (2014, October). Informed consent: Is it attainable with students in schools? *ASCA School Counselor, 52*(1), 6–8.

Tarasoff v. Regents of the University of California, 551 p. 2nd 334 (California, 1976).

Therapists bear a duty to commit, says U.S. district court judge. (1987). *Mental Health Law Reporter,* pp. 4–5 (sample issue).

Van Hoose, W. H., & Kottler, J. (1978). *Ethical and legal issues in counseling and psychotherapy.* San Francisco: Jossey-Bass.

Wade, M. E. (2015, April). Handling conflicts of personal values. *Counseling Today, 56*(1), 16.

Ward v. Wilbanks, No. 09-CV-11237 (E.D. Mich. July 26, 2010).

Wilson, J., Thomas, D., & Schuette, L. (1983). Survey of counselors on identifying and reporting cases of child abuse. *School Counselor, 30,* 299–305.

Zingaro, J. (1983). Confidentiality: To tell or not to tell. *Elementary School Guidance and Counseling, 17,* 261–267.

ADVOCACY IN SCHOOL COUNSELING

5

RELATED STANDARDS OF PRACTICE

CACREP CORE	2.F.d, 2.F.e
CACREP SCHOOL COUNSELING	5.G.2.a, 5.G.2.f

Goal: To recommend a place for advocacy in school counseling and suggest implementation strategies for a balanced program.

Children and adolescents are among the most powerless and vulnerable people in 21st-century society. They can be moved from home to home and from school to school with little or no recognition of their needs or rights. The following is an example:

> Marcus was a 6-year-old boy. He lived in one of the wealthiest suburbs of Denver. He was adopted when he was 5 years old, not long after he appeared on a local television news program that featured children who needed a home. Marcus appeared to be a handsome, strong, healthy youngster during his television appearance, and several callers to the television station requested opportunities to meet Marcus and to consider adopting him. An affluent couple in Denver, who had tried unsuccessfully for years to give birth to a child, adopted Marcus and set out to provide a wonderful home for him. Shortly after the adoption, the couple learned that Marcus had a serious disease that would consume much of their time and wealth to manage. The couple, fearing the loss of their wealth and freedom, neglected Marcus and rejected him emotionally. Marcus came to the attention of his school counselor because of the neglect and rejection he faced at home.

What should a school counselor do in a case like this one? How can the counselor advocate for kids like Marcus? What advocacy skills does the counselor need? What dilemmas will school counselors face as they advocate for students? Advocacy is an important role for school counselors; this chapter discusses that role.

THE LEGACY OF ADVOCACY

THE SOCIAL REFORM MOVEMENT AND SCHOOL COUNSELING

Aubrey (1977) suggested the process by which social reformers made an impact on the problems when he described the relationship between the social reform movement and vocational guidance:

> The linkage between this movement and vocational guidance was largely built on the issue of the growing exploitation and misuse of human beings. This linkage centering on the two conditions of economic waste and human suffering was to be used time and again as a means of pricking the conscience of the public, especially legislators. Lawmakers, visibly absent among the ranks of social reformers, were forced to be responsive to the persistent and ceaseless cries of social reformers. As a consequence, Congress in 1917 passed the landmark Smith-Hughes Act for secondary vocational education and teacher training. This beginning of enabling legislation was to be strengthened during the next twenty years.
>
> (p. 290)

Cremin (cited in Aubrey, 1977) is credited for noting that some reformers viewed the schools as vehicles for improving individuals' lives. Referred to as humanitarians and progressives, these reformers included Horace Mann and John Dewey, who founded the Progressive Education Association. Cremin (1965) was among those who viewed school counselors as the professionals in the schools whose role and functions most epitomized the goals of the progressive movement. In pointing out that Cremin's thought was more of a compliment than a reality, Aubrey observed that the tendency to elevate school counseling idealistically beyond reality reached its zenith with the publication of John Brewer's *Education as Guidance* in 1932. Brewer's point of view and that of the progressives faded during World War II and the postwar years.

THE POST–WORLD WAR II YEARS

In the years immediately following World War II, the United States found itself among the wealthiest and most powerful of nations. Many social problems of the late 19th and early 20th centuries had abated, and some goals of the reformers had been achieved.

School counseling entered a period of rapid expansion following the passage of the National Defense Education Act of 1958 (NDEA). Much attention was devoted to training new counselors, retraining employed counselors, and developing counselor education programs. The support provided by the NDEA for these efforts was predicated on the assumption that the needs of the nation will be served if its youth are guided into careers that will strengthen the nation in its struggle against communism and keep it strong and prosperous.

The need for social reform still existed. It did not have the high priority in school counseling and in education it had once enjoyed, however, and those who insisted on telling others the right answers, as some early reformers did, were not very popular. An indication of some social problems in the middle of the 20th century was provided by Wrenn (1962) in *The Counselor in a Changing World.* He cited racial discrimination, occupational restrictions on women, the influence of automation on employment opportunities, increasing divorce rates, and inner-city income and cultural deprivation among the challenges for which new directions in school counseling were needed.

THE CALL FOR SCHOOL COUNSELORS TO BE CHANGE AGENTS

The 1960s and early 1970s were a period of great social unrest in the United States. Exacerbated by a growing confusion over the country's military involvement in Vietnam, many young Americans clashed with their elders over national priorities, social mores, and personal rights and responsibilities. The Vietnam War and the Civil Rights and women's rights movements were leading factors in the polarization of attitudes. A return to militancy toward social problems developed concurrently with the appearance of individuals whose voices sounded a demanding, uncompromising, and accusing tone.

Contributors to the professional counseling literature during this era encouraged counselors to respond to the conditions proactively. Terms like *activist, advocacy, social action,* and *change agent* became prominent in the literature (cf. Hansen, 1968; Harris, 1967; Rousseve, 1968; Shaw, 1968; Stewart & Warnath, 1965; S. C. Stone & Shertzer, 1963). Clearly, school counselors were being challenged to try to change the circumstances causing various social problems and alleviating the effects. Focusing on the problems of urban United States in particular, though also alluding to related problems in rural and suburban areas, Menacker (1974) advocated an interventionist role for school counselors. He argued as follows:

> The most fundamental guidance issue, finally, is the response that guidance ought to take to the concept that the student's out-of-school psychological, social, and physiological environment (food, housing, parents, peers, and so on) are more important determinants of school achievement than anything that occurs inside the school building.
>
> (p. 23)

Menacker (1974) insisted that school counselors should respond to "the forces outside the school as those within it and, in so doing, actively support the student" (p. 22). His recommendation placed school counselors idealistically in the role of advocates. Herr (1979) sees this as

> a source of both vulnerability and promise—vulnerability in the sense that many of the problems encountered by school counselors are of long duration of resolution, promise in the sense that the school counselor is a symbol of hopefulness that the school is a caring, humane place that has regard for individual purpose among all students.
>
> (p. 11)

SOCIAL ADVOCACY REVISITED

Advocacy was not on the front burner in school counseling during the 1980s. Attention to the advocacy concept came primarily from champions for multiculturalism and multicultural counseling competencies in the 1990s. In 1999, the American School Counselor Association (ASCA) issued a position statement on multicultural counseling that called for facilitation of student development through an understanding of and appreciation for multiculturalism and diversity. In the ASCA National Model for School Counseling Programs (ASCA, 2012), advocacy is one of four themes upon which the National Model framework is based. Within the Model, school counselors are viewed as uniquely well positioned to serve as advocates for students and families in order to enhance student achievement.

Similarly, the Transforming School Counseling Initiative emphasized the importance of school counselors advocating for access to rigorous education for all students (House & Hayes, 2002). School counselors are viewed as advocates for school-community collaboration in the school-community collaboration model (Adelman & Taylor, 2002; Stinchfield & Zyromski, 2010). They are encouraged to take the lead in planning and advocating for less costly, more comprehensive, and more efficient interventions for students and their families.

Kiselica and Robinson (2001) remind us that advocacy has several synonyms that may be found in the professional literature and that essentially mean the same thing. *Advocacy counseling, social action,* and *social justice* are among the most recent synonyms. Bradley and Lewis (2000) define advocacy as the act of speaking up or taking action to make environmental changes on behalf of clients. Dinsmore, Chapman, and McCollum (2002) supplement the definition by pointing out that advocacy can focus on responding on behalf of clients or empowering clients to work on their own behalf. Furthermore, Lee (1998) reminds us that the goal of advocacy in school counseling is to help clients challenge institutional and social barriers that are impediments to academic, career, or personal-social development. Comparing advocacy to the more traditional responsive counseling competencies such as counseling and consulting, Kiselica and Robinson (2001) point out that advocating for clients expands the counselor's focus. That is, the focus is expanded from intrapsychic concerns to include responding to extrapsychic forces that may be detrimental to clients. Their analysis implies that different competencies may be needed as well.

Furthermore, being advocates for the school counseling profession is important as well. The goals for a balanced approach to school counseling presented in Chapter 2 included being advocates for all students and for the school counseling profession. Advocacy for the profession may be manifested through individual actions and via participation in and support of professional counseling associations.

CHALLENGES OF THE 21ST CENTURY

THE CURRENT LITANY OF CHALLENGES

In the first decade of the 21st century, U.S. society was faced with social issues as challenging as ever. The struggle for equality continues for individuals with disabilities, racial and ethnic minority groups, women, senior citizens, homeless individuals and families, immigrants, migrants, and gays and lesbians. Suicide is a national problem among adolescents, especially sexual minority students. The traditional family has declined as the norm, with the children of many single parent, dual-working parent, and disintegrated families left to fend for themselves. The technology environment provides access to communication using social media platforms. In turn, this creates a paradox as it offers a world full of technological interactions and yet promotes isolation. Because of rapid changes in the economy, the workplace, and employment opportunities, many Americans have found themselves unemployed after years of employment or underemployed, with a corresponding decline in their standard of living. The same conditions threaten to engulf those young people who, for one reason or another, fail to cope with the expectations of the workplace and condemn themselves to unfulfilling futures living below the economic subsistence level.

RESPONDING TO THE CHALLENGES

The litany of problems cited in the previous paragraph can make one feel depressed and overwhelmed. They represent current and future challenges with which society must continue to struggle. The schools and school counselors are in the midst of this struggle; they cannot ignore the problems because individuals affected by the problems attend and will attend the schools. And, these problems will prevent those children from being successful academically. Like it or not, the schools have become more than a place to impart knowledge. Consequently, professional school counselors are in a unique position to act as agents of systemic change that have an impact on not only the individual, but also the school and community (Beck, Rausch, & Wood, 2014). Clearly, school counselors have a place in this scene as collaborators with other professional colleagues. School counseling was born in the social reform movement of another era, the legacy lives on, and it will continue to flourish.

In a call for social action in counseling, Lee and Sirch (1994) point out that the new millennium will usher in "a more global view of human need and potential" (p. 91). While striving to present their vision of an enlightened world society, Lee and Sirch also recommend two ways the counseling profession may promote their vision through social action, which they refer to as *counseling for an enlightened world society*.

First, counselors must believe in the vision of an enlightened world society and, in so doing, adopt *a sense of social responsibility*. Lee and Sirch (1994) view this commitment as manifesting itself in philosophical commitment to the need for global social change and a willingness to become *social change agents* in the spirit of the models promoted by the activist contributors to the counseling literature of the 1960s and 1970s. Second, counselors are challenged to work with clients from diverse cultural backgrounds, to be able to facilitate client development via traditional intervention and prevention strategies, and to help clients "assess the meaning of life and significant relationships within it" (p. 95).

Lee (2001) issued a challenge for school counselors as follows:

> [Demographic trends indicate that] as never before, U.S. schools are becoming a social arena where children who represent truly diverse behavioral styles, attitudinal orientations, and value systems have been brought together with one goal—to prepare them for academic, career, and social success in the twenty-first century.
>
> (p. 257)

Lee (2001) continued by challenging counselors to be able to respond to students representing an expanded set of worldviews in order to ensure them access to services that promote optimal academic, career, and psychosocial development. Finally, he challenges us to "move beyond the myth of a monolithic society to the reality of cultural diversity" (p. 261).

As was pointed out in Chapter 4, advocacy has been highlighted in the 2014 *ACA Code of Ethics* (Standard A.7.a.) within the section on Roles and Relationships at Individual, Group, Institutional and Societal Levels. This entry in the *Code* implies that failure to advocate for clients when appropriate is unethical.

In our opinion, the pervasiveness of these social problems and the call for advocacy require school counselors to respond with patience and care. Setting goals and working with others to achieve them is a better strategy than working independently and impulsively to resolve issues. Demanding change may be less palatable to decision makers than leading the way with information and reasoned debate. When singular efforts fail, planning and renewed efforts are needed. These social problems may not be eradicated for a generation or more. Yet some individuals can be helped. Many counselors attempting to help many individuals can be very influential. The remainder of this chapter elaborates on advocacy competencies and provides vignettes in which the competencies are demonstrated.

A CLOSER LOOK AT ADVOCACY

POPULARITY OF THE INTRAPSYCHIC COUNSELING APPROACH

The popularity of Carl Rogers's nondirective or person-centered approach to counseling in the mid-20th century led to an atmosphere in which most school counselors viewed their role as somewhat clinical in nature. Much emphasis was placed on individual counseling, one-to-one relationships, and counseling interventions. In developmental counseling—the counseling of individuals who were dealing with developmental issues such as selecting courses of study, planning for the future, coping with schoolwork, and getting along with others—many counselors also used client-centered response modes. That client-centered counseling dominated the repertoires of many counselors indicated that they found it effective. Numerous clients were helped by school counselors who were using a predominantly client-centered model or other models that allowed them to work mainly in their offices, responding to referrals from colleagues and self-referrals by students.

EMERGENCE OF AN EXTRAPSYCHIC COUNSELING APPROACH

Although effective for some student clients, the intrapsychic counseling model is also a passive, reactive one in which student clients are expected to take responsibility for helping themselves. Therefore, the solutions to problems, choices, and challenges confronting these students are often viewed as being within the grasp of the clients themselves if they can figure out how to solve the problems, make the choices, and meet the challenges successfully. In this approach, school counselors use listening and responding skills to create an accepting and empathic environment for their clients. Clients are helped because they can use that environment to feel understood, to clarify their thoughts and feelings, and to move freely toward decisions or feel better about themselves and their circumstances. As an alternative method, counselors can share the wisdom of their experience to offer student clients advice based on the expectation that the clients will be responsible for carrying out that advice. To sum up, in the mid-20th century, most school counselors used helping models drawn primarily from psychological theories that stressed passive verbal interaction and self-directed client activity (Menacker, 1976). It is not a helping model that encourages advocacy, nor is it a training model that produces counselors who are active interventionists. Into this setting came the unrest of the 1960s. With that unrest came dissatisfaction with the accepted counseling models because school counselors seemed too passive and uninvolved and because some clients could not achieve their goals through their own self-directed efforts. Several descriptive terms were used to label different approaches being advocated; yet advocates of these approaches seemed to recommend that school counselors become more active, more directive and challenging, and more helpful to individuals confronted by issues whose resolutions were beyond their own self-directed efforts. A sample follows.

Menacker (1974) highlights the importance of a nontraditional, more active role for school counselors in the urban schools. His position is based on his conclusions that the out-of-school environment of urban students is more important than anything that occurs inside the school building and that urban school bureaucracies are inert and resistant to change, which challenges counselors to adopt an activist, interventionist role to prevent themselves from becoming part of a stifling bureaucracy. Recommended manifestations of this role include the following:

- Adopting a multiple school counseling program control model in which central counseling officials, principals, local school counselors, teachers, students, and parent-community representatives are all involved in planning, monitoring, implementing, and evaluating the counseling program;

- Resisting bureaucratic pressures to achieve maintenance goals and instead advocating goals that serve students and promise to improve their circumstances;

- Engaging in environmental alteration when such changes seem appropriate, both in the school and in the community as a community resource specialist.

In his activist theory, Menacker (1976) advocates a shift away from philosophical underpinnings deeply rooted in psychology and toward a greater emphasis on sociology, anthropology, and political science. He believes this will bring about increased understanding of the importance of social class and race in schooling, the impact of social change on communities and the schools, the importance of socioeconomic status, the importance of reference groups, and the effect on learning of the environment outside school. Menacker believes that a pervasive amount of activist philosophy in the approach of school counselors will change their traditional work patterns and their relations with other professionals. New work patterns will include spending more time away from the office and the school interacting with employers, parents, and community leaders and will lead to different work patterns (e.g., evening and weekend hours). New relations will occur when clients find counselors advocating more assertively for students, sometimes appearing more like attorneys or ombudsmen than mediators.

Implementation of Menacker's activist theory is founded on the following principles:

- Direct counselor activity is focused on concrete action that objectively helps students. Activist counselors can achieve empathy through direct, concrete helping activities.

- There should be mutual client-counselor identification of environmental conditions that may facilitate or retard goals and self-development. Counselors should attempt to capitalize on the positive and to eliminate the negative student client elements.

- Activist school counseling recognizes the distinction between student client goals and values and those of educational institutions. Thus, rather than always adjusting the student, it may be necessary to acknowledge that the institution is sometimes the pathological element that needs time to adjust or to be adjusted.

Standing out among Menacker's principles are the ideas that direct helping activities can achieve empathy and that the institution may need to be adjusted. Traditional empathy takes the form of verbal and nonverbal responses by counselors that lead clients to feel understood. One might hypothesize that acts of direct help when help is needed also make clients feel understood. Therefore, empathy might be achieved in ways other than listening and responding passively. Few will claim that the schools are perfect institutions. Yet the tendency for bureaucratic thinking among school personnel often leads to the expectation that students and parents, even teachers and counselors, must adjust to the system. The traditional goal of verbal counseling often has been to help individuals adjust to the system. Menacker would have counselors attempt to alter the system in those instances when it is the system, and not the student, that seems wrong or pathological and to help students adjust only when it is they who are wrong. Field and Baker (2004) found evidence of a consistent call for advocacy since the 1970s, and the words of Bailey, Getch, and Chen-Hayes (2003), published 30 years after Menacker's, seem to echo his position: "Students need an advocate who will recognize when student needs are not being heard or met and when they are being squashed emotionally and intellectually by the very system designed to enhance their emotional, physical, and intellectual wellbeing" (p. 420).

Beyond the importance of activist counseling for all students lies the potential for helping disadvantaged students. Sue (1992) summarizes the position succinctly:

> Evidence continues to accumulate, for instance, that economically and educationally disadvantaged clients may not be oriented toward "talk therapies," that self-disclosure in counseling may be incompatible with cultural values of Asian Americans, Latinos and American Indians, that the sociopolitical atmosphere may dictate against working openly with the counselor, and that some minority clients may benefit from the counselor's active intervention in the system.
>
> (p. 14)

In an approach he labels *synergistic counseling,* Herring (1997a, 1997b) believes that if school counselors are to serve as advocates for culturally different students, they will be challenged to employ a *cultural- and ethnic-specific model.* Herring describes synergistic counseling as going beyond eclecticism and the communication skills approaches. The basic themes are that traditional counseling models are incomplete and that school counselors will be more helpful if able to employ counseling strategies that are responsive to students' goals, cultures, and environments. Cultural and environmental factors, as well as psychodynamics, are important in the helping process.

THE SCHOOL COUNSELOR AS ADVOCATE: A CASE STUDY

When interviewing a 17-year-old male student who was having academic difficulties, a rural high school counselor learned that the client had moved away from home and was living in his own apartment. The student was working as many hours as possible after school in a local food market in an effort to earn enough money to support himself. He had too little time for his studies and was often so tired that he overslept or fell asleep in school. The counselor's response was to contact county social services agencies whose services were available to the student. These were services about which the student was uninformed. By contacting the targeted agencies on the student's behalf, the counselor was able to help the client receive assistance that made it possible for him to afford to live alone and finish his high school education. In this case, the counselor recognized the client's needs, knew or found out how they could be met, took the initiative to intercede for a client who was too naïve to help himself, and changed the circumstances that were impeding the student's successful academic performance.

ADVOCACY BEHAVIORS OF SCHOOL COUNSELORS

Field and Baker (2004) reported findings from a study designed to investigate how school counselors define advocacy and what advocacy behaviors they employ. There were nine school counselor participants, and the data were acquired from semistructured interviews and focus groups. The participants defined advocacy as focusing on students, exhibiting specific advocacy behaviors, and going beyond business as usual. They identified several behaviors in their advocacy repertoires, and Field noted that many of those behaviors "fit within a reactive framework of school counseling or reacting to the individual student after a problem has existed for some time." She concluded, "Other than appealing to people in power, none of these behaviors focus on changing the systems that may be creating or contributing to students' academic, personal, or social problems" (p. 62). This observation mirrored what Baker and Hansen (1972) reported 30 years earlier when a national sample of school counselors indicated a preference for helping students help themselves over more active responses.

More recent research findings, however, suggest that school counselors are engaging in more proactive practices. In their qualitative study with 16 participants, Singh, Urbano, Haston, and McMahan (2010) found school counselors do engage in consciousness raising, initiate difficult dialogues, build relationships, use data for marketing purposes, educate others about the advocacy role, and use political savvy skills to navigate their systems. The latter finding supports Stone and Zirkel's (2010) call for school counselors to develop their skills of political acumen. Although this research seems promising, we cannot assume that all school counselors are ready to take on the role as advocates given the many associated challenges.

CHALLENGES ASSOCIATED WITH ADVOCACY

Activism has a traditional place in school counseling, along with the more passive, traditional models. Passive and active counseling strategies are different, however, and the special challenges that face counselors who attempt to achieve activist goals are addressed in closing this section. Among these challenges are the possibility of appearing to be an adversary to those one is trying to influence and the real possibility of becoming burned out. Consequently, Bemak and Chung (2008) noted that school counselors may fall into the nice counselor syndrome, which is defined as those who maintain the status quo rather than advocating for underserved populations and stressing socially just policies with other school personnel. This claim is supported by Singh et al.'s (2010) qualitative study that found advocacy was a political process that required one to take a stance that was often quite difficult. Further, one could not maintain a neutral position while engaging in social advocacy. It is clear that advocacy requires school counselors to understand the political climate of the educational environment before taking action.

Pyrrhic Victories

In a classic example of a school counselor who demanded that the system do things the way he truly believed it should, Ponzo (1974) reflects on what he learned from his Pyrrhic victory—one in which he achieved his immediate goals but destroyed his relationships with some fellow professionals and part of the community:

> For a host of reasons, systems—human, animal, and social—tend to resist change. The strength of this resistance is dependent on the system's awareness of its need to change, its confidence in its ability to change, and its perception of the entity that proposes to bring the change about. It is prudent as well as necessary for a change agent to consider these factors as part of the change process. In Lincoln I attempted to bring about change without considering those factors. I barged in as if I were asked, wanted, and trusted. I failed to recognize that my "client" was very security conscious and had its borders well guarded. I failed to recognize that I was an outsider looking in. I failed to recognize that much of my behavior created additional barriers to change rather than removing existing ones.
>
> (p. 29, used with permission)

Were he to do it over again, Ponzo would change his strategies, adopting a more diplomatic approach:

- One must understand himself or herself. Your own personality is a strong tool, but it can be administered in dosages that are too heavy.

- One must understand the system. This corresponds to developing a facilitative relationship with a student client. Empathy, warmth, concreteness, and understanding serve to prevent the system (client) from fearing you.

- Learn how the system works. The chances for success increase if one is a consultant who facilitates change rather than a foreign intruder who demands it.

- Noble dreams must be translated into achievable program goals. This will increase the probability of success and decrease the probability of failure and abandonment.

One of Ponzo's recurring themes is the recommendation to learn the system and then use that knowledge to negotiate differences and initiate new proposals. Counselors will be successful more often if others in the system view them as competent. Counselors are then in a better position to promote competing goals in an appropriately assertive manner and to take positions that are not necessarily popular. The ultimate negotiating goal is to have all sides gain something in the end, with everyone believing that they won something and that the counselor's goals were accomplished.

Burnout

An overly literal interpretation of the information about advocacy can lead a counselor to work night and day every day of the week. Few individuals can keep up that pace without burning out. Therefore, the advocacy model, to be effective, must provide for prevention against burnout. Individuals who engage in advocacy need rest and recreation. More than 30 years ago, Gunnings (1978) provided two useful suggestions for preventing burnout and enhancing the effectiveness of advocates. One suggestion is to give school counselors 12-month contracts so that they will have time to develop community contacts. A second suggestion is to provide additional funding to reduce the ratio of counselors to students, especially in districts requiring high levels of advocacy. Additional strategies are released time during weekdays for counselors who work evening and weekend hours, periodic sabbatical leaves, and supportive counseling and supervision services for counselors. Counselors are also encouraged to make proactive efforts to prevent becoming burned out. Skovholt (2001) recommends a self-care action plan based on a thorough analysis of one's own other-care/self-care balance and of external factors such as stress at work that may contribute to burnout. Sheffield and Baker (2005) noted proactive approaches that have been used by counselors such as keeping up-to-date, reading professional books and journals, and attending workshops and conferences.

If the legacy of advocacy is to be kept alive, school counselors who accept the challenge need to be skillful change agents, not martyrs, so that advocacy goals can be achieved and clients served. Such counselors need to protect themselves from burnout and to be protected by enlightened supervisors and administrators. Otherwise, they will be used up by the same systems they are trying to help their clients understand and manage; the losses will be great because some will leave the profession, and many will continue to function at a level much less proficient and helpful than they should, cheating both themselves and their clients.

COMPETENCIES FOR ADVOCACY IN SCHOOL COUNSELING

ADVOCATING ON BEHALF OF STUDENTS

There are situations when it seems clear to counselors that students face challenges that lie beyond their coping capacity. These are opportunities to be advocates for our student clients. These are also situations that present significant challenges. What do I do? How do I do it? What are the consequences? Will I place myself, or my job, at risk? These questions represent a myriad of challenges school counselors who would be advocates on behalf of their student clients will face. In this section, we address the "How do I do it?" question with a set of recommendations taken from recent contributions to the professional literature.

Lee (2001) believes that counselors need to possess cultural awareness, that is, an understanding of the diverse cultural realities of all students. This includes an awareness of one's own cultural blind spots. Also required are an awareness of the systemic barriers to quality education that clients face and knowledge of, and competence in, how to challenge the barriers effectively.

Marinoble (1998) suggests that a strategy for challenging systemic barriers successfully is trying to influence school policies, curriculum, and staff development when appropriate. For example, school counselors might lobby for including sexual orientation in the language of nondiscrimination clauses of teacher contracts and school policies about treatment of students and parents, for establishing and enforcing school policies forbidding homosexual slurs and jokes, and for permitting mention of gay and lesbian topics in school publications. Dahir and Stone (2009) suggest using data to inform practices, develop programs that are equitable, and highlight any inequities that exist in schools, thereby engaging in social advocacy work.

Kiselica and Robinson (2001) highlight the importance of a capacity for appreciating human suffering as well as a capacity for being able to commit to advocating for those in need. To influence groups that might help students or that may be affecting them negatively, counselors are challenged to understand group change processes. As emphasized earlier by Menacker (1974), organizations or systems (e.g., schools and school systems) sometimes engage in practices or policies that are harmful to students. In advocacy challenges of this nature, Dinsmore, Chapman, and McCollum (2000) recommend being able to (a) ensure that students and their families receive accurate information, (b) serve as a mediator for students and organizations, (c) negotiate with organizations on behalf of students, (d) engage in lobbying efforts on behalf of students, and (e) submit articulate complaints.

Another approach is to try to influence significant others such as colleagues and members of the community by raising the level of discussion (D'Andrea & Daniels, 1997). Similar comments were shared by Stone and Zirkel (2010) that political acumen and collaboration are important skills for school counselors to develop. One such potential discussion topic is racism and how it impedes opportunities for many students to be successful academically. School counselors must collaborate with school and community resources to promote systemic change. However, this cannot occur until the school counselor understands how to be politically savvy and develop influential relationships.

In closing this section, we share strong words about advocating on behalf of clients from Kiselica and Robinson (2001): "We are convinced that it is not possible for us as counselors to engage in genuine social action unless we discover a personal moral imperative to serve as a drawing force behind our work" (p. 396).

ADVOCATING FOR STUDENTS TO WORK IN THEIR OWN BEHALF

Helping students work in their own behalf begins with the basic listening and responding skills presented in Chapter 8. Kiselica and Robinson (2001) stress the importance of being able to listen and respond to clients who need advocates and to help them communicate effectively for themselves. An example would be to help a gay youth who wants to do so to be able to "come out." Arredondo and D'Andrea (2001, 2002) agree that all communication skills are appropriate in counseling relationships. They stress that the importance of realizing which skills to use and how to use them may vary across cultural groups. Ethnic and cultural differences across clients highlight the importance of multicultural competence.

This focus on multicultural competence was introduced in the Multicultural Counseling Competencies and Standards (Sue, Arredondo, & McDavis, 1992) and later revised as the Multicultural and Social Justice Counseling Competencies (Ratts, Singh, Nassar-McMillan, Butler, & McCullough, 2015) as found in Appendix C. This revision highlights how the counseling profession has moved toward practices that examine the intersection of privilege, power, and oppression, each of which has potential to influence the client-counselor relationship. Note when viewing the competencies in Appendix C that attitudes and beliefs, knowledge, skills, and action are highlighted. It is our hope that this textbook and your training program will provide you with the opportunity to examine your attitudes and beliefs, build your knowledge, and use your skills to engage in action. We also firmly believe that this is a lifelong process and one that you will carry with you throughout your professional career.

ADVOCACY COMPETENCIES FOR SCHOOL COUNSELORS

Trusty and Brown (2005) state that "Because advocacy cuts across multiple school counseling roles, occurs on multiple levels, and is conceptualized broadly, it is logical to conclude that everything school counselors do is advocacy" (p. 259). Responding to this challenge, Trusty and Brown offer a way of conceptualizing advocacy in order to develop advocacy competencies. Space limitations make it impossible to provide all of their structure, and they have elaborated on their ideas in Brown and Trusty (2005). An overview is presented here.

Three advocacy competency categories have been identified. The categories are dispositions, knowledge, and skills. Within each category, there are several subgroupings. Within the disposition category is advocacy disposition, family/support empowerment disposition, social advocacy disposition, and ethical disposition. For example, school counselors who have an advocacy disposition

> are aware of and embrace their professional advocacy roles. They are autonomous in their thinking and behavior. There is altruistic motivation with the major concern being students' well-being. Advocates are willing to take risks in helping individual students and groups of students meet their needs.
> (Trusty & Brown, 2005, p. 260)

The knowledge competencies consist of knowing about resources, parameters (e.g., school policies and procedures), dispute resolution mechanisms (e.g., mediation and conflict resolution), advocacy models, and systems change. Advocacy skills include communicating, collaborating, assessing problems, solving problems, organizing, and taking care of oneself. Trusty and Brown (2005) point out that, although advocacy knowledge and skills can be provided through well-designed training programs, dispositions tend to be associated with beliefs and values that individuals acquired before entering training programs. Failure to have or develop advocacy dispositions will probably lead to failure to acquire advocacy skills as well. Therefore, influencing dispositions in the desired direction is an important basic component of acquiring competence as an advocate. Choosing individuals who have basic advocacy dispositions then is an important part of the training program selection process. Although this may seem like an easy task, research by Parikh, Post, and Flowers (2011) found from a national survey of 298 practicing school counselors that their political ideology and belief in a just world do influence one's inclination to engage in social justice advocacy work.

Keys components of employing advocacy dispositions are autonomy and school climate. If school counselors achieve sufficient autonomy, they are better able to gain self-confidence and form important collaborative relationships with other professionals. If the school climate is a culture of autonomy, the environment is more likely to be democratic, value individual expression and change, and focused on the needs of students. If the school climate is one of conformity, the environment will value the needs of the professionals in the schools over those of the students. To be successful advocates, school counselors are challenged to accept advocacy concepts and possess the knowledge and skills required to be a successful advocate. Potential for success as an advocate is also influenced by one's school climate.

Brown and Trusty (2005) offer a step-by-step model of the advocacy acquisition/ implementation process: (a) develop an advocacy disposition, (b) develop advocacy relationships and knowledge, (c) define the advocacy problem, (d) develop advocacy plans, (e) implement advocacy plans, (f) make an evaluation, and (g) celebrate or regroup. This stepped model is similar to the rational approach to ethical decision-making model presented in Chapter 5, the decision-making counseling model in Chapter 9, and the collaborative consultation model in Chapter 11. An important aspect of the position taken by Brown and Trusty is that there is a rational stepped approach to being an advocate that one can employ after having acquired the appropriate disposition, knowledge, and skills.

The *developmental advocate* role for school counselors proposed by Galassi and Akos (2004) provides a hypothetical application of the proposal by Brown and Trusty (2005). The requisite advocacy *disposition* is a belief that promoting the optimal development of all students is the primary mission of school counselors. The requisite advocacy *knowledge* and *skills* for developmental advocates are composed of (a) learning to be a leader in the school educational community; (b) being able to collaborate with stakeholders (e.g., students, teachers, and administrators) to build developmental supportive learning environments; (c) being able to recommend new strategies for the developmental needs of an increasingly diverse student population; (d) being able to offer proactive educational intervention approaches that help students acquire skills that enhance their academic, career, and personal/social development; and (e) knowing what the developmental needs of *today's students* are. These components of the developmental advocate model recommended by Galassi and Akos appear to represent the advocacy competencies highlighted earlier and fit within the advocacy acquisition/implementation process proposed by Brown and Trusty (2005) and Trusty and Brown (2005).

EXAMPLES OF ADVOCACY IN SCHOOL COUNSELING

The following examples are a mixture of cases from school counselors in various school levels and environments. We attempted to present a variety of student clients needing advocacy and of approaches to advocacy, yet we realize that there are numerous other possible examples. The narrative will reveal both specific and implied advocacy competencies. Our format is to first provide background about the advocacy challenge. The overview will be followed by a narrative summary of the advocate's response and an analysis of the advocacy process involved.

EMPOWERING HER TO BE ALL THAT SHE CAN BE

Background

That women have not achieved a status equal to men is a widely accepted and documented proposition. One domain in which these differences have clearly manifested themselves is occupational opportunities (Bartholomew & Schnorr, 1994; Pedersen, 1988). Bartholomew and Schnorr highlight the need to enhance the confidence of many young women to enable them to take advantage of career opportunities opening up to them, especially in mathematics and science. The several recommendations Bartholomew and Schnorr offer for responses by counselors add up to a challenge to conceive and implement a broad range of efforts aimed at enhancing the self-esteem of female students so that they will view themselves as capable of pursuing expanding career opportunities.

Summary

When meeting with a 12th-grade female student to discuss her plans for college, a female counselor asked her if she was ready to solidify her acceptance to her first choice college. The client, who was a better than average student, stated that she is ready but now confused about her major. When the counselor asked her to elaborate, the student noted that she wanted to drop her AP biology class because she was not doing so well. After reviewing previous grades and test scores, the school counselor noted she was more capable of making a passing grade in her class. After some questioning, the student responded in a manner that indicated she was not feeling supported by her male teacher. She noted that her numerous attempts to ask questions were ignored.

The counselor's advocacy responses were as follows: She noted her successful history in her previous advanced science courses. The school counselor then suggested a parent-teacher-student conference to resolve any issues and find ways to support her in class. The student agreed to this meeting. Acting as the mediator, the school counselor held a meeting and asked the student to share what she was experiencing and inquire how the teacher could support her. The conclusion was that the teacher did not realize the student was feeling this way and offered after-school support to which the parent also agreed. The student remained in the class the entire year, earned a B grade, and enrolled in her first choice university as a biology major.

Analysis

Much of the activity in this advocacy response occurred in the counselor's office. She recognized the student's need for someone to support her in her desire to do well in biology and yet acknowledge her feeling of being ignored by her teacher when asking for assistance. The school counselor acted as a mediator in the conference by offering a space for the student to voice her concerns in a safe setting. Instead of speaking for the student, the school counselor empowered her to ask for the help she needed.

AN ADVOCATE FOR THE FAMILY IN THE SCHOOL

Background

Exceptional children have a physical, emotional, or intellectual status that places them outside the normal range and, therefore, causes them to be categorized as having a disability. The welfare of this constituency historically concerned counselors, but they had little direct contact with such children until November 1975. Any question about whether school counselors believed in equity for exceptional children became academic with the passage of PL 94–142, the Education for All Handicapped Children Act, in 1975. This piece of federal legislation made equity for exceptional children mandatory across the United States and challenged school counselors to implement their social activism tradition.

PL 94–142 is very specific about what is to be done. One specific ingredient of the law is that all individuals between the ages of 3 and 21 have to be given a free, appropriate public education in some form and setting. That education is to be provided, to some degree, in the same environment with able individuals. This concept is known as *mainstreaming*. Implementation of the mainstreaming concept is specified through annual individualized educational plans (IEPs) that are developed for every child. IEPs must include information about the child's current level of functioning, annual goals, measurable short-term objectives, and an inventory of specific educational services the child requires. IEPs are drawn up by multidisciplinary teams of teachers, administrators, and pupil service specialists (including counselors) in cooperation with parents. Parents of exceptional children are granted specific due process rights that include the right to independent educational evaluations, the option of requesting hearings by impartial officials, and the inspection of all evaluative records. Chief among the categories of people whose education is governed by PL 94–142 are those children evaluated as being deaf, deaf-blind, hard of hearing, multihandicapped, orthopedically impaired, seriously emotionally disturbed, speech impaired, and visually impaired or having an intellectual disability, a specific learning disability, or other health impairment.

Passage of the Education for All Handicapped Children Act Amendments (PL 99–457) in 1986 expanded the mainstreaming concept to working with both the child and the family through individualized family service plans. This legislation calls for school personnel to work closely with the family and the child to identify early intervention services. Greer, Greer, and Woody (1995) believe that PL 99–457 expands the role of counselors in the mainstreaming process.

Concern about programming in schools that seemed to be defeating the principles in PL 94–142 led to enactment of the Education for All Handicapped Children Act Amendments of 1990 (PL 101–476). PL 101–476 calls for *inclusion*, which means that all students, no matter the severity of their disability, must be included in all aspects of school life. The present vignette is drawn loosely from Hourcade and Parette (1986).

Summary

A school counselor received a telephone call from the parents of a child with epilepsy who revealed that the child needed an anticonvulsant medicine administered while in school. Unfortunately, unenlightened school personnel resisted responding to the parents' request, and their family physician referred them to the school counselor. The counselor recognized that the family needed an advocate to act as a liaison between them and the school—a champion for their position.

First, the counselor informed the parents that he would try to act as a liaison if they wished. With their approval, the counselor diplomatically informed the unenlightened school personnel about the student's rights under the applicable federal legislation, the parents' due process rights, and the responsibilities of the school personnel. Upon achieving cooperation from the targeted school personnel, the counselor informed the parents and proceeded to coordinate the process of ensuring that the student received the requisite anticonvulsant medicine. Coordinating the process involved informing/educating all school personnel who were to participate in the process about their responsibilities and roles, arranging the medicine administrations (e.g., times and places, excuses from classes for the student), ensuring the client was cognizant of the system that had been set up, informing the parents about what to expect and their due process rights, keeping notes about important events and agreements in the process, monitoring the process as it took place, and evaluating the success of the advocacy intervention.

Analysis

In this vignette, the counselor was appropriately informed about the related legislation while also understanding the client's rights and the school's responsibilities. The counselor also viewed the student's family as part of the client system and realized they needed help from someone familiar with the school system and personnel. Beyond that, the counselor was willing to take the risk of advocating for them and upsetting the previously uncooperative school personnel. It also appears as if the counselor knew how to approach the school personnel in a manner that got their attention and cooperation. Finally, the counselor was willing and able to coordinate the process once it was initiated.

A PROACTIVE EFFORT TO EXPAND THE RANGE OF POSSIBILITIES

Background

This example is based on a project reported by Vontress (1966). Advocacy is a theme that runs through the multicultural literature (cf. Bailey & Paisley, 2004; Bemak, Chung, & Siroskey-Sabdo, 2005; Casas & Furlong, 1994; Chung, 2005; Dixon, Tucker, & Clark, 2010; Gibbs, 1973; Kopala, Esquivel, & Baptiste, 1994; Luftig, 1983; Rogler, Malgady, Constantino, & Blumenthal, 1987; Ruiz & Padilla, 1977). Pallas, Natriello, and McDill (1989) advocate a role for counselors outside the schools that might be conceived of as a community resource specialist, working with families and communities, helping them learn to use their power, and reintegrating them with the schools. Acting in this manner causes a counselor to become known in the community as someone who cares. LaFromboise and Jackson (1996) suggest that doing whatever is possible to help clients control their own lives leads to empowerment, that is, clients exerting interpersonal influence, improving performance, and maintaining effective support systems. Vontress (1966) described an all-out attempt to widen the range of possibilities for African American children in a large inner-city school.

Summary

Viewing themselves as advocates for all the children in their school, the counselors developed and initiated a plan for a school-community collaboration program. They conducted an analysis of the needs of the students and their families, particularly those needs they were unable to meet through the services their staff could provide. Then, by concentrating on what needed to be done, they initiated a number of intervention strategies such as evening parent conferences, home visits, driving parents to visit colleges, talking to newspaper reporters, making television appearances, meeting with civic leaders, and finding part-time jobs for students. This multifaceted set of interventions consisted of working with students individually and reaching out to several targeted constituencies (e.g., families, the school board, and business/community groups).

Analysis

Realizing that they were unable to meet all the important needs of their student clients, these counselors were willing to extend their services by engaging in advocacy activities. To accomplish their goals, the counselors were willing and able to engage in activities that might be depicted as public relations and social work. They understood that enriching the current environment and opportunities for their students might have positive long-term benefits for their lives. Their efforts also resulted in the formation of school-community partnerships that had potential for being continuous.

ADVOCACY FOR SEXUAL MINORITY YOUTHS

Background

Marinoble (1998) writes,

> A favorite self-esteem activity among elementary school children involves listening to a story about a "very special person" who can be seen by opening a colorful box. One-by-one the children lift the lid, peer inside, and see their own reflection in a mirror. . . . Most children giggle with glee, pride, or self-consciousness. It is fun, and it encourages children to feel good about the

> person they see. . . . For some children though, the mirror begins to develop a blind spot—a part of themselves they cannot see or, at best, cannot bring into focus. As these children progress through childhood and adolescence, their schools, families, and communities often collaborate to reinforce the blind spot. The results of this collaboration may range from mild to tragic. The blind spot is homosexuality—a sexual orientation that appears to be natural for approximately 10% of the population.
>
> (p. 4, used with permission)

"Gay adolescents face the same developmental challenges as their heterosexual counterparts, with the added burden of attempting to incorporate a stigmatized sexual identity" (Fontaine, 1998, p. 13). For some sexual minority youths, the burden may be too much to bear. Suicide is the number one cause of death among these youths, 2 to 3 times more than among heterosexual youths (Cooley, 1998; Logan & Williams, 2001; McFarland, 1998). Higher rates of substance abuse, psychiatric treatment, school problems, and running away from home have been documented as well (Remafedi, 1987; Remafedi, Farrow, & Deisher, 1991). For others, the burden may be sufficiently challenging to require counseling interventions. Collectively, Black and Underwood (1998), Cooley (1998), Fontaine (1998), Marinoble (1998), Omizo, Omizo, and Okamoto (1998), and Savage, Harley, and Nowak (2005) provide an inventory of burdens that is both impressive and saddening: identity confusion and conflict, depression, family disruptions, fear of exposure, internalized hostility, peer relationship problems, self-doubt and low self-esteem, social isolation, unfriendly environments (e.g., institutional homophobia), powerlessness, and concerns and doubts about the future. Although heterosexual youths face many of these challenges as well, some are clearly more applicable to homosexual youths (fear of exposure, unfriendly environments) or have the potential for being more severe if one has a homosexual orientation (identity confusion and conflict, family disruptions, peer relationship problems, social isolation, concerns and doubts about the future).

Many sexual minority youths attend schools in which institutionalized homophobia ranges from outright intolerance to benign neglect. McFarland and Dupuis (2001) report about the decisions in three court cases that collectively indicate schools must ensure safe educational environments for gay and lesbian students. Two examples of advocacy interventions found in the professional literature are presented here.

Summaries

Bauman and Sachs-Kapp (1998) provide an example of counselors helping an alternative high school in Fort Collins, Colorado, manifest its goal to achieve tolerance toward diversity. The focus of the counselors' efforts was to create school-wide workshops on a variety of diversity issues, the most controversial of which was sexual orientation, that were well organized and facilitated by students. The counselors recruited and trained those students who would lead the workshops. An overview of the workshops follows.

Student leaders were trained in a for-credit minicourse. Team building, self-awareness enhancement, demonstrations of effective teaching and facilitating skills, and practice with constructive feedback were features of the training program. Students were not required to attend the workshops. An alternative workshop covering fear and intolerance in more general terms was offered by a popular teacher. A daylong format involving the entire school was followed. A guest speaker keynoted the workshops with a presentation that focused on individual humanity being more important than sexual orientation when dealing with people. Three panels followed, all of which the students experienced via a rotation format. Guest panel members, chosen by students, included gay, lesbian, and bisexual individuals (one panel); individuals whose family members were gays, lesbians, and bisexuals (a second panel); and professional psychologists considered experts in human behavior (a third panel). All three panels were requested by students to focus on the theme "How Hate Hurts." Following the panel rotations, small discussion groups, consisting of no more than 10 students and one or two staff members, were facilitated by the trained students. These groups focused on processing the experience and talking about feelings. The leaders followed a structured format they learned during their training. The closing event was an exercise for all in attendance scripted by the counselors and led by a popular teacher. Students who were willing to identify themselves as being gay, lesbian, or bisexual or as having friends and family members who are *(the targets)* were invited to move silently to the opposite side of the room from the remainder of those present *(the nontargets)*.

Ninety-five percent of students opted to participate in the primary program. Follow-up evaluation survey data indicated that, on a 5-point scale, the average rating of the educational value of the workshop was 3.8.

Muller and Hartman (1998) provide suggestions for group counseling, including issues that may be the focus of the group intervention (homophobia, loneliness and isolation, identity issues, alienation from families, suicide, substance abuse). They describe a counseling support group that was conducted in a suburban Maryland public high school. The general goal for this group was to provide an atmosphere for universality, hope, and interpersonal learning. Overt methods for identifying prospective members included hanging posters in hallways encouraging sexual minority youths to see a counselor if they wanted to talk about their concerns, posting rainbows and pink triangles around the school with invitations from the counselors, posting antihomophobic slogans in the school counseling area, and the counselors wearing buttons declaring support for sexual minority youths. Teachers known to be trusted by sexual minority youths were informed about the proposed group. Seven students eventually responded and participated. An overview of the group intervention follows.

Two heterosexual female counselors led the group. Both had extensive preparation. Goals for the group counseling process focused on identifying and discussing feelings, developing coping skills, and building a support system. Twenty-five weekly sessions of 45 minutes each were held; meeting times were rotated to prevent students from missing the same class more than once a month. A more detailed description of the content and methods is offered in Muller and Hartman (1998), who state: "Many sessions were devoted entirely to interpersonal issues which arose in the group. Anger and resentments among members and resulting feedback enriched sessions and became the focus of the group on many occasions" (p. 41).

Analysis

Both interventions involved groups organized by counselors in their schools. The first group required prevention programming competencies, and the second group counseling competencies. Probably speaking for the organizers of both group interventions, the author-counselors in the second intervention point out the importance of being aware of their own assumptions and beliefs and of having the support of their principal in advance of and during the program. As well, they state that school system policies on any kind of sexual harassment must be in effect (Muller & Hartman, 1998). Beyond competence, awareness, and acquiring support, the counselors were also risk takers, willing to demonstrate their advocacy for sexual minority youths in a potentially hostile school and community environment. All the elements just cited required careful planning by the counselors. They also had to be able to organize and manage the programs efficiently and successfully.

BULLY-BUSTING ADVOCATES FOR VIOLENCE PREVENTION/INTERVENTION

Background

The following case is hypothetical and based on information presented in Roberts and Morotti (2000) and Hanish and Guerra (2000). School violence has received considerable national attention in recent years, especially in the context of horrific instances where students take the lives of other students and teachers (Sandhu, 2000). Bullying is one manifestation of violence in schools, and in some recent instances reported in the press, those who took the lives of classmates were bullying victims who responded in a very drastic manner. In our vignette, the counselor views the bully and the bully's target as individuals in need of an advocate.

Summary

Reports from a couple of teachers indicate that a middle school eighth-grade boy has been bullying a much smaller, shy, and introverted sixth-grade boy for two months since students returned from summer vacation. The counselor's first step was to call in the target, or victim, in order to get acquainted, establish rapport, and decide when it was appropriate to ask about the bullying. Feeling comfortable with the counselor, the target related a tale of physical and mental abuse that had him both frightened and angry. The counselor immediately indicated that the target student's tale had been believed, that an effort would be made to help him and immediately, and that the student was invited to come to the counselor's office immediately if either an act of bullying occurred or he felt like retaliating.

The counselor initiated a plan to work with the target and the bully concurrently. To help the target, the counselor (a) met with the victim to help him process his feelings about the situation and determine proactive strategies for protecting and feeling better about himself, (b) worked with teachers and administrators to make necessary modifications in the school climate to help the victim and reduce the likelihood that the bully would have opportunities to act, and (c) met with the victim's parents to help them process their concerns, determine what they could do to help, and understand that something constructive was being done at the school.

Concurrently, the counselor met with the bully. The first step was to make the contact nonthreatening and listen to what the bully had to say about himself and the situation. Eventually, specific unacceptable behaviors and their possible consequences were described to the bully. The counselor attempted to find opportunities to help the bully achieve increased self-awareness leading to change. Targets for the self-awareness effort were the bully's home environment and the sources of vicarious reinforcement for the bullying behaviors. This led to the counselor working with both the bully and his parents in an effort to induce change. Finally, once the effort was under way, the counselor provided attention, support, and long-term follow-up.

Analysis

The counselor recognized the need for advocacy—for the victim and the bully—immediately. In addition, the counselor responded quickly, and the response was multifaceted. Interventions involved both the victim and the bully, and they were undertaken concurrently. The multifaceted response involved clients, school personnel, school climate, and parents. The counselor as an advocate achieved collaboration with others and served as a coordinator of the intervention process.

ADVOCATING FOR THE PROFESSION

Perhaps professional self-advocacy, the road less traveled, is the approach that needs to be emphasized in the 21st century. Although advocacy directed toward achieving universal recognition of the desired identity for school counselors by individual counselors and counselors within school systems is necessary, it is probably also not sufficient (Baker, Kessler, Bishop, & Giles, 1993). A profession that agrees on its mission, role, and functions may be more likely to achieve dramatic change collectively rather than individually. Advocacy for this purpose must occur in each locality *and* collectively, beginning at the grass roots (Baker, 2001).

A PROFESSIONAL ADVOCACY VIGNETTE

The following vignette is based on recommendations found in Johnson (2000). Our case describes a group of school counselors who decide to become advocates for their own professional identity.

Summary

The scenario that we present can conceivably happen anywhere, and we hope it will happen in numerous school systems. A group of school counselors within a school system decided to advocate for themselves as primary players in their educational system. Their first step was to conduct internal discussions among themselves and determine a shared, clear vision that consisted of goals and objectives for the program, functions required to achieve those goals, and the estimated time and resources required to achieve those goals.

This first step was carried out as follows: The counselors conducted a needs assessment of students, teachers, parents, administrators, and community members. A more detailed coverage of needs assessments is found in Chapter 4. The needs assessment data were used to identify goals for their program (e.g., What outcomes do we want to achieve over the next 5 years?). This led to writing a mission statement that reflected their vision for the future, one that can be understood by their publics and used when promoting their cause. Next, they developed a school counseling program plan outlining objectives, activities, services, and expected outcomes across all grade levels. They established a calendar designating what services would be provided and when. The counselors included professional development for themselves within the plan. Going into more detail, the counselors created formal job descriptions for themselves at each level. They invited input from school administrators, union officials, professional organizations, and state legislative and education department representatives. Finally, the counselors selected a strong leader for their unit, someone who could be their advocate throughout the school system. The second step was to determine a strategy for promoting the plan that had been developed. This led to an ongoing public relations campaign designed to inform students, parents, teachers, administrators, the community, and the school board. All components of the plan were systematically integrated. The strategy included (a) presentations about the role of the school counseling program and accountability data about the effects of its services; (b) membership in school-community–based committees and publication of a newsletter for parents and the community that informed readers about program goals, roles, and accomplishments; (c) development of a booklet that informed readers about specific services to special populations; (d) visits to all classrooms in the fall to introduce the counseling program to teachers and students; (e) preparation of an annual accountability report that was distributed to building and central administrators, the school board, and appropriate parent and community groups; (f) invitations to teachers and administrators to visit classroom guidance sessions; (g) arrangements with local service clubs and organizations to offer counselors as speakers on topics related to the mission; (h) development of professional portfolios for each counselor to be made available to the public; and (i) a website that provided information about the mission, accountability data, a calendar of school counseling activities, and links for students and the community.

Analysis

The counselors in this vignette appeared to believe in themselves and the value of their program. They were proactive in their efforts, united as a team, and clear about their goals. They worked their way through a plan to achieve their goals systematically and became advocates for themselves and their profession. Indirectly, they were also advocates for their students, schools, and community, all of whom would become beneficiaries of the accomplishments of the program. The plan was based on an awareness of good practice derived from professional standards. Their strategy for promoting the plan was multifaceted and reached out to all their stakeholders. The public relations efforts exposed their important services to the various publics, were enhanced by accountability data, and brought attention to their mission. Because this is a hypothetical vignette, we cannot report on the actual outcomes. We believe that professional advocacy strategies of this nature have excellent potential for successful outcomes.

ACHIEVING ADVOCACY GOALS THROUGH POLITICAL ACTION

We believe that grassroots efforts such as were depicted in the earlier vignette are necessary for the school counseling profession to enhance itself in the 21st century. In addition, counselor educators and national professional organizations, such as the ASCA and American Counseling Association (ACA) and their affiliates, will benefit from working together. The next generation of school counselors will have to be more active than their predecessors if the counselor role challenge is to be resolved. That resolution will require being active rather than passive in responding to the challenges, being informed, being committed to providing the best possible counseling services, becoming skilled at being successful advocates, and supporting the efforts of national, regional, and state professional counseling associations that are directed toward achieving uniformity and clarity in the school counselor's role.

The ACA provides significant resources for school counselors to use in order to achieve advocacy goals through political action. Clicking the "Government Affairs" tab on its website (www.counseling.org) will open several political action vistas. The "Take Action" (http://www.counseling.org/government-affairs/actioncenter) provides an inventory of important pending federal legislation with accompanying background about each item. Taking advantage of the opportunity to be an advocate is made easy through recommended content for letters to one's legislators as well as the e-mail addresses of those legislators. In fact, one can use the ACA's recommended model and send an e-mail message from the website. The "Recent Updates" provides online archives about important legislation. External Links provides access to a number of home pages, including the

White House, the U.S. Department of Education, and the National Institute of Mental Health. The American School Counselor Association (ASCA has a Legislative Affairs link that provides a summary of recent events with links to Congress, this week's legislative update, and legislative alerts (www.schoolcounselor.org/school-counselors-members/legislative-affairs).

You will find that state ACA and ASCA divisions also have developed political action programs to encourage members to respond to both federal and state issues. For example, the North Carolina School Counselor Association has a government relations committee (http://www.ncschoolcounselor.org/) that works closely with ASCA and continues to search for new pathways to inform members and help them achieve advocacy goals.

ACHIEVING ADVOCACY AT THE LOCAL LEVEL

Being active in one's community will help school counselors to understand the culture of their clients and identify their support networks. For example, local religious leaders may help school counselors identify previously untapped resources for school-community collaboration. Secular community agencies are also sources of community understandings and advocacy collaborations. Advocacy can become cyclical. When school counselors advocate for their clients and communities, the clients and communities, in turn, may become advocates for the school counselors and their programs. This cyclical advocacy process leads to shared goals and potential for empowering all who are involved. One of the attributes of advocacy is school counselor leadership, a topic that we elaborate upon in the next chapter.

COMPREHENSIVE SCHOOL COUNSELING PROGRAM COMPONENT

1.   Examine the standards from Category 1 of the ASCA Mindsets & Behaviors for Student Success: K-12 College- and Career-Readiness Standards for Every Student guide. How would you advocate *all* students to have the opportunity to reach each of those standards? Choose one of those standards and create a school-wide plan.

REFLECTION POINT

1.   How do you feel about being a student who advocates for improving the educational environment? How does this role prepare you for your advocacy role as a school counselor? What are your overall thoughts about advocacy in school counseling?

2.   Brainstorm the following advocacy scenarios with your classmates and instructor.

You are an elementary school counselor, and a parent of a second-grade student has approached you with the following concern. Her daughter is complaining that her class is boring and all of the students who were in her first-grade class last year are in the other second-grade class this year. The teacher is also very strict and sometimes physically disciplines unruly students. The mother looked into the situation and came to the conclusion that the principal, when making room assignments for the current year, got her daughter's name mixed up with another child with a similar name, and the two were switched accidentally. Otherwise, all of the students in the two classes are the same as the previous year. When she shared this observation and concerns about her child's unhappiness in school the principal denied that a mistake was made and refused to make any changes.

You are a counselor in a comprehensive high school with a large student to counselor ratio (700 to 1). In addition, you are teaching half time in the social studies department. On the other hand, you are expected to carry out the same counseling program responsibilities as your full-time school counselor colleagues. These responsibilities include scheduling all of your students before classes begin and making changes in schedules as needed or requested when school begins and over the duration of the school year, advising the student council and providing oversight for their massive fundraising scheme each year, supervising the junior and senior proms when your advisees are in those grades, and supervising the student awards program and graduation when your advisees are seniors. The tasks seem overwhelming and impossible for one part-time counselor to do, and it is taking its toll on you both mentally and physically. Quitting is not an option at the present.

APPLICATION TO TECHNOLOGY

1. Conduct research on a special population (students with autism, homeless families, refugees, LGBT youths, and so forth) and create a PowerPoint presentation that can be given in a school setting. The purpose of the presentation would be to educate teachers, administrators, and staff on best practices of working with that minority population. Be sure to consider cultural differences and how you will create a culturally responsive environment.

REFERENCES

Adelman, H. S., & Taylor, L. (2002). School counselors and school reform: New directions. *Professional School Counseling, 5*, 235–248.

American Counseling Association. (2014). *ACA code of ethics.* Alexandria, VA: Author.

American School Counselor Association. (2012). *The ASCA National Model: A framework for school counseling programs* (3rd ed.). Alexandria, VA: Author.

Arredondo, P., & D'Andrea, M. (2001, April). Changing paradigms in organizations. *Counseling Today, 43*, 38, 44.

Arredondo, P., & D'Andrea, M. (2002, June). What do culturally competent practices look like? *Counseling Today, 44,* 28, 32.

Aubrey, R. E. (1977). Historical development of guidance and counseling and implications for the future. *Personnel and Guidance Journal, 55,* 288–295.

Bailey, D. F., Getch, Y. Q., & Chen-Hayes, S. (2003). Professional school counselors as social and academic advocates. In B. T. Erford (Ed.), *Transforming the school counseling profession* (pp. 411–434). Upper Saddle River, NJ: Merrill-Prentice Hall.

Bailey, D. F., & Paisley, P. O. (2004). Developing and nurturing excellence in African American male adolescents. *Journal of Counseling and Development, 82,* 10–17.

Baker, S. B. (2001). Reflections on forty years in the school counseling profession: Is the glass half full or half empty? *Professional School Counseling, 5,* 75–83.

Baker, S. B., & Hansen, J. C. (1972). School counselor attitudes on a status quo—Change agent measurement scale. *School Counselor, 19,* 243–248.

Baker, S. B., Kessler, B. L., Bishop, R. M., & Giles, G. N. (1993). *School counselor role: A proposal for ridding the profession of an "old ghost."* Unpublished manuscript. University Park: Penn State University.

Bartholomew, C. G., & Schnorr, D. L. (1994). Gender equity: Suggestions for broadening career options of female students. *School Counselor, 41,* 245–256.

Bauman, S., & Sachs-Kapp, P. (1998). A school takes a stand: Promotion of sexual orientation workshops by counselors. *Professional School Counseling, 1*(3), 42–45.

Beck, M. J., Rausch, M. A., & Wood, S. M. (2014). Developing the fearless school counselor ally and advocate for LGBTQIQ youth: Strategies for preparation programs. *Journal of LGBT Issues in Counseling, 8,* 361–375.

Bemak, F., & Chung, R. C. (2008). New professional roles and advocacy strategies for school counselors: A multicultural/social justice perspective to move beyond the nice counselor syndrome. *Journal of Counseling & Development, 86,* 372–381.

Bemak, F., Chung, R. C., & Siroskey-Sabdo, L. A. (2005). Empowerment groups for academic success: An innovative approach to prevent high school failure of at-risk urban African American girls. *Professional School Counseling, 5,* 377–389.

Black, J., & Underwood, J. (1998). Young, female, and gay: Lesbian students and the school environment. *Professional School Counseling, 1*(3), 15–20.

Bradley, L., & Lewis, J. (2000). Introduction. In J. Lewis & L. Bradley (Eds.), *Advocacy in counseling: Counselors, client & community* (pp. 3–4). Greensboro, NC: ERIC Clearinghouse on Counseling and Student Services.

Brewer, J. M. (1932). *Education as guidance.* New York: Macmillan.

Brown, D., & Trusty, J. (2005). *Designing and leading comprehensive school counseling programs: Promoting student competence and meeting student needs.* Belmont, CA: Thomson Brooks/Cole.

Casas, J. M., & Furlong, M. J. (1994). School counselors as advocates for increased Hispanic parent participation in schools. In P. Pedersen & J. C. Carey (Eds.), *Multicultural counseling in schools: A practical handbook* (pp. 121–156). Boston: Allyn & Bacon.

Chung, R. C. (2005). Women, human rights, and counseling: Crossing international boundaries. *Journal of Counseling and Development, 83,* 262–268.

Cooley, J. J. (1998). Gay and lesbian adolescents: Presenting problems and the counselor's role. *Professional School Counseling, 1*(3), 30–34.

Cremin, L. A. (1965). The progressive heritage of the guidance movement. In R. L. Mosher, R. E. Carle, & C. D. Kehas (Eds.), *Guidance: An examination* (pp. 3–12). New York: Harcourt, Brace & World.

Dahir, C. A., & Stone, C. B. (2009). School counselor accountability: The path to social justice and systemic change. *Journal of Counseling & Development, 87,* 12–20.

D'Andrea, M., & Daniels, J. (1997). Continuing the discussion about racism: A reaction by D'Andrea and Daniels. *ACES Spectrum, 58*(2), 8–9.

Dinsmore, J. A., Chapman, A., & McCollum, V.J.C. (2000, March). *Client advocacy and social justice: Strategies for developing trainee competence.* Paper presented at the Annual Conference of the American Counseling Association, Washington, DC.

Dinsmore, J. A., Chapman, A., & McCollum, V.J.C. (2002, March). *Client advocacy and social justice: Strategies for developing trainee competence.* Paper presented at the Annual Conference of the American Counseling Association, New Orleans, LA.

Dixon, A. L., Tucker, C., & Clark, M. A. (2010). Integrating social justice advocacy with national standards of practice: Implications for school counselor education. *Counselor Education and Supervision, 50*(2), 103–115.

Field, J. E., & Baker, S. B. (2004). Defining and examining school counselor advocacy. *Professional School Counseling, 8,* 56–63.

Fontaine, J. H. (1998). Evidencing a need: School counselors' experiences with gay and lesbian students. *Professional School Counseling, 1*(3), 8–14.

Galassi, J. P., & Akos, P. (2004). Developmental advocacy: Twenty-first century school counseling. *Journal of Counseling and Development, 82,* 146–157.

Gibbs, J. T. (1973). Black students/White university: Different expectations. *Personnel and Guidance Journal, 51,* 463–470.

Greer, B. B., Greer, J. G., & Woody, D. E. (1995). The inclusion movement and its impact on counselors. *School Counselor, 43,* 24–132.

Gunnings, T. S. (1978). Guidance and counseling in special settings. In *The status of guidance and counseling in the nation's schools: A series of issue papers* (pp. 147–156). Washington, DC: American Personnel and Guidance Association.

Hanish, L. D., & Guerra, N. G. (2000). Children who get victimized at school: What is known? What can be done? *Professional School Counseling, 4,* 113–119.

Hansen, L. S. (1968). Are we change agents? *School Counselor, 15,* 245–246.

Harris, P. R. (1967). Guidance and counseling: Where it's been—where it's going. *School Counselor, 15,* 10–15.

Herr, E. L. (1979). *Guidance and counseling in the schools: Perspectives on the past, present, and future.* Falls Church, VA: American Personnel and Guidance Association.

Herring, R. D. (1997a). *Counseling diverse and ethnic youth: Synergistic strategies and interventions for school counselors.* Ft. Worth, TX: Harcourt Brace College Publishers.

Herring, R. D. (1997b). *Multicultural counseling in schools: A synergistic approach.* Alexandria, VA: American Counseling Association.

Hourcade, J. J., & Parette, H. P., Jr. (1986). Students with epilepsy: Counseling implications for the hidden handicapped. *School Counselor, 33,* 279–285.

House, R. M., & Hayes, R. L. (2002). School counselors: Becoming key players in school reform. *Professional School Counseling, 5,* 249–256.

Johnson, L. S. (2000). Promoting professional identity in an era of educational reform. *Professional School Counseling, 4,* 31–40.

Kiselica, M. S., & Robinson, M. (2001). Bringing advocacy counseling to life: The history, issues, and human dramas of social justice. *Journal of Counseling & Development, 79,* 387–397.

Kopala, M., Esquivel, G., & Baptiste, L. (1994). Counseling approaches for immigrant children: Facilitating the acculturative process. *School Counselor, 41,* 352–359.

LaFromboise, T., & Jackson, M. (1996). MCT theory and Native American populations. In D. W. Sue, A. E. Ivey, & P. B. Pedersen (Eds.), *A theory of multicultural counseling and therapy* (pp. 192–203). Pacific Grove, CA: Brooks/Cole.

Lee, C. C. (1998). Counselors as agents for social change. In C. C. Lee & G. R. Walz (Eds.), *Social action: A mandate for counselors* (pp. 3–16). Alexandria, VA: American Counseling Association.

Lee, C. C. (2001). Culturally responsive school counselors and programs: Addressing the needs of all students. *Professional School Counseling, 4,* 257–262.

Lee, C. C., & Sirch, M. L. (1994). Counseling in an enlightened society: Values for a new millennium. *Counseling and Values, 38,* 90–97.

Logan, C., & Williams, C. B. (2001, April). Ethical issues in counseling gay youth. *Counseling Today,* 41–42.

Luftig, R. L. (1983). Effects of schooling on the self-concept of Native American students. *School Counselor, 30,* 251–260.

Marinoble, R. M. (1998). A blind spot in the mirror. *Professional School Counseling, 1*(3), 4–7.

McFarland, W. P. (1998). Gay, lesbian, and bisexual student suicide. *Professional School Counseling, 1*(3), 26–29.

McFarland, W. P., & Dupuis, M. (2001). The legal duty to protect gay and lesbian students from violence in school. *Professional School Counseling, 4,* 171–179.

Menacker, J. (1974). *Vitalizing guidance in urban schools.* New York: Dodd, Mead.

Menacker, J. (1976). Toward a theory of activist guidance. *Personnel and Guidance Journal, 54,* 318–321.

Muller, L. E., & Hartman, J. (1998). Group counseling for sexual minority youth. *Professional School Counseling, 1*(3), 38–41.

Omizo, M. M., Omizo, S. A., & Okamoto, C. M. (1998). Gay and lesbian adolescents: A phenomenological study. *Professional School Counseling, 1*(3), 35–37.

Pallas, A. M., Natriello, G., & McDill, E. L. (1989). The changing nature of the disadvantaged population: Current dimensions and future trends. *Educational Researcher, 18*(5), 16–22.

Parikh, S. B., Post, P., & Flowers, C. (2011). Relationship between belief in a just world and social justice advocacy attitudes of school counselors. *Counseling and Values, 56,* 51–72.

Pedersen, J. S. (1988). Constraining influences on the vocational guidance of girls from 1910 to 1930. *Career Development Quarterly, 36,* 325–336.

Ponzo, Z. (1974). A counselor and change: Reminiscence and resolutions. *Personnel and Guidance Journal, 53,* 27–32.

Ratts, M. J., Singh, A. A., Nassar-McMillan, S., Butler, S. K., & McCullough, J. R. (2015). *Multicultural and social justice counseling competencies.* Retrieved from http://www.counseling.org/docs/default-source/competencies/multicultural-and-social-justice-counseling-competencies.pdf?sfvrsn=20

Remafedi, G. (1987). Adolescent homosexuality: Psychosocial and medical implications. *Pediatrics, 79,* 331–337.

Remafedi, G., Farrow, J. A., & Deisher, R. W. (1991). Risk factors in attempted suicide in gay and bisexual youth. *Pediatrics, 87,* 869–875.

Roberts, W. B., Jr., & Morotti, A. A. (2000). The bully as victim: Understanding bully behaviors to increase the effectiveness of interventions in the bully-victim dyad. *Professional School Counseling, 4,* 148–155.

Rogler, L. H., Malgady, R. G., Constantino, G., & Blumenthal, R. (1987). What do culturally sensitive mental health services mean? The case of Hispanics. *American Psychologist, 42,* 565–570.

Rousseve, R. J. (1968). The role of the counselor in a free society. *School Counselor, 16,* 6–10.

Ruiz, R. A., & Padilla, A. M. (1977). Counseling Latinos. *Personnel and Guidance Journal, 55,* 401–408.

Sandhu, D. S. (2000). Foreword. *Professional School Counseling, 4,* iv.

Savage, T. A., Harley, D. A., & Nowak, T. M. (2005). Applying social empowerment strategies as tools for self-advocacy in counseling lesbian and gay male clients. *Journal of Counseling and Development, 83,* 131–137.

Shaw, M. C. (1968). *The function of theory in guidance programs. Guidance Monograph Series I.* Boston: Houghton Mifflin.

Sheffield, D. S., & Baker, S. B. (2005). Themes from retrospective interviews of school counselors who experienced burnout. *Hecettepe University Journal of Education, 29,* 177–186.

Singh, A. A., Urbano, A., Haston, M., & McMahan, E. (2010). School counselors' strategies for social justice change: A grounded theory of what works in the real world. *Professional School Counseling, 13,* 135–144.

Skovholt, T. M. (2001). *The resilient practitioner: Burnout prevention and self-care strategies for counselors, therapists, teachers, and health professionals.* Boston: Allyn & Bacon.

Stewart, L. H., & Warnath, C. F. (1965). *The counselor and society.* Boston: Houghton Mifflin.

Stinchfield, T. A., & Zyromski, B. (2010). A training model for school, family, and community collaboration. *The Family Journal: Counseling and Therapy for Couples and Families, 18*(3), 263–268.

Stone, C. B., & Zirkel, P. A. (2010). School counselor advocacy: When law and ethics may collide. *Professional School Counseling, 13,* 244–247.

Stone, S. C., & Shertzer, B. (1963). The militant counselor. *Personnel and Guidance Journal, 42,* 342–347.

Sue, D. W. (1992). The challenge of multiculturalism: The road less traveled. *American Counselor, 1,* 7–14.

Sue, D. W., Arredondo, P., & McDavis, R. J. (1992). Multicultural counseling competencies and standards: A call to the profession. *Journal of Counseling & Development, 70,* 477–486.

Trusty, J., & Brown, D. (2005). Advocacy competencies for professional school counselors. *Professional School Counseling, 8,* 259–265.

Vontress, C. (1966). *Counseling the culturally different adolescent: A school community approach.* Moravia, NY: Chronicle Guidance Publications.

Wrenn, C. G. (1962). *The counselor in a changing world.* Washington, DC: American.

LEADERSHIP AND COLLABORATION IN SCHOOL COUNSELING

6

RELATED STANDARDS OF PRACTICE

CACREP CORE	F.1.b, c
CACREP SCHOOL COUNSELING	G.1.d, G.2.a,d

Goal: To discuss and advocate the role of leadership and collaboration in school counseling and identify leadership and collaboration competencies.

Back in the early 2000s, an urban elementary school counselor in the Southeastern United States worked to decrease the number of discipline referrals in her school. Although she was a solo counselor with a caseload of 400 students, she observed that students were spending too much time out of class and not enough time on academic engagement. She approached the principal about collecting data on the discipline referrals that were sent to the front office. The principal was hesitant to keep this kind of data, as it would reflect poorly on her school. She agreed to let the school counselor collect the data with the condition that it be shared only with her at the close of the semester.

For 12 weeks, the school counselor recorded data related to offense stated in the discipline referral, grade level, and teacher. Then, at the close of the semester, she shared the data with the principal. Her reaction was of shock. She could not believe that in a school of 400 students, the school counselor had recorded over 200 referrals. Given the data illustrated the significance of the issue, the principal convened a leadership team to examine the concern and asked the school counselor take the lead. That January, before students

Baby steps?
Slowly integrated
Change.

came back to school, the school counselor, with the support of the principal and leadership team, presented the data to the teachers and staff. This was the first step in changing a culture that was detrimental to the academic achievement of the students in that school. Months following that presentation, a new school-wide discipline plan was developed, teachers received training on classroom management, and the referrals were reduced by 80%.

This level of systemic change could not have occurred without the use of data, focused leadership, and collaboration from the entire school staff.

Innovative school counselors have, throughout the history of the profession, made important contributions to the evolution of school counseling. These contributions have typically not been publicized or recorded in textbooks. The names of these dedicated counselors have typically remained only in the minds of the children they have served. Nevertheless, the leadership of these creative professionals has contributed much to the profession.

Individuals often enter school counselor preparation programs because they want to work closely with students, parents, and teachers. Seldom do these aspiring counselors consider the leadership skills that are required to build and maintain successful school counseling programs. This chapter focuses on school counselors as leaders and collaborators.

DEMAND FOR LEADERSHIP AND COLLABORATION IN SCHOOL COUNSELING

LEADERSHIP

As mentioned in Chapter 1, First Lady Michelle Obama's Reach Higher Initiative has further highlighted the necessary leadership of school counselors in helping to close the postsecondary attainment gaps. Schools counselors use data to make decisions about comprehensive school programming, and these skills also align with the need to increase college access for all students. As you might already sense, school counselors must develop leadership skills to help create this level systemic change, as it can be accomplished only through collaboration, which is also one of American School Counselor Association National Model (ASCA, 2012) themes, and depicted in this chapter.

Leadership has not been a traditional function in the repertoire of school counselors. According to Schwallie-Giddis, Maat, and Pak (2003), the seeds of the current interest in leadership may be traced to the 1980s when school counseling was omitted from the "most quoted and read national publication" about school reform, *A Nation at Risk* (Gardner, 1983). This "real wake-up call" is said to have caused the counseling profession to undertake a number of initiatives that highlighted leadership and collaboration as important components of the school counselor role and functions.

One of those initiatives was the Transforming School Counseling Initiative (TSCI), which called for school counselors to be the leaders and advocates who would remove systemic barriers that impede academic achievement for all students. Given this was no small task, school counselors had to develop leadership skills and collaborate with other stakeholders. Not far behind, the ASCA National Model (ASCA, 2003) was published and included the notion of school counselor as leader.

In fact, the pathway to the current state of affairs for the ASCA includes the development of National Standards (Campbell & Dahir, 1997) and the National Model (ASCA, 2012). According to Schwallie-Giddis et al. (2003), "Leadership is defined as the ability to lead; the capacity to be a leader. A leader is someone who leads others along the way, one who guides (Morris, 1980)" (p. 171).

There are multiple avenues for school counselors to engage in leadership. One such avenue is illustrated by Baker, Robichaud, Dietrich, Wells, and Schreck (2009), who provided examples of how school counselors can engage in leadership through consultation. Consultation provides an opportunity to provide both direct and indirect services, thus ensuring that school counselors have a wider reach relative to their caseloads. Another avenue is through the collection and use of data. McMahon, Mason, and Paisley (2009) suggest that school counselors engage in educational leadership by the collection and use of data, thereby also promoting accountability.

The ASCA National Model (ASCA, 2012) highlights leadership as one of four themes. We quote the document as follows:

> **Leadership**
>
> School counselors serve as leaders who are engaged in systemwide change to ensure student success. They help every student gain access to rigorous academic preparation that will lead to greater opportunity and increased academic achievement. Working as leaders, advocates and collaborators, school counselors promote student success by closing the existing achievement gap whenever found among students of color, poor students or underachieving students and their more advantaged peers. School counselors become effective leaders by collaborating with other professionals in the school to influence systemwide changes and implement school reforms. In this way, school counselors have an impact on students, the school, the district, and the state.
>
> (p. 24)

Note the mention of systemic change, advocacy, and collaboration—the remaining three ASCA National Model themes. As well, you are encouraged to note the emphasis on access to rigorous academic preparation, equal access to academic achievement in order to close the achievement gap, counselors promoting school success, and involvement in school reform.

COLLABORATION

While promoting the TSCI, Paisley and Hayes (2003) tied the leadership idea to the ASCA National Standards (ASCA, 2003) by envisioning modern school counselors as leaders who advocate for the academic, career, social, and personal success of all students. It appears as if the constructive work undertaken by the TSCI and the ASCA may also lead toward achieving school-community collaboration goals. Adelman and Taylor (2002) articulate the school-community collaboration goals: "School counselors and all other school personnel concerned must find their way to the leadership tables so that system-wide changes are designed and implemented" (p. 240). The goal is to connect schools, families, and communities (Taylor & Adelman, 2000). As leaders, school counselors will establish collaborations that connect schools with home and community resources. In so doing, considerable effort will be required to link health and human services with the schools.

In this initiative, the leadership emphasis appears to be on linking schools with community services in order to achieve school-community collaboration. This approach focuses on the perceived need to enhance the services available to students and their families in order to respond to social, emotional, and physical health barriers to student academic success by bringing outside services into better relationships with the schools.

Lewis and Borunda (2006) provide a dimension to leadership that they depict as *participatory leadership*. In this approach, leadership is spread out among stakeholders democratically. In their own words:

> Participatory leadership emerges from engagement in collaborative efforts to bring about systemic change in specific schools by advocating for and engaging all students in ways in which they are challenged to meet high expectations, provided care and support, and given opportunities to participate in activities they find meaningful.
>
> (p. 408)

In this approach, attributes of participatory leaders include (a) drawing upon democratic traditions, (b) bringing in and listening to diverse voices, (c) engaging all students in authentic dialogues that help individuals and communities define success for themselves and participate in activities that are meaningful, and (d) discovering outcomes that indicate what "works in helping all students to fulfill their potential in their local schools" (Lewis & Borunda, 2006, p. 408). Collaboration, a theme of the National Model (ASCA, 2012) is described as follows:

> **Collaboration**
>
> School counselors work with all stakeholders, both inside and outside the school system, to develop and implement responsible educational programs that support the achievement of identified goals for every student. School counselors build effective teams by encouraging genuine collaboration among all school staff to work toward the common goals of equity, access and academic success for every student.
>
> (p. 25)

Clearly, collaboration appears to be a vehicle through which school counselors achieve leadership goals. The ASCA focus on collaboration emphasizes *working* with all stakeholders, *building* effective teams, *creating* effective working relationships, *understanding and appreciating* contributions of others in achieving educational equity, and *serving* as a vital resource to families, educators, and community agencies.

Keys and Green (2005) define *collaboration* as "A specific process that occurs among individuals who have come together to solve problems" (p. 392). Keys and Green present six characteristics that make an interaction collaborative in nature: (1) there is voluntary participation; (2) all involved parties respect each other as equals; (3) the participants have mutual goals; (4) although levels of responsibility may differ, problem-solving is a shared responsibility; (5) tangible (e.g., personnel) and intangible (e.g., knowledge) resources are shared, and (6) accountability for outcomes is shared.

Keys and Green (2005) accurately point out that collaboration with outsiders has not been a traditional feature of the public school systems. Consequently, school personnel are challenged to understand that many of their students have environmental and psychosocial problems preventing them from being successful students that school systems are unable to address by themselves. Luongo (2000) cites evidence that suggests that from 30% to 40% of children receiving services from core social institutions such as child welfare, criminal justice, and behavioral health are also in need of special services in the schools.

These circumstances promote a need for collaboration. In the school environments where collaboration with outsiders is the road less traveled, enlightened school counselors may be the professionals who can bring the important stakeholders together in order to achieve school-community collaboration. Meaningful collaboration may be achieved via intelligent leadership initiatives undertaken by school counselors. Leadership initiatives that lead to successful school-community collaborations bring the leadership and collaboration concepts to life. That is, when the leadership and collaboration concepts are understood and appreciated by school counselors and they engage in successful leading and collaborating, ideas will be translated into action. That is the ultimate goal. Without school counselors who lead and collaborate, leadership and collaboration become inert ideas.

Young, Millard, and Kneale (2013) provide another example of collaboration through participation in professional learning communities. There are some important characteristics of professional learning communities. Examples include a shared belief system that governs instructional practices, collaborative teaming, and results orientation. The authors also connect the ASCA National Model (ASCA, 2003) to the work of professional learning communities. The commonalities include use of data to examine the effectiveness of programs, high standards for all students, and outcome data as a focus (Young et al., 2013).

BASIC INGREDIENTS OF LEADERSHIP AND COLLABORATION IN SCHOOL COUNSELING

ARE LEADERS BORN OR MADE?

This question has been studied for some time, and we do not intend to address it in this edition of the textbook. We are aware that leadership has not traditionally been treated as an important function in the training of school counselors. Indeed, we believe that many individuals who entered school counseling previously did not view themselves as leaders. Otherwise, they may have entered training programs for educational administrators.

There also are conditions in the schools that make leadership a challenge for school counselors. Haettenschwiller (1971) describes counselors as being in a weak or boundary position within the power and status framework of the schools, receiving demands from parents, administrators, and teachers who are able to bestow both positive and negative sanctions. Furthermore, school counselors may often find themselves in environments where some of their more influential colleagues and supervisors have beliefs that are contrary to the counselors' preferences and ideals (Willower, Hoy, & Eidell, 1967). This may cause them to be silent or pay lip service to the preferences of their more dominant colleagues.

It seems as if some individuals are by nature and nurture more likely to seek or respond to leadership opportunities successfully. Others may not want to be, or be capable of being, good leaders. With regard to school counselors already in the field, perhaps the best thing that can be done is to inform and attempt to motivate them about the importance of leadership and help them if they are so inclined. With regard to future students, counselor educators who believe in the importance of leadership can attempt to select individuals who are willing and able to be leaders as well as become competent in all the other aspects of the profession. Having done so, they can then provide training opportunities that enhance the potential to be successful leaders. Perhaps practicum and internship experiences will help. On the other hand, it may not be until counseling students are on the job in the real world that they will have the opportunity to emerge as leaders. Then, they will have to be both willing and able.

UNDERSTANDING LEADERSHIP CONCEPTUALLY

More recently, there has been focused research and literature discussing school counselors as leaders (Baker et al., 2009; Janson, Stone, & Clark, 2009; Sink, 2009; Young et al., 2013). Dollarhide (2003) has applied important writings about leadership from adult education, management theory, educational administration, and political science to school counseling in a manner that will help you apply the concept of leadership to practice. Important ingredients of this understanding of leadership are contexts and skills. Borrowing from the work of Bolman and Deal (1997), Dollarhide presents four contexts in which leadership might occur in school counseling. Each leadership context calls for school counselors to engage in corresponding leadership activities and apply requisite skills.

Structural Leadership

According to Dollarhide (2003), the structural leadership context will lead to activities involving the building of effective comprehensive school counseling programs. The structural leadership process includes having a technical mastery of implementation and maintenance strategies. Perceived requisite skills for structural leadership are counseling, consulting, teaching, advocacy, and evaluation/accountability, all of which are common components of graduate school counselor training programs.

Human Resource Leadership

Activities associated with human resource leadership are believing in people and communicating that belief, being visible and accessible, and empowering others. As is the case with structural leadership, the skills associated with human resource leadership (i.e., communicating, empowering, trust building, and listening) are traditional components of school counselor training programs.

Change Agents

Political Leadership

Dollarhide (2003) depicts political leadership as "a more nontraditional role for many counselors [that] may cause. . . . anxiety and dissonance" (p. 305). Political leadership activities in school counseling include assessing power distribution in school buildings and districts, building linkages with important stakeholders, persuading, and negotiating. Requisite skills are relatively complex and difficult to teach comprehensively in traditional training programs. Therefore, political leadership skills associated with negotiation, persuasion, collaboration, and advocacy may have to be acquired and polished on the job as school counselors after completing one's training program. Training programs most certainly can begin the process by introducing concepts and basic skills and motivating trainees to believe in the importance of being successful leaders politically.

Symbolic Leadership

The symbolic leadership context draws on "using symbols and metaphors to capture attention, framing experience in meaningful ways for followers, and discovering and communicating a vision" (Dollarhide, 2003, p. 305). This form of leadership focuses importance on relationships with students, families, and communities; articulating and maintaining faith in visions; and inspiring others through effective modeling. The associated skills for symbolic leadership are designing symbols, expressing meaning, inspiring others, and modeling for others. As was stated about political leadership skills, some of the symbolic leadership skills may need to be acquired beyond the training program as school counselors develop professional identities and mature into expert and trustworthy role models.

Viewing a Leadership Vignette Contextually

Excerpts from an example presented by Dollarhide (2003) are presented in order to enhance understanding. A newly hired school counselor was attempting to develop a comprehensive school counseling program based on the ASCA National Standards (Campbell & Dahir, 1997) in a rural setting where the existing program emphasized scheduling, testing, and discipline. The leadership contexts were used to formulate a change agent strategy.

The first priority was to design a viable program. Reducing inappropriate functions was a second priority. Symbolic and human resource leadership skills were employed initially when the counselor shared a passionate vision about the potential outcomes of her proposed school counseling program with influential stakeholders. Next, structural leadership skills were used to design a viable middle school counseling program. Teachers and parents were consulted. Finally, political leadership was addressed through seeking support from the school principal and establishing an advisory board to help with the design, implementation, and evaluation of the program. Eventually, the counselor weaved all four leadership contexts together into her own leadership style.

The vignette indicates that various leadership contexts may come into play during a leadership episode. Therefore, it behooves school counselors to acquire skills across all of the four leadership context categories in order to enhance their effectiveness. Furthermore, a conceptual understanding of the four contexts and their related skills will make school counselors better prepared to achieve leadership goals, such as those presented in this vignette, and analyze the process while engaged in change agent strategies.

COMPETENCIES IN BASIC LEADERSHIP AND COLLABORATION IN SCHOOL COUNSELING

It appears to us that the basic competencies are rather complex combinations of many specific behaviors. We have derived a set of behaviors that seem appropriate for leaders and collaborators. We also believe that these behaviors will be appropriate when used successfully. Using the behaviors successfully depends on a combination of one's genetic proclivities and one's socialization. It is not necessary to exhibit all the following behaviors in order to be a leader because there are numerous ways one can lead, depending on the circumstances. For example, one person may exhibit leadership qualities by taking charge during the process of developing and implementing a school counseling program. Another individual may demonstrate leadership in more subtle ways, such as being a mediator during a dispute, recruiting volunteers for collaborations, or helping community and school representatives build a sense of community. The following behaviors were taken from the work of Adelman and Taylor (2002), Bemak (2000), Bemak and Cornely (2002), Dahir (2001), Gysbers and Henderson (2000, 2001), Hatch and Bowers (2002), House and Hayes (2002), Keys (2000), and Rowley, Sink, and MacDonald (2002). The order in which they are presented does not reflect an opinion of their importance. We have tried to order them in a manner that makes sense to us. When reading this information, reflect on the position of Chickering and Gameson (1987) who globally describe leadership as being untidy rather than orderly, the art of facilitating one's own growth as well as that of others, and being aware that your presence makes a difference in every situation. A leader in school counseling should be able to do the following:

- Cause, lead, implement, and maintain a comprehensive school counseling program;

- Form and lead committees, including chairing committees, planning agendas, and establishing meeting schedules;

- Coordinate the objectives, strategies, and activities of a comprehensive school counseling program;

- Serve as a missionary for the program;

- Develop mechanisms for educating and involving others;

- Develop support systems for yourself and other school counseling personnel.

- Conduct meetings, make commitments for action, form and convene steering committees, form and convene school and community advisory committees, establish work groups, and meet with district administrators and school boards;

- Demonstrate leadership skills as an active member of programs and committees;

- Identify and use complementary skills;

- Mediate conflicts;

- Recognize differences such as race, gender, experience, preferred learning styles, and work roles and use that information to engage in creative problem solving even though it may involve conflict;

- Recognize opportunities for empowerment;
- Know how work groups operate, especially teams, and how to build effective teams;
- Recruit volunteers to assist in school programs;
- Build a sense of community in the schools;
- Know how to effectively manage school and community bureaucracies;
- Build a consensus and work collaboratively with a broad range of professionals and concerned citizens in order to achieve a sense of community;
- Keep your fingers on the pulse of the needs of students and on the mission and goals of the school;
- Adopt a systems perspective;
- Facilitate family-school partnerships;
- Break down bureaucratic turf boundaries;
- Work collaboratively with school administrators;
- Bring community services into the schools and coordinate them;
- Develop mutual prevention/intervention programs with community agencies;
- Work closely with other support personnel in the schools (e.g., school psychologists, school social workers, nurses, and special educators);
- Support, consult, and work with teachers;
- Collect and share data (e.g., document obstacles to student growth and development);
- Develop a crisis team that is educated in emergency response procedures;
- Inform administrators about the contributions you plan to make rather than asking them what to do.

EXAMPLES OF LEADERSHIP AND COLLABORATION BY SCHOOL COUNSELORS

TRANSFORMING THE SCHOOL CULTURE: AN EXAMPLE OF LEADERSHIP

This vignette is based on a report by Littrell and Peterson (2001) about an elementary school counselor in Oregon whose goal was to transform the school's culture from one of negativity and high stress to one of problem solving at all levels. The counselor had a vision of a school in which all children were problem solvers. Littrell and Peterson depicted the counselor as having a guiding vision, defined values and beliefs, a willingness to confront the school about her vision, and the ability to clarify how she functions in the system.

We do not know the exact sequence of steps in which the counselor engaged. The following specific acts of leadership were reported by Littrell and Peterson. The counselor adopted a four-step problem-solving model that helped her to think systematically.

Through a combination of previous experience, meetings, and consultation, she learned about and understood the school climate. Having a vision and knowledge of the school climate, the counselor introduced "a new, but natural and familiar, 'language' that was easy for all to understand—the language of problem solving" (Littrell & Peterson, 2001, p. 314). For example, she would ask such questions as "What is the problem?" and "What have you tried so far?" Through teaching the language of problem solving, she bonded with students. Eventually, parents picked up the problem-solving language as well.

Eventually, the counselor designed and implemented a developmental curriculum that was based on problem solving. For example, second graders learned 10 ways to solve conflicts. Having established a problem-solving curriculum in classrooms, the counselor also found ways to implement the curriculum content elsewhere (e.g., a problem-solving wheel in the principal's office). In response to numerous referrals by teachers of students who were classroom behavior problems, the counselor created several counseling groups or clubs, beginning with six that were topic focused (e.g., students who get everything done and want to do more and students who need to develop their own unique strengths).

The counselor's systematic approach led to identifying four factors that influenced her individual counseling: (1) accenting client strengths, (2) providing a caring relationship, (3) knowing her counseling theories and techniques, and (4) providing hope. Viewing the entire school as a community, the counselor built partnerships at all levels (e.g., the lunchroom supervisor, the new junior high school counselor, teachers, and parents). As a leader, the counselor engaged in advocacy activities such as lobbying legislators in order to influence policy and mobilizing local merchants to acquire clothing for poor children. The report also highlighted the counselor's effectiveness at planning and organizing, her attempts to ensure self-renewal, and an incidence of her efforts being self-sustaining six years later.

Littrell and Peterson (2001) conclude their report as follows:

> [She] was not a perfect counselor; however, we chose to study her because her work as a school counselor was exemplary and inspiring. The uniqueness of our model is in the emphasis on the counselor as a person and on the counselor's ability to assess the context and align vision, identity, beliefs/values, capabilities, and behaviors in the interest of creatively conceiving and realizing a programmatic vision. Our hope is that this model helps counselors to be visionary educational leaders.
>
> (p. 318)

SCHOOL-BASED CLINICIANS: AN EXAMPLE OF COLLABORATION

The following vignette was derived from a report by Porter, Epp, and Bryant (2000). The school-based clinicians in the vignette are part of a larger program sponsored by the Community Psychiatry Department of Johns Hopkins University in Baltimore,

Maryland. The Johns Hopkins program partnership includes the departments of social services, juvenile justice, health, and police, and the mental health clinicians include professional counselors, psychologists, arts therapists, and social workers.

Our example took place in an urban high school in which the clinician was a welcome guest because of high incidences of challenging mental health problems. The clinician worked with the difficult mental health cases in order to allow the school counselors to provide developmental guidance and college counseling services to a broad range of students.

The school's director of guidance implemented a collaborative system that could be established in other schools. She created a school mental health team that consisted of all the school counselors, a vice principal, a school nurse, a faculty member, and the school-based clinician. The guidance director chaired the committee and served as coordinator.

The school was referring clients to a clinician from an outside agency that was being paid by Medicaid. Therefore, a system of oversight and referral was needed. According to Porter et al. (2000), the committee was egalitarian, multidisciplinary, and free of turf battles. On the other hand, there were a number of challenges from within the school and the community. For example, the magnitude of presenting problems challenged the committee to figure out how to respond within the confines of their resources and not become overwhelmed. Also, some members of the faculty were less than friendly and cooperative, and the committee had to engage in quiet diplomacy in that domain. Occasionally, the committee faced dilemmas about which they were divided (e.g., reporting child abuse) and had to recognize the value of their common mission.

Porter et al. teased out the following lessons about collaboration that can overcome the potential barriers: (a) use the multidisciplinary team meetings to solve problems and make decisions, (b) ensure cultural sensitivity of clinicians through training, (c) develop a common language across the represented disciplines, (d) develop open and flexible attitudes, and (e) standardize procedures. Porter et al. (2000) conclude,

> School counselors are in a unique position to facilitate the collaborative process needed to ensure the provision of comprehensive, accessible mental health services. Collaboration is a major challenge, but when professionals are able to use their varied skills and experiences in a complimentary, collaborative way, they can transcend any barriers.
>
> (p. 322)

SCHOOL COUNSELORS AS LEADERS AND COLLABORATORS

Based on a survey of school counselors in South Carolina, Bryan and Holcomb-McCoy (2004) reported that school counselors across all levels indicated their involvement in school-community-family partnership collaborations was important. We find the potential for school counselors to be leaders and collaborators as just depicted exciting. School counseling is a human service career, and school counselors are exposed to numerous situations that challenge their ability to serve all clients who are in need. We believe that leadership and collaboration are avenues through which school counselors can be of greater service to a broad range of clients. Perhaps the most important ingredients are the desire and will to do so.

The structural leadership context introduced in this chapter lists building effective comprehensive school counseling programs as a goal and teaching as one of the competencies. In the next chapter, we focus on the teaching function in school counseling.

COMPREHENSIVE SCHOOL COUNSELING PROGRAM COMPONENT

1. Identify stakeholders in your school and community with whom you will collaborate in efforts to support all students.
2. Identify strategies you will use to advocate for multicultural populations in your school.
3. Conduct a presentation at a local, state, regional, or national conference on a topic of your choice.

REFLECTION POINT

1. What do you think about the school counselor as a leader and collaborator whose primary goal is to improve educational fulfillment and academic achievement of all students?
2. Interview one or more school counselors and ask their opinion about whether they should be leaders.
3. Follow up with the school counselors who believe that they should be leaders, and ask them to provide an inventory of circumstances in which they believe school counselor leadership is needed and appropriate.
4. Discuss the interrelationships among leadership, collaboration, and advocacy.
5. Make an inventory of both your leadership strengths and challenges.
6. Make an inventory of the disadvantages associated with failing to provide leadership, collaboration, and advocacy as a school counselor. Then, make an inventory of the potential beneficiaries of good school counseling leadership. Finally, compare the two inventories and process your reactions to the comparisons.
7. Brainstorm the following advocacy scenarios with your classmates and instructor.

You have just graduated from a master's degree program in school counseling, found a job with which you are pleased, become integrated into the school setting, and want to make a contribution to your profession beyond what is being accomplished at your school. Yet you are not sure what to do. You've landed a new school counseling position and found that the counselors in your school are not thought of very well. They are scapegoats for many of the administration's shortcomings and the objects of many unkind jokes around the school. As well, the counselors tend to engage primarily on one-to-one counseling on demand and keep to their offices and the office suite all day, more or less avoiding contact with faculty members unless they are approached by them.

Your school counseling colleague has angrily informed you about the problem that he is having with local mental health counselors and has stated that he will never refer one of his clients to them again. Previously, he made a referral and never received any feedback from the agency. Upon inquiring about the case, he was informed that they will not tell him anything because of client confidentiality. He wonders whether it is useless to make any referrals if they will not help him become better informed to be of service to the referred students when they are in school.

APPLICATION TO TECHNOLOGY

1.   Consider your audience (teachers, parents, students, other stakeholders) and create a presentation to educate that audience about your role as a professional school counselor.

2.   Post to your professional school counseling website how you will serve as a leader in your school (using data, collaborating with community, advocacy, etc.).

REFERENCES

Adelman, H. S., & Taylor, L. (2002). School counselors and school reform: New directions. *Professional School Counseling, 5,* 235–248.

American School Counselor Association. (2003). *The ASCA national model: A framework for school counseling programs* (1st ed.). Alexandria, VA: Author.

American School Counselor Association. (2012). *The ASCA National Model: A framework for school counseling programs* (3rd ed.). Alexandria, VA: Author.

Baker, S. B., Robichaud, T. A., Dietrich, V.C.W., Wells, S. C., & Schreck, R. E. (2009). School counselor consultation: A pathway to advocacy, collaboration, and leadership. *Professional School Counseling, 12*(3), 200–206.

Bemak, F. (2000). Transforming the role of the counselor to provide leadership in educational reform through collaboration. *Professional School Counseling, 3,* 323–331.

Bemak, F., & Cornely, L. (2002). The SAFI model as a critical link between marginalized families and schools: A literature review and strategies for school counselors. *Journal of Counseling & Development, 5,* 322–331.

Bolman, L. B., & Deal, T. E. (1997). *Reframing organizations: Artistry, choice, and leadership* (2nd ed.). San Francisco: Jossey-Bass.

Bryan, J., & Holcomb-McCoy, C. (2004). School counselors' perceptions of their involvement in school-family-community partnerships. *Professional School Counseling, 7,* 162–171.

Campbell, C. A., & Dahir, C. A. (1997). *Sharing the vision: The national standards for school counseling programs*. Alexandria, VA: American School Counselor Association.

Chickering, A., & Gameson, Z. (1987). Principles for good practices in undergraduate education. *AAHE Bulletin, 39,* 3–7.

Dahir, C. (2001). The national standards for school counseling programs: Development and implementation. *Professional School Counseling, 4,* 320–327.

Dollarhide, C. T. (2003). School counselors as program leaders: Applying leadership contexts to school counseling. *Professional School Counseling, 6,* 304–309.

Gardner, D. (1983). *A nation at risk: The imperative for educational reform.* Report of the National Commission on Excellence in Education. Washington, DC: Government Printing Office.

Gysbers, N. C., & Henderson, P. (2000). *Developing and managing your school guidance program* (3rd ed.). Alexandria, VA: American Counseling Association.

Gysbers, N. C., & Henderson, P. (2001). Comprehensive guidance and counseling programs: A rich history and a bright future. *Professional School Counseling, 4,* 246–256.

Haettenschwiller, D. L. (1971). Counseling Black college students in special programs. *Personnel and Guidance Journal, 50,* 29–36.

Hatch, T., & Bowers, J. (2002, May/June). The block to build on. *ASCA Counselor, 39,* 13–17.

House, R. M., & Hayes, R. L. (2002). School counselors: Becoming key players in school reform. *Professional School Counseling, 5,* 249–256.

Janson, C., Stone, C., & Clark, M. A. (2009). Stretching leadership: A distributed perspective for school counselor leaders. *Professional School Counseling, 13*(2), 98–106.

Keys, S. G. (2000). Living the collaborative role: Voices from the field. *Professional School Counseling, 3,* 332–338.

Keys, S. G., & Green, A. (2005). Enhancing developmental school counseling programs through collaboration. In C. Sink (Ed.), *Contemporary school counseling: Theory, research, and practice* (pp. 390–405). Boston: Lahaska Press/Houghton Mifflin.

Lewis, R. L., & Borunda, R. (2006). Lived stories: Participatory leadership in school counseling. *Journal of Counseling and Development, 84,* 406–413.

Littrell, J. M., & Peterson, J. S. (2001). Transforming the school culture: A model based on an exemplary counselor. *Professional School Counseling, 4,* 310–319.

Luongo, P. (2000). Partnering child welfare, juvenile justice and behavioral health with schools. *Professional School Counseling, 3,* 308–313.

McMahon, G., Mason, E., & Paisley, P. (2009). School counselor educators as educational leaders promoting systemic change. *Professional School Counseling, 13,* 116–124.

Morris, W. (Ed.). (1980). *The American heritage dictionary of the English language.* Boston: Houghton Mifflin.

Paisley, P. O., & Hayes, R. L. (2003). School counseling in the academic domain: Transformations in preparation and practice. *Professional School Counseling, 6,* 198–205.

Porter, G., Epp, L., & Bryant, S. (2000). Collaboration among school mental health professionals: A necessity, not a luxury. *Professional School Counseling, 3,* 315–322.

Rowley, W. J., Sink, C. A., & MacDonald, G. (2002). An experiential and systemic approach to encourage collaboration and community building. *Professional School Counseling, 5,* 360–365.

Schwallie-Giddis, P., Maat, M., & Pak, M. (2003). Initiating leadership by implementing the ASCA National Model. *Professional School Counseling, 6,* 170–173.

Sink, C. (2009). School counselors as accountability leaders: Another call for action. *Professional School Counseling, 13*(2), 68–74.

Taylor, L., & Adelman, H. S. (2000). Connecting schools, families, and communities. *Professional School Counseling, 3,* 298–307.

Willower, D. J., Hoy, W. K., & Eidell, T. L. (1967). The counselor and the school as a social organization. *Personnel and Guidance Journal, 46,* 228–234.

Young, A. A., Millard, T., & Kneale, M. M. (2013). Enhancing school counselor instructional leadership through collaborative teaming: Implications for principals. *NASSP Bulletin, 97*(3), 253–269.

PREVENTION PROGRAMMING IN SCHOOL COUNSELING: SERVING ALL STUDENTS PROACTIVELY

7

RELATED STANDARDS OF PRACTICE

CACREP CORE	2.F.4.f., 2.F.5.j., 2.F.6.a.b., 2.F.8.e.
CACREP SCHOOL COUNSELING	5.G.3.c.d.

Goal: To offer evidence of the importance of developmentally appropriate prevention programming, propose basic competencies for prevention programming, and provide examples.

> The Cornish Test of Insanity comprised a sink, a tap of running water, a bucket, and a ladle. The bucket was placed under the tap of running water, and the subject was asked to bail the water out of the bucket with the ladle. If the subject continued to bail without paying some attention to reducing or preventing the flow of water into the pail, he or she was judged to be mentally incompetent.
>
> (Morgan & Jackson, 1980, p. 99)

The need for prevention may never have been greater than it is now. Substance abuse and school violence are examples of matters that need to be addressed creatively through prevention programming. Violent and disruptive behavior among students present especially serious challenges for school counselors (Bryan, Day-Vines, Griffin, & Moore-Thomas, 2012). Bullying among school-age youths is pervasive (Pergolizzi et al., 2009). School counselors may need to "reconnect the past to the present" and revisit a time when preventive programs were at the center of school counseling practice (DeKruyf, Auger, & Trice-Black, 2013).

We have had many opportunities to hear school counselors discuss their hopes and aspirations for preventive programming in classrooms. The following account from an elementary school counselor is among the most poignant we have heard:

> I meet with small groups of children every week, giving them an opportunity to discuss their feelings about many aspects of their lives. These groups help the children to feel welcome at school and to know the benefits of self-disclosure and listening. Recently, while discussing the topic "the saddest thing that ever happened to me," a fourth-grade girl reluctantly raised her hand. When I looked toward her, she brought her hand down quickly. She seldom said anything in the group and generally appeared shy and reserved in social situations. Several other youngsters contributed to the group topic before her hand went up again. I looked toward her, and she lowered her hand. Two other members of the group spoke. Her hand went up again and remained up this time. I called on her. She spoke with great care: "The saddest thing I ever saw was my grandfather hanging from a rope in our barn." She had been holding this in for weeks and finally felt trusting enough to share this traumatic experience from her life. She was relieved. I invited her to meet with me later to discuss this matter.

The flow of problems to counselors' offices can never be reduced unless counselors plan and implement preventive intervention programs. It is important, therefore, that school counselors devote a major portion of their time and effort to preventing the onset of emotional problems in children. In cooperation with teachers, counselors conduct classroom programs that include listening activities and other techniques that are designed to help children and adolescents (a) feel worthy as persons and as students, (b) recognize their feelings about themselves and about learning, (c) feel comfortable about expressing these feelings openly and honestly, and (d) acquire developmentally appropriate knowledge and coping skills.

DEMAND FOR PREVENTION PROGRAMMING IN SCHOOLS

School counseling programs need to be balanced between intervention responses and proactive prevention programming. Proactive prevention programming is the mainstay of the prevention function and is pedagogical in nature. The word *pedagogical* identifies these activities because they are primarily instructional; *pedagogy* is the "art, science, or profession of teaching" (*Merriam-Webster's Collegiate Dictionary,* www.merriam-webster.com). Although pedagogics is seldom associated with counselor education, there is no denying that school counselors engage in instructional or pedagogical activities when delivering many group programs. These prevention programs have various labels:

classroom guidance, group guidance, guidance teaching, developmental guidance, guidance-related courses or units, and wellness programs. This textbook uses the term *proactive prevention programming*. We use this term because it allows us to present a set of pedagogical competencies that are needed to deliver classroom guidance, group guidance, developmental guidance, or any such school counselor program that is pedagogical in nature. The word *proactive* indicates that the activities involved are anticipatory. *Prevention* indicates that the goals are to prevent problems and enhance human development. The word *programming* indicates that the process involves systematically arranging a sequence of intentional applications based on goals and objectives derived from an underlying conceptual rationale. School counselors are challenged to be competent teachers/pedagogues in order to offer proactive prevention programs. Providing a balanced school counseling program seems to require competence as teachers.

As Cinotti (2014) has explained, the profession of school counseling, throughout its existence, has struggled with competing professional identity constructs that have influenced the roles and responsibilities of school counselors. He noted further, however, that the American School Counselor Association's (ASCA) most recent position statements have indicated that school counselors are responsible for planning and initiating activities that enhance the academic, career, and personal/social development of students. The ASCA has long used the term *developmental guidance* when referring to strategies that promote the academic, career, and personal/social development of children and adolescents. Excerpts from the ASCA's 1978 position statement (reviewed and revised in 1984) on developmental guidance indicate that, aside from differing semantics, the association seems to agree that proactive prevention programming is an important school counseling function:

> Developmental guidance should be an integral part of every school counseling program and be incorporated into the role and function of every school counselor. During recent years a number of counselor educators and school counselors have advanced the proposition that counseling can and should be more proactive and preventive in its focus and more developmental in its content and process.... Developmental guidance is a reaffirmation and actualization of the belief that guidance is for all students and that its purpose is to maximally facilitate personal development.... The program should be systematic, sequential, and comprehensive.... The program should be jointly founded upon developmental psychology, educational psychology, and counseling methodology.
>
> (n.d., p. 33)

The ASCA National Model (ASCA, 2012) with the National Standards therein represents a significant effort of the ASCA to operationalize the developmental guidance concept highlighted earlier. Gysbers and Henderson (2000) have advocated a K–12 curriculum for school counselors consisting of "guidance" classes designed to help all students meet the competencies presented in the ASCA National Standards (ASCA, 2014). Comprehensive school counseling programs include these kinds of classes and other forms of prevention and developmental programming.

> Some students have the good fortune to attend schools where they have supportive, personal relationships with their school counselors and receive valuable comprehensive school counseling . . . far too many students attend schools where this is not the case.
>
> (Lapan, 2012, p. 84)

Childhood and adolescence are opportune times to prevent many problems. Therefore, the school years are an excellent time for programs designed to help children and adolescents get the most out of their school experience and cope better with life's challenges. This is also a good time to identify at-risk individuals and to prevent them from being overwhelmed by the problems they are at risk of experiencing. Proactive prevention programming usually has several common features: It is structured, planned in advance, presented in a group format, and led by individuals working from a predetermined plan. Carey and Dimmitt (2012) have cited research showing that school counselors who deliver prevention programs—as prescribed by the ASCA National Model (ASCA, 2012) through traditional comprehensive developmental guidance—may help to decrease suspension rates, decrease discipline rates, increase attendance, and enhance student achievement as measured by some state achievement tests in math and reading.

Many school counselors enter the profession with degrees in education and with teaching experience. Traditional counselor education programs are designed to provide them additional competencies such as counseling and assessment skills. School counseling trainees, however, increasingly come from fields outside education, especially in states that do not require teaching experience as a prerequisite for school counseling certification or licensure. Because these individuals are not trained in pedagogics, it is important to train them as competent instructors, as well as competent counselors. School counseling students, it seems, will benefit from opportunities to become competent at pedagogics during their training in order to provide balanced school counseling services.

Training experiences for school counselors might include opportunities to learn about structured, developmentally appropriate proactive group prevention and intervention programs for students, teachers, and parents in addition to opportunities to learn skills for presenting and delivering such programs effectively to students representing the students' own as well as other worldviews. Counselors planning and presenting structured programs to groups of students will be more successful if they are competent technically—at developing lesson plans and supplementing instruction with activities that are interesting and that complement the instructional goals—as well as competent multiculturally—able to make programs meaningful to individuals representing all worldviews.

All of the best paradigms for enhancing school counseling recommend proactive prevention programming competencies for school counselors. In line with the ASCA National Model, Bowers, Hatch, and Schwallie-Giddis (2001) state that prevention programming should include a guidance curriculum. Further, Gysbers and Henderson (2001) indicate that the curriculum should cover kindergarten through 12th grade and include classroom activities delivered via structured groups. Indeed, the competencies in the ASCA National Model (ASCA, 2012) offers a foundation for proactively designing strategies and producing activities to enhance student achievement and success in academic, career, and personal-social development.

Representing the Transforming School Counseling Initiative, House and Hayes (2002) use the words *planner* and *program developer* among the desired competencies for school counselors. The Education Trust hopes to produce school counselors who can promote student achievement through well-articulated developmental school counseling programs. Through these programs, school counselors will teach students how to help themselves via improved organizational, study, and test-taking skills. House and Hayes also promote school counselor involvement in staff development for school personnel focused on learning how to promote high expectations and standards.

In the school-community collaboration paradigm, part of an interconnected system for meeting the needs of all students is having systems for promoting healthy development and preventing problems (i.e., primary prevention). Examples given are drug and alcohol education, parent involvement, and conflict resolution (Adelman & Taylor, 2002).

PROGRAMMING FOR PREVENTION

IMPORTANT INITIAL CONDITIONS

Presenting a plan for prevention programming must have several important initial conditions. First, a school environment in which administrators view teachers and counselors as unique, yet equally important, professionals is essential. Second, participants should understand at the outset that a balanced program is a basic goal. Third, all individuals who influence the counselors' role should understand what prevention means.

The first of these conditions, though very important, is somewhat beyond the purview of this book. On the one hand, if not treated as equal to the teachers, counselors will have a difficult time. On the other hand, the balanced program advocated here may help bring about desired changes in administrative attitudes because potential outcomes are visible. The second condition, the goal of a balanced program, has already been addressed. Therefore, let's look at ways to help influential individuals understand the meaning of prevention.

The word *prevention* means different things to different people. For instance, the general population longs to have such pervasive problems as AIDS, violence, adolescent suicide, substance abuse, unemployment, and teenage pregnancy prevented and all students successful academically and in life. That is certainly a tall order and one that creates great expectations. These expectations have led to identification of students needing intervention responses. Therefore, the public demands prevention, and rightly so. Unfortunately, AIDS, violence, adolescent suicide, substance abuse, unemployment, and teenage pregnancy are actually outcomes, the causes of which are varied and subtle. Therefore, planning to prevent any one of those negative outcomes before it occurs is very difficult.

Stakeholders also associate some positive or developmental outcomes—such as social skills competence, appropriate assertiveness, multicultural competence, self-esteem, good self-concept, and academic success—with prevention programming. When this is the case, it is hoped and perhaps expected that planned prevention programming will cause the participants to have enhanced social skills, appropriate assertiveness, multicultural competence, greater self-esteem, improved self-concepts, or good grades. Although these appear to be agreeable and important outcomes, the words represent very general concepts that beg to be made specific and measurable enough to serve as criteria for prevention programming efforts: Programmers need to be able to associate content with identifiable outcomes. These conditions suggest challenges for prevention programmers, who must develop programs with specific activities that lead to measurable outcomes. Thus, the best thing programmers can do to prevent pervasive problems such as adolescent suicide while enhancing the desired personal qualities is to demonstrate a logical connection between their prevention programs and the desired outcomes. For example, many children who learn to cope better with anxiety, communicate better with their peers, understand the features of their developmental stages, and become more assertive when faced with peer pressure are less likely to abuse drugs and more likely to feel good about themselves. The success of such prevention programs may have to be shown simply by participants acquiring competence and knowledge (ASCA, 2012).

Thus, participants need to demonstrate that they have become more assertive and less anxious or that they have learned information about developmental stages. From these demonstrations, it will have to be assumed that participants are better prepared to cope and less likely to succumb to problem behavior because it is impossible to measure whether something was prevented. We believe that the ASCA National Standards (ASCA, 2014) will help school counselors who are attempting to resolve this challenge.

In addition to helping stakeholders become aware of misperceptions about prevention, it is important to help them understand what prevention is. Shaw and Goodyear (1984) provide a definition that is both applicable to school settings and generalizable to other situations. It focuses chiefly on primary prevention. Taken in part from Cowen (1982), Shaw and Goodyear's (1984) summarized definition the focus should be on groups not actually experiencing significant levels of concerns, should be intentional, and are appropriate for prevention activities.

Primary prevention programs are designed to help all children and adolescents cope better with the developmental tasks they must face. Some children and adolescents are more vulnerable to life's challenges and are more at risk for trouble. They can be helped with prevention programming, too. In these cases, at-risk children can be identified and offered prevention programming targeted to them specifically. An example is to offer assertiveness training to preteens and young teenagers who are likely to have difficulty resisting peer pressure to participate in substance-abusing behaviors. Such services may also be offered on a one-to-one basis. This form of early efforts to keep small or potential problems from becoming more serious is classified as *secondary prevention* (Shaw, 1973). The term *tertiary prevention* is confusing, because in this case the word *prevention* is associated with what are essentially remedial intervention goals. In tertiary prevention, one-to-one and group counseling are used to serve individuals already experiencing problems, to prevent those problems from getting worse, to prevent relapses, and to help resolve the problems (Shaw, 1973). Providing aftercare for adolescents who have returned to school from a temporary sojourn in a drug treatment facility is an example of tertiary prevention that is also part of the responsive counseling intervention function of school counseling. Prevention programming may be designed to reach all students before problems exist or to reach at-risk students before remediation is necessary. In this textbook, primary and secondary prevention are treated globally as prevention.

Stakeholders who influence the counselor's role must understand that major features of prevention programs are the group delivery mode and the intention to help students become better prepared to cope with future events, including developmental tasks. Such stakeholders must also realize that the goal of prevention is to enhance individual development. Understanding this, these stakeholders will probably entertain suggestions for reducing counselor time devoted to intervention and administration and for initiating prevention programming into the regular classroom schedule. Beyond a general understanding of prevention, stakeholders who influence the counselor's role also need information concerning what specifically can be accomplished through prevention programs and how those programs might be implemented.

Intended to address the concerns of counselors who want to achieve program balance through an increasing emphasis on prevention programming, the foregoing information is not meant as a call for eliminating the equally important responsive counseling intervention services that school counselors are expected to provide. The goal is balanced programs. Achieving suitable balance requires a commitment to be informed, organized, systematic, and diplomatic.

GOING UPSTREAM

Here is a paraphrase of a metaphor sometimes used to support prevention activities: Once upon a time, two people were strolling alongside a stream and enjoying the scenery when suddenly another person appeared in the stream, struggling to keep from drowning. The two strollers jumped in immediately and saved the struggling individual. No sooner had they accomplished this then another struggling person appeared, and another, and another, and another. As the two rescuers struggled to save as many of the increasingly larger group of unfortunates as they could, the task became more and more hopeless. Suddenly, one of the two rescuers went to the shore and ran upstream. In response to the other's inquiry about what was going on, the person running upstream said, "I'm going to find out who's throwing all these people into the stream" (Shaw, 1973).

The metaphor supports prevention. To achieve the advocated balance between prevention and intervention, some counselors will remain downstream to rescue potential drowning victims, whereas others will go upstream to reduce the number of individuals in need of rescuing. Notice that the word *reduce* is used instead of *eliminate*. It is important to realize that the current state of the art of school counseling is such that, whether the focus is on intervention or prevention, success cannot be predicted in absolute terms. Counselors can provide successful interventions for some students, and their prevention programs will be more successful for some individuals than for others. A balanced approach combining careful counseling intervention responses and prevention programming has promise for more success than either approach alone because successful prevention programming reduces the need for interventions, and the existence of a complementary intervention thrust provides help for those for whom prevention programming is not enough.

LARGE GROUP GUIDANCE

Large group guidance is the primary delivery system for prevention programming and developmental curricula (Sears, 2005). The ASCA (1999) lists large group guidance as one of the four primary school counselor interventions. The remaining three are individual and group counseling, consultation, and coordination. Sears (2005) defines large group guidance as "an intervention to deliver a curriculum or a series of planned activities to help students anticipate problems before they occur" (p. 190). Recently, the ASCA (2012) presented a *school counseling core curriculum* framework consisting of

> a planned, written instructional program that is comprehensive in scope, preventive in nature, and developmental in design. School counselors plan, design and evaluate the curriculum. The curriculum is delivered to every student by school counselors and other educators as appropriate.
>
> (p. 85)

BASIC INGREDIENTS OF PREVENTION PROGRAMMING

POINT OF VIEW

Because large group guidance is analogous to teaching, it might be argued that the basic ingredients are drawn from the field of education. Education is an applied field, just as counseling is, and like counseling, education has drawn from various disciplines for its foundations. For instance, psychology contributes ideas about human learning, philosophy is the source of ideas about the human condition, and sociology helps educators understand the role of the schools in the greater society. Basic education is also influenced by local, state, and national politics and by applied economics because the schools are primarily supported by taxes. Therefore, when counselors act like teachers and engage in large group guidance, they are not necessarily mimicking a field that is foreign to them.

The traditional training that counselor education programs impart includes knowledge and competencies that prepare counselors for prevention programming. However, the preparation is often not formalized or specified in traditional counselor education programs. Therefore, the field of education is the source of ideas for formalizing and specifying the ingredients of the prevention programming in counseling. What results is a marriage of ingredients from traditional counseling programs and from education that provides an organizing structure for prevention programming training in counselor education training programs.

This combination may not seem necessary for school counseling students who are experienced teachers with formal training in education. On the other hand, it is important to remember that teachers are trained to focus on the enhancement of cognitive abilities; in some cases, they learn to divorce thinking about the affective domain from their professional mindset. Experienced teachers and counselor education students from other disciplines who are being trained as school counselors are challenged to focus on both the cognitive and affective domains in their prevention programming. Therefore, there is a place for formalized instruction in prevention programming within counselor education programs.

The competencies to be introduced are valid for all forms of prevention programming. Prevention programming can take different forms depending on the circumstances. For instance, the programming can be direct or indirect. The term *direct programming* indicates that programs are delivered directly to audiences (e.g., the school counselor leads groups designed to help students become better problem solvers). Indirect programming, on the other hand, indicates that audiences receive programs from third parties (e.g., the school counselor helps classroom teachers prepare for and deliver programs designed to help their students become better problem solvers).

The competencies are also valid for prevention programming that falls within a core curriculum or is independent of a curriculum. Some schools and school districts have guidance curriculums. That is, school counselors have their own set of courses (i.e., curriculum) in schools just as the academic disciplines do, and they have their own recognized area of specialization. They have prevention programs based on enhancing specific developmental goals that are sequenced by grade levels. Time for delivering the programs is scheduled by school administrators and recognized by classroom teachers. Essentially, school guidance counseling is accepted as an equally important curriculum and treated accordingly.

Many school counselors work in environments where they do not have core curriculums. They arrange to deliver prevention programs via large group guidance independently of the curriculum by working around the schedule. This requires cooperation from school administrators and teachers and leads to less comprehensive prevention programming than is the case with core curriculums. For example, during the fall semester of an academic year, a hypothetical elementary school counselor might present a unit to enhance self-esteem in the classes of kindergarten teachers who want to cooperate and also might provide a study skills program for students who are interested and whose teachers will let them leave the classroom to participate.

Whether prevention programs are delivered via core curriculums or by working around the academic curriculums, the programs can be either direct or indirect. Prevention programs can be delivered directly and indirectly in core curriculums and in programs that are adapted to the academic curriculum. Whichever of these circumstances may occur, the competencies to be presented remain valid.

FORMALIZING AND SPECIFYING PREVENTION PROGRAMMING

Foundations

According to the ASCA (2012), the fruits of prevention programming should be available to all students and should be focused on promoting maximum personal development. Dagley (1987) recommends that these general principles focus on school counselor activities devoted to enhancing individual development on distinct goals related to lifelong learning, personal effectiveness, and life roles. Table 7.1 presents a summary of Dagley's proposal. The goals and outcomes in Table 7.1 offer an inventory of the foundations on which school counselors' prevention programming is based.

Like the counseling function, prevention programming is immersed in a developmental context. One example of the developmental perspective is the work of Havighurst (1972), who identified developmental tasks that must be mastered at various developmental stages in order to achieve happiness and be able to cope with later tasks. Examples of Havighurst's tasks are (a) learning to relate emotionally to family members (infancy and childhood), (b) learning appropriate social roles (middle childhood), and

TABLE 7.1   *Foundations on Which Prevention Programming Is Based*

Personal Effectiveness Competencies	Self-Understanding (identity, autonomy, acceptance, validation)
	Human Relations (respect, empathy, social interest, conflict resolution)
	Health Development (intimacy, leisure, growth stages)
Lifelong Learning Competencies	Communication (reading and writing, listening, expressiveness, assertiveness)
	Information Processing (study and analysis, evaluation, problem solving)
	Personal Enrichment (time management, renewal, change)
Life Roles Competencies	Daily Living (child rearing, consumerism, community involvement)
	Career Planning (values clarification, decision making, planning, goal setting)
	Employability (self-placement, work habits, educational and occupational preparation)

Source: "A New Look at Developmental Guidance: The Hearthstone of School Counseling," by J. C. Dagley, 1987, *School Counselor, 35,* p. 103. Copyright 1987 by American Counseling Association.

(c) preparing for an economic career (adolescence). The ideas of Havighurst remind us that human development is complex and varied and that individuals develop at different rates although common themes are found within age groups. Knowledge of human development appears to be an imperative foundation for prevention programming by school counselors.

Thus, prevention programming is often based on developmental theory. That is, the goals and objectives of the programs are designed to achieve outcomes that enhance the development of the recipients and help them to meet important developmental tasks. An example is the ASCA National Standards for Students (ASCA, 2014). The Standards are presented in three general clusters: academic development, career development, and personal/social development. The following example indicates how the idea of using developmental theory to identify goals/objectives and competencies that can be acquired and measured in order to achieve the goals/objectives gets played out. Standard A under Academic Development is "Students will acquire the attitudes, knowledge and skills that contribute to effective learning in school and across the life span." Competency A.A3 states, "Achieve School Success." The following indicators are presented under A.A3 to be used to determine if the goal-driven competency is achieved: take responsibility for their actions; demonstrate the ability to work independently, as well as the ability to work cooperatively with other students; develop a broad range of interests and abilities; demonstrate dependability, productivity and initiative; and share knowledge.

Sears (2005) points out that, although developing large group guidance programs based on developmental theory is useful for primary prevention programming, many students are faced with challenges that block their ability to respond successfully. Sears's recommendation is to use large group guidance interventions to assist at-risk students (i.e., secondary prevention) by helping them to learn skills that they should have learned previously at home or in the schools. Designed to replace previously learned dysfunctional responses, these programs might focus on such goals as helping at-risk students to achieve self-control, manage their anger, and learn how to peacefully resolve conflicts. This idea suggests that prevention programming might best consist of two layers. The first layer is to focus on all students (primary prevention), and the second layer focuses on at-risk students (secondary prevention) who are unable to take sufficient advantage of the primary prevention programming.

Ingredients

Prevention programming seems to require careful planning. Adherence to specific steps is as important to prevention programming as it is to counseling and consulting interventions. The major steps in prevention programming are planning, delivering, transferring, and evaluating. *Planning* includes assessing the needs of the prospective recipients, setting goals and objectives, researching, and recruiting and selecting participants. *Delivering* includes lesson planning, instructing, demonstrating, and directing. *Transferring* involves providing opportunities for students to transfer their learning to the real world. The ingredients of the delivering component are also important in transferring. *Evaluating* includes assessing, analyzing, and reporting. Together, these ingredients are the basic components of proactive prevention programming.

BASIC COMPETENCIES IN PREVENTION PROGRAMMING

PLANNING

Assessing Needs

Counselors are encouraged to engage in the measurement and assessment activities that will help them identify the perceived, expressed, and assumed needs of their public. Fall (1994) refers to this first step as asking questions. Direct measurement and assessment of perceived and expressed needs involve counselors in sampling and surveying activities with accompanying skills. Assumed needs can be learned from reading the professional and popular literature. Results of needs assessments may be reported to interested individuals and entities; thus, reporting is an important skill. Needs assessment, whatever the method, sets the stage for setting goals and objectives.

Setting Goals and Objectives

The terms *goal* and *objective* have been used both interchangeably and separately—*goal* meaning a more general purpose, and *objective* meaning the more specific purposes assigned to general goal achievement. Whichever meanings counselors assign to these terms, the requisite skills are constant. Counselors are challenged to translate needs into goals. For instance, if a local needs assessment survey results in a public demand for the school system to do something about the drug abuse problem among teenagers, one goal will be to reduce drug abuse in that group. One objective related to that goal will be to teach adolescents at risk of abusing drugs to respond to peer pressure more assertively. Notice that the example goal and objective are stated in measurable terms. This allows the individuals delivering such programs to assess their ability to achieve the goals and objectives; that is, instances of increased or decreased drug use and acquisition of assertiveness skills can be measured. The results can be offered as evidence of achieving or not achieving the program goals and objectives. Counselors and their publics will be better served if they state their goals and objectives in measurable terms.

Researching

Having established goals and objectives, counselors may use them to determine the content of their prevention programming. Necessary content may be material with which they are familiar or unfamiliar. When necessary, counselors may have to locate, read, and abstract material from various resources. Therefore, they will benefit from being familiar with available libraries; catalogs of publications, media, and assessment instruments; consultants; relevant professional organizations; and various governmental, service, private, fraternal, and special interest organizations that may have useful information. The Internet has expanded the potential for school counselors to engage in this researching function in the 21st century. There is a limit to the knowledge base that counselors should be expected to have at the outset. In other words, counselors will not be able to deliver all programs for all people on demand. What kinds of prevention programming should counselors be able to deliver initially?

One possibility is that counselors are able to use the competencies they acquired during graduate school. Much of what was learned in counselor education programs can be translated into prevention programming. Some examples are basic interpersonal communication and challenging skills training, decision-making and problem-solving training, peer helper training, teaching individuals to cope with and change irrational thinking, a variety of applications of behavioral rehearsal (e.g., applying for jobs, meeting new people, coping with stressful relationships), self-management training, assertiveness training, relaxation training, career information-seeking and information-processing, career planning, gaming, cartooning, playing, clarifying and sharing values, support groups, process groups, and parent and teacher groups that focus on any of this content. This is a relatively comprehensive list that can be expanded through research and experience, leaving the impression that counselors can offer much through their prevention programming.

Recruiting and Selecting Participants

On occasion, prevention programming might be offered on a voluntary basis, and counselors will need to recruit volunteers successfully. This involves using information-sharing skills and being able to motivate children and adolescents, as well as being truthful. Circumstances may lead counselors to select possible participants from a pool of volunteers, or counselors may have to determine group membership for individuals in the pool. When engaging in selection activities, counselors again may use their information-sharing skills. For example, they may be challenged to explain their selection decisions to inquiring individuals. In addition, they may use diagnostic and assessment skills to match the right opportunities with the appropriate individuals.

DELIVERING

Lesson Planning

Lesson planning involves several important components. The ideas culled from researching can be organized around the goals and objectives to form a coherent plan for delivering a program. Lesson plans are organized on a global and unit basis. A global lesson plan covers the entire program, detailing the proposed goals and events sequentially. The events are daily or single-unit lesson plans. Basic ingredients of lesson plans are objectives, materials/resources, identification of the audience, an outline of the planned action steps for presenting the program, identification of information individuals need to participate in the lessons, homework assignments, and evaluation strategies. A sample lesson plan follows:

LESSON PLAN FOR AN ANXIETY MANAGEMENT PROGRAM

Objectives (stated so that each objective identifies specific desired outcomes behaviorally that can be measured)

- Participants will be able to generate at least one self-defeating and one self-improving thought without assistance or coaching.
- Participants will contribute to a discussion about applying self-statements to stressful situations in their lives.

Materials/Resources

- Chalkboard, whiteboard, or overhead projector to record information generated during the discussion.
- Assertiveness handouts to be distributed as homework for the next lesson.

Audience

- Male and female ninth-grade students who have volunteered to participate in the program.

Action Steps

- Have participants generate a list of anxiety-provoking situations.
- Review the notion of self-improving thoughts.
- Have participants generate and share one self-defeating and one corresponding self-improving thought for the anxiety-provoking situations they previously listed.
- Discuss how the self-statements may be applied in a stressful situation.
- Distribute assertiveness handouts.
- Introduce assertiveness training and review the important components of appropriate assertive responses by reading the handout aloud.
- Ask participants to read the assertiveness handout and to practice applying coping self-statements in real-life stressful situations as homework.

Evaluation Strategies (parallel to the stated behavioral objectives)

- Participants keep a record of the self-defeating and self-improving thoughts as they occur in their daily experiences.
- Observe participation during the discussion.

Fall (1994) provides an example of a situation that might require a global plan. A fifth-grade teacher asks an elementary school counselor for assistance with initiating a classroom guidance unit. Goals for the teacher include learning about group membership and developing skills for leading a group. Related objectives might be that the teacher will learn how to include all students in the group activities and how to get the students to work cooperatively in the group activities. Action steps might include providing printed information and helping the teacher understand and process that information. The counselor might follow this by demonstrating the targeted skills and by providing opportunities for the teacher to practice those behaviors via simulations. The counselor offers constructive feedback until the teacher is ready to engage in classroom guidance with the students.

Counselors are also challenged to create environments that ensure their lesson plans will be successful. In a school setting where there is no core curriculum, this involves arranging for rooms, adapting or developing the master schedule so that targeted individuals can participate, informing administrators and teachers of the program goals and obtaining their cooperation, and securing the cooperation of resource persons such as librarians, speakers and presenters, media coordinators, and custodians—all of whom are vital to the success of the program. Pursuing the example just presented, the counselor might ask the teacher to have the students engage in reading and writing assignments related to the guidance unit. For example, students might be encouraged to write in journals about preassigned topics that coincide with objectives for the guidance unit (Fall, 1994).

Instructing

The term *instructing* as used here refers to behaviors through which people who assume the instructor's role in prevention programming engage in the direct or indirect imparting of information to members of the group. Different forms of direct instructing occur in prevention programming situations. Lecturing, explaining, and reading are prominent examples. Video, audio, film, and graphic media are indirect methods to impart information, as are printed and computer-generated materials. Providing information is an important component of prevention programming, and counselors will be challenged to do this in ways that are interesting and motivating. It seems as if it is as important to prevention programming for counselors to lecture, explain, and read to audiences interestingly as it is for them to listen empathically and to respond facilitatively during responsive counseling interventions. It seems as if it is equally important for counselors to select and prepare media aids and handout materials that are interesting and motivating. Experience indicates that successful instructing leads to a mutually facilitative relationship between the leader and the members of a group, just as successful basic communicating leads to a facilitative counseling relationship. In both instances, acquisition of a facilitative relationship is the foundation for achieving goals successfully.

Demonstrating

Guidance curriculum programs often focus on teaching such skills as communicating with other people more proficiently, making rational decisions, and asserting oneself. In these instances, counselors are challenged to demonstrate the skills adequately. The process is social modeling (Bandura & Jeffery, 1973). Models can be living people, or they can be symbolic—people in films or videos. Counselors may serve as models themselves, select and train others to serve as models, or develop or locate appropriate symbolic models to provide adequate demonstrations. In addition, counselors will benefit from being familiar with research on modeling to enhance the effectiveness of their demonstrations.

For example, effects are enhanced when there is a similarity between the model and the participants—a model who is coping well, though not perfectly, may be more effective than one who has mastered the skills. Repeated demonstrations are often necessary (Cormier, Nurius, & Osborn, 2013). For example, a counselor might help a teacher by demonstrating how to interact with students when trying to get them to work cooperatively in a group. If the counselor is viewed as a competent, coping model, the probability of helping the teacher is enhanced. Achieving the goal occurs through communicating to the teacher that the counselor is not perfect and does not expect the teacher to be perfect but is performing to the best of his or her ability and appears to the teacher to be providing useful suggestions. Successful demonstrating sets the stage for participants to rehearse the skills. As participants rehearse or practice, counselors direct.

Several important behaviors are associated with directing. While helping participants acquire the desired skills, counselors may coach them through the steps and repetitions, provide encouragement, give accurate and useful feedback, determine helpful homework assignments, and discern when the participants have achieved a desirable level of skill or have gone as far as they can to achieve the targeted objectives. Coaching involves instructing and providing cues that help participants determine how they are doing or what to do next. Coaching may be manifested through recommending repeated practices, altering the time devoted to practicing, arranging and rearranging the sequence of practice activities, or offering verbal or physical support (Cormier et al., 2013).

Encouraging is best done via applications of learning principles such as positive reinforcement, withdrawal of reinforcement, and time-outs. Feedback provides participants information about the quality of their rehearsing efforts. Counselors contribute by providing feedback that helps participants recognize what is desirable and undesirable about their efforts. When offering prevention programs, it is important to dispense feedback judiciously and with as much care and empathy as is provided when engaging in counseling interventions. Keeping up-to-date on research about feedback is as important as it is for modeling. For example, participants may have opportunities to assess their own performances, verbal assessment may be supplemented with objective assessment, and verbal feedback may contain encouragement and suggestions for improvement (Cormier et al., 2013).

Appropriate homework assignments can help participants acquire the desired skills and knowledge and lay the foundation for developing desirable ideas. Helpful homework also lays the foundation for transfer of training. Counselors can give assignments to teachers (indirect delivery), and teachers or counselors can give assignments to the student participants (direct delivery). Counselors might ask teachers to practice in front of a mirror at home, reading information about leading small, structured groups, and instructing and encouraging students to work cooperatively. Teachers and counselors can ask students who are to be working cooperatively on an activity to distribute components of the activity among themselves voluntarily and set a date for each to have the assigned component ready for sharing and for integrating the components into one joint endeavor. The assignments help the participants engage in constructive, goal-directed activities that, if accomplished successfully, provide evidence that the participants have achieved skills commensurate with the goals of the project.

To be effective at giving homework assignments, counselors may need to explain the purpose and to inform participants about what they are to do, where it is to occur, how often it is to occur, and how it is to be recorded (Cormier et al., 2013). At some time during the rehearsal and homework cycle, counselors will probably need to decide whether participants are achieving targeted levels of accomplishment. If the decision is affirmative, counselors can focus on transfer of training, closure, and evaluation. If the decision is negative, they can determine whether the best alternative is to recycle the participant(s) or to end the training. To make these decisions, counselors will be challenged to assess, to diagnose, and to make rational decisions. In so doing, counselors may find it necessary to apply all the basic and challenging counseling skills as carefully as they do when engaging in counseling interventions.

TRANSFERRING

The ultimate goal of prevention programming is transfer or generalization of training to one's natural environment. Goals, training activities, and homework assignments serve us best when they reflect a plan to help participants apply what is being taught to the real world. Procedures for achieving this transfer of training have been identified and discussed previously.

EVALUATING

Assessing the effects of all counseling functions is important. Suffice it to say that evaluation is among the requisite prevention programming skills. This evaluation must consider (a) whether prevention programming objectives have been met, (b) the perceptions of stakeholders concerning prevention programs, and (c) the cost-effectiveness of those programs.

EXAMPLES OF PREVENTION PROGRAMMING

In this section, we present information about prevention programs that have been or could be developed. Each program is presented with its own heading. We did this because the problems to be prevented and the areas of human development to be enhanced seem very important in these times. As a group, the examples represent the three important domains advocated by the ASCA National Model (ASCA, 2012): academic development, career development, and personal/social development.

HELPING STUDENTS TO BECOME SELF-REGULATED LEARNERS

A schematic for helping students to become self-regulated, successful learners is offered by Lapan, Kardash, and Turner (2002). Self-regulated learning is a process where goals are set by the learners who work to regulate and monitor their behavior and thinking (Pintrich, 2000). Self-regulated learners can control planning, performing, and completing stages of the learning process and focus on mastering tasks, improving skills, and understanding information. They also use a variety of strategies and tend to attribute poor performance to ineffective strategies rather than inability.

Lapan et al. (2002) elaborate on the value of helping students to become more engaged in academics, especially in consideration of national initiatives to help all students to be successful learners. Their presentation covers the importance of many of the competencies in a balanced program. In this chapter, we focus on their suggestions that can be translated into prevention programming.

The information presented by Lapan et al. (2002) suggests that school counselors could develop and initiate proactive prevention programs designed to help any student become a self-regulated learner. They offer the following categories of learning strategies that are known to enhance academic performance. The goals of a prevention program would be to teach students these effective learning strategies and to motivate them to use the strategies. The strategies are the ability to (a) separate important from nonessential information, (b) identify main ideas, (c) relate new information to prior knowledge, (d) take effective notes, (e) organize information into useful subsets, (f) monitor whether information is truly understood, and (g) construct internal images that represent the meaning of information studied.

The following tactics for teaching effective learning strategies, recommended by Lapan et al. (2002), could be melded into a prevention program: (a) explain the effective learning strategy to the participants, (b) model/demonstrate the strategy while sharing thoughts aloud, (c) have participants practice the strategy continuously on several important learning tasks, (d) use both covert (e.g., mental imagery) and overt (e.g., physical performance) rehearsals, (e) have students practice with their peers, (f) help participants learn ways to monitor and evaluate their own performance, (g) help students realize concrete benefits of using the strategies, and (h) involve participants in the process of modifying and constructing new strategies.

TEACHING COPING SKILLS

Teaching children and adolescents how to cope successfully with life's various stressors may prepare them for such events in advance of occurrences (primary prevention) or help them manage challenges that are already influencing their lives (secondary prevention). For example, Hains (1992, 1994) reports on the effectiveness of teaching youths to recognize, monitor, and alter stress-arousing or anxiety-provoking thoughts. Romano, Miller, and Nordness (1996) describe a stress management and student well-being curriculum for elementary school students that consists of six 45-minute lessons integrated into the fifth- and sixth-grade curriculums, including the importance of physical exercise, good nutrition, focusing on and identifying feelings and expressing them positively, communicating well with one's parents, and learning problem-solving skills. Some components of the program engage their parents as well. Deffenbacher, Lynch, Oetting, and Kemper (1996) found that teaching sixth-through-eighth-grade students with high anger thresholds to identify anger-provoking situations, acquire specific relaxation skills, and learn how their thought-influenced anger led to increased control of their expressions of anger. The sequential training includes learning how to calm down while visualizing anger-provoking situations and replacing the anger-producing thoughts with controlling thoughts that are more calming. Shechtman (2001) demonstrated that prevention goals can be achieved in small groups as well as in large group interventions. She reported being able to reduce aggressive behaviors and enhance social skills of young children via a small counseling group intervention.

An example of a coping skills training program is found in Kiselica, Baker, Thomas, and Reedy (1994). Participants in the program were ninth graders enrolled in a guidance class in a rural high school. They met once per week during 60-minute sessions for 8 weeks. The program combines elements of Meichenbaum and Deffenbacher's (1988) stress inoculation training, assertiveness training (Galassi & Galassi, 1977), and progressive muscle relaxation (Bernstein & Borkovec, 1973).

After receiving instruction about stress, stressors, anxiety, and anxiety-related symptoms, participants generate examples of their own anxiety-provoking experiences. Next, participants are taught progressive muscle relaxation through a series of exercises, learning how to transfer the skills to in vivo situations. Then, participants are taught to elicit the relaxation response by repeating a cue word during anxiety-provoking situations. The following step is to teach participants how to identify negative thoughts that lead to self-defeating behaviors and replace them with self-improving thoughts, learning how the process (cognitive-restructuring) works. This process is combined with progressive muscle relaxation in practice sessions and in vivo homework. Following discussion of the importance of appropriate assertiveness, participants engage in simulations designed to enhance their assertiveness skills.

Combining cognitive restructuring with progressive muscle relaxation and assertiveness training approaches coping with anxiety arousal from a multimodal perspective. Because the school environment is a source of many anxiety-arousing experiences for children and adolescents, stress-inoculation training holds promise for providing coping skills that can be learned and generalized to the real world via proactive primary and secondary prevention programming (Baker, 2001).

PREJUDICE PREVENTION

Ponterotto and Pedersen (1993) believe that adolescents, because they are learning to depend on their cognitive skills and are becoming more comfortable with abstract thinking, are at a stage when prejudice prevention may be developmentally appropriate. Concluding that prejudice is caused by stereotypical beliefs that become more important than real people, Ponterotto and Pedersen recommend several exercises designed to increase awareness of ethnic, racial, and cultural identity. An example is the Label Game, the objective of which is to discover what others believe about each individual participant.

The steps in this exercise are (a) prepare a set of labels containing positive adjectives (e.g., friendly, generous, helpful) and attach one to the forehead or back of each participant so that the label cannot be seen by its wearer; (b) have participants mingle while discussing a topic of interest without any additional structure; (c) instruct participants to treat each individual in a manner that reflects the label he or she is wearing; (d) instruct participants not to inform each other about the content of the labels; and (e) instruct each participant to attempt to guess his or her own label before it is removed.

Debriefing includes asking the participants to share with each other how they used feedback from interacting with others to figure out the content of their own labels. They also discuss how it feels to be labeled and treated as if the label were accurate. Components of the exercise are used to introduce such concepts as stereotyping, prejudice, and communication barriers. It is hoped that participants become aware that we do label each other, that there are differences important to each person's identity, and that the differences are not always bad: Diversity is an important reality. The remaining components of the program are designed to help participants engage in meaningful and enjoyable activities that lead to processing important information related to prejudice prevention.

PREVENTION OF SCHOOL VIOLENCE AND BULLYING

School violence and bullying are pervasive problem in schools today, so many state regulatory agencies have mandated that schools be responsive to these threats to children's safety (Sacco, Silbaugh, Corredor, Casey, & Doherty, 2012). Like most education issues, school violence and bullying are complex matters, requiring substantial attention from school counselors, school administrators, and teachers.

Psychologist Harry Stack Sullivan (1947) wrote, "In most general terms, we are all much more simply human than otherwise, be we happy and successful, contented and detached, miserable and mentally disordered, or whatever" (p. 7). He believed that human beings often think of themselves as alienated—alone in the world—having problems and concerns unlike those of other people. This construct, known as the "delusion of uniqueness," appears to be at the core of school violence—where children and adolescents, alienated from their peers and feeling unconnected with the school community—and often subjected to bullying—turn to planning and implementing violent acts that bring wide attention on television news and various Internet venues, including social networks.

As school counselors design proposals for the prevention of bullying, for example, they need to take into consideration, at minimum, these constituencies—school administrators, teachers, students, parents and guardians, and law enforcement personnel.

School Administrators

School counselors should work with school leaders to (a) be available and visible in hallways and other public places in school and to observe student behavior firsthand, (b) establish school-wide codes of conduct that value acceptable behavior and set consequences for bullying and other unacceptable actions, and (c) plan events that make positive school values evident and clear.

Teachers

School counselors should work to (a) collaborate with teachers on classroom programs that feature activities and materials demonstrating the value of positive behaviors and highlighting the negative impact of bullying behaviors, (b) be with teachers as they discuss matters related to bullying and other behaviors that may lead to violence, and (c) stand with teachers as they manage the challenges of student behavior within and outside the classroom.

Students

School counselors should work to (a) be where students are and readily available to reinforce positive student interactions, (b) know students who are likely candidates for bullying and to intervene when necessary, and (c) show students care and empathy beyond the walls of the counseling office.

Parents and/or Guardians

School counselors should work with parents to (a) coach children in healthy antibullying behaviors (e.g., walking away from bullies and ignoring bullies), (b) model behaviors that exemplify effective communication of dissatisfaction and anger, and (c) spend time at school whether simply visiting on occasion or being active in parent/teacher associations.

Law Enforcement Personnel

School counselors should work with school resource officers and law enforcement personnel to (a) build positive, trusting school and community relationships, (b) collaborate in understanding the laws surrounding bullying behavior, and (c) be aware of the warning signs of bullying and other behaviors that contribute to school violence.

CONFLICT RESOLUTION

An important response to widespread concern about violence in the schools has been the development and implementation of conflict resolution programming. Attempts to implement conflict resolution programming vary from individual programs to those integrated into the core curriculum of a school system.

Carruthers, Carruthers, Day-Vines, Bostick, and Watson (1996) described the core conflict resolution curriculum in the Wake County, North Carolina, public schools. The goals are to (a) help make the schools orderly and peaceful, (b) use conflict as an instructional tool, (c) teach participants to generalize what they have learned to future interpersonal interactions, and (d) reinforce the core curriculum goals and objectives. This curriculum has a developmental overlay in which the focus shifts across grade levels to make units relevant to students at different grade levels (e.g., greater emphasis on interpersonal relations in the early grades, conflict resolution in the upper elementary grades, conflict at the middle school level, violence at the high school level). Examples of four objectives recommended for specific subjects in the curriculum are as follows:

- *Kindergarten:* The student will dramatize the appropriate behavior when confronted with various warning signs, sounds, and symbols (subject: health living);
- *Second grade:* The student will demonstrate the ability to infer (subject: science);
- *Fourth grade:* The student will propose alternatives to impulsive behavior (subject: healthful living);
- *Seventh grade:* The student will exercise social and interpersonal persuasion (subject: healthful living).

One popular form of conflict resolution is *peer mediation,* which can be provided as a total school program, as an elective course, or by training selected mediators (Lupton-Smith, Carruthers, Flythe, Goettee, & Modest, 1996). Lupton-Smith et al. describe three peer mediation programs, one of which is in a middle school with the in-school suspension coordinator serving as the program coordinator. In the preliminary stage, a core group of school staff members are trained, and the entire staff agrees to refer conflicts between students to mediation before treating them as discipline problems. All sixth graders receive 10 days of conflict resolution instruction in their health classes and are informed about the function of peer mediation in their schools via short assemblies. Parents are informed at an open house. Selected student mediators receive 20 hours of training that focuses on (a) engaging in self-introspection, (b) considering how to deal with conflict, (c) learning how to use active listening skills in the mediation process, and (d) practicing in simulated sessions. Time is set aside for peer mediation sessions each day in a 30-minute period after lunch known as *teen development time.* Mediation sessions take place in a room adjacent to the coordinator's office with the door between the two rooms left open.

The importance of recruiting and selecting a diverse set of peer mediators is highlighted by Day-Vines, Day-Hariston, Carruthers, Wall, and Lupton-Smith (1996). They propose that, rather than be represented proportionally, all segments of the school's population should be represented equally.

COMPREHENSIVE DEVELOPMENTAL GUIDANCE

Considerably broader in perspective than the programs just covered, comprehensive developmental guidance programs, as perceived by Gysbers and Henderson (2000), are integrated into the school's curriculum. Primary characteristics of these programs are as follows: They (a) are similar to other programs in education (focused on student outcomes, have activities designed to help students achieve the outcomes, are facilitated by professionally recognized personnel, use curriculum-enhancing resources, and employ student evaluation); (b) are based on developmental principles; (c) represent a full range of guidance services (e.g., assessment, referral, placement, consultation); and (d) involve all school staff members.

The underlying theme or theoretical perspective of the guidance curriculum is *life career development.* "Life career development is defined as self-development over the life span through the integration of the roles, settings, and events in a person's life" (Gysbers & Henderson, 2000, p. 62). Four domains of human growth and development are emphasized in life career development: (1) self-knowledge and interpersonal skills; (2) life roles, settings, and events; (3) life career planning; and (4) basic studies and occupational preparation. The major delivery systems are the school counseling and instructional programs.

Prevention programming is an essential ingredient in comprehensive developmental guidance whether in the school counseling or the instructional program of a school, school district, or state school system. A concrete example, taken from Gysbers and Henderson (2000), is the following curriculum goals for a school district: Students will (a) understand and respect themselves and others; (b) behave responsibly in the school, family, and community; (c) develop decision-making skills; (d) use their educational opportunities well; (e) communicate effectively; and (f) plan and prepare for personally satisfying and socially useful lives. These goals will generate competencies that, in turn, generate educational strategies and materials to support them. For the goal "develop decision-making skills," the recommended competencies are (a) making wise choices, (b) managing change successfully, and (c) solving problems. Subcompetencies for "making wise choices" are (a) awareness of how decisions are made, (b) exploration of use of the process, and (c) implementation of the decision-making process.

More than as a method of implementing the prevention programming concept, Gysbers and Henderson (2000) view their idea as a way to reconceptualize school guidance and reform education. This developmental guidance model is the framework for the school counseling core curriculum in the ASCA National Model (ASCA, 2012).

A MODEL SUBSTANCE ABUSE PREVENTION PROGRAM

Swisher, Bechtel, Henry, Vicary, and Smith (2001) describe a substance abuse prevention program that may be integrated into school curriculums under the leadership of school counselors. Adoption of Drug Abuse Prevention Training (Project ADAPT) is an initiative funded by the National Institute on Drug Abuse that was instituted and evaluated over a 5-year period prior to publication by Swisher et al. (2001). Project Adapt employs Botvin's (1998) Life Skills Training concept by helping teachers to integrate targeted skills, concepts, and content into their subject matter curriculums. Because teachers are to be involved actively in the design and delivery of this programming, school counselors are viewed as excellent sources of consultation, modeling, and coaching. For example, Botvin's program includes such activities as group discussions, role-plays, and hands-on activities. School counselors may also contribute by helping teachers find and use developmentally appropriate teaching aids, recruiting capable teachers, and assessing the effects of program implementation. Project ADAPT staff members reported that participating teachers displayed a considerable amount of creativity and initiative.

The goals of Botvin's program are that student participants will (a) learn to resist social pressure to use alcohol, tobacco, and other drugs; (b) develop an enhanced sense of self-direction; (c) be better able to cope with anxiety; (d) acquire improved decision-making skills; (e) improve their basic communication and social skills; (f) acquire increased knowledge about the risks associated with using alcohol, tobacco, and other drugs; and (g) develop healthy beliefs and attitudes consistent with avoiding substance abuse. Swisher et al. (2001) present a sample lesson plan matrix from a rural middle school that implemented the program. It indicates how specific life skills training components such as decision making, coping with anxiety, and assertiveness are infused/integrated into various curriculums. For example, decision making was approached in geography via a travel exercise in which routes had to be chosen on a map. In earth science, the students considered the pros and cons of space travel. They were taught the steps in personal decision making in a personal development course.

HELPING PARTICIPANTS IMPROVE ACADEMIC ACHIEVEMENT AND SCHOOL SUCCESS BEHAVIOR

Research has shown a relationship between student problem behaviors and academic achievement (Wanzek, Roberts, & Al Otaiba, 2013). Johnson and Hannon (2014), for example, have examined the relationship between academic achievement and reports from teachers and parents about student problem behaviors. Problem behaviors can disrupt instruction in the classroom and can hinder activities designed to facilitate learning.

On the basis of reviews of research that identified clusters of skills needed for school success, a combined group counseling and group guidance program titled Student Success Skills was designed for fifth-, sixth-, eighth-, and ninth-grade students (Brigman & Campbell, 2003). This report focuses on the group guidance component. The skills clusters derived from the aforementioned reviews were (a) cognitive and meta-cognitive skills such as goal setting, progress monitoring, and memory skills; (b) social skills such as interpersonal skills, social problem solving, listening, and teamwork skills; and (c) self-management skills such as managing attention, motivation, and anger.

The topics for the group guidance program were based on the three skill clusters. The school counselors involved in this program were trained to provide a specifically structured presentation to the participants. Components of a typical presentation were as follows: The first part of a presentation was designed to introduce the topic and stimulate participant motivation to care about the topic. Participants were also asked to share what they already know about the topic. In the second part, school counselors presented information about the specific component to be covered (e.g., goal setting) in a manner that engaged the participants in the process. The third part found the participants applying the information previously presented in small group discussions. The younger children were divided into pairs. In the final part of a presentation, the participants summarized and set personal goals. In general, the program goals were to have participants reflect on what they did and learned in the sessions and discover ways to transfer that knowledge to the real world.

DESIGNING PROACTIVE PROGRAMS TO ACHIEVE PREVENTION AND DEVELOPMENTAL GOALS: THE CHALLENGE

In a survey of elementary, middle, and high school counselors selected randomly from the membership of the ASCA, Bowman (1987) posed several important questions about the state of "small group guidance and counseling" in basic education. He found that counselors at all levels agree that these are important functions, although high school counselors find them less practical. A variety of topics such as decision making, communication skills and peer helping, self-concept, study skills, career, behavior, and family were identified as having been presented across grade levels with different emphases because of developmental needs. Finding time to engage in prevention programming, coping with resistance from others, and feeling competent in a pedagogical domain were the three categories in which the majority of respondents' professed problems occurred.

It seems clear that counselor education programs face a challenge: helping graduates learn about prevention programming and how to implement prevention programs. School counselors are challenged to know how to plan, deliver, and evaluate such programs; they also will benefit from ideas for coping with the practical challenges of competition for time and space, resistance, and ignorance that are associated with working in school systems. For instance, creative counselors, when attempting to resolve the time challenge, use lunch break groups, form groups of students attending the same study halls, make their groups an option during general activity periods, alternate class periods on a weekly basis to prevent participants from missing the same class every week, and cooperate with teachers to make their prevention programming ideas units in the teachers' classes.

EVALUATING PREVENTION PROGRAMMING: ONE PATHWAY TO ACHIEVING ACCOUNTABILITY

THE CHALLENGE OF PROVIDING EVIDENCE OF PREVENTION PROGRAMMING COMPETENCE

Evaluation of student results, school counselor performance and program completeness is essential to ensuring the effectiveness and relevance of school counseling programs, and it requires the collection and use of data (ASCA, 2012). On the surface, it appears as if evaluating prevention programs or guidance curricula should be a relatively straightforward process. Yet there is more to consider than what initially comes to mind, making this evaluation and accountability process a considerable challenge. That which initially comes to mind may proceed as follows: Prevention programming often is manifested by delivering programs to participants in large group settings. The programs are based on previously determined goals and objectives. Therefore, the evaluation will consist of determining whether the goals were achieved by examining or observing the participants at the close of the program.

Unfortunately, following this line of thinking may lead to collecting data that do not conclusively rule out alternative explanations for the results of the end-of-program assessments and observations because methods for controlling the alternative explanations have not been employed. Alternative explanations for the findings are caused by a myriad of other events in the lives of the participants (e.g., assignments in other classes, reading related materials, learning similar information elsewhere, the effects of one's home environment, and natural maturation). These other events may have a concurrent impact while they are involved in the prevention programming.

In order to control the alternative explanations of the perceived gains found in end-of-program evaluations, professional school counselors will have to use program designs and assessment strategies that are usually beyond their master's level training and expertise. These evaluation activities may be difficult or impossible to undertake in most K–12 school settings. For example, practitioner research designs that help program evaluators rule out alternative explanations of results-based data will require using control groups that would receive no programming or alternative programming with which the programs to be evaluated (aka treatment programs) could be compared. These methods are referred to as true experimental or quasi-experimental designs, and they require some form of random assignment of individual participants to groups (true experimental design), individual groups to treatment or control conditions (quasi-experimental design), or individual program presenters to treatment and control conditions. In addition, the results-based data from the respective evaluations usually must be analyzed via inferential statistical models such as analysis of variance (ANOVA).

We suspect that most of you, our readers, and professional school counselors will find the information presented in the previous paragraph both foreign and overly challenging to understand and implement. Experimental and quasi-experimental research is more often the domain of university faculty members than of professional school counselors.

One way to cope with the challenge of being overwhelmed by these evaluation designs is for professional counselors to work with university faculty members as "effective evaluation teams composed of skilled researchers and school-level practitioners using a variety of salient research methods" (Sink, 2005, p. 11). Although this is an excellent idea that may possibly be implemented somewhere, we believe that most professional school counselors will be unable to participate in such teams either because they do not have sufficient access to skilled researchers or because it will be impossible to implement experimental or quasi-experimental research designs in their settings.

A PROPOSAL FOR MEETING THE CHALLENGE

We understand that the following proposal will not meet the rigorous standards of experimental research. Yet we believe that it offers professional school counselors who do not have the experimental approach available to them a way to evaluate their prevention programming interventions in order to provide data that will help achieve accountability to themselves and their stakeholders. We present an overview here, and an example will follow.

Imagine that a prevention program has been designed or selected on the basis of perceived or expressed needs of students in one's school. All matters concerning preparation and implementation are in place, and specific goals and objectives have been stated. Outcome data should be collected at the beginning and end of the program.

The most useful outcome data will be that which can be directly measured or observed, that is, participants' assessment of the value of the program and whether they understood or retained the information presented and the skills taught. These results are not unlike those general attributes assessed in typical teacher-led classrooms, and control groups and the like are not required to achieve accountability in teacher-led classrooms.

Prevention programs may have goals and objectives that go beyond achieving participant support for the value of the program and evidence of delivering information and teaching skills successfully. Goals such as influencing attitudes like self-esteem and achievement motivation and enhancing academic performance (e.g., grades) are worthy yet virtually impossible to employ in our model because they require using the aforementioned experimental conditions to substantiate or rely on distal data.

Although such goals may be stated, we recommend that they be presented as hoped-for outcomes that seem to follow logically if the program intervention is well-received by the participants and the targeted information and skills are presented successfully. Logical assumptions about results can be supported by information drawn from published research. That is, professional counselors can cite the results of published research studies in support of their assumption that the present program may influence targeted attitudes or future behaviors even though one is unable to measure the effects at the end of the targeted program intervention. This establishes the importance of presenting prevention programming for which there are published outcome studies that support the merits of the targeted program goals and objectives (Brown & Trusty, 2005a). We offer more on this idea later.

The ASCA (2012) National Model states, "Having benefited from school counselors' interventions, students are more ready to learn academically and to be successful in school" (p. 140). In our example, a middle school counselor created a 6-week prevention program intervention designed to accomplish the following proximal objectives. Participants will (a) learn the basic principles of critical thinking, (b) apply critical thinking skills in a simulated exercise successfully, and (c) indicate that the intervention program was of value to them. The counselor collected proximal outcome data as follows.

To evaluate the first objective, immediately during the first meeting of the intervention, the participants completed an objectively scored test (e.g., multiple choice and true/false questions) covering the information about critical thinking that will be presented during the program. The same test was given during the final meeting, and the differences between pretesting and posttesting were used to determine whether the objective was achieved.

The second objective was assessed by having the participants engage in a simulated critical thinking exercise following the presentation-related information and a leader demonstration. The simulations were observed and rated on a predetermined performance scale in order to assess whether the second objective was accomplished.

To evaluate the third objective, all participants completed a survey about their attitudes toward the value of the program during the second and the last sessions. The first survey assessed their expectations after having experienced one session, and the second survey assessed their attitudes upon completion of the program. Both surveys provide information about whether the third objective was achieved.

Thus far, our proposal includes focusing on targeting outcome data that can be attributed to a specific intervention (i.e., participants' perceptions of the value of the program, acquisition of information presented, and acquisition of skills taught). These results lend themselves to paper-and-pencil objectively scored assessments similar to those used by classroom teachers and observations of participants demonstrating competence at skills that were taught. A final component of this proposal is to implement and evaluate the same prevention programming interventions numerous times and, if possible, in a variety of settings (e.g., different grade levels) (Brown & Trusty, 2005b). An accumulation of repeated successful outcomes increases the body of evidence in support of apparently successful prevention program interventions and enhances overall program accountability. This repeated presentation process also reduces concerns over the lack of control groups.

FINDING INFORMATION ABOUT THE EFFECTS OF PREVENTION PROGRAMS

There are many sources available, and the present listing is probably not exhaustive. Therefore, we recommend that individual professional school counselors continuously maintain a vigilant search for information that speaks to the merits of prevention programming interventions before employing them in their own settings, especially if they do not have the resources to conduct experimental or practitioner research in their schools.

Internet Resources

The following Internet sites may be fruitful. Like all such domains, some of the information presented is not necessarily useful to specific individuals. Thus, users are challenged to review the information carefully and selectively. One useful resource is offered by the Society for Prevention Research (www.preventionresearch.org/). Click on "Resources," then "Publications." Users will gain access to prevention research in a number of journals such as *Prevention Science, American Journal of Community Psychology,* and *The Journal of Primary Prevention.*

A second potentially useful Internet resource is the What Works Clearinghouse (www.whatworks.ed.gov). This site requires user patience that may prove fruitful. On an ongoing basis, the site presents information on studies of educational programs that were screened and identified as effective. Many of these studies are of programs outside of the school counseling or prevention domains.

A third source offered through the Ronald H. Fredrickson Center for School Counseling Outcome Research and Evaluation (www.CSCOR.org) is its publication of school counseling research briefs that provide continuous access to research-based information about school counseling, some of which may focus on prevention programming interventions. This site was introduced in Chapter 4.

Published Literature Reviews

On occasion, university scholars will collect and review sets of research studies on aspects of prevention programming interventions. The primary interest of these reviewers is usually to assess the merits of the research designs used and look for important themes about programmatic successes to report. School counseling practitioners may benefit most from identifying those program interventions that appear to work and with whom and then locating the sources that more fully describe the specific intervention programs in the reference sections of the reviews. At present, we are aware of only a few such reviews that may be of value to you and, like many journal publications, they may be somewhat dated—not covering more recent research. We list these reviews by author and date herein, and more complete retrieval information is in the reference section of this chapter. They are as follows: Baker, Swisher, Nadenichek, and Popowicz (1984), Baker and Taylor (1998), Borders and Drury (1992), and Whiston and Sexton (1998).

Using These Resources Successfully

The resources we listed earlier are the beginning of a multistage process in which professional school counselors are challenged to participate in order to receive the full fruits of their labors. In the first stage, users of the Internet sites or readers of the review articles seek and find information about prevention programs that may work. A second stage finds the counselors locating specific sources that have been identified in the first stage and reading them in a quest for information about the particulars of the highlighted programs. A third stage occurs when school counselors develop their own programs based on the information provided in the acquired sources. Delivering and evaluating the programs are the final stages. A quest for useful resources leads one through acquisition, preparation, and delivery stages to a point where evaluation leading to accountability is required to complete the process.

WHAT IF I'M NOT EDUCATED AS A TEACHER AND DREAD THE THOUGHT OF LEADING LARGE GROUP GUIDANCE CLASSES?

One of our counselor education interns in a large, public high school wrote the following in the final report about her internship:

> There were four counselors at my internship school. Each of them was able to lead *SELF BUILDING* sessions for students in about three classrooms during the semester of my internship. I observed some of the sessions; the counselors were well received, and the kids seemed to be very involved in the sessions. Interestingly, many kids were quite self-disclosing during the sessions. After one of the best sessions (with a class of seniors about ready to graduate), I asked the counselor who led the session how she felt about leading these kinds of classroom group activities. She responded that she would like to spend most of her time doing prevention and development classes with kids. She added, however, I was not educated to be a teacher.

This is a real issue for a number of students preparing to become school counselors and among those who are in the school counseling profession. Neuman (2006), who was a family counselor prior to entering the school counseling domain, offers a refreshing approach to coping with the challenge. She stated: "I would dread the thought of doing it. My voice is not loud and classroom management was not my forte. I've had a lot of training to be a counselor, but very little to be a teacher" (p. 5).

To her credit, Neuman (2006) recognized the challenge and decided to try to overcome it. The steps in her quest included (a) thinking of classroom guidance as just a big group (as in group counseling); (b) beginning the sessions by establishing ground rules just as in other groups (e.g., listen, be respectful to the teacher and others, and participate); (c) varying the activities; (d) incorporating learning styles and multiple intelligence information into her teaching style (e.g., visual cues to help children remember the lessons); (e) observing other counselors teaching large group guidance sessions; (f) using appropriate self-disclosure as a part of the lessons (i.e., letting the students know you are not perfect); (g) using the Internet and books to find useful materials; (h) knowing the students' needs; (i) making the lessons fun; and (j) continuing to work on her own attitude and presentation skills.

We close this section with the following observations from Neuman (2006): "The students look forward to my lessons and ask me when I'm coming back. Do I still dread the weeks when I teach? Well, not as much as I used to and it's something I'll continue to work on" (p. 5). So dreading large group presentations is something that needs to be recognized and worked on over time in order to be able to be a complete school counselor in the 21st century. School counselors who share this sentiment may want to consider some of the following activities in moving toward increased engagement in prevention programming.

COMPREHENSIVE SCHOOL COUNSELING PROGRAM COMPONENT

1.   Create a classroom guidance unit on a topic such as antibullying, academic success skills, or transitioning. Align the lessons with national and state school counseling standards and create a plan for measuring effectiveness. Remember to include perception, process, and outcome data.

REFLECTION POINT

1.   Take an inventory of prevention programming experiences and competencies you already possess. What additional competencies do you need to be more proficient at prevention programming? Why?

2.   Debate one theme of this chapter—for example, prevention programming competence is equally as important in school counseling as is clinical competence.

3.   Analyze, discuss, and/or debate the following statement: School counselors need not have been classroom teachers to offer prevention programming successfully.

4.   Prepare a document explaining how a counselor might convince parents or administrators that prevention programming is a valid school counseling function.

5.   Make an inventory of ideas from the section "Examples of Prevention Programming" that are most appealing to you. What are your reasons for selecting these ideas?

6.   Critique the merits of the evaluation/accountability proposal made in this chapter.

APPLICATION TO TECHNOLOGY

1.   Identify social media that can be used to enhance effective information sharing.

2.   Look on the Internet for a statistical package that can be used to analyze the data from the recommendation for evaluating prevention programs by comparing the results of assessments collected at the beginning of the program and then again at the end (e.g., correlated t tests, paired t tests, independent samples t tests).

REFERENCES

Adelman, H. S., & Taylor, L. (2002). School counselors and school reform: New directions. *Professional School Counseling, 5,* 235–248.

American School Counselor Association. (1978, April 1). A new look at developmental guidance. *ASCA Counselor, 16*(2–3), 11–12.

American School Counselor Association. (1999). *Role statement: The school counselor.* Alexandria, VA: Author.

American School Counselor Association. (2012). *The ASCA National Model: A framework for school counseling programs* (3rd ed.). Alexandria, VA: Author.

American School Counselor Association. (2014). *ASCA national standards for students.* Alexandria, VA: Author.

Baker, S. B. (2001). Coping skills training for adolescents: Applying cognitive behavioral principles to psychoeducational groups. *Journal for Specialists in Group Work, 26,* 219–227.

Baker, S. B., Swisher, J. D., Nadenichek, P., & Popowicz, C. L. (1984). Measured effects of primary prevention. *Personnel and Guidance Journal, 62,* 459–463.

Baker, S. B., & Taylor, J. G. (1998). Effects of career education interventions: A meta-analysis. *Career Development Quarterly, 46,* 376–385.

Bandura, A., & Jeffery, R. W. (1973). Roles of symbolic coding and rehearsal processes in observational learning. *Journal of Personality and Social Psychology, 26,* 122–130.

Bernstein, D. A., & Borkovec, T. D. (1973). *Progressive relaxation training.* Champaign, IL: Research Press.

Borders, L. D., & Drury, S. M. (1992). Comprehensive school counseling programs: A review for policy makers and practitioners. *Journal of Counseling and Development, 70,* 487–498.

Botvin, G. J. (1998). *Life skills training: Promoting health and personal development.* Princeton, NJ: Princeton Health Press.

Bowers, J., Hatch, T., & Schwallie-Giddis, P. (2001, September–October). The brain storm. *ASCA Counselor, 42,* 17–18.

Bowman, R. P. (1987). Small-group guidance and counseling in schools: A national survey of counselors. *School Counselor, 34,* 250–262.

Brigman, G., & Campbell, C. (2003). Helping students improve academic achievement and school success behavior. *Professional School Counseling, 7,* 91–98.

Brown, D., & Trusty, J. (2005a). School counselors, comprehensive school counseling programs, and academic achievement: Are school counselors promising more than they can deliver? *Professional School Counseling, 9,* 1–8.

Brown, D., & Trusty, J. (2005b). The ASCA National Model, accountability, and establishing causal links between school counselors' activities and student outcomes. *Professional School Counseling, 9,* 13–15.

Bryan, J., Day-Vines, N. L., Griffin, D., & Moore-Thomas, C. (2012). The disproportionality dilemma: Patterns of teacher referrals to school counselors for disruptive behavior. *Journal of Counseling and Development, 70*(2), 177–190.

Carey, J., & Dimmitt, C. (2012). School counseling and student outcomes: Summary of six statewide studies. *Professional School Counseling, 16,* 146–153.

Carruthers, W. L., Carruthers, B.J.B., Day-Vines, N. L., Bostick, D., & Watson, D. C. (1996). Conflict resolution as a curriculum: A definition, description, and process for integration in core curricula. *School Counselor, 43,* 345–373.

Cinotti, D. (2014). Competing professional identity models in school counseling: A historical perspective and commentary. *The Professional Counselor, 4,* 417–425.

Cormier, S., Nurius, P. S., & Osborn, C. J. (2013). *Interviewing strategies for helpers: Fundamental skills and cognitive-behavioral interventions* (7th ed.). Boston: Cengage Learning.

Cowen, E. L. (1982). Primary prevention research: Barriers, needs, and opportunities. *Journal of Primary Prevention, 2,* 131–137.

Dagley, J. C. (1987). A new look at developmental guidance: The hearthstone of school counseling. *School Counselor, 35,* 102–109.

Day-Vines, N. L., Day-Hariston, B. O., Carruthers, W. L., Wall, J. A., & Lupton-Smith, H. (1996). Conflict resolution: The value of diversity in the recruitment, selection, and training of peer mediators. *School Counselor, 43,* 392–410.

Deffenbacher, J. L., Lynch, R. S., Oetting, E. R., & Kemper, C. C. (1996). Anger reduction in early adolescents. *Journal of Counseling Psychology, 43,* 149–157.

DeKruyf, L., Auger, R. W., & Trice-Black, S. (2013). The role of school counselors in meeting students' mental health needs: Examining issues of professional identity. *Professional School Counseling, 16*(5), 271–282.

Fall, M. (1994). Developing curriculum expertise. A helpful tool for school counselors. *School Counselor, 42,* 92–99.

Galassi, M. D., & Galassi, J. P. (1977). *Assert yourself! How to be your own person.* New York: Human Sciences Press.

Gysbers, N. C., & Henderson, P. (2000). *Developing and managing your school guidance program* (3rd ed.). Alexandria, VA: American Counseling Association.

Gysbers, N. C., & Henderson, P. (2001). Comprehensive guidance and counseling programs: A rich history and a bright future. *Professional School Counseling, 4,* 246–256.

Hains, A. A. (1992). Comparison of cognitive-behavioral stress management techniques with adolescent boys. *Journal of Counseling & Development, 70,* 600–605.

Hains, A. A. (1994). The effectiveness of a school-based, cognitive-behavioral stress management program with adolescents reporting high and low levels of emotional arousal. *School Counselor, 42,* 114–125.

Havighurst, R. J. (1972). *Human development and education.* New York: Longman Green.

House, R. M., & Hayes, R. L. (2002). School counselors: Becoming key players in school reform. *Professional School Counseling, 5,* 249–256.

Johnson, K., & Hannon, J. L. (2014). Measuring the relationship between parent, teacher, and student problem behavior reports and academic achievement: Implications for school counselors. *Professional School Counseling, 18,* 38–48.

Kiselica, M. S., Baker, S. B., Thomas, R. N., & Reedy, S. (1994). Effects of stress inoculation training on anxiety, stress, and academic performance among adolescents. *Journal of Counseling Psychology, 41,* 335–342.

Lapan, R. T. (2012). Comprehensive school counseling programs: In some schools for some students but not in all schools for all students. *Professional School Counseling, 16*(2), 84–88.

Lapan, R. T., Kardash, C. M., & Turner, S. (2002). Empowering students to become self-regulated learners. *Professional School Counseling, 5,* 257–265.

Lupton-Smith, H., Carruthers, W. L., Flythe, R., Goettee, E., & Modest, K. H. (1996). Conflict resolution as peer mediation: Programs for elementary, middle, and high school students. *School Counselor, 43,* 149–157.

Meichenbaum, D. H., & Deffenbacher, J. L. (1988). Stress inoculation training. *Counseling Psychologist, 16,* 69–89.

Morgan, C., & Jackson, W. (1980). Guidance as a curriculum. *Elementary School Guidance and Counseling, 15,* 99–103.

Neuman, N. (2006, Winter). Classroom guidance doesn't have to be a chore. *North Carolina School Counselor Association News, 5.*

Pergolizzi, F., Richmond, D., Macario, S., Gan, Z., Richmond, C., & Macario, E. (2009). Bullying in middle schools: Results from a four-school survey. *Journal of School Violence, 8*(3), 264–269.

Pintrich, P. R. (2000). The role of goal orientation in self-regulated learning. In M. Boekaerts, P. R. Pintrich, & M. Zeidner (Eds.), *Handbook of self-regulation* (pp. 452–502). New York: Academic.

Ponterotto, J. G., & Pedersen, P. B. (1993). *Preventing prejudice: A guide for counselors and educators.* Newbury Park, CA: Sage.

Romano, J. L., Miller, J. P., & Nordness, A. (1996). Stress and well-being in the elementary school: A classroom curriculum. *School Counselor, 43,* 268–276.

Sacco, D. T., Silbaugh, K., Corredor, F., Casey, J., & Doherty, D. (2012). *An overview of state anti-bullying legislation and other related laws.* Cambridge, MA: Born This Way Foundation, Harvard University. Retrieved from http://cyber.law.harvard.edu/sites/cyber.law.harvard.edu/files/State_Anti_bullying_Legislation_Overview_0.pdf

Sears, S. (2005). Large group guidance: Curriculum development and instruction. In C. A. Sink (Ed.), *Contemporary school counseling: Theory, research, and practice* (pp. 189–213). Boston: Lahaska Press/Houghton Mifflin.

Shaw, M. C. (1973). *School guidance systems.* Boston: Houghton Mifflin.

Shaw, M. C., & Goodyear, R. K. (1984). Introduction to the special issue on primary prevention. *Personnel and Guidance Journal, 62,* 444–445.

Shechtman, Z. (2001). Prevention groups for angry and aggressive children. *Journal for Specialists in Group Work, 26,* 228–236.

Sink, C. A. (2005). Comprehensive school counseling programs and academic achievement—A rejoinder to Brown and Trusty. *Professional School Counseling, 9,* 9–14.

Sullivan, H. S. (1947). *Conceptions of modern psychiatry.* Washington, DC: William Alanson White Psychiatric Foundation.

Swisher, J. D., Bechtel, L., Henry, K. L., Vicary, J. R., & Smith, E. (2001). A model substance abuse prevention program. In D. C. Locke, J. E. Myers, & E. L. Herr (Eds.), *The handbook of counseling* (pp. 551–560). Thousand Oaks, CA: Sage.

Wanzek, J., Roberts, G., & Al Otaiba, S. (2013). Academic responding during instruction and reading outcomes for kindergarten students at-risk for reading difficulties. *Reading & Writing, 27,* 55–78.

Whiston, S. C., & Sexton, T. (1998). A review of school counseling outcome research. *Journal of Counseling and Development, 76,* 412–426.

INDIVIDUAL AND GROUP COUNSELING: RESPONDING TO SELECTED NEEDS IN SCHOOLS

8

RELATED STANDARDS OF PRACTICE

| CACREP CORE | 2.F.2.b.c, 2.F.5.a.b.j.n., 2.F.6.b., 2.F.8.e. |
| CACREP SCHOOL COUNSELING | 5.G.3.f. |

Goal: To provide evidence of the demand for counseling interventions from school counselors and to propose a set of basic counseling competencies for a balanced school counseling program.

"Throughout its history, the professional identity of school counselors has been an elusive and fluid construct" (DeKruyf, Auger, & Trice-Black, 2013, p. 271). Characterized in school counselors' own words:

> I was speaking recently with a 10-year-old who watched his mom deal with chemotherapy for breast cancer. He said, "I'm always afraid my mom is going to die." How can I deal with this child's fears?
>
> I was called on a Saturday afternoon to be with the parents of a 16-year-old who was hospitalized in critical condition after a serious car accident. The parents were recently divorced and trying to manage their grief together in spite of their breakup. I'm not sure how to help these parents.
>
> My colleague counselor has a drinking problem. She often misses work on Monday morning and is constantly asking me to go drinking with her on the weekends. How can I ever hope to organize and focus the

counseling program at my middle school when my colleague needs more help than most of the students and parents at my school?

State mandated, end-of-grade, competency tests have created tremendous anxiety among teachers and parents. Consequently, I'm seeing more and more students who say that they are smart but not good test-takers. They are scared to death to fail one of these tests. One student said to me, "I have forgotten how to add fractions. Will you help me before the test tomorrow?" Who has the best answer for dealing with this student—Ellis or Rogers (or neither)?

I am leading a group for parents who have adopted children of foreign descent. It is a wonderful group of folks. They are trying to talk me into learning Spanish. I think I will take on the challenge. My counseling could really benefit—and I think my entire counseling program will be stronger if I am able to speak the native language of so many of my students.

I have been hired as a middle school counselor about halfway through my Master's program in school counseling. I have a provisional license. I am feeling a lot of pressure to finish my program in counselor education and pass the Praxis exam. How can I think about and run an effective program at my school when I'm under so much pressure myself?

These demands require skills that are learned through preservice preparation and through on-the-job experience. This chapter explores some of the demands and the skills required to meet the demands.

DEMAND FOR COUNSELING INTERVENTIONS

The schools are a microcosm of society. Many problems that occur in the greater society also exist in the schools, affecting children and adolescents alike. Current circumstances seem to place more and more responsibility on educators for responding to childhood and adolescent manifestations of society's problems. In some instances, such responsibilities are actually imposed, as was the case with PL 94–142, which mandated that all children with disabilities be accommodated in the mainstream of basic education. Other problems have become the responsibility of the schools simply because they cannot be ignored and, for a variety of reasons, are not successfully treated elsewhere. One way to view this phenomenon is as an imposition, because the primary function of the schools is to impart knowledge. Another way to view the phenomenon is that it is inevitable because the schools as a microcosm of the greater society share responsibility for responding to the problems. Beyond that, it seems illogical to expect the acquisition and use of knowledge to occur for many individuals whose personal and social problems are not recognized.

Like the greater society, the schools have experienced varied success in responding to personal and social problems. There are many reasons for this, some of which are related to the expertise of the professional staff. Most teachers and principals are not trained to intervene in students' personal and social problems. Specialists in social work, psychology, reading, speech, hearing, and the like are available only part time. Among the full-time professional staff of the schools, the individuals most likely trained to provide interventions for personal and social problems are school counselors. Support for this position is found in *Ethical Standards for School Counselors* of the American School Counselor Association (ASCA, 2010) under the heading "Responsibilities to Students": "The school counselor is concerned with the total needs of the student (educational, vocational, *personal*, and *social*) [italics added]." Therefore, without debating whether this system is fair, it seems obvious that school counselors will be challenged to prepare to provide responsive counseling interventions.

The Transforming School Counseling Initiative (TSCI) (Education Trust, 1997) viewed counseling the whole child as an important role for school counselors, especially academic counseling for learning and achievement and supporting student success (House & Hayes, 2002). ASCA, influenced by the TSCI, has since developed the ASCA Student Standards (ASCA, 2013) and the ASCA National Model (ASCA, 2012), both of which emphasize counseling the whole child within academic, career, and personal/social domains.

In ASCA's (2012) National Model for School Counseling Programs, counseling is considered a responsive service. As a responsive service, counseling is viewed from two perspectives (Gysbers & Henderson, 2001). Individual counseling is part of an individual planning process for which the goals are to help students monitor their career, academic, and personal development. Personal counseling is for students who experience problems with relationships, personal concerns, or normal developmental tasks. Most issues addressed in personal counseling will relate to the three domains identified by the ASCA (2013): academic development, career development, and personal/social development. The school-community collaboration model specifically alludes to the school counselor's important, responsive role in a system of care (i.e., treatment of severe and chronic problems such as emergencies and crises) and systems of early intervention (i.e., responding early after the onset of problems) (Adelman & Taylor, 2002).

The competencies for counseling in schools, as presented in this textbook, lend themselves to preparing school counselors to function successfully in each of the initiatives just cited. School counselors who possess these competencies will be able to provide individual and personal counseling as defined in the ASCA National Model (2012), academic counseling, crisis counseling, early interventions, and a host of other categories of important counseling services that are not highlighted in the paradigms.

BASIC INGREDIENTS OF COUNSELING INTERVENTIONS

POINT OF VIEW

Counseling is essentially a direct service that may be devoted primarily to a responsive intervention goal. It is an important function that requires considerable training to learn and develop the requisite skills. It also requires time to acquire the experience necessary for making appropriate decisions during counseling interviews and in case planning. Counseling is at the heart of the responsive intervention function.

The more popular personality and counseling theories on which school counseling is founded were derived from the experiences of psychoanalysts and clinical psychologists (e.g., Sigmund Freud, Alfred Adler, Erik Erikson, Carl Rogers, Albert Ellis) and the research of experimental and social cognitive psychologists (e.g., B. F. Skinner, Albert Bandura). These foundations are useful, but counselor educators and school counselors find themselves translating the information, which is devoted to enhancing long-term psychoanalysis and psychotherapy, into appropriate models for short-term counseling of children and adolescents, most of whom are coping with normal developmental issues.

Historically, the fields of psychoanalysis, psychotherapy, and counseling have endured conflict among disciples of various theoretical camps over which approach is superior. Although differences of opinion still exist, time seems to have diffused some of them. The most common response by less invested persons to such disputes has been to advocate an eclectic approach. Supporters of eclecticism are quick to define what it is and is not. *Eclecticism* is a counselor's systematic, studied, and intelligent assimilation of ideas from differing theoretical perspectives into a personal hybrid that is defensible and identifiable. This individual eclectic theory is then adapted to the specific clientele and setting. Eclecticism is not a random set of acts and thoughts drawn from previous life experiences in response to immediate events.

Eclecticism appears to be the appropriate approach for school counseling. Sue (1992) points out that an eclectic approach may also be the path to achieving multicultural competence in one's counseling interventions by becoming culturally flexible:

> In counseling, equal treatment may be discriminatory treatment. And differential treatment is not necessarily preferential. Minority groups want and need equal access and opportunities, which may dictate differential treatment. Counselors must be able to shift their counseling styles to meet not just developmental needs of their clients but also the cultural dimensions. There has to be recognition that no one style of counseling is appropriate for all populations and situations.
>
> (p. 14)

In the spirit of Herring's (1997) synergistic model, rather than use counseling interventions universally for all students, school counselors will make the most appropriate use of the interventions selectively, having taken into account the attributes of individual student client characteristics such as ethnicity, environment, culture, and gender. Sue, Ivey, and Pedersen (1996) refer to this as being aware of a *third presence* in counseling relationships: counselor, client, and culture. You are encouraged to think about the following hypothetical students when reading the remainder of this chapter or when identifying your own alternative clients. How would the individual attributes of the following students influence you in choosing from the menu of basic counseling competencies and strategies and in responding to student client resistance or reluctance?

John is a third-generation Italian American teenager whose close-knit family has recently moved to a metropolitan area of the southeastern United States. The family consists of two parents and six older siblings (three males and three females), all devout Roman Catholics. They own a restaurant, and all the family members work in some way in that business.

Jennifer is a biracial middle school student; she has two younger sisters. Her father is African American, and her mother is Asian American (Thai). The family is currently homeless because of a series of misfortunes that caused both parents to lose good jobs. The family is receiving welfare assistance.

Brianna is a second grader whose mother is an employed single parent. Brianna just transferred to a new school and is having difficulty making friends because she is considered an outsider. Her younger sister has a hearing disability.

Tomas dropped out of school a year ago because of substance abuse problems. Tomas has returned to school in an effort to graduate and get a diploma. He belongs to a gang whose negative attitudes about his decisions have caused him to be conflicted.

Because this book is intended to be used for training school counselors, the basic ingredients of eclectic school counseling are presented here. It is assumed that school counselors receive training to acquire basic competencies before accepting their first paid counseling positions. What follows, then, are recommended ingredients of the counseling intervention function competencies. It is also assumed that counselors will become lifelong learners after basic training. As lifelong learners, they will surely enhance that basic training through thoughtful analyses of their own counseling experiences, and intelligent applications of information from readings, workshops, conferences, and collegial discussions will enhance the basic competencies.

FOUNDATIONS

School counselors are challenged to understand several important sets of knowledge to apply basic skills successfully. Such knowledge provides the necessary environment for successful counseling. Therefore, these foundation ingredients are addressed first. The list is presented here in no particular order; other writers may identify additional or different foundations:

- Knowledge about human ego defenses, such as rationalization, denial, and intellectualization;
- Awareness that the United States is becoming increasingly pluralistic culturally;
- Knowledge of the developmental tasks associated with childhood and adolescence;
- Knowledge of changing social attitudes and conditions and economic opportunities;

- Awareness that the vast majority of student clients need counselors who will help them overcome deficits and learn ways to cope better;
- Self-awareness, leading to self-acceptance and a genuine interest in the welfare of all members of one's student clientele.

TYPES OF RESPONSIVE COUNSELING INTERVENTIONS

Early Identification and Treatment

Intervention differs from prevention in that it is reactive, rather than proactive, and is offered only to those referred for interventions, rather than to the entire population. *Early identification and treatment* is a phrase that describes the situation of at-risk individuals experiencing a problem or deficit that has not yet overwhelmed them, although they do need individualized help. The following simulations are examples of early identification and treatment cases. The majority of intervention cases with which school counselors work probably fall into this category.

An elementary school counselor is working with a child who has been disruptive in class. The short-term goal in this case is to help the child learn better ways to gain attention; the long-term goal is to prevent the child from becoming alienated, labeled negatively by teachers, or academically deficient.

A middle school counselor uses teacher-to-parent progress reports as a means of identifying students at risk of failing courses. On finding those who want assistance and for whom learning or behavioral deficits can be identified, the counselor reaches out to them in an effort to provide individual or possibly small group counseling interventions that will help them. The purpose of an intervention is to help these students pass their courses and learn more appropriate or new, more useful behaviors. Over the long term, it is hoped that what was learned or changed will generalize to other challenging situations and that the recipients will have enhanced self-esteem because of their accomplishments.

At the secondary school level, a counselor who provides an empathic, facilitative relationship for youths experiencing grief over the loss of a loved one or the failure of a friendship may be able to prevent the impact of such experiences from being overwhelming. The immediate goal is to prevent self-deprecating or self-abusive (e.g., suicidal) responses. The long-term goal is that students will not only come to terms with the immediate incapacitating experience but also generalize the accomplishments of that struggle to similar challenges in the future.

Remedial Interventions

Individuals needing remedial interventions are those with a history of chronic or borderline-chronic maladaptive thoughts and behaviors. Examples are the child who is known to be a school phobic, the adolescent who is or has been addicted to drugs or alcohol, and the chronic truant. These individuals usually represent a relatively small percentage of the total school population but may make up a substantial portion of the population in some individual schools or districts. Yet they require disproportionately more time per individual than do those receiving prevention and early identification and treatment services. Students who fall within the remedial intervention category represent a small but hardcore segment of the school population, and school counselors are challenged to consider them among the potential recipients of their counseling responses in a balanced counseling program. Suggested approaches for helping those whose needs are within the expertise of school counselors are presented in this chapter. Those who cannot be helped directly may be assisted through intelligent referrals and school-community collaborations.

PREVENTION PROGRAMMING AND RESPONSIVE COUNSELING INTERVENTIONS MAY OVERLAP

Although prevention and intervention differ by definition, secondary prevention and early identification and treatment are found in an overlapping region. In the world of school counseling practitioners, this overlap should not matter. Prevention and intervention also differ with respect to the ratio of counselor time spent per client. Prevention programs are economical in this regard because counselors are able to serve several individuals at once through group activities. Responsive counseling interventions, in contrast, are often delivered on a one-to-one basis, although small group counseling may be offered to individuals with similar needs and a willingness to share their problems with peers. Multiple one-to-one or small group counseling sessions are usually required to achieve responsive counseling intervention goals. Therefore, if cost-effectiveness is the primary accountability criterion, prevention services are certainly more cost-effective than responsive counseling intervention services. Using cost-effectiveness as the sole criterion for judging a school counseling program is a mistake, however, because prevention programming will then dominate, and those needing responsive counseling interventions will go underserved. A balanced program serves both predicted and remedial developmental needs; an unbalanced program ignores an important needs area. A balanced counseling program serves all students at all grade levels, responding systematically to the developmental needs of children and adolescents.

DEVELOPMENTAL PERSPECTIVE

The primary means of delivering responsive counseling interventions is through individual and small group counseling. Counseling is a dynamic, continuous process, and counselors are aided by road maps to help them find their way. On the assumption that all counseling has beginnings and endings—sometimes prematurely—a road map serves as a means of deciding what to do next (e.g., when the student client's goals have been identified) and analyzing the situation when problems occur (e.g., when engaged in

TABLE 8.1   *The Ivey, Ivey, and Zalaquett (2014) Paradigm*

Stage	Goal
1	Empathic relationship—Build rapport with and provide structure for the student client
2	Story and strengths—Listen to the student client's story and search for positive assets
3	Mutual goal setting for the student client
4	Restory—Work with student client to explore alternatives, confront incongruities and conflicts, and decide on a constructive action plan
5	Action—Help student client generalize and act on action plan

Source: Data from *Intentional Interviewing and Counseling: Facilitating Client Development in a Multicultural Society* (8th ed.) by A. E. Ivey, M. B. Ivey, & C. P. Zalaquett, 2014, Belmont, CA: Brooks/Cole Cengage Learning.

helping the student client achieve previously established goals and the student suddenly resists). Several such road maps can be found in the professional literature. They often take the form of a stage-wise paradigm, appearing developmental, which counseling often is, and linear, which counseling often is not. The comment about the nonlinearity of the counseling process is important and usually is a disclaimer from authors of stage-wise models. One well-known stage-wise model applicable to school counseling was developed by Ivey, Ivey, and Zalaquett (2014).

Ivey et al.'s (2014) paradigm consists of five stages, which they have subdivided for discussion and increased understanding. Each stage is characterized by goals and related counseling skills. Once familiar with this model or one like it, counselors can use it in making decisions about their own behaviors, analyzing student client needs, and assessing progress in counseling relationships. A summary of the Ivey et al. paradigm is presented in Table 8.1.

THE NATURE OF COUNSELING INTERVENTIONS IN SCHOOLS

Unlike the classic therapeutic hour that psychotherapists in private practice or counselors in college and university counseling centers set aside for appointments with clients, school counselors engage in a greater variety of counseling interventions, many of which are very brief. In addition, school counselors, because of the press of time or competence limits, are less likely to see student clients for more than one or a few consecutive appointments. Most school counseling interventions are short-term rather than long-term. Some interventions are short-term because the nature of the student's needs demands nothing else. Others are shortened because a referral is better.

Other factors that impinge on the length of school counseling sessions are (a) the large number of students that each counselor is to serve; (b) little time available for students to see a counselor because of tight academic scheduling; (c) concern about taking students away from their classroom studies for too long; (d) in secondary schools, scheduling periods that are about 40 to 45 minutes in length; and (e) school systems that do not provide activity periods or study halls for students. Faced with having to conduct brief or limited counseling interventions, school counselors are challenged to be efficient. Important to efficiency in brief/limited counseling is being able to establish a working alliance and to determine student client goals expeditiously. Equally important is being able to provide the student something of value immediately. Some things of value can be as diverse as feeling understood and receiving something concrete such as valuable information or relief from negative affect (e.g., anxiety). Fortunately, Ivey et al.'s (2014) helping model lends itself to conducting brief/limited counseling interventions. Being organized from the outset is also important. In the next section, we use the five stages in the Ivey et al. (2014) paradigm as a foundation for presenting an overview of the basic counseling competencies required of counselors in both individual and small group counseling.

The information presented in the next section is offered as an overview for those of you who may not yet have taken courses in counseling theories and methods, career counseling and development, assessment, prepracticum, and practicum—with the caveat that the information is not intended to be a substitute for, or a primer in, the content of these courses. Indeed, the aforementioned courses will cover these topics more substantively with accompanying opportunities to observe counseling demonstrations and to engage in supervised practice with corresponding constructive feedback. Consider the following information as suggestions for good practice with examples inserted for clarification. You are encouraged to revisit this information during or after taking the courses in your training program similar to those generic courses just listed.

STAGE 1: EMPATHIC RELATIONSHIP

RESPONDING TO CLIENT AVERSION TO COUNSELING

Client aversion takes two forms: reluctance and resistance (Doyle, 1992; Ritchie, 1986). Reluctant clients do not want to be involved in a counseling relationship initially; resistant clients behave in counterproductive ways while involved in the counseling process. Resistance can be a trait or a state in that clients may be resistant throughout the counseling process (trait) or may resist engaging in goal-directed behaviors periodically (state). Reluctance and resistance are natural challenges—part of the counseling process.

Reluctance

School counselors work in a setting in which they do not always control referrals made to them, and their functions are viewed differently by teachers, administrators, and parents. For example, teachers may refer students to counselors because they are puzzled, baffled, or frustrated by the students' behaviors and want someone to change the students so that they will behave as desired in the classroom. Viewing counselors as behavior management specialists or wishing the counselors were such specialists, some teachers refer their troublesome students to counselors. Often, the referred students have not been appropriately prepared for the referral and are reluctant to participate. Administrators sometimes do the same thing; for instance, principals may send misbehaving students to the counselor's office after having administered disciplinary action, expecting the counselor to modify student behavior, validate the principal's disciplinary decisions, or initiate additional discipline. In all these cases, students are very likely to be reluctant to visit the counseling office.

Parents sometimes view counselors as their agents in the school, persons who will gather information about their children or who will support the parents' wishes. Viewing counselors as their agents, parents may expect them to initiate interviews with students at the parents' request. In such interviews, students are often reluctant to participate or cooperate. They may be reluctant because they are unfamiliar with counseling or the counselor or because they do not know why they have been summoned to the counseling office. In some of these instances, counselors are faced with student clients who enter the relationship negatively. When individuals make inappropriate referrals or have unrealistic expectations of counselors, perhaps the best way to cope with the predictably reluctant student clients is to find acceptable ways to avoid engaging in such interviews.

Suggestions for coping with reluctance recommend that counselors draw on their basic counseling skills to earn the student's trust and on their challenging skills to explain the counseling relationship and determine student-based goals (information sharing, goal setting). Trust and structure are important in counteracting student reluctance (Ritchie, 1986). The goal is to restructure the relationship to one in which counselors and students work together in mutual understanding toward achieving student goals. If, during the process of trying to accomplish this, counselors can replace student reticence, suspiciousness, and defensiveness with trust, they will appear trustworthy and competent to their student clients. Janis (1983) calls this "motivating power." Having become what Janis calls "referent persons," counselors are able to use their motivating power to challenge student clients to achieve their goals successfully.

Keat (1990a) points out that children may often be reluctant parties at the beginning of counseling relationships because adults initiate the counseling and establish the outcome goals. He recommends that counselors try to convince reluctant children that counselors are special adults, different from other adults in their lives. Suggestions for employing this idea include (a) demonstrating that counselors have influence over other adults in the children's lives and can effect changes; (b) presenting themselves as adults who can help children by engaging them in activities they find useful, such as learning to relax and cope better with stress, or by giving them therapeutic gifts, such as tape-recorded information or readings; and (c) showing a genuine interest in the children's interests.

Resistance

Ritchie (1986) believes that the instances of resistance in counseling far outnumber those of reluctance, making it a more pervasive challenge. This seems true because a limited number of reluctant students enter a counselor's life, but all students exhibit resistance at some time. The reasons for resistance vary. Some students do not understand what they are to do. Others lack the skills to carry on as expected. Fear of failure and other immobilizing emotions may prevent students from responding. Sometimes students receive more reinforcement for engaging in unproductive behaviors than in productive ones. Sometimes students do not want to admit to needing to change or, if admitting it, do not want to change.

Suggestions for coping with resistance vary because the reasons for resistance vary. Corey, Corey, Callanan, and Russell (1992) and Ritchie (1986) advocate an eclectic approach that can be summed up as using what works best from among available strategies. Cormier, Nurius, and Osborn (2013) offer what might be called a systematic eclecticism (they recommend finding the cause of the resistance and responding accordingly). Causes of resistance may be categorized as being attributable to student client variables (e.g., pessimism, anxiety), environmental variables (e.g., unable to change environment), or counselor or counseling process variables. Inventories of suggestions for coping with resistance present a variety of strategies crossing different theoretical underpinnings and having no absolute guarantees (Corey et al., 1992; Cormier et al., 2013; Cowan & Presbury, 2000; Ritchie, 1986). Consequently, counselors may have to draw on many of their basic skills and creativity when faced with student resistance. What can be stated positively is that counselors are challenged to be prepared because resistance will occur during their careers, manifesting itself in forms ranging from the very subtle to the outrageous.

INTENTIONALITY

Counselors who have adequate developmental road maps will be able to respond to student clients intentionally from a culturally appropriate framework. As defined by Ivey et al. (2014):

> Intentionality, along with cultural intentionality, is acting with a sense of capability and deciding from among a range of alternative actions. The intentional individual has more than one action, thought, or behavior to choose from in responding to changing life situations. The culturally intentional individual can generate alternatives in a given situation and approach a problem from multiple vantage points, using a variety of skills and personal qualities, *adapting styles to suit different individuals and cultures.*
>
> (p. 8)

Intentionality is enhanced when counselors possess a repertoire of appropriate behaviors or responses to changing situations and can choose freely from among these options—the epitome of eclecticism.

OPENING INDIVIDUAL AND GROUP COUNSELING SESSIONS

Opening Individual Counseling Sessions

Because the opening influences the remainder of the interview, effectiveness in opening interviews is crucial. Interview openings are of two types. When student clients are self-referred or referred by a third party and their needs are unknown, they are invited to talk. Open invitations beginning with "How," "What," or "Tell" will help counselors induce client talk (e.g., "How can I help?" "What brought you here?" "Tell me what I can do for you."). Open invitations to talk encourage student clients to share anything they choose and direct attention to their needs. In so doing, counselors set the stage for listening to the student client's stories and gathering data. Two examples follow:

- A high school student is seated in the office of a school counselor, having made an appointment previously, and the counselor smiles at the student client and asks, "How can I help you today?"

- An elementary school counselor encounters a child who is sobbing and obviously distressed. After helping the child calm down enough to be able to talk, the counselor states, "Tell me what happened."

A second type of counseling interview opening occurs when the counselor requests a meeting with a student, placing the counselor in a position of having to explain the purpose of the meeting. A clear explanation is important. The following suggestions for explaining the purpose of an interview are based on Ivey and Gluckstern's (1974) ideas. First, be effective in self-expression (e.g., appropriate eye contact, body language, and verbalizations). Second, share all the important information. Third, make the explanation specific and clear. Fourth, check whether the student understands the explanation before proceeding. Two examples follow:

- A junior high school counselor has initiated a plan to get acquainted with all students assigned to her, and when inviting each student into the counselor's office, she explains, "I am trying to get to know my advisees so that I can serve them better. Do you have time to visit with me for about half hour today? Good, I would like to ask some questions to help us get acquainted. You are not expected to answer them unless you wish to do so. Also, feel free to ask me questions that are of interest to you. I'll be asking some questions about your interests, experiences, and goals for the future and sharing some information about the counseling program while also responding to questions you might have. Before we begin, do you have any questions about what I just said?"

- In an elementary school, a counselor is meeting with an upper elementary school student who has been referred for counseling by her parents, who are concerned about their child's inability to make friends. After making the student welcome, the counselor explains: "If it is OK with you, I would like to talk about friendships. As you know, your parents told me you would like to make some new friendships. I hope to be able to help you make some new friends. Do you want to see what we can do together? Good, I am going to ask some questions about what you do when making friends so that I can get a good idea of what is happening. Then, we can think about what else might need to be done for you to be happy about making friends. It may be hard work for both of us. What are your thoughts at the moment?"

Opening Group Counseling Sessions

Opening individual and group counseling sessions have both similarities and differences. Most group counseling begins after a selection process, so explanations during the first session take the form of a review. Group counseling leaders are better served by giving directions and negotiating rules and expectations. Being believable, thorough, and specific and checking whether members understand are also important when opening group counseling sessions. Explanations, directions, and negotiations are enhanced by exercises designed to get the group off to a good start. An example follows in which the leader of a middle school counseling group to which the members have been referred for acting-out behaviors in classrooms that have led to in-school suspensions is negotiating rules, specifically about confidentiality:

> At times, some of us will share information that is private and that we believe is important for the others to know or because we can't help ourselves. I believe that information should be kept in the group and used only for the benefit of the person who shared the information and the other members of the group. That's called keeping private personal information confidential. I believe that, to be a successful group, we all need to agree that the information shared in our group sessions will be treated as confidential. Is there anything I just said that is confusing and needs to be clarified?

STAGE 2: STORY AND STRENGTHS

The stories students tell about themselves and their lives are key sources of data and information for school counselors. An entire approach to counseling, known as narrative counseling, focuses on students' stories. Narrative counseling is centered in multiculturalism and views students' problems as expressed through stories and helps students construct meaning through the language in their stories (Nafziger & DeKruyf, 2013). Narrative counseling is based on student strengths (Gehart, 2013) and views students as the experts of their own lives (Lambie & Milsom, 2010).

BASIC ATTENDING

One way that counselors convey their desire to understand and help student clients is by their physical behaviors. Physical attending behaviors promote communication and understanding. Egan (2013) offers basic attending behaviors that counselors may use with student clients. As a group, these behaviors may be identified by the acronym SOLER, from the first letter of the key words *Squarely, Open, Lean, Eye,* and *Relaxed.* These terms are described in following sections. The SOLER behaviors are important attending behaviors in North American culture and may not have similar positive effects with students from all other subcultures. Alternative behaviors may be necessary with some students; counselors are challenged to adjust to such variations in their student clientele by being culturally intentional.

Face the Student Client Squarely

When the counselor's body is positioned toward the client, psychological contact with the student client is heightened. As a result, counselor involvement is communicated.

Adopt an Open Posture

The counselor's posture during a counseling interview conveys the degree of involvement. Suggestions often state what not to do, rather than what to do. For instance, crossing arms and legs or placing objects such as books, clipboards, and desks between the counselor and the client may lessen the client's perception of counselor involvement. Egan (2013) offers sage advice about these suggestions when he states that they can be taken literally or metaphorically; that is, crossed legs may not always communicate lack of involvement. Counselors crossing their legs might think about whether that act interferes with communication of involvement with the student client.

Lean Forward Slightly

A forward lean is another posture that conveys involvement. The degree of forward lean serves best when it is a natural reaction to whatever the student client is communicating. Egan (2013) points out that leaning too far forward and leaning backward are both potentially counterproductive behaviors in that the former may convey too much closeness, whereas the latter may convey disinterest.

Maintain Good Eye Contact

Counselor involvement is also conveyed via eye contact. Students who find eye contact with the counselor when seeking a sign of involvement are likely to conclude that the counselor is trying to understand. Staring, of course, is a counterproductive application of this principle because student clients will be uncomfortable. Occasionally looking away is acceptable; it is sometimes necessary so that counselors can gather their thoughts, and it prevents staring. Looking elsewhere often during the interview, however, conveys disinterest (Egan, 2013). With younger children, adult counselors may have to get down to the children's level to make eye contact by sitting or kneeling on the floor or an object close to the floor.

Try to Be Relatively Relaxed

Counselors who rigidly conform to the SOLER guidelines will probably make student clients uncomfortable and distracted. Counselors who feel comfortable with their own behavior are more likely to be natural in their counseling. Only then will they be able to concentrate on their student clients. Being relaxed and attentive follows from a genuine interest in the welfare of students.

Psychological Attending

Being able to attend to student clients psychologically is equally important. Psychological attending manifests itself through listening carefully and focusing on the core or theme of what is being said and felt and then conveying having done so via verbal responses and physical behaviors.

OBSERVING

An important counseling competency is to be able to observe the nonverbal behavior of student clients in order to better understand what they are feeling internally and expressing verbally. An important component of this process is to be able to identify discrepancies and respond to them appropriately. Nonverbal behavior that may provide important information for counselors includes facial expressions and body language. Verbal behaviors that are important to observe include key words that may occur often, whether student clients present information abstractly or concretely, whether issues are attributed to themselves ("I statements") or to others, and discrepancies in the stories shared by the student clients. Counselors are challenged to observe these behaviors and use the awareness of them to help student clients tell their stories successfully (Ivey et al., 2014).

LISTENING AND RESPONDING

The following listening and responding behaviors are considered basic components of the successful counselor's repertoire of counseling skills. They are necessary for successful listening and responding and achieving the goals of the data gathering stage. Whether engaged in individual or group counseling, school counselors are challenged to help student clients explore their problem situations and identify their resources. Several basic counseling or interviewing skills have been recommended for accomplishing the goals associated with successfully initiating counseling relationships. These basic skills remain important throughout all stages of counseling relationships. The basic verbal skills are paraphrasing information, reflecting feelings, clarifying unclear material, summarizing information and feelings, inviting student clients to talk, and questioning appropriately.

Paraphrasing Information

By briefly rephrasing clients' verbal presentations, counselors can help them focus on the content of their messages (Cormier et al., 2013). Therefore, counselors are challenged to be able to restate the information and ideas that clients share. An example of an elementary school counselor paraphrasing the content of a child's verbal message follows:

Student: I don't like school. No one will play with me, and it's not fun. I hate all of them and wish they would move away. Sometimes I don't want to come to school.

Counselor: No one will play with you, and school is not fun.

Reflecting Feelings

Counselors are also challenged to recognize the affective components in student client messages. Sometimes student clients label their feelings, although on other occasions they only imply them by their behavior and statements. Being able to recognize important client feelings and label them (e.g., "You seem frustrated," "That made you happy," "There is sadness in your words") helps student clients recognize their feelings and explore them more deeply (Cormier et al., 2013). Continuing with the child who is expressing her dislike of school, a reflection in response to the same student client statement might be:

Counselor: The way the other children treat you hurts your feelings and makes you unhappy.

Clarifying Unclear Material

Sometimes students are vague or their messages are unclear; occasionally, counselors just get lost when trying to follow student client material. Clarifying clears up vague or missed messages, verifies the accuracy of what was heard, and encourages client elaborations (Cormier et al., 2013). Clarifications can take the form of questions and paraphrases/reflections or can be open-ended questions or invitations. An example is based on the unhappy upper elementary school student introduced earlier:

Student: Yes, they hurt my feelings. I wish I could just stay at home. They make me so unhappy that I want to go away.

Counselor: Please tell me what you mean when you say "I want to go away."

Summarizing Information and Feelings

Identification and clarification can be enhanced by rephrasing parts of the student client's message, including information and feelings. Summarizing facilitates a student's thinking by tying multiple elements together and identifying themes or patterns (Cormier et al., 2013). A summary of what has been presented thus far about the child client might be as follows:

Counselor: I think we have gotten off to a good start today. You have shared some important information with me about how bad you feel when being rejected by other children, how much you would like to make friends, and how hopeful you are that we can work together to try to help you be happier.

Inviting Student Clients to Talk

Open invitations have been mentioned as important for beginning counseling interviews. Open-ended questions are also useful for obtaining further information ("Tell me more"), encouraging further student client exploration ("How did that affect you?"), eliciting specific examples ("What happened then?"), and motivating the student to continue to communicate ("Could you elaborate on . . .") when a pause occurs in the interview (Cormier et al., 2013). In the section on clarifying unclear material, the counselor used a "Tell me" open invitation. The counselor could have responded with alternative open invitations and achieved the same goal (e.g., "What does 'I want to go away' mean?" or "Could you elaborate on what you are thinking when saying 'I want to go away'?").

Questioning Appropriately

All individuals know how to ask closed-ended questions, which require a yes-or-no response. Such questions have a place in counseling if they are used to narrow the topic being discussed ("Is there a reason for that?"), obtain specific information ("Is this decision still important to you?"), identify parameters of a problem ("Have you identified what causes that reaction?"), or focus the interview ("Do you want to talk about your goals?") when necessary (Cormier et al., 2013). Care is recommended, however, when using closed-ended questions to prevent the interview from becoming an interrogation or from coming to a halt. Their use may indicate that the counselor has run out of questions or may lead the student to wait for the next question before responding. Consider the following two hypothetical responses in which closed-ended questions are used. The first is an example of an interrogation and is not recommended; the second is an example of using closed-ended questions that are facilitative:

Student: Yes, they hurt my feelings. I wish I could just stay at home. They make me so unhappy that I want to go away.

Counselor: Who hurt your feelings?

Student: All of those kids.

Counselor: What kids? Name them for me.

Student: Amy, James, Sammy, and Alicia.

Counselor: Have you been staying at home?

Student: No.

Counselor: OK, did these children say mean things to you?

Student: Yes.

Counselor: Did they hurt you?

Student: Yes.

Counselor: Did you tell your parents and your teacher about this?

Student: Yes.

Counselor: What do you want me to do about this?

Student: I don't know.

Counselor: Can you be more specific?

Student: Yes, they hurt my feelings. I wish I could just stay at home. They make me so unhappy that I want to go away.

Counselor: Please tell me what you mean when you say "I want to go away."

Student: Sometimes I feel like running away or moving away or going to my grandmother's house and living there. Then those kids will be sorry for what they did and I can play with someone who is nice.

Counselor: So you have thoughts about running or moving away. Have you ever run away? (closed-ended question)

Student: No, I can't do that because I'd miss my mom and dad and it would be scary.

Notice that the closed-ended question received a response similar to that of an open-ended question because it was preceded by a paraphrase ("So you have thoughts . . .") and an open invitation to talk ("Please tell me . . ."), both of which created a facilitative atmosphere rather than an interrogative one. The closed-ended question introduced an important element (has the client acted on thoughts of running away?).

Depending on how they are used, questions can be part of basic counseling or challenging responses. If the goal is to elicit, in basic counseling, then questions are being used for listening/responding purposes. If the goal is to probe, the questions are being used as challenging skills. The same relationships are true in open invitations.

Open-ended questions are preferred whenever possible. They are a form of invitations to talk and serve counselors well at the beginning and during counseling sessions. Consider the potential effect of the changes in the earlier scenario where closed-ended questions were used by the counselor:

Student: Yes, they hurt my feelings. I wish I could just stay at home. The make me so unhappy that I want to go away.
Counselor: What does "going away" mean?
Student: Sometimes I feel like running away.
Counselor: In what ways will running away make you feel better?

Open-ended questions provide more latitude for student clients to consider information and feelings to share with counselors than closed-ended questions will accomplish. Consequently, more important information usually is shared and the helping process is enhanced accordingly.

Integrating the Skills

The following example from a simulated counseling session provides examples of the respective basic verbal listening and responding skills.

An elementary school student is seated in the office of a school counselor. The counselor smiles at the student client and asks, "How can I help you today?" (open-ended question/invitation to talk):

Student: I don't like school. No one will play with me, and it's not fun. I hate all of them and wish they would move away. Sometimes I don't want to come to school.
Counselor: No one will play with you, and school is not fun, (paraphrase) and the way the other children treat you hurts your feelings and makes you unhappy. (reflecting feeling)
Student: Yes, they hurt my feelings. I wish I could just stay at home. They make me so unhappy that I want to go away.
Counselor: Please tell me what you mean when you say "I want to go away." (clarifying unclear material)
Student: Sometimes I feel like running away or moving away or going to my grandmother's house and living there. Then those kids will be sorry for what they did and I can play with someone who is nice.

Counselor: So you have thoughts about running or moving away. (paraphrase) Have you ever run away? (closed-ended question)

Student: No, I can't do that because I'd miss my mom and dad and it would be scary.

Student client continues to identify and clarify her concerns and the counselor must close the interview.

Counselor: I think we have gotten off to a good start today. You have shared some important information with me about how bad you feel when the other children are mean to you, how much you would like to make friends, and how hopeful you are that we can work together to try to help you be happier. (summarizing information and feelings)

During his presentation on March 25, 2002, at the American Counseling Association (ACA) convention, William Glasser referred to the preceding competencies as "making nice" and stated his belief that anyone who cannot make nice does not belong in the counseling profession. He appeared to allude to a belief that the basic counseling skills are necessary for all counselors in every counseling situation.

STAGE 3: MUTUAL GOAL SETTING

Through telling their stories, individual student clients and counseling group members learn how to present issues. They may also need help in setting goals. Setting goals is challenging and often requires stronger responses from counselors—responses that are more directive and influential than the ones listed previously. Whereas the previous responses focus on helping student clients understand their own material better, challenging responses evolve from counselor perceptions and are, therefore, more direct in their influence. Cormier et al. (2013) describe these as *action responses* because they exert such direct influence on clients. For all these reasons, student clients may respond in a negative fashion.

Unproductive student client responses such as anger, denial, and attacks on the counselor may set the relationship back, cause a stalemate, or lead to student withdrawal from the counseling relationship. Challenging responses, in contrast, may cause student clients to acquire insights impossible to achieve by themselves, accept responsibility for their behavior, and change their thoughts or behaviors or both constructively. Because challenging responses are so powerful, they are best used sparingly—only when needed—and skillfully. Rather than single behaviors, as are the previously cited skills (e.g., paraphrasing, reflecting, summarizing), the challenging skills are sets of behaviors that are logically combined to achieve specific goals. Important basic challenging skills include interpretation, self-sharing, confrontation, immediacy, information sharing, and goal setting. A common aspect of the challenging skills is to present them tentatively to allow student clients to negotiate their responses, rather than be forced to defend themselves. Examples of each follow. Ivey et al. (2014) use the term *interpersonal influencing skills* as a synonym for challenging skills.

REFLECTION OF MEANING AND INTERPRETATION/REFRAME

The reflection of meaning and interpretation/reframe process occurs when a counselor challenges a student client to think about what is implied rather than stated by the client's words and behaviors. Usually preceded by a paraphrase, reflection, and/or summary of what the student did say, an interpretation/reframe is the counselor's hypothesis of what was implied or stated tentatively (e.g., "You decided not to apply at an Ivy University. I wonder whether your decision is related to doubts about your ability to succeed in that college."). Successful interpretations evolve from insights acquired by counselors from their clinical experiences and from closely following material presented by the student client. When successful, interpretations provide clients either a new view of their material or another explanation for their thoughts and behaviors (Cormier et al., 2013).

SELF-DISCLOSURE AND FEEDBACK

Self-disclosure and feedback takes place when counselors share something about themselves with their student clients. Usually prompted by a paraphrase, reflection, and/or summary of something about the student, the counselor presents related information and feelings with an attempt to be brief and an invitation for the client to use the information therapeutically (e.g., "You're afraid of flunking out of State University during the first semester and being too embarrassed to face your family. I remember having similar thoughts when trying to decide whether to take this job at Comprehensive High School. I wasn't sure whether the students would accept me, and I had to understand that I might not achieve my goal of working in a high school counseling center if I wasn't willing to take that risk. There seem to be some similarities between your situation and that one of mine."). Successful self-disclosure helps student clients learn how to share and discover perspectives they had not considered previously (Egan, 2013). Effectiveness at self-sharing seems to require being selective and not overdoing the sharing by offering material that adds to the student's burden, is too verbose, or causes the roles to shift (i.e., client becomes attentive responder to counselor who is engaging in excessive self-talk).

LOGICAL CONSEQUENCES

Logical consequences occurs when counselors help student clients examine the logical consequences of alternative choices and actions. Best preceded by a summary of the detected choices, the logical consequences process contains a tentative description of what the counselor has observed along with an invitation to think about the consequences (e.g., "You say that not attending college has something to do with your fear of failure. Have you thought about what the decision not to go to college means to your future plans?"). The logical consequences process can help student clients consider alternative ways to perceive their issues and become more aware of the potential positive and negative consequences (Ivey et al., 2014).

IMMEDIACY

Immediacy achieves direct, mutual interactions between counselor and student client when the counseling relationship itself is at issue. A counselor's summary of what is interfering with the counseling relationship is followed by a statement of the counselor's feelings about what is happening and the counselor's goals in bringing attention to the situation. The immediacy response concludes with an invitation to the student to participate in negotiating an amicable resolution. For example, a student client accuses a middle-class European American counselor of overemphasizing concerns about possible academic difficulties as a college student because the student client is African American and from a lower socioeconomic background. The student client wonders whether the counselor is discouraging college attendance because of racist intentions. The counselor responds, "You think I believe college will be difficult for you because I am White and you are Black and I am a racist, and that both surprises and hurts me. We seem to be in danger of being at odds with each other because you interpreted my comments in a way I did not intend. I apologize for my part in that, and I want to get us back on the right track. Do you think we can resolve this, and if so, do you have any recommendations?"

Immediacy serves as a means of engaging student clients in mutual assessments of problems in the counselor-client relationship that interfere with progress.

INFORMATION SHARING

Information sharing occurs when student clients need information that may challenge them to view circumstances differently. Cormier et al. (2013) suggest that information giving can include the sharing of facts about experiences, events, alternatives, or people. Following a summary of the student client's understanding of the information in question, the counselor asks whether the student is aware of, and interested in, additional information the counselor possesses. The counselor then shares the information, checking the student's reaction. For example, "You heard that all freshmen at an Ivy University must take calculus and an advanced year of foreign language in the first semester. Are you aware that there is an alternative? . . . No? Would you like to know what it is? . . . Incoming freshmen at Ivy University who do not have the background to take calculus or an advanced year of foreign language are allowed to take other courses appropriate to their high school preparation. How does that affect your thinking?"

Information sharing helps clients identify and evaluate alternatives they were not aware of previously, helps dispel myths they may harbor, and motivates them to examine issues they may have been avoiding (Cormier et al., 2013).

GOAL SETTING

Understanding that most student clients need help in adjusting or coping, learning new and better ways of behaving and thinking, and overcoming deficits in their environment, counselors may view themselves as participants in the counseling process, helping students identify and achieve their goals. Goal setting is at the heart of this participatory relationship between counselors and clients, and counselors are challenged to help student clients find a sense of direction, as well as share the responsibility for clients achieving their goals (Egan, 2013). Several basic counseling intervention skills are involved in the goal-setting process.

Initially, counselors explain the purpose of goal setting; this involves information-sharing skills. The basic verbal responses (paraphrasing and summarizing) will help students identify and evaluate their options (What are the possible goals?). All the basic verbal and challenging skills may be needed to help student clients select their goals, clarify them, determine whose goals they really are, decide how to achieve them, and then proceed to achieve them. Helping students set goals focuses their attention on acting constructively, gets them involved in the helping process, makes them aware of what needs to be accomplished, encourages them to act on their own behalf, and informs them that the counselor is a capable partner in the helping process. A hypothetical interaction between that elementary school counselor and the unhappy student introduced earlier provides an example of one of the many approaches counselors might pursue when trying to help clients set goals:

Counselor: So we have talked about how bad you feel and how angry you are at the others. Tell me what you want right now.

Student: I wish they would all disappear in a cloud of smoke!

Counselor: I can see how that might make you feel better right now. Are you sure that is all you want?

Student: Well, I wish someone would be nice to me.

Counselor: Do you think that is something for us to work on—figuring out how to get someone to be nice to you?

The counselor has discovered a possible goal in the student's comments and offered it as a possible goal. At this point, the counselor and student may engage in negotiating whether this would be a viable goal.

STAGES 4 AND 5: RE-STORY AND ACTION

In the logic of the five-stage counseling paradigm, building an empathic relationship, listening to the students' stories, and mutual goal setting usher in constructive student action designed to achieve their goals. The options available to counselors when helping students act on their goals are far ranging, and many counselors spend their careers trying to learn more about ideas in the counseling literature and to become more accomplished at applying those skills. This book focuses on selected basic action strategies, not all possible action strategies. The strategies presented here are suggested because they are appropriate for helping most student clients achieve their goals. Therefore, the suggestions that follow are presented as basic action strategies for the school counselor's repertoire. Some strategies may be more appropriate for counseling children, some more appropriate for counseling adolescents, and others useful for both children and adolescents. When perusing the next section, you are reminded to think about the information on *eclecticism* presented earlier in this chapter.

You are also reminded that the purpose of the following information is to provide an overview, rather than to be a substitute for other courses in one's training program. In this section, an overview of action strategies that appear to be useful is presented. Competence in these strategies will come from comprehensive training associated with course work in one's counselor education training program. After his comments about the necessity of the basic counseling skills (i.e., "making nice") during the 2002 ACA convention, William Glasser stated that the "hard work" follows, that is, helping student clients achieve their goals. Each of the strategies is presented as a way of responding to specific challenges that are common to student clients.

HELPING STUDENTS WHO NEED EMPATHY AND SUPPORT

Children and adolescents benefit from knowing that someone cares and is trying to understand their circumstances. They respond best to counselors who provide support and understanding by creative facilitative mutual relationships. These student clients may be experiencing grief, confusion, pain, or apathy, and their goal may be to adjust, to understand, or to feel accepted. The skills popularly associated with client- or person-centered counseling (Rogers, 1951) are commonly used in supportive counseling. Interestingly, they are the same skills cited previously as the basic verbal counseling responses (e.g., paraphrasing content, reflecting feelings, clarifying unclear material). Thus, in this instance the action strategy takes the form of continuing counseling responses designed to help students tell their stories in advance of goal setting. What differs is the use of these responses to help clients achieve their goals.

For example, a high school counselor is meeting with a student who is traumatized by the sudden death of a classmate killed in a car accident. Realizing that the student client needs to identify and clarify feelings, the counselor uses paraphrases, reflections, clarifications, and summaries to provide an empathic atmosphere. Eventually, the counselor learns that the student "just needs someone to talk to." Deciding that needing someone to talk to is the student's immediate goal, the counselor continues to respond in much the same manner as was done initially to provide a supportive environment for the student client to work through and process the thoughts and feelings that led to seeking help from the counselor.

HELPING STUDENTS MAKE DECISIONS

Many children and adolescents are confronted with choices, and making the best decisions is critically important to them. This is another arena in which counselors can be of service. Counselors are faced with a broad range of student problems that require decision-making assistance. For instance, choices are to be made when seeking a job, selecting a college, or determining whether to pursue a vocational-technical curriculum. Choices are also to be made in the personal-social domain, such as whether to forgive a transgressing peer or to pursue dangerous activities.

When engaging in decision-making counseling as an action strategy, counselors have at their disposal several rational, stepped, decision-making counseling paradigms. As Horan (1979) points out, they all have four major components in common; therefore, counselors will be able to follow these paradigms and assist many of their student clients successfully by helping them do the following:

- Define the problem as involving a decision,
- Identify the alternative response options (by using basic clarifying and exploring skills),
- Determine the advantages and disadvantages of each option, and
- Make a tentative choice (by using basic clarifying, exploring, and challenging skills).

Decision-making counseling involves a unique combination of the aforementioned basic responding and challenging skills in a strategy founded on the counselor leading the student through a set of predetermined helping steps. For example, the high school student who was traumatized by the death of a classmate, having processed thoughts and feelings with the help of a supportive counselor, reaches a point of having to decide whether to tell someone about witnessing alcohol abuse by the driver of the car before the accident occurred (the problem is defined as involving a decision). Using the decision-making steps, the counselor helps the student client decide what the alternatives are (e.g., tell someone, tell no one, or have someone else tell). Following identification of the alternatives, the counselor helps the student client consider the advantages and disadvantages of each one. For instance, the counselor might say (using an open-ended question): "What are the advantages of telling someone?" Having discussed the advantages, the counselor will then ask, "What are the disadvantages?" After seemingly having together exhaustively discussed the various advantages and disadvantages, the counselor then asks the student which alternative seems to be the best choice. The response may be to make a choice, to not make a choice (which is actually a choice—to do nothing), or to think about the choices further—perhaps acquiring more information or opinions in the process. If more time is needed, the counselor invites the student client to return and continue if desired. If a choice is made, the counselor helps the student make plans for implementing it and returning to meet with the counselor and process the effects.

One prominent application of the decision-making counseling framework that may occur often for school counselors is when working with students who are trying to make career-related decisions. Such decisions include but are not restricted to school-to-school transitions, school-to-work transitions, and school-to-postsecondary education decisions. Examples of questions that may be best approached by the decision-making framework are What do I want to do when I grow up or after graduation? What courses should I take in high school in order to prepare me for the transition to work or postsecondary education? To which postsecondary schools should I apply? Which postsecondary school should I select from those that have accepted me? and How do I decide what to do about financial aid for postsecondary education?

An important ingredient of the decision-making process is helping student clients acquire and process relevant information that will inform them about the advantages and disadvantages of their options. School counselors are challenged to be aware of the various sources of information that may be available and to find ways to help student clients find that information. It is impossible to know everything that may be important for a variety of clients. Yet it is possible to acquire and commit to memory information about certain options that are of common interest to many student clients (e.g., admission requirements to local and state postsecondary training institutions) and to be aware of a number of resources that are available in printed materials or on the Internet.

Helping students identify useful information and acquire it is an initial step that is enhanced by a helping them to process it. That is, once the information is acquired, student clients may also need help making sense of it and putting it to use in the decision-making process. In this phase, counselors use their listening and responding skills to help students make sense of the information and put it to good use. In some cases during the decision-making process, professional school counselors may be challenged by student clients who are approaching the process irrationally.

HELPING STUDENTS TO THINK RATIONALLY

Although humans have the capacity to engage in thinking processes, that capacity is not always used rationally. Some irrational thoughts common among school-age individuals are "People don't like me because my nose is big," "Men who choose careers in nursing are sissies," "The principal is mean because she doesn't smile at me," and "I've got to do what the others are doing or else they won't like me." It is safe to conclude that much irrational thinking occurs during childhood and adolescence and that it often leads to maladaptive responses. Many student clients whom school counselors encounter need help in identifying and coping with their irrational thoughts, and school counselors can use proven strategies to help them.

Rational-emotive behavior therapy (*REBT;* Ellis, 2007) provides a system for seeking out irrational beliefs in what students present and for pointing out the unfortunate consequences of those beliefs. For instance, the counselor working with the African American student client discussed earlier in this chapter in the material on immediacy and believing that the accusation of racism was emotionally rather than factually based might borrow from REBT as follows to introduce to the student client the counselor's view of how the situation occurred and to induce mutual discussion:

Counselor: So when I mentioned challenges I thought you would face as a college student, you thought my motives were racist, and that led to your being angry, losing confidence in me, and telling me off.

Basic verbal counseling and challenging responses can be used to help the student become aware of irrational thinking. Counselor-client interactions can be quite challenging, and students may either recognize their irrational cognitions or leave counseling.

Ellis and others offer systems for teaching student clients to think more rationally. *Cognitive self-instruction* is a system for identifying self-defeating thoughts and teaching clients to replace them with coping thoughts (Meichenbaum, 1993, 1994). *Reframing* helps student clients learn more rational ways of perceiving situations (Gendlin, 1996). These and other strategies for teaching students to think more rationally follow the establishment of students' goals as being the acquisition of more rational coping responses. The common ingredients of these strategies are (a) explaining the procedure to the student (information sharing), (b) demonstrating the strategy (serving as a model), (c) helping the student rehearse the new behavior and cognitions (practicing), and (d) encouraging the client to use the skills in the real world (by using basic counseling and interpersonal influencing skills when encouraging them).

The most challenging aspect of irrational ideation counseling occurs at the beginning: Counselors try to identify the irrational components of the student client's cognitions and the behavioral consequences. Then they may find themselves disputing the student's irrational thinking patterns, which sometimes is very difficult to do. It follows that counselors who are rational thinkers themselves are more likely to help student clients think more rationally.

HELPING STUDENTS TO ACQUIRE COPING SKILLS

Competence Enhancement Counseling

It is not uncommon for school-age clients to set goals successfully and then feel stymied because they do not feel competent to achieve their goals. When these feelings of incompetence are products of inexperience, lack of information, or mild performance anxiety, counselors can help students enhance or learn the requisite skills. As a result, student clients will be better prepared to cope with the targeted situations and others like them, and they may feel better about themselves for having coped and acquired new or enhanced skills.

Participant modeling, also called *behavioral rehearsal*, is a competence-enhancing counseling strategy for the school counselor's basic action strategies repertoire (Bandura, 1986). The ingredients are modeling, rehearsal with feedback, and transfer of training. The strategy is explained to the student (information sharing), the targeted behavior is demonstrated by a model (observational learning), the client engages in repeated practice sessions—as many as needed—with possible repetitions of the modeling if necessary (basic counseling and challenging skills), and an effort is made to transfer the acquired or enhanced skills to the real world when the student is ready. Among the sample cases that have been presented in this chapter, the elementary school student experiencing difficulty making friends might be helped through friendship training provided by the counselor's employing participant modeling as just described.

Another case that lends itself to behavioral rehearsal is the high school student who, after receiving supportive and decision-making counseling assistance from a counselor following the death of a classmate in a car accident, decides to tell someone about having witnessed alcohol abuse by the driver of the car but is concerned about not being clear and convincing in the presentation. The counselor offers to help the student client feel more confident by employing the participant modeling strategy. After exploring the student's concerns about telling someone, the counselor helps the student decide who it will be. Counselor and student then determine together how that person might act and how the student should act. Next, counselor and student engage in a series of practice sessions in which the two exchange playing the roles of the student and the person to whom the student is relating the information. When the counselor plays the student's role, modeling occurs; when the student plays the student's role, the counselor provides encouragement and helpful feedback after each rehearsal. Successive approximations are employed until the student client either feels ready to carry out the decision or decides to delay action, to not act, or to rethink the alternatives.

Competence enhancement counseling is similar to teaching when counselors engage in participant modeling or behavior rehearsals with student clients. Therefore, counselors are better prepared to be effective if they are familiar with such strategies as induction aids, reinforcing statements, coaching, and arranging the subskills of the targeted behavior into a hierarchy (Cormier et al., 2013).

Assertiveness Counseling

Children and adolescents who are unable to respond to others with appropriate levels of assertiveness are at risk of undesirable consequences that range from feeling unfulfilled (e.g., unable to approach others socially) to being endangered (e.g., unable to resist peer pressure to engage in life-threatening behaviors such as substance abuse or unprotected sexual intercourse). Realizing that there is a fine line between assertiveness and aggressiveness, counselors can help students who are not assertive enough by enabling them to receive compliments, make normal requests of others, express affective feelings such as fondness and displeasure, initiate and maintain conversations, express their legitimate rights, and refuse illegitimate requests. Furthermore, school counselors can assist students with recognizing their deficits, establishing appropriate goals, and being appropriately assertive (Galassi & Galassi, 1977; Lange & Jakubowski, 1976).

When students engage in maladaptive, nonassertive behaviors, counselors may help them replace those behaviors with adaptive responses. When students have deficits, new behaviors can be taught. As with other instructional counseling intervention strategies, the first step is to explain the purposes and procedures for the training. Second, the counselor teaches student clients how to appraise situations and decide how to behave (information-sharing skills). Third, demonstration and practice with feedback are used to teach the actual assertion skills (observational learning and reinforcement menus). Finally, the skills are implemented in the real world. One of the easiest ways to encourage appropriate assertiveness is to reinforce such behaviors when student clients exhibit them.

In the example of the student client being helped to tell someone about the alcohol abuse of the driver in the car accident through participant modeling, one might conclude that the student client was lacking in assertiveness and may have been helped to be more assertive through competence enhancement counseling. Therefore, it seems appropriate to conclude that although not all participant modeling involves enhancing assertiveness, it is a very useful strategy for helping individuals learn to be more assertive.

SELF-MANAGEMENT BY STUDENT CLIENTS

Counselors have direct influence over their student clients only during periods of direct contact during counseling interviews or group sessions. Interviews and sessions seldom occur more than once per week and often less than that. It is fortunate if counselors spend as much as 45 minutes per week with student clients individually or in groups. Consequently, student clients are responsible for their own behavior most of the time. The influence of counselors may increase a bit when they arrange with third parties to assist in intervention programs. In those cases, however, their influence is indirect.

Because student clients involved in various counseling programs are on their own most of the time, it behooves counselors to introduce a system of self-management to help students be successful with their counseling interventions. In essence, student clients assume control of their own intervention programs. Counselors remain important partners in the arrangement, however, because they introduce the self-management system and because they receive dependable information about student progress. Therefore, counselors assume indirect control over the intervention program, with the self-management system serving as the third party. More work by the student may occur between counseling sessions than during them. This is good because much more time is devoted to the intervention program than if student action is restricted to the counseling sessions.

Self-management programs require workable systems that are taught to students. Appropriate homework assignments provide clear explanations (information sharing), teach student clients how to carry them out (pedagogical skills), and assess student success with self-management activities (e.g., self-evaluation, standard setting, self-reinforcement, self-monitoring, stimulus control; Cormier et al., 2013).

An interesting secondary effect of self-management activities is that clients often experience more success than they might have otherwise simply because they pay more attention to the targeted behaviors.

In an example of self-management programming (self-monitoring) for a middle school student, a counselor and the student have agreed that academic performance in school may improve if the student becomes involved in a self-managed schoolwork program. To initiate the program, the counselor explains to the student how it works:

Counselor: I think the best way to do this is for you to set aside 2 hours for homework each evening and to write down on the chart I am giving you what you need

Student: to accomplish (goals), what you accomplish (outcomes), and how you feel about it (opinions) without spending too much time doing the record keeping. The chart is like a weekly and monthly calendar, and you can see how things are progressing. What do you think?

Student: Sounds good to me.

Counselor: OK! Now let's decide when you will start, and set up a series of meetings between the two of us to analyze how you are doing and determine what to do next.

HELPING STUDENTS WHO DO NOT EXPRESS THEMSELVES WELL VERBALLY

Verbal interactions between counselors and their clients are not the only way to achieve counseling goals; in fact, nonverbal strategies may be better in some cases. Although the following strategies all include some verbal material and interactions, they are classified here as nonverbal because of the special importance of nonverbal material and activities.

Play therapy offers counselors an avenue into the world of young children that is less successfully traveled through verbalizations. Through play therapy, counselors are able to learn what children are thinking. Here, counselors can communicate with children indirectly by using basic counseling skills to inquire about the play activities. Understanding the play therapy process and having at one's disposal the necessary space or, at least, equipment is imperative (e.g., toys, games, materials; Keat, 1990b). Barlow, Strother, and Landreth (1985) recommend that teachers and principals be aware of the goals and benefits of play therapy to make them more understanding partners in the helping process.

O'Connor (1991) believes that play therapy can be adapted for children at all levels of functioning. Children at higher levels will find the treatment more cognitive than experiential. Therefore, it is important to have a sense of a child's level of cognitive development before initiating play therapy activities. When done well, play therapy provides an opportunity for children to have a new understanding with corresponding response options. Further information is available in the following sources: O'Connor and Schaefer (1994) provide a menu of theoretical approaches to play therapy (e.g., Adlerian, time-limited, and cognitive-behavioral); ideas for adapting play therapy to adolescent clients; and descriptions of several play therapy techniques. Schaefer and Cangelosi (1993) offer recommendations for a wide variety of play therapy techniques (e.g., using puppets, sand play, water play, using food, finger painting, checkers or chess, and gaming consoles). Ideas for using play therapy in concert with specific presenting problems are suggested by Landreth, Homeyer, Glover, and Sweeney (1996; e.g., abuse and neglect, aggression and acting out, attachment difficulties, grief, reading difficulties, and social adjustment). For more on play therapy, see Landreth (2002) and the Center for Play Therapy at the University of North Texas (www.coe.unt.edu/cpt/).

Kahn (1999) believes that art therapy is an effective medium for counseling adolescents in several important ways by helping them with developmental tasks such as individuation and separation from their families. This is accomplished by aiding them to achieve control over their expressions, stimulate their creativity, have pleasurable experiences, and employ media options that reflect personal and age group symbols and metaphors. She also believes that school counselors can establish art stations in their offices, using a variety of materials, each selected for specific reasons (e.g., felt-tip markers can be used quickly and are relatively easy to control). Stressing that counselors do not need to be artistically talented themselves, Kahn points out that the process should be planful, normalized, and explained to parents, teachers, and administrators. She also stresses the importance of informing students that they are engaged in a communication process rather than a talent show and of maintaining the confidentiality of the artwork done by students—it is not for exhibition. Kahn closes with the presentation of a stage-wise art therapy case with a high school junior who returned to school following alcohol abuse rehabilitation. In the last seven sessions, the client was able to summarize insights acquired about the role of alcohol in his schooling and interpersonal relationships coupled with a record free of alcohol-related or disciplinary actions.

Other physical activities in which student clients can engage therapeutically are drawing and writing. Whereas drawing is useful for children and adolescents, writing is probably more useful with adolescents and possibly older children. These activities provide alternative avenues for students to express themselves and may also be therapeutic action stage strategies. The process will be enhanced by counselors who can explain the strategies, help students carry them out, and help them find meaning in their drawings and writings.

Film, video, audio, and printed media are also nonverbal resources that counselors can employ as action strategies for children and adolescents. Again, counselors are challenged to be able to explain the purposes and procedures involved in these strategies, help their student clients carry them out, and help them find meaning in the messages. Knowing where to find media sources that are appropriate for specific student needs (e.g., grief, substance abuse, divorce) is a challenge. It behooves counselors to use media sources to enhance their intervention repertoires, and they may learn about media resources through catalogs, advertisements, annotated bibliographies, and journals.

HELPING STUDENTS VIA A BRIEF COUNSELING PROCESS

Models for brief counseling have appeared in the school counseling literature recently (Bruce, 1995; Littrell, 1998; Murphy, 2008). Bruce (1995) describes a brief counseling approach that is time limited by design, rather than by default. Essential components of this approach are (a) a strong working alliance between counselors and students, (b) affirmation and use of student strengths and resources, (c) high levels of counselor and student client affective and behavioral involvement, and (d) establishment of clear, concrete goals. Synonyms for brief counseling include *solution-focused counseling, brief solution-focused counseling,* and *brief solution-oriented interviewing and counseling.* Murphy (1994, 2008), referring to the approach as solution-focused counseling, believes that counselors should focus on increasing their student clients' existing success, rather than on trying to eliminate problems. In this approach, counselors help students identify exceptions and encourage them to engage in the exceptions more often. An example follows:

> A middle school counselor is seeing a female student whose presenting problem is stated vaguely as wanting to be more successful academically. The counselor quickly helps the student assess the problem in concrete terms. In this hypothetical case, the student and the counselor agree that academic success involves her doing her homework more consistently and correctly and then getting higher grades. Next, the counselor helps the student client identify solutions to the problem that the student attempted previously, looking for exceptions (specific circumstances in which the presenting problem does not occur or occurs with less intensity; Murphy, 2008). The student client indicates that when she takes her schoolwork home and completes it in a quiet environment and in a timely manner, she seems to be more successful. The counselor then helps the student determine short-term goals that are concrete, achievable, and measurable, establishing a deadline for achieving the goals. With the counselor's assistance, the student client decides that she wants to feel that she is getting her homework done successfully for the next month with the hope of improving her grades. They agree that the student will set aside a specific amount of time each evening to complete her homework in a quiet place at home.

The student now has control of her own solution, and measurable, achievable goals have been established. The plan just described could conceivably have been accomplished in one counseling session. Follow-up sessions are in order to determine how well the student is doing and whether the goals need to be revisited. Murphy (2008) refers to these as "booster sessions." Counselors use their social influence to help students own and maintain their accomplishments. Another feature of the approach is the possibility that the effects of the intervention strategy will generalize to other aspects of the student client's life. Bruce and Hopper (1997), LaFountain, Garner, and Eliason (1996), and Murphy (2008) report research that provides some empirical support for the claims of proponents of this approach, indicating that it has promise for school counseling both in individual and group counseling relationships.

One criticism of the brief counseling approach is that the building a counselor-client relationship or working alliance based on empathy may be overlooked in an attempt to move quickly to setting goals. Aware of this concern, Ivey and Ivey (2007) have demonstrated that all five stages in their helping model can be incorporated into the brief counseling process. Should there be instances in which school counselors fail to establish rapport with student clients successfully yet are able to provide concrete assistance, one might argue that providing concrete assistance is a form of empathy as Menacker (1976) proposed in his theory of activist guidance.

HELPING STUDENTS THROUGH SMALL GROUP COUNSELING

Sometimes a group mode is the most effective vehicle for achieving intervention goals. Group counseling interventions, for example, have been used to develop and foster resiliency in middle school students. Data from these interventions have shown that some students may increase in their grade point averages and personal-social functioning following the interventions (Rose & Steen, 2014). Small group counseling may also be used to enhance academic motivation (Rowell & Hong, 2013) and to improve the organizational and time-management skills of underachieving students (Berger, 2013).

Group counseling has advantages over individual counseling. Krieg (1988) points out that group members may keep fellow members honest, preventing them from manipulating counselors as easily as they might during individual sessions. Dinkmeyer (1969) suggests that group relationships are more realistic than individual relationships between adult counselors and children or adolescents. When in group settings, counselors can observe social interactions among the members, peers may serve as role models, peer feedback is available, student clients have opportunities to help their peers, and they may become aware that they are not alone in their circumstances.

Group counseling differs from group guidance (i.e., prevention programming), group therapy, and sensitivity training. The distinctions are important considerations for school counselors. Two basic differences between group guidance and group counseling are the roles of the leaders and the goals of the groups. Group guidance goals are determined by the leaders and are usually instructive and preventive in nature. The role of the leader is pedagogical—instructing, informing, directing, and leading. Group counseling goals are determined by the needs of the members, and the role of the leader is therapeutic—using counseling skills to help members of the group achieve individual and common goals. Group counseling is appropriate for the schools and is within the scope of the school counselor's training. The members are usually volunteers who are functioning normally and possibly are at risk. Topics are personal, often related to normal developmental concerns, and are shared by the members. Desired outcomes include greater self-understanding, self-acceptance, and resolution of targeted concerns.

The basic individual counseling and challenging skills are important ingredients of group counseling. Counselors also use skills more specific to group counseling, such as forming groups, teaching members about group processes, understanding the finer points of the small group process contrasted with individual counseling, and mediating between and among members. Group counseling is not without challenges. Scheduling time for counseling groups in the schools is more difficult than scheduling individual counseling sessions. The difficulty of bringing groups of students together for counseling is compounded by the need to find student volunteers who share the same goals and can be scheduled together. When working in groups, many counselors find that maintaining a leadership role is more difficult than working with individuals. Maintaining confidentiality is more challenging in small counseling groups because several individuals might breach it, rather than only two.

Group counseling appears to be more cost-effective than individual counseling, and sometimes that may be true. More important, group counseling may be the most successful strategy for school counselors to use to help some student clients. Therefore, it appears to be an important part of the school counselor's repertoire. An example of a group counseling intervention for elementary school children points out that successful group counseling has many features that often do not come to the attention of casual observers (Corey & Corey, 1997):

> Students ranging in age from 6 to 11 years were referred to group counseling by a principal, their teachers, and the school nurse. The students were experiencing a host of problems that, in turn, influenced their academic performance. The counselor's goal was to alleviate school problems and prevent arrested development by helping the students cope with underlying problems. She hoped to identify maladaptive behaviors, teach the students to express their emotions constructively, and provide an atmosphere where they could express their emotions freely while understanding that problems are caused by the way they act on feelings, rather than by the feelings themselves. Important ingredients of the counseling process were as follows:
>
> The counselor worked with the students individually and in small groups.
> The students received tutoring from empathic tutors concurrently with the counseling.
> The students and their parents agreed to participate only after informed consent sessions.
> The counselor had continuous meetings with parents, teachers, the school nurse, school psychologists, and the principal during the helping process.
> The counselor engaged in social action activities as needed to help the students and their families receive clothing, food, money, and special services.

Several groups were formed. Those deemed most successful consisted of 3 to 5 students of the same age and gender. In forming the groups, which were open to new members at any time, the counselor attempted to combine withdrawn and outgoing students and to keep together students experiencing similar problems. The typical group met twice per week for 30 to 60 minutes. Students could leave a session before it ended, although they were encouraged to stay. A termination date was set in advance, and the students were prepared for termination as it approached.

Activities designed to help the students express their emotions safely included role playing, play therapy, acting out special situations, painting, finishing stories started by the leader, puppet shows, playing music, and dancing. Most students manifested observable behavior changes. The leader commented that although the group provided an excellent setting for the students to learn and practice relational skills, the individual counseling provided opportunities to pay each student more attention and to develop a trusting relationship.

Hoag and Burlingame (1997) reported findings from a meta-analytic review of studies of group counseling that had been published between 1974 and 1997, and the findings are very encouraging. Fifty-six studies were included in the review. Most studies (approximately 74%) took place in schools, 20% involved school counselors as leaders, and 25% involved mixtures of school counselors and other school professionals such as school psychologists and school social workers. The overall effects of the 56 studies were labeled as *moderate;* however, there was a wide range of effectiveness across the 56 studies. Disruptive behavior, anxiety, adjustment to divorce, cognitive performance, social skills, and self-esteem were among the outcomes that appeared to be targeted successfully in the counseling groups. Two demographic variables were influenced differently. In the socioeconomic status category, middle-class students received more from group counseling then working-class students generally. Regarding settings, group counseling conducted in clinics was more successful than in schools.

HELPING STUDENTS EXPERIENCING CRISES

Although not labeled as such, school counseling offices are often viewed as drop-in counseling centers. Some students never drop in and have to be invited. Others make appointments. Some drop in to see whether a counselor is available. Emergencies or crises occur in the schools, as well as in the greater society. Some emergencies are handled in the main office, by nurses, or by other staff members. Students in crisis also find their way to the counseling office, and it behooves counselors to have crisis counseling skills in their intervention repertoire. For example, students grieving over the suicide of a classmate may be overwhelmed. Others who have just had a traumatic experience (e.g., a physical beating, taunts and insults from peers, a suddenly broken relationship, a rejection letter from a prospective college or employer, receipt of disappointingly low scores on a college entrance exam) may panic. In these cases and others like them, counselors do not have the advantage of making appointments or opening the interviews in a relatively calm working atmosphere.

Crisis counseling is an immediate, time-limited treatment process. Students are clearly unable to employ the usual coping mechanisms, and counselors do not have time to move patiently through the usual counseling steps. Because students in crisis are extremely amenable to being assisted, counselors who act quickly and appropriately can be very helpful. Even in crisis situations, counselors can follow potential helping stages (Caplan, 1961). First, the counselor can assess how effectively the student is functioning and whether an immediate referral is necessary (determine whether the student needs medical attention). Second, if an immediate referral is not needed, the counselor can help the student cope with powerful affect, accept that affect, and find out the causes of the affect (use basic counseling skills). Third, some sort of immediate resolution or plan to resolve the problem is negotiated with the student (use basic counseling and interpersonal influencing skills). Next, after determining whether it is appropriate for the student to be allowed to leave (e.g., determine whether the student is expressing suicide ideation) or whether the student wishes to end the interview, the counselor will determine whether termination, referral, or an appointment is in order.

All that has been suggested about crisis counseling thus far is clearly within the basic counseling repertoire of school counselors. Interestingly, school counselors cannot choose whether to include crisis counseling in their repertoires. Crises will seek them out, and they will be expected to respond successfully. Therefore, it is important for their students' welfare and their own reputations that school counselors be prepared to respond to crises. A strategy that counselors may employ to be prepared for crises is to conduct controlled simulations of possible crisis interventions, following them with analyses of their performances to rectify problems encountered during the simulations.

Roberts (1995) provides an example of how a small, rural school system that was prepared in advance responded to a crisis. A 14-year-old student with a long, troubled history took his life 3 weeks after classes had dismissed for summer vacation. Although the school had a crisis prevention-intervention team, it was not prepared to respond during the summer vacation. Under the circumstances, the school counselor collected accurate information about the event, contacted those members of the team who could be located to ensure that they knew the facts and could dispel rumors, and secured commitments from some of them to volunteer to hold conferences with students they had contact with in the community. Most of the immediate postvention responsibilities were handled by the counselor, the principal, and the school secretary.

The school served as the center for communications about everything, including the facts about the suicide and information about the funeral. Care was taken to protect the family's privacy and to prevent speculation and rumors. Telephone calls were answered and messages returned. The counselor scheduled supportive interviews with students and others in need (e.g., nurses in the hospital emergency room) on request. Members of the deceased student's peer group and their parents were contacted to provide support and to encourage the parents to provide support as well. Home visits were made to these students to provide immediate assistance, inform them about sources of help in the future, and assess their emotional stability. Local media outlets were requested to handle the matter tactfully. The school was kept open to assist students and adults from early morning until late at night for 5 days following the suicide.

Long-range postvention continued through the summer and into the next school year. For example, all faculty members were briefed at the first teachers' meeting, faculty members feeling guilt were seen by the counselor, and the student's peer group members were monitored for 18 months.

TERMINATING THE COUNSELING PROCESS: HELPING STUDENT CLIENTS GENERALIZE AND ACT ON THEIR ACTION PLANS

Individual and group counseling relationships are analogous to lives in that they have beginnings and endings. The endings may be good because the student clients are ready, they may be difficult because the students are resistant, or they may be bad because they occur prematurely. Ward (1984) recommends that termination be viewed as one of several stages in the counseling process. Indirectly supporting the termination-as-a-stage concept, Krieg (1988) advocates devoting 10% of the life of a group to termination.

Cummings (1986) suggests that therapy and counseling can be thought of as analogous to medicine without adopting the medical treatment model. He thinks that the ending of a counseling relationship is considered an interruption rather than a termination. Physicians treat patients for problems (e.g., the flu), and when the treatments are completed, the physician-patient relationship is interrupted. The relationship may be reactivated to treat different or recurring problems (e.g., headaches). The relationship is, therefore, continuous, with intermittent contacts when needed. If responsive counseling interventions are viewed similarly, then termination will not be treated as a permanent event. School counselors are encouraged to view termination as an interruption in the counseling process.

The basic counseling and challenging skills are important as counselors engage in terminating or interrupting individual and group counseling relationships. These skills provide an appropriate climate for carrying out the activities required to accomplish the following goals:

- Evaluating student client readiness,
- Resolving affective issues between students and counselors or among group members,
- Maximizing transfer of training to the real world,
- Enhancing student client self-reliance and confidence,
- Coping with and responding to premature terminations,
- Enhancing the prospects of student clients being able to cope successfully after the terminations,
- Making successful referrals when needed, and
- Ensuring that student clients are aware of their counselors' availability after the terminations. (Corey et al., 1992; Ward, 1984)

Achieving these goals is challenging because the issues are varied and because student clients respond differently to the circumstances associated with termination/interruption. School counselors can achieve the goals eclectically, using what works from their repertoire of skills.

Although counseling interventions are conceivably available to all students, and counselors are employed to serve all student clients to the best of their ability, as Yalom (1975) points out, the matching of interventions, counselors, and student clients is less than perfect. Freedom to terminate or interrupt is an important option because it is a source of protection for the student client. Although counseling interventions in the schools are imperfect, counselors can do much to increase the probability that the interventions are good by having a desire to serve and help their student clients and by being knowledgeable about counseling and skillful at it. School counselors have the freedom to choose whether to do everything in their power to provide effective counseling interventions.

EVALUATING INDIVIDUAL AND GROUP COUNSELING

THE CHALLENGE OF PROVIDING EVIDENCE OF COUNSELING INTERVENTION COMPETENCE

There are many challenges associated with evaluating the impact of small group counseling. These challenges are similar to those posed by evaluating prevention and development strategies. Evaluating individual counseling is also challenging. To evaluate individual counseling efforts requires a strategy that treats each case independently of the others, and this approach at first glance probably seems overwhelmingly difficult to manage and report. In addition, the process and content of individual and small group counseling sessions is subject to ethical confidentiality standards. So how do school counselors evaluate counseling interventions and demystify for stakeholders what goes on behind those closed doors in the counseling suites?

A PROPOSAL FOR MEETING THE CHALLENGE

A Case-by-Case Approach

We propose that each individual student client or member of a small counseling group be considered an independent counseling intervention and evaluated accordingly. Our proposal is based on the following assumptions. Each student client has a specific goal, or specific goals, that will be targeted mutually by the counselor and student prior to determining how to achieve the goals. Progress toward achieving the goals can be measured over time. This second assumption is more elusive in some cases than in others because not all counseling goals are equally measurable. Therefore, not all counseling interventions will lend themselves to this approach. Yet enough interventions may qualify to allow professional counselors using this approach to provide sufficient evaluation data about their individual counseling interventions in order to be accountable to stakeholders in this domain. Continuing with our assumptions, confidentiality can be maintained by assigning pseudonyms or numbers to each intervention case when reporting the findings.

Our proposal is based on a research approach referred to as single-subject experimental designs (Heppner, Kivlighan, & Wampold, 1999). The common characteristics of single-subject designs are (a) mutually specify the counseling intervention goals so counselor and student clients are in agreement and working together to achieve them, (b) identify objectively scored behaviors or measures of goal attainment that student clients can use successfully and that provide meaningful data for record keeping, (c) collect assessments of the behavior and goal attainment measures over time segments that are appropriate for the targeted goals (e.g., hours, days, weeks, or months), and (d) establish baseline data on the behavior and goal attainment measures before attempting to institute a plan or program to achieve the goals. We offer an example at this point in order to help you understand the process.

A Case Example

Liu and Baker (1993) reported the progress of efforts to help a 4-year-old Chinese girl who was experiencing culture shock when attending a day-care center at a large U.S. university. The child's progress in response to a counselor's friendship training program was charted graphically. The evaluation design, known as ABA, is one of several single-case designs that can be used to plot the progress of individual student clients (Heppner et al., 1999). In this case, A represents the time when no intervention occurs, and B represents the time when the intervention is in progress. Thus, the first A-phase allows a counselor to collect baseline data, the B-phase provides information about a student client's progress during the intervention, and the second A-phase offers data depicting the student's progress after the intervention is completed. In this case, student progress is visible and relatively easy to determine. The process itself is also relatively easy. A key factor in using this approach is being able to identify outcomes that lend themselves to observing and counting behaviors. When working with cases of this nature, the single-case design is useful for school counselors. From an accountability perspective, counselors can present graphic representations from several cases, with student clients' identity protected, as evidence of effectiveness (i.e., accountability). This offers promise for counselors who feel nagged by criticisms that no one knows what is being done that is worthwhile behind the closed doors to their counseling sessions.

Collect Case Data in a Portfolio

We suggest that school counselors use the AB single-case design to evaluate their counseling interventions. This requires data collection during a baseline phase and during the intervention. In addition to being a useful accountability strategy, this evaluation approach has promise for helping clients manage their progress toward goal attainment better and offers counselors data to help them work with specific student clients more efficiently and effectively. The following list gives examples of behaviors and attitudes that can be assessed in single case designs and suggests how behaviors and goals that do not lend themselves to clearly defined behaviors can be assessed. The behaviors provided in the list are one set that can be used if appropriate. Other behaviors will be peculiar to individual cases. The process remains constant, however. That is, the mutual goals set by counselors and student clients focus on either trying to increase or decrease the targeted behaviors.

Targeted counseling intervention goals that do not lend themselves to identifying behaviors that can be reduced or increased over time can be assessed by easily employed goal attainment scales. When employing goal attainment scales, student clients rate their perceptions/attitudes on a scale with low and high dimensions (e.g., "On a scale of 1 *[low]* to 10 *[high]*, how do you rate yourself on what we accomplished today?" [How you feel today, how close we are to making and achievable action, etc.])?

Assess Changes in Academic Performance Behaviors Over Time (Counselors and Student Clients Keep Records of Changes in the Following Behaviors)

- Grades or grade-point averages
- How often homework is completed
- Increased time devoted to homework/studies
- Decrease in wasted time
- Increased attendance.

Assess Ratings of Targeted Attitudes/Perceptions Over Time (Counselors and Student Clients Keep Records of Changes in Ratings on a Scale of 1 *[low]* to 10 *[high]*)

- How do you feel about your relationships with other students today?
- How do you rate your friendships today?
- How do you rate the decision you made today?
- How do your rate your relationship with (fill in the blank) today?
- How do you rate the relationship with your math teacher today?

Students involved in individual and small group counseling spend significantly more time away from sessions with counselors than they do in the sessions. Therefore, establishing systems for helping student clients monitor their progress toward achieving targeted counseling goals when away from their schools and their school counselors is an important component in their successfully achieving targeted counseling goals. Cormier et al. (2013) point out that the mere act of paying attention to one's counseling goals through self-monitoring activities encourages the clients toward achieving their goals. We recommend that counselors bring this idea to the attention of their student clients and help them set up systems for conducting the self-monitoring process. Unfortunately, if counselors merely suggest that their student clients engage in this activity without helping them set it up, the probability that no self-monitoring will occur is considerable.

School counselors are capable of helping numerous students who are experiencing personal developmental challenges through individual and group counseling interventions. Preparation for engaging in responsive counseling interventions successfully is a component of counselor education training programs. We have pointed out as well that the individual and small group counseling process is amenable to evaluation strategies that can lead to achieving accountability in this domain. Unfortunately, some students are unable to be successful in school because they manifest problems that are beyond the training and scope of what school counselors can respond to effectively.

FINAL THOUGHT

Throughout this chapter, we discuss individual and group counseling in schools. Counselor Education graduate students often have differing abilities and interests related to counseling interventions. Recently, we heard a student comment that she became a counselor education student primarily because of her interest in working individually with students. She was surprised to learn in her first school counseling course that some school counselors spend more time doing group interventions than individual interventions. She wondered what her future as a school counselor would be like. Would she be able to fulfill her desire to work individually with students or would she be spending more time in group work? Also, how much control would she have in making decisions about the interventions (individual or group) to use as a school counselor?

COMPREHENSIVE SCHOOL COUNSELING PROGRAM COMPONENT

1. Create a plan for receiving referrals to the school counselor.
2. Conduct an inventory of your community and create a referral resource list for the following:
   a. Students with disabilities
   b. LGBTQ populations
   c. College access
   d. Health care
   e. Homelessness
   f. Immigrant populations that are unique to your community

REFLECTION POINT

School counselors who have questions about planning and implementing individual and group counseling strategies may want to consider some of the following activities in moving toward increased engagement in prevention programming:

1. Analyze a counseling model in terms of the following:
   a. Basic steps
   b. Basic competencies
   c. Multicultural potential

2. Make an inventory of responsive counseling intervention competencies that are new to you and learn more about them.

3. From the responsive counseling intervention competencies suggested in this chapter, select those that you think are debatable and debate their merits.

4. Analyze, discuss, and/or debate the intent of the following statement: "School counselors have neither the credentials nor the training required to provide therapy, but they can offer therapeutic counseling."

5. Discuss or debate the merits of eclecticism and multicultural competence in school counseling.

6. Among the various competencies cited in the chapter, identify those that are important or mostly important for counselors working in the elementary, middle, and secondary schools; identify those that are universal across all three levels. Which list is the largest? Why do you think it is the largest?

7. Compare the suggested basic competencies in this chapter with those taught in the curriculum in your own training program. Analyze your findings.

8. Evaluate the concept that the freedom to terminate counseling is an important protection for clients.

9. Discuss the merits of brief, solution-focused counseling.

10. Debate the merits of the recommendations for evaluating individual and small group counseling presented in this chapter.

APPLICATION TO TECHNOLOGY

1. Watch a film or a talk show and analyze the differences among conversing, interviewing, and counseling.

2. Create an online spreadsheet that can help you keep track of specific community resources.

REFERENCES

Adelman, H. S., & Taylor, L. (2002). School counselors and school reform: New directions. *Professional School Counseling, 5,* 235–248.

American School Counselor Association. (2010). *Ethical standards for school counselors.* Alexandria, VA: Author.

American School Counselor Association. (2012). *The ASCA National Model: A framework for school counseling programs* (3rd ed.). Alexandria, VA: Author.

American School Counselor Association. (2013). ASCA National Model 3.0: When it's time to change. *ASCA School Counselor, 49,* 10–13.

Bandura, A. (1986). *Social foundations of thought and action: A social cognitive theory.* Upper Saddle River, NJ: Prentice Hall.

Barlow, K., Strother, J., & Landreth, G. (1985). Child-centered play therapy: Nancy from baldness to curls. *School Counselor, 32,* 347–356.

Berger, S. (2013). Bring out the brilliance: A counseling intervention for underachieving students. *Professional School Counseling, 17,* 86–96.

Bruce, M. A. (1995). Brief counseling: An effective model for change. *School Counselor, 42,* 353–363.

Bruce, M. A., & Hopper, G. C. (1997). Brief counseling versus traditional counseling: A comparison of effectiveness. *School Counselor, 44,* 171–184.

Caplan, G. (1961). *An approach to community mental health.* New York: Grune & Stratton.

Corey, G., Corey, M. S., Callanan, P., & Russell, J. M. (1992). *Group techniques* (2nd ed.). Pacific Grove, CA: Brooks/Cole.

Corey, M. S., & Corey, G. (1997). *Groups: Process and practice* (6th ed.). Pacific Grove, CA: Brooks/Cole.

Cormier, S., Nurius, P. S., & Osborn, C. J. (2013). *Interviewing strategies for helpers: Fundamental skills and cognitive behavioral interventions* (7th ed.). Belmont, CA: Brooks/Cole Cengage Learning.

Cowan, E. W., & Presbury, J. H. (2000). Meeting client resistance and reactance with reverence. *Journal of Counseling & Development, 78,* 411–419.

Cummings, N. A. (1986). The dismantling of our health system. *American Psychologist, 41,* 426–431.

DeKruyf, L., Auger, R. W., & Trice-Black, S. (2013). The role of school counselors in meeting students' mental health needs: Examining issues of professional identity. *Professional School Counseling, 16,* 271–282.

Dinkmeyer, D. (1969). Group counseling theory and techniques. *School Counselor, 17,* 148–152.

Doyle, R. E. (1992). *Essential skills and strategies in the helping process.* Pacific Grove, CA: Brooks/Cole.

Education Trust. (1997). *Transforming school counseling initiative.* DeWitt Wallace-Reader's Digest Grant. Washington, DC: Author.

Egan, G. (2013). *The skilled helper: A problem-management and opportunity development approach to helping* (10th ed.). Belmont, CA: Brooks/Cole Cengage Learning.

Ellis, A. (2007). *Rational-emotive behavior therapy: It works for me—It can work for you.* New York: Penguin Random House Prometheus Books.

Galassi, M. D., & Galassi, J. P. (1977). *Assert yourself! How to be your own person.* New York: Human Sciences Press.

Gehart, D. (2013). *Theory and treatment planning in counseling and psychotherapy.* Belmont, CA: Brooks/Cole.

Gendlin, E. T. (1996). *Focusing oriented psychotherapy: A manual of experiential methods.* New York: Guilford.

Gysbers, N. C., & Henderson, P. (2001). Comprehensive guidance and counseling programs: A rich history and a bright future. *Professional School Counseling, 4,* 246–256.

Heppner, P. P., Kivlighan, Jr., D. M., & Wampold, B. E. (1999). *Research design in counseling* (2nd ed.). Belmont, CA: Wadsworth.

Herring, R. D. (1997). *Multicultural counseling in schools: A synergistic approach*. Alexandria, VA: American Counseling Association.

Hoag, M. J., & Burlingame, G. M. (1997). Evaluating the effectiveness of child and adolescent group treatment. *Journal of Clinical Child Psychology, 26*, 234–246.

Horan, J. J. (1979). *Counseling for effective decision making*. North Scituate, MA: Duxbury.

House, R. M., & Hayes, R. L. (2002). School counselors: Becoming key players in school reform. *Professional School Counseling, 5*, 249–256.

Ivey, A. E., & Gluckstern, N. B. (1974). *Microcounseling: An introduction*. North Amherst, MA: Microtraining Associates, Incorporated.

Ivey, A. E., & Ivey, M. B. (2007). Intentional interviewing and counseling: Facilitating client development in a multicultural society (6th ed.). Pacific Grove, CA: Thomson Brooks/Cole.

Ivey, A. E., Ivey, M. B., & Zalaquett, C. P. (2014). *Intentional interviewing and counseling: Facilitating client development in a multicultural society* (8th ed.). Belmont, CA: Brooks/Cole Cengage Learning.

Janis, I. L. (1983). The role of social support in adherence to stressful decisions. *American Psychologist, 38*, 143–160.

Kahn, B. B. (1999). Art therapy with adolescents: Making it work for school counselors. *Professional School Counseling, 2*, 291–298.

Keat, D. B. (1990a). Change in child multimodal counseling. *Elementary School Guidance and Counseling, 24*, 248–262.

Keat, D. B. (1990b). *Child multimodal therapy*. Norwood, NJ: Ablex.

Krieg, E. J. (1988). *Group leadership training and supervision manual for adolescent group counseling in schools* (3rd ed.). Muncie, IN: Accelerated Development.

LaFountain, R. M., Garner, N. E., & Eliason, G. T. (1996). Solution-focused counseling groups: A key for school counselors. *School Counselor, 43*, 256–266.

Lambie, G., & Milsom, A. (2010). A narrative approach to supporting students diagnosed with learning disabilities. *Journal of Counseling & Development, 88*, 196–203.

Landreth, G. L. (2002). *Play therapy: The art of relationships* (2nd ed.). New York: Brunner-Routledge.

Landreth, G. L., Homeyer, L. E., Glover, G., & Sweeney, D. S. (1996). *Play therapy interventions with children's problems*. Northvale, NJ: Jason Aronson.

Lange, A., & Jakubowski, P. (1976). *Responsible assertive behavior*. Champaign, IL: Research Press.

Littrell, J. M. (1998). *Brief counseling in action*. New York: Norton.

Liu, Y. C., & Baker, S. B. (1993). Enhancing cultural adaptation through friendship training. *Elementary School Guidance and Counseling, 18*, 92–103.

Meichenbaum, D. H. (1993). Stress inoculation training: A 20-year update. In P. M. Lehrer & R. L. Woolfolk (Eds.), *Principles and practices of stress management* (2nd ed., pp. 373–406). New York: Guilford.

Meichenbaum, D. H. (1994). *A clinical handbook: Practical therapist manual for assessing and treating adults with post-traumatic stress disorders*. Waterloo, Ontario: Institute Press.

Menacker, J. (1976). Toward a theory of activist guidance. *Personnel and Guidance Journal, 54*, 318–321.

Murphy, J. J. (1994). Working with what works: A solution-focused approach to school behavior problems. *School Counselor, 42*, 59–72.

Murphy, J. J. (2008). *Solution-focused counseling in schools* (2nd ed.). Alexandria, VA: American Counseling Association.

Nafziger, J., & DeKruyf, L. (2013). Narrative counseling for professional school counselors. *Professional School Counseling, 16*, 290–302.

O'Connor, K. J. (1991). *The play therapy primer: An integration of theories and techniques.* New York: John Wiley.

O'Connor, K. J., & Schaefer, C. E. (Eds.). (1994). *Handbook of play therapy: Vol. 2. Advances and innovations.* New York: John Wiley.

Ritchie, M. H. (1986). Counseling the involuntary client. *Journal of Counseling & Development, 64,* 516–518.

Roberts, W. B., Jr. (1995). Postvention and psychological autopsy in the suicide of a 14-year-old public school student. *School Counselor, 42,* 322–330.

Rogers, C. (1951). *Client-centered therapy.* Boston: Houghton Mifflin.

Rose, J., & Steen, S. (2014). The achieving success everyday group counseling model: Fostering resiliency in middle school students. *Professional School Counseling, 18,* 28–37.

Rowell, L., & Hong, E. (2013). Academic motivation: Concepts, strategies, and counseling approaches. *Professional School Counseling, 16,* 158–171.

Schaefer, C. E., & Cangelosi, D. M. (Eds.). (1993). *Play therapy techniques.* Northvale, NJ: Jason Aronson.

Sue, D. W. (1992). The challenge of multiculturalism: The road less traveled. *American Counselor, 1,* 6–14.

Sue, D. W., Ivey, A. E., & Pedersen, P. B. (1996). *A theory of multicultural counseling and therapy.* Pacific Grove, CA: Brooks/Cole.

Ward, D. E. (1984). Termination of individual counseling: Concepts and strategies. *Journal of Counseling & Development, 63,* 21–25.

Yalom, I. D. (1975). *The theory and practice of group psychotherapy* (2nd ed.). New York: Basic Books.

REFERRAL AND COORDINATION IN SCHOOL COUNSELING

9

RELATED STANDARDS OF PRACTICE

CACREP CORE	2.F.5.k.m.
CACREP SCHOOL COUNSELING	5.G.2.k., 5.G.3.l.m.

Goal: To explain the unique circumstances of the referral and coordination functions in school counseling. To propose competencies for counselor-initiated referrals and a system for managing referrals to school counselors. To highlight the place of coordination in the referral process.

Lakisha, an 8-year old living in North Florida with her grandmother and grandfather, came to school almost every day wearing long-sleeved sweaters and heavy wool pants. When teachers questioned her about wearing such heavy clothing in a warm climate, Lakisha responded simply that she liked the way the clothes looked. She would then lower her eyes and walk away quickly. One teacher, suspicious that something was wrong, asked the school counselor to speak with Lakisha. Noticing that Lakisha moved with great care and with a grimace on her face, the counselor immediately referred Lakisha to the school nurse, who examined Lakisha and discovered burns and bruises on her arms and legs. The counselor and school nurse immediately contacted social services and began the difficult process of investigating and repairing the tragedy of Lakisha's existence. The process required the coordination of many professionals and involved diligence to avoid having Lakisha's case lost in a sea of bureaucracy.

DEMAND FOR REFERRAL AND COORDINATION IN SCHOOL COUNSELING

In previous chapters, a case was made for balanced school counseling programs consisting of equally important responsive counseling and proactive prevention emphases in comprehensive school counseling programs. Individual and small group counseling and prevention programming were presented as important competencies in a balanced program. All professionals are limited in expertise and time; they refer individuals to others whose services are more appropriate. In addition, school counselors receive referrals from other professionals who are also limited in expertise and time. Consequently, professional school counselors are challenged to have the skills to make referrals, manage the referrals they receive, coordinate the process once the referrals have been made or accepted, and collaborate with important service providers beyond the school settings. The case of Lakisha described earlier depicted a situation where several referrals occurred with a school counselor directly involved in the processes.

Referring and coordinating are functions that fit within a broader school counselor role concept that appears to be increasingly important. Atkinson and Juntunen (1994) use the label *school-home-community liaison* for this role. As liaisons, school counselors work with students, parents, and members of the community to identify and use valuable human services inside and outside the school system that meet both remedial and enhancement goals for students, and then coordinate the acquisition and use of the services, acting at times like brokers.

Collaboration between the schools and their communities seems to be increasingly important. Students are faced with problems that require comprehensive services, many of which are beyond the capacities of the services the schools can provide. Hobbs and Collison (1995) found evidence that collaboration between the schools and local agencies (in their study, youth services teams in four communities in Oregon) is increasing. They believe that school counselors need to reassess their role in the context of the community rather than the school and to develop or enhance collaboration skills.

Downing, Pierce, and Woodruff (1993) picture this collaboration in the context of developing networks among the community's professional helpers inside and outside the schools, a challenging yet potentially fruitful undertaking. Bryan and Holcomb-McCoy (2004) highlight the importance of including families in these partnerships.

Our focus in this chapter is on two types of referrals. They are treated separately and referred to as either counselor-initiated referrals or referrals to counselors. Because counseling is a human services profession, it is important that counselors help student clients receive needed services. At times, the needed services are beyond the scope and setting of school counseling. In such cases, school counselors help student clients through a referral process. The direction of these referrals is away from school counselors toward other professionals or sources of help. These are counselor-initiated referrals. Prospective referees are encouraged to use the school's counseling services voluntarily and, in so doing, to understand the goals and limitations of those services. At other times, school professionals (e.g., teachers, administrators) and individuals outside the schools who are interested in students' welfare (e.g., parents) look to counselors as a source of help for their students/children and make referrals to counselors. This process works best when the prospective referees clearly understand the counselors' range of competencies. All parties are served best when school counselors inform others about their services and manage efficiently the referrals they receive.

In the American School Counselor Association's (ASCA, 2012) National Model, referral is depicted as an indirect service through which school counselors seek help for students from professional resources in and out of the school when necessary. The Model highlights the potential for making referrals that provide needed assistance to students and their families in the academic, career, and personal/social development domains. The school-family-community collaboration writers point out the importance of collaborating cooperatively with family and community resources in order to make needed services available to students and their families in a systematic manner.

SCHOOL COUNSELOR–INITIATED REFERRALS

POINT OF VIEW

In the American Counseling Association's (2014) *Code of Ethics* and in the ASCA's (ASCA, 2010) *Ethical Standards for School Counselors,* referrals are presented as a mandate to do what is in the student client's best interests. Note the emphasis on competence and values in the two sections of the ACA *Code* that were addressed in Chapter 4.

If counselors **lack the competence** [bold type added] to be of professional assistance to clients, they avoid entering or continuing counseling relationships. Counselors are knowledgeable about culturally and clinically appropriate referral resources and suggest these alternatives. If clients decline the suggested referrals, counselors discontinue the relationship.

(ACA, 2014, Section A.11.a)

Counselors refrain from referring prospective and current clients based solely on the counselor's personally held **values, attitudes, beliefs, and behaviors** [bold type added]. Counselors respect the diversity of clients and seek training in areas where they are at risk of imposing their values onto clients, especially when the counselor's values are inconsistent with the client's goals or are discriminatory in nature.

(ACA, 2014, Section A.11.b.)

Professional school counselors . . . Make referrals when necessary or appropriate to outside resources for student and/or family support. Appropriate referrals may necessitate informing both parents/guardians and students of applicable resources and making proper plans for transitions with minimal interruption of services. Students maintain the right to discontinue the counseling relationship at any time.

(ASCA, 2010, A.5.a)

Two delicate issues that counselors face in the referral process are the related possibilities of referring student clients prematurely and of counseling them too long. On the one hand, busy counselors may wrongly view referral as a way to divest themselves of part of their counseling burden. Then referral sources become repositories for excess workloads. The motives behind such referrals are primarily selfish. Premature referrals may also result from counselors' feelings of inadequacy, low risk-taking thresholds, or failure to appreciate their own ability. Although counselors' intentions may be honorable, the outcomes are still premature referrals.

On the other hand, counselors may continue working with student clients too long for selfish reasons, such as a need to feel responsible for achieving successful closure with their student clients. This mistaken motivation serves the needs of the counselors, rather than those of the students. Counselors may also work with student clients too long for altruistic reasons, as when students convince them that no one else can help or refuse to be referred. Kimmerling (1993) refers to deciding when to refer as "When Saying No Is the Right Thing to Do" (p. 5).

Shertzer and Stone (1981) offer suggestions for resolving these referral fallacies. First, counselors realize that referral is not merely a technique they use when operating a clearinghouse. Second, they understand that referrals are not limited to emergencies. Many emergencies can be averted by timely referrals. Third, referrals are not admissions of failure. Instead, they are intelligent decisions to provide the best possible assistance to student clients.

When approaching the referral decision, counselors are forced to look within themselves and beyond their work settings to ask several important questions. These questions draw on evaluations of their competencies, the competencies of their referral sources, and their own motives. Assessing one's competencies realistically can be difficult and painful. Although counselors are the main sources of information about their own competencies, respected colleagues can provide wise counsel.

Knowing the competencies of potential referral sources requires careful intelligence gathering. Sources of information are numerous, and using them requires considerable effort. Information can be acquired through cooperative research with colleagues. Weinrach (1984) suggests that referees can make the referral process more mutual by demystifying it. What counselors and students should know about referees includes their qualifications, expertise, and orientation; intake procedures, fee structures, and scheduling methods; whether the services are publicly or privately provided; follow-up procedures; and general attitudes toward clients.

Motives can be controlled if counselors hold their students' welfare above their own needs. This is continuous because student client cases change and counselors grow in experience and competence. In all, the decision process requires honest introspection and a willingness to spend time and energy gathering information.

A unique aspect of the referral function in school counseling is that most student clients are minors. Therefore, the referral process is complicated by the need for parental knowledge and cooperation. At times, all seems well until the students' parents or guardians become involved. Parents may be the source of students' attitudes that lead to ignoring or rejecting referral suggestions, and usually parents cannot be forced to respond as desired. On other occasions, students who are minors may themselves make the referral process extremely difficult. They may not want their parents or guardians to know about the issues leading to referral suggestions, or they may ignore or reject referral suggestions. Children and adolescents are less likely than adults to understand the referral process and to be objective about it.

School counselors face the additional challenge of working with parents or guardians through their children, often without authority to require desired responses. Because of this two-tiered decision-making situation, school counselors are challenged to be more adept at making referrals than many other helping professionals. They also face the dilemma of deciding whether to continue counseling students who fail to accept referral suggestions or to discontinue the relationships. Discontinuing counseling services under these circumstances is ethically acceptable. Yet failing to respond to referral suggestions may be caused by parental attitudes, leaving students caught in the middle and counselors struggling to determine whether their own services are better for the student clients than none.

An additional challenge for school counselors is managed care. Many families may be insured by health insurance plans that place restrictions on one's freedom to choose service providers. Therefore, even though student clients and their parents are cooperative, their insurance may not cover the services being recommended or the services can be provided only by a restricted group of preferred or contracted providers. Counselors will then be challenged to become aware of a larger cohort of approved providers across various organizations serving their student clients' families.

FOUNDATIONS

Counselor-initiated referring and coordinating beg for a systematic approach. A system helps counselors know in advance what to do and makes the process more efficient for everyone. The process is more likely to progress effectively, and student clients are more likely to be treated appropriately. The five-stage helping model adapted from Ivey, Ivey, and Zalaquett (2014) for counseling is applicable to referring and coordinating, too. The five stages can be expressed as establishing an empathic relationship, listening to the student's story and searching for positive assets, mutually setting goals for the student, working with the student to explore alternatives and decide on an action plan, and helping the student to generate an action plan. The following suggested competencies are woven into the fabric of these stages.

BASIC COMPETENCIES FOR SCHOOL COUNSELOR–INITIATED REFERRALS

ESTABLISHING AN EMPATHIC RELATIONSHIP, LISTENING TO THE STUDENT'S STORY, AND SEARCHING FOR POSITIVE ASSETS

Counselors are challenged to know themselves and their referral sources—to evaluate realistically their own competencies as well as those of other referral sources. Beyond that, counselors who have sufficient knowledge about their student clients make educated decisions about referral sources. The basic counseling competencies are again paramount because most referrals begin as counseling or consulting relationships. An example follows:

> A high school teacher refers a student to a high school counselor after witnessing a noticeable change in the student's affect indicating that the student seemed depressed. The student responds to the counselor's invitation to have an interview. The counselor explains that the teacher is concerned about the student's welfare and has asked for help to be provided if needed. The student confirms that things are not good and agrees to talk with the counselor. Beginning the relationship as if it were a potential counseling intervention, the counselor asks the student tell her story. Using the basic responsive counseling skills, the counselor helps the student client try to identify and clarify the challenges while also seeking information about positive assets and concludes that the student seems quite depressed and is also at a loss to offer specific reasons for the depressed affect.

MUTUALLY SETTING GOALS FOR THE STUDENT

Bringing a counseling relationship to the point where goals are established helps counselors determine whether a referral needs to be suggested. Thus, the basic influencing skills are also part of the referral process. Because many student clients and their parents do not necessarily think they need specialized help outside the school system, counselors may have to use interpersonal influencing skills to challenge them to consider and accept a referral suggestion (e.g., interpretation/reframe, logical consequences, information sharing, immediacy). An example follows:

> The case of the depressed high school student moves to the goal-setting stage when the counselor, after having met with the student for two sessions to identify and clarify the situation, concludes that the student client is deeply depressed, seemingly unable to identify causes, and apparently in need of help that is beyond the scope of the counselor's competence. The counselor indicates to the student that the best source of help may be a referral to a clinician in private practice (e.g., psychologist or psychiatrist).

Counselor: We have talked extensively about how miserable you seem to feel, and you have indicated a desire to get some relief. I agree that you need and should get some relief, and I also think that the best way to get relief is to see a professional who is a specialist and can devote the proper amount of time that is needed to help you, doing so in a setting that is more private than being seen here at school.

Student: I don't know. That sounds expensive, and I don't know if my parents will agree to it. Besides, I don't want people to think I am crazy and have to see a "shrink."

Counselor: So you are concerned about the cost and what people will think, perhaps what you think about yourself as well (reflection of meaning). Are you familiar with the services of Wellsprings?

Student: No. What do they do?

Counselor: They may be able to help you without it being too expensive and without your thinking of yourself as needing to see a "shrink." Do you wish to know more?

Student: Yes.

The counselor then proceeds to provide accurate information about Wellsprings (information sharing). After sharing the information, the counselor asks, "Well, what do you think?"

Student: I don't know, it sounds pretty involved to me. I don't think I will have enough time, and my parents probably will object to my going there.

Counselor: It sounds involved, and you worry about what your parents will say. On the other hand, you have indicated to me that things are really bad and you have to get some help, and I have pointed out that the kind of help you seem to need is not really available here in school, leading me to suggest Wellsprings. We can explore other alternatives, but before we do, I'm wondering if you need to think first about how badly you want help and whether you and your parents are willing to make the commitment needed to take that first step. I want to help you, but I also think you need to take a good look at what you have just been saying. What do you think? (logical consequences)

In the foregoing interaction, the counselor employed three influencing responses: reflection of meaning, information sharing, and logical consequences. All are presented caringly and tentatively in the hope that the student client will accept a referral suggestion to achieve expressed goals.

WORKING WITH THE STUDENT TO EXPLORE ALTERNATIVES AND HELPING TO GENERATE AN ACTION PLAN

Sometimes, counseling relationships move into the action stage before a referral suggestion is considered, or the act of referring becomes the restorying and action stages of the helping relationship. In either case, where and how to refer become the basic referring objectives, and how to coordinate a successful referral becomes the third basic action strategy objective. Referring and coordinating competencies are devoted to responding to those questions.

Deciding where to refer student clients requires knowing a variety of referral sources. Acquisition of such information demands investigative skills, using time and energy to search the Internet, attend meetings of professional organizations, confer with colleagues, interview potential service providers, and evaluate advertisements. School counselors may also have opportunities to acquire useful information from service organizations. Hollis and Hollis (1965) suggest that awareness includes identification of sources, a working knowledge of their services, knowledge of ways to use the services, and development of reciprocal services. Box 9.1 lists various referral sources with which school counselors in any community might develop referral agreements.

Box 9.1 Potential Referral Resources Available to School Counselors

Local Volunteer Organizations

Churches—Clergy
Counseling Services
Emergency Financial Assistance
Health Councils
Hospitals
Information Services
Job Placement Services
Medical Societies
Nursing Services
Parents Without Partners
Planned Parenthood Association
Private Schools
Rape Crisis Centers
Referral Services
Runaway Hotlines
Sheltered Workshops
Thrift Shops

Government Agencies and Services

Bureau of Employment Security
Bureau of Special Health Services
Bureau of Vocational Rehabilitation
Child Welfare League of America
Child Welfare Services
Civil Service Commission
Community Action
County Board of Assistance

County Health Services
Department of Agriculture
Department of Consumer Services
Department of Human Services
Department of Public Welfare
Family Planning Centers
Foster Home Care
Home Health Services
Human Relations Commission
Mental Health/Mental Retardation
State Department of Health
State Hospitals
State Schools
Upward Bound
Youth Service Bureau

National Nonprofit Organizations

Al-Anon
Alateen
Alcoholics Anonymous
Altrusa International
American Association of University Women
American Bar Association
American Cancer Society
American Heart Association
American Red Cross
Catholic Social Services
Chamber of Commerce
Easter Seals
Economic Opportunity Commission
Goodwill
Junior Chamber of Commerce
Lions Club International
Lutheran Social Services
March of Dimes Foundation
Narcotics Anonymous
National Association for the Advancement of Colored People
National Association of Business and Professional Women
National Federation of the Blind
National Runaway Hotline
Optimist International
Rotary International
Salvation Army
YMCA
YWCA

School District Services

Administrators
Adult Education
Counseling Colleagues
Intermediate Service Units
School Nurses
School Psychologists
School Social Workers
Speech and Hearing Specialists
Teachers
Other Pupil Personnel Specialists

Proprietary Services

Attorneys
Boarding Houses
Chiropractors
Clinical Psychologists
Counseling Psychologists
Counselors
Employment Agencies
Nurses
Occupational Therapists
Opticians
Optometrists
Osteopaths
Physical Therapists
Physicians
Preparatory Schools
Professional Résumé Services
Psychiatrists

Multiculturally aware counselors will develop resource lists of "educational and community support services to meet the socioeconomic and cultural needs of culturally diverse students and their families" (ASCA, 1989, p. 322). Recognizing the importance of cultural sensitivity in the referral process, Atkinson and Juntunen (1994) recommend that counselors be familiar with services offered both in ethnic communities and in the larger community. They also suggest that referrals can be traditional—that is, to remediate problems—and can be made to enhance the development of ethnic students. In the latter instance, the coordinating function comes into play as counselors refer students to such programs as Big Brothers and Big Sisters and children's workshops and to such organized, sponsored athletic programs as Little League baseball that may enhance their development. Although those recommendations are from writers whose focus is on serving ethnic minority students, the ideas are useful for, and applicable to, serving all students. Examples of referrals made to enhance development are as follows:

> A middle school counselor pursuing the school-home-community liaison role engages in the following related activities as a part of his or her overall functioning as a school counselor during 1 week.

- The counselor coordinates arrangements for a group of students to visit nearby colleges and technical schools;
- The counselor, in conjunction with cooperating local employers, arranges for part-time work for several students who are borderline delinquents;
- The counselor recommends a Big Brother to an 11-year-old male student and coordinates a meeting between the student and a volunteer recommended by the Big Brother organization;
- A female student who has been attending an after-school drama workshop because the counselor recommended and arranged it stops by the office and reports that she is enjoying the activity.

After adequate information has been gathered, a system for storing and retrieving it is necessary. Options include personal memory and filing systems. In this age of micro-computers, the information can be stored relatively easily. Simplicity of organization and efficient retrieval are mandatory, so new information can be added, old information updated, and existing information accessed easily.

Community asset mapping is a process that holds promise for finding and organizing referral resources. "Community asset mapping can engage members of the school and surrounding neighborhoods in working together to identify the resources that are already readily available to them without having to rely on financial assistance" (Griffin & Farris, 2010, p. 249). The process consists of four basic steps: (1) developing a multidisciplinary team; (2) examining and assessing current resources and identifying new ones (i.e., individuals, citizens associations, and institutions within or near the community); (3) contacting individual and community resources (i.e., current and potential services and attitudes); and (4) developing and maintaining community asset maps.

Including *cultural brokers* among the multidisciplinary teams is recommended. These individuals are acculturated to the families in the service areas and able to help bridge potential school-family cultural gaps. Recommendations for the asset maps include (a) making them multilingual if necessary, (b) providing information guides and visual maps, and (c) realizing that the process is dynamic (i.e., the map is never completed).

Counselors are challenged to be willing to serve as reciprocal referral sources. It seems logical that counselors do for others that which others request them to do. To implement a reciprocal arrangement, formal or semiformal agreements can make both parties aware of the services each is prepared to deliver to the other on request.

Carrying the idea of organization a step farther, a follow-up system can be considered. Among the benefits is the acquisition of helpful information about the student clients and about the referral service. The follow-up can contain information from both parties covered in the referral service agreement. One example of a reciprocal feedback proposal follows:

> A school counselor successfully arranges for a referral of a student client to Dr. X. Per their agreement, Dr. X supplies the counselor with appropriate information about the client after acquiring signed permissions from the client or the client's parents. The counselor expects this feedback from Dr. X and will seek it out if necessary.

Because student clients are the most important parties in the referral process, follow-up data from them are a valuable source of information about the adequacy of referral services. Some sort of client survey is suggested. Important questions can be incorporated into these surveys by using any one of several available formats. Here are some areas to cover by questions in client surveys:

- The student client's level of satisfaction with the counselor's manner when making the referral suggestion,

- The accuracy of the counselor's description of these referral services to the student,

- The student client's level of satisfaction with the helper's services,

- The student client's perception of the competence of the new helper, and

- The client's level of satisfaction with the new helper or the combination of original and referred helpers.

Such surveys measure client satisfaction perceptions about the referral services. A more comprehensive evaluation of the referral services also includes procedures for acquiring outcome data derived from referral objectives and use-of-time data that determine cost-effectiveness of the referral services.

The follow-up procedures just described, including the survey, fall into the coordinating domain. As such, counselors are attempting to ensure success for referrals and to assess how successful the referring and coordinating efforts were.

How to Refer Student Clients

Perhaps the most important facet of the referral process is the referral suggestion. Brammer, Abrego, and Shostrom (1993) think that the way the referral suggestion is introduced and explained has considerable influence on the chance for success. Two challenges confront counselors when suggesting referrals. Clients may feel abandoned or rejected by the suggestion and they may reject the suggestion. Responding to the first challenge requires sensitivity and good communication skills. The second challenge requires resilience and persistence; if rejected, counselors are challenged to keep seeking answers to the challenge.

To avoid confusion when referrals are made, counselors determine whether referrals are partial or complete. A *partial referral* results in the continuation of the original counseling relationship, with supplementary services being provided by the referral source. For instance, after recommending a referral physical examination and pregnancy test, the counselor meets with the young woman again to discuss her possible alternatives once the medical results are known. A *complete referral* is just what the term implies: The client is referred to another helper, and the counselor who made the referral completely disassociates from the case unless approached for consultation by the referee with client permission.

Carey, Black, and Neider (1978) propose a plan for increasing the success of referral suggestions. They believe that student client expectations about complete referrals are seldom fulfilled. Thus, partial referrals are likely to be the best choice in many cases. They suggest looking at the problem from the student's point of view, which is often a troubled one. They conclude that two variables, student client motivation and confidence, have a strong effect on the success of any referral. Both variables can be influenced strongly by counselors. Carey et al. (1978) offer the following suggestions for increasing student client motivation and confidence:

- Eliminate some student client dilemmas by recommending partial referrals. This should increase student motivation.

- Know your referral sources well. Counselors who do are less likely to project ambiguity to student clients.

- Communicate appropriate and important information about student clients to the referral sources. Telling the student that you've done this provides an additional safeguard and increases student client motivation and confidence in the referral.

- Give specific information about cost, time, location, and the like to student clients to help make their decision easier.

- When necessary or prudent, help student clients by becoming active in the referral process. This may require making direct contact with referral sources to arrange for appointments or accompanying or transporting clients to appointments.

Becoming active in the referral process to the point of arranging appointments and providing transportation, however, gets counselors into the arena of legal and ethical decisions. It also raises the issue of whether such acts are acceptable according to the school district policies where one is employed. Deciding to accompany or transport minor student is predicated on thorough consideration of ethical standards, legal precedents, insurance liability, and school district policies. School districts may rightly be concerned about accident liability and also liability for paying for completed services that were recommended.

It is virtually impossible to develop a foolproof, cookbook-type method for making referral suggestions. The following suggestions may increase the chances of success. When reading and processing the suggestions, reflect on the hypothetical case about the depressed high school student presented earlier in this chapter, and think about how well the counselor followed the suggestions made here. Those suggestions that offer ideas that will be incorporated during the implementation of the constructive action stage are accompanied by extensions of the counselor-client interactions introduced earlier in the chapter.

- *Assess a student client's readiness carefully before making the suggestion.* In so doing, attempt to determine the psychological and emotional climate. It is important to know the student client's ability to cope not only with making the decision but also with the implications of making such a suggestion. In the hypothetical case of the depressed high school student, the counselor first explored the student's presenting problem and the student's assets and assessed his or her own capabilities before introducing the referral suggestion.

- *Treat the student client as you would like to be treated.* Consider the following questions and their implications:

> Would [the student] want the counselor to be attentive and non-threatening? Objective and factual? Completely honest? Partially honest? Should the counselor "sell" the referral service, or does the student client want an objective evaluation with a choice of optional resources? Does the student want the counselor to assist with the arrangements, or would he or she rather do it alone?

- *Whenever possible, discuss the potential referral with prospective referees before making the referral suggestion.* This can be accomplished without divulging confidential information. Counselors can describe the specifics without mentioning identifying information, or they can present case information hypothetically. Make the referral suggestion to the student after selecting potential referees, informing them about the case, and deciding to make the referral suggestion. The way the counselor introduced the idea of making a referral to Wellsprings indicates a familiarity with its services that predates the interview with the student.

- *Be able to explain that the referral suggestion is congruent with the student client's goals and why the referee will be better able to meet those goals.* Avoid implying that problem severity is the main reason for the referral. Doing so may lead students to think negatively about themselves. Allow ample time for presenting and discussing the referral suggestion with the student client. Offer specific information about names, orientations of referees, fees, and procedures. Communicate an interest in knowing how the referral fared for the student—to the point of arranging follow-up meetings and providing support. The hypothetical case is continued below:

Student: (In response to the counselor's confrontation) I guess you are right. I do need to do something about this situation because it seems to be getting worse instead of better. But it's so hard. I don't have any energy, and it seems overwhelming to go to that place and start telling my story all over again.

Counselor: You realize something needs to be done, yet there seems to be no energy, making it appear almost impossible. Perhaps knowing that I can be of some help in the process and will be here for you even though you are seeing someone outside the school may help. What do you think?

Student: You'll help me and will see me, too. How?

Counselor: Before you do anything, I'll see to it that you and your mother receive all the information needed to better know the people at Wellsprings, what they do, how they operate their services, and how much it may cost. Also, I'll work with you here at the school in cooperation with whomever you are working at Wellsprings. That is usually the way it is done. It makes the whole process run more smoothly when someone here at the school coordinates these arrangements. So what do you think about that?

Student: It sounds good, but I haven't really told my mother about how bad I feel or about seeing you. Will you help me tell her?

Counselor: Yes. Let's explore how we can do that.

- *When student client and parental permissions are granted, cooperate with referees by providing helpful information when it is requested.*

- Parental resistance to a referral suggestion may be natural because problems involving their children threaten family systems and may seem to reflect badly on the core of the parents' being. They wish to protect their family systems. Counselors may have to *use interpersonal influencing skills to persuade resistant parents of the seriousness of the problem.* Amatea and Fabrick (1984) recommend, as one approach, that the counselor hold back on tentativeness and assume the stance of an authoritative expert. The hypothetical case continues after the counselor has helped the student client tell the parents about the referral and the counselor and client have explained what has transpired thus far:

Parent: As you know, I am a single parent, and this all sounds to me like it could be very expensive. I don't know if my insurance will cover this, and I'm also not sure it is as serious as you say. Can't my child just shake it off and straighten things out with your help and mine?

Counselor: You have doubts, and that is a reasonable response. I agree that your child has the capacity to get better and that both of us can be helpful. However, I also believe that additional help is needed, both in terms of time and expertise, and that help is available at Wellsprings. Before thinking about the cost, let's think about the effect this situation is having on your child and what the human costs will be if sufficient help is not provided. What are your thoughts about that?

Parent: Well, I like the idea of your helping us get information before making a decision. What do we do now?

Counselor: I think we should ask your child to explain just how serious it is and then look carefully at the options, and if seeing someone at Wellsprings turns out to be part of the plan, we need to gather information that will answer your questions. Then, I hope you'll be ready for a decision. I'll try to help you as much as I can, whatever the decision.

- *Give very careful consideration to the arrangements for the first meeting and for follow-up procedures.* A successfully accomplished referral suggestion can be damaged severely by expecting the student client to make the next move. Experts are divided on this issue. Some think that student clients should initiate contacting referees (Amatea & Fabrick, 1984); others think that referees should initiate contacts (in this case, family therapists; see Bobele & Conran, 1988); and others suggest that counselors should be willing to help student clients and parents initiate contacts (C. J. Downing, 1985). The natural compromise is for counselors to be prepared to use all three approaches because circumstances will dictate which is best. Some student clients are very independent; others need help with making arrangements. Be sure to deal with this part of the referring/coordinating process carefully and conscientiously. What do the circumstances dictate in our hypothetical case?

- *Engage in this process with an awareness of the implications involved when entering into the referral process with student clients and referees who represent different worldviews* (e.g., gender differences, different cultural backgrounds). This concern leads to being able to take cultural differences and levels of tolerance into consideration when trying to select referees for student clients.

- *Understand that referrals are only one step in the counseling process.* They are not the ending of the helping relationship. For example, the counselor in the hypothetical case running through this chapter may make arrangements for a partial referral in which the student client continues to see the counselor while seeing a helper at Wellsprings, and the counselor serves as a coordinator of services the student client is receiving in and out of school.

How to Coordinate a Successful Referral

Where referring ends and coordinating begins is somewhat unclear. It makes no difference whether referrals are partial or complete. Coordinating remains important in either approach. Important coordinating competencies include being able to (a) keep track of whether student clients and referees met, (b) submit all information and materials that are needed by the referee, (c) help the student while not interfering with the work of the referee if the referral is partial, (d) serve as a consultant to the referee when necessary, and (e) evaluate the effects of the referral. What follows is an application of these recommendations to the hypothetical case running through this section of the chapter.

> Soon after the referral was made, the school counselor checks with the student and finds out that a relationship with a therapist at Wellsprings has been successfully initiated. Upon the request of the referee at Wellsprings, and with the approval of the parent, the counselor provides pertinent information about the student from the cumulative records without violating confidentiality or the FERPA standards. Next, the counselor meets with the student client periodically to address issues that are appropriate and have been recommended by the referee at Wellsprings. As the helping process continues, the referee contacts the school counselor for consultation about the case, and the counselor responds cooperatively. Finally, when appropriate, the counselor gathers information from the student, parent, and referee that will help determine how effective the referral seemed to be. As well, the data are used to find ways to improve the process.

Clearly, making a good referral and coordinating it successfully require considerable thinking and conscientious organizing. To ignore the importance of devoting the necessary thought and effort to this task is to flirt with the danger of reducing the effectiveness of the school counseling program.

The information presented here recommends preferred practices. Data collected from a sample of 149 Ohio school counselors and analyzed by Ritchie and Partin (1994) provide evidence of differences between the recommendations and the realities of professional practice, leaving room for improvement. Included in their summary are the following comments:

> Our findings indicate that school counselors are faced with a host of concerns. . . . Emotional concerns, family concerns, alcoholism, drug abuse, and suspected child abuse were the concerns most frequently referred. . . . Although counselors claimed to be familiar with referral resources in their school, . . . they were less familiar with referral resources outside of school. . . . Many counselors expressed a need for more formal training in ethical referral practices.
>
> (p. 270)

School-Family-Community Collaboration

School counselors are able to accomplish only so much through a coordination process such as that described earlier. The school-family-community collaboration paradigm introduced by Bryan and Holcomb-McCoy (2004) highlights the importance of establishing working alliances with family and community resources in order to deliver the many services students and their families need to enhance student readiness for academic achievement. Keys and Bemak (1997) encourage school counselors to view themselves as leaders in a process of integrating their programs within a broader system of community services. Adelman and Taylor (2002) believe that schools will not be able to address current barriers to learning without working collaboratively with community-based organizations and families. The primary steps in this process for school counselors are (a) accepting the collaboration concept as having merit; (b) influencing counselor, administrator, and teacher colleagues about the merits of the idea; (c) identifying relevant community services; (d) influencing community services representatives of the merits of the idea; (e) creating a grand implementation design in collaboration with other stakeholders; (f) working with significant stakeholders to implement the design; (g) establishing your role within the design (e.g., coordination); and (h) monitoring the process (i.e., evaluation and accountability).

MANIFESTATIONS OF SCHOOL COUNSELOR–INITIATED REFERRING AND COORDINATING

THE SCHOOL COUNSELOR AS A REFERRAL SERVICE COORDINATOR

Referral service coordinating encompasses a blend of counseling, consulting, and referral services. Taken from DeVoe and McClam (1982), the following is a summary of proposed phases of referral service coordinating with examples of their implementation in the case of Brenda, a student with many overwhelming problems.

After establishing counseling relationships leading to awareness of goals and priorities, counselors may determine what information about a case is needed, collect critical information, organize it, and assess it to identify problems and goals. DeVoe and McClam call this the *information retrieval phase*. Brenda is a young woman experiencing failure in school, abuse of drugs, possible child abuse, and possible pregnancy. Information about her perception of her problems is acquired via an accepting, participatory counseling relationship. In addition, physicians, teachers, school psychologists, social workers, and neighbors are asked for information that can help identify Brenda's needs. In some instances, those questioned are referees in partial referrals.

After receiving the information, counselors may determine how their own expertise can meet student needs and where referrals are needed. Evaluating one's professional capability, making appropriate referrals, establishing a timeline, and determining follow-up procedures make up the *information assessment phase*. With Brenda, the counselor realizes that some problems are beyond her own expertise and/or require more time and attention than she can offer. She then pursues a plan of joint, cooperative actions, setting up the information assessment phase.

While continuing to offer legitimate counseling services, the counselor acts as a coordinator of referral services. As coordinator, the counselor orchestrates the referral process and mobilizes the referral services by making referrals and devising plans for communications among referral services. In so doing, the counselor acts as an advocate for Brenda, ensuring that she does not get lost in the system. As the professional who is providing direct, caregiving services to Brenda in school, the counselor occupies the most strategic position for coordinating the helping services, including following up on referral services and incorporating them with the direct services when appropriate.

DeVoe and McClam (1982) view referral service coordination as a way for school counselors to alleviate concerns about not being able to meet all their student clients' needs while also providing a more comprehensive set of services. Effective referral service coordination results in more effective counseling interventions. In the referral service coordination scenario described, the counselor used referrals as one means of helping the student client while serving as a liaison between the various persons and agencies involved in providing services for Brenda.

SCHOOL COUNSELORS AND STUDENT ASSISTANCE PROGRAMS

Designed for At-Risk Students

Student assistance programs (SAPs) are approaches that the schools use to reach out to and help a variety of at-risk students. SAPs are helpful to school counselors because they bring into play sources of help, in responding to the challenges at-risk students present, that are more systematic and comprehensive than individual counselors are usually able to be when working independently with at-risk students and trying to make referrals.

Modeled on the concept of the employee assistance programs (EAPs) established in business and industry, SAPs are designed to identify high-risk students experiencing decreased productivity (declining academic performance) because of chemical abuse and other suspected mental health problems. Identification is followed by intervention and referral to appropriate community services. An aftercare component is provided to support those returning to school after having received counseling intervention services. One important distinction between EAPs and SAPs is that EAPs provide adult employees with voluntary participation and an option to resign; SAPs, in contrast, often demand that adolescent students participate or face expulsion (Roman, 1989). This circumstance occurs because the school differs from the workplace.

The school atmosphere favors acceptance of referral suggestions, although it is also more subject to abuse and exploitation unless great care is exercised. Because of legitimate national concern about chemical abuse and prevention of mental health problems, SAPs became increasingly popular in the late 1980s. As Roman points out, the rapid transfer of the core technology from the workplace (EAPs) to the school (SAPs) posed both advantages and disadvantages. High-risk adolescents and the school personnel trying to help them gain the advantages because SAPs offer additional systematic opportunities for help. Inconsistency of services is one disadvantage, however, because there is no national consensus on the definition of SAPs.

Three approaches to organizing SAPs have emerged (Borris, 1988). Some SAPs follow an externally based model, in which a specialized staff is available for services outside the school. Others have employed an internally based model, in which a specialized staff is available for services inside the school. Because it is the most common and cost-effective model, a third approach, the core team idea, is described in detail here.

Core Team Student Assistant Programs

Core team members are trained to screen, refer, intervene with, and support dysfunctional students. Diversity in team membership is recommended to represent all kinds of school personnel and to provide a variety of pathways to discovering potential student clients. Therefore, central office and building administrators, teachers, counselors, nurses, school psychologists, and other specialists are members of core teams. Certified providers outside the school district can give specialized training, usually short term and intense, to core team members. The training often includes a knowledge base about SAPs, group process, chemical dependency and the disease concept, suicide prevention/ intervention, symptoms of mental illness, theories of adolescent development, treatment recovery, continuity of care, and action planning. Some of these topics are similar to the basic training programs of school counselors. Simulations and rehearsals of confrontations with targeted adolescents and their parents/guardians are often included in the training. Having been trained, core team members in turn provide training to other school personnel through in-service programs. Such faculty in-service training creates an informed and helpful professional staff supportive of the core team.

Core teams network with referral sources just as counselors do as part of their liaison function. In this instance, the networking involves a team of professionals that includes counselors, rather than counselors acting independently. Identification of at-risk students can therefore involve all professional school personnel because of the pyramid-like nature of core teams and the in-service training of others. Self-referrals and referrals from peers, parents, and others are welcomed. When at-risk students are identified, the core teams are responsible for investigating the referrals and meeting with the students and their parents/guardians if further action is deemed appropriate.

Informing and involving parents/guardians varies from school to school; the nature of such contacts seems to be independent rather than a universal policy. Meetings with parents are informational in that the core teams share their findings and recommendations. The meetings may also be confrontational because of the possibility of denial and resistance from the students and/or their families. In these situations, school systems are often empowered to threaten suspension as a form of caring coercion if cooperation is not achieved. This occasional resorting to coercion may cause school counselors to be concerned about students' perceptions of them. This issue has not yet been resolved beyond the individual decision-making level.

Recommended intervention plans vary because of differing circumstances where SAPs exist. When appropriate services are provided outside the schools, core teams are responsible for assessing the readiness of returning students and for providing after-care services. When necessary services are not readily available, which is the case in many communities, or targeted families cannot afford the services, or both, core teams may have to devise alternative intervention programs. Sometimes such alternative services are provided by school personnel and are offered in the schools during or after the school day.

The nature of the problem also affects where students receive help. Students with discipline and attendance problems might receive help in the school, whereas students with substance abuse problems require more specialized help off-site. In some instances, counselors are among the staff professionals with competencies that enable them to serve as referees as well as referral recommenders. For example, Zubrod (1992) describes a situation where a school counselor provided ongoing counseling groups for students referred to the school's SAP. In this case, the counselor was able to help many participants achieve improved mental health, and all who indicated substance abuse problems reported change in a positive direction. Confidence in the viability of the group counseling program, which was high at the outset, continued throughout.

Aftercare is another challenge facing core teams. A system must be established and monitored for accepting the referred student back in school or for determining whether problem behaviors have been changed successfully. Beyond that, support is needed to prevent or detect relapses or both. Aftercare seems to be natural for counselors as part of their responsive counseling intervention function (i.e., tertiary prevention). One way school counselors provide aftercare for these students is through ongoing counseling groups that returning students can join to process things in a safe environment while trying to adapt to having returned to the school after a substantial absence (e.g., Zubrod, 1992).

SAPs offer counselors an exceptionally useful adjunct to their referral services, whether they are members of core teams or are making referrals to core teams or to external and internal experts. Advantages include the team concept, the targeting of dysfunctional behaviors by informed staff members, and the comprehensive and systematic nature of the program.

SAPs are designed to identify, inform, and refer many more students than counselors can independently under their less-formalized referral services. To ensure appropriate counselor involvement in SAPs, Zimman and Cox (1989) make several recommendations:

- The program should be mandated by the school's administration to avoid turf battles between counselors and teachers,

- Services within the SAPs should be spelled out clearly to avoid confusion over what is to be referred internally (e.g., to counselors) and what is to be referred externally,

- Coordinators should be designated in a manner that conveys the broadest possible ownership of the program,

- The headquarters of the SAP program should be located in an office near but not within the counseling or administrative offices to give the program separate status,

- Responsibilities of all professionals should be clarified in advance, and

- Allowances should be made for individual differences among counselors and grade-level differences among students when implementing the program.

A relatively recent idea, SAPs have already had a significant influence on the basic education scene. Designed originally to serve high school adolescents, SAPs were gradually being implemented in junior high, middle, and elementary schools.

REFERRALS TO SCHOOL COUNSELORS

REFERRALS FROM OTHER PROFESSIONALS AND PARENTS

Being a referee for other professionals and parents can be a source of professional satisfaction, as well as frustration. Satisfaction is achieved from knowing that coworkers and parents know and appreciate one's efforts. Frustration occurs when the process is misunderstood, expectations are unrealistic, and referrals are made inappropriately. Consider, for example, the following hypothetical and real cases:

- Tina's mother, Mrs. Jones, calls the counselor and requests an interview. In the interview, the counselor learns that Mrs. Jones is terribly worried about Tina's behavior in and out of school. She requests help from the counselor to find out what is wrong and perhaps bring about a cure.

- Gene has just arrived in the counselor's office. He is accompanied by Ms. Smith, the principal, who finds Gene's behavior reprehensible. The principal requests that the counselor "straighten Gene out" and hints at more drastic methods if this does not work.

- Taking a survey of teacher-initiated referrals during one week of school, a counselor creates the following list: six cases of students fighting, four cases of classroom acting out, two cases of smoking, and one case of inappropriately affectionate behavior in the hallways.

- A analysis of 313 referral documents and findings from focus group interviews with 10 elementary school teachers led Jackson and White (2000) to conclude that many teachers tend to view referrals from the perspective of a medical model. That is, many teachers assume that children are not responsible for their problems. Therefore, they attribute responsibility to the referees (i.e., school counselors), expecting them to solve the problem for the child (and possibly for the teacher as well).

These four frustrating scenarios demonstrate some pitfalls awaiting counselors who respond to referrals indiscriminately. Indeed, these cases dictate the challenge to organize the system by which referrals are made to counselors. The examples offer several ideas about how this aspect of the referral service can be organized. The ideas are organized around three basic questions: Who is my client? What is the proper referral procedure? and What is a legitimate referral?

Who Is My Client?

Mrs. Jones's request places the counselor in a dilemma from which there is no escape if the counselor attempts to serve her and her daughter at the same time. Initially, Mrs. Jones requests to be the client, but it is her daughter who is to receive the direct responsive counseling process. If the counselor initiates a counseling relationship with Tina, she will become a client. Then, from an ethical perspective (and legally in some states), Mrs. Jones can no longer be a client because whatever Tina shares with the counselor becomes confidential and the counselor cannot share it with Tina's mother without Tina's permission. If the counselor decides to accept Mrs. Jones as a client, then consultation is in order. Then, Tina is the client and Mrs. Jones the consultee. A more detailed coverage of consultation is presented in Chapter 10. With Mrs. Jones as the client, the counselor's services to Tina are indirect; that is, the counselor helps Tina by consulting with Mrs. Jones, who works directly with Tina. When Mrs. Jones's goals become clear to the counselor, it is time to clarify the issues and negotiate which client to serve directly. A third option is to work out a system for serving both clients if an understanding of mutually acceptable goals can be achieved. Mrs. Jones's request indicates a misunderstanding of the counseling services and naïveté about counseling ethics, problems counselors handle systematically or individually on a case-by-case basis.

What Is the Proper Referral Procedure?

Ms. Smith, the principal, expects the counselor to cure student Gene quickly and dramatically. This appears to be a manifestation of the medical model belief reported above from Jackson and White (2000). The counselor is challenged to clarify for Ms. Smith what are and what are not legitimate expectations (referrals). Among other things, clarification involves requesting information from Ms. Smith about what transpired before the referral, what behavioral goals Ms. Smith has for Gene, and what outcomes she expects. In fairness to the counselor, this information will be the content of negotiations with Ms. Smith. This is also a "Who is my client?" situation because it is not Gene who initiated the request for a responsive counseling intervention. Ms. Smith wants an intervention to change Gene's behaviors. As is the case with Mrs. Jones and Tina, the "Who is my client?" question needs to be resolved quickly.

Ms. Smith essentially commands the counselor to perform a service. In this case, the counselor is not forewarned, availability of the counselor's services is assumed, and outcome expectations are vague. Such a situation underscores the need for communication with superiors and colleagues to establish a clearly defined referral system.

Diplomacy is in order, leading to a systematic plan wherein the needs of all parties are being served, and both the principal and counselor believe they are winners.

What Is a Legitimate Referral?

The two hypothetical cases and the findings by Jackson and White (2000) require thought about whether counselor involvement in the interventions is appropriate. Neither Tina nor Gene asks the counselor for help. The list of reasons for the referrals demands that one ask whether demonstrations of affection or smoking in school are counseling problems or matters of rules and mores that should be regulated by either administrators or community consensus. The findings from the Jackson and White study indicate that expectations of teachers and others may be inappropriate when making referrals, placing school counselors in no-win situations. This raises two questions: How do the counselors help teachers and other referees understand that all involved parties, including students and teachers, are potentially involved in achieving solutions to problems that cause referrals? and Do school counselors view themselves as miracle workers or super-counselors who can fix all problems referred to them, or do they understand that all players, including teachers, students, and parents, are involved helping students realize their potential?

Another issue is the fact that all the referrals involved some form of acting out. No referral involved a student who exhibited symptoms of being overly passive or withdrawn. This narrowness of focus in recognizing problems indicates that members of the school staff seem not to be aware of a broader range of potential problems. The situation offers an opportunity to design an in-service presentation for other members of the faculty and staff.

A report by Wagner (1976) offers food for thought about referral patterns of elementary school teachers. Teachers were invited to make referrals to groups helping students enhance personal problem-solving skills. Data from the teachers' responses showed they consistently recommended more boys than girls for this kind of help. This finding led Wagner to hypothesize that girls' problems in adjusting to home and school are more difficult to observe from their school-related attitudes and behaviors than boys' are and that perhaps expectations of boys in elementary school need further investigation. The latter hypothesis was based on Wagner's observation that, in general, boys are encouraged to be independent, active, and mobile but that exhibiting these behaviors in classrooms often leads to teacher distress and disciplinary referrals.

Are Referrals Being Made Appropriately?

Another serious problem is the absence of referrals to the school counselor. Some colleagues and parents are apathetic or poorly informed. This suggests that counselors need to establish systems for receiving referrals and to make those systems known.

Ingredients of any system are bound to differ among communities, schools, and counseling goals. Despite such differences, some basic suggestions are relevant to most school districts:

- Distribute information about the services that school counselors provide (e.g., counseling, consulting, information).
- Include examples of how those services are carried out (what kind of counseling is offered and the outcomes to expect).
- Make public a referral system, explaining the process for making referrals to counselors and providing necessary forms. Make the system simple, efficient, and multiculturally appropriate.
- Include procedures for providing feedback to referral sources.
- Explain the policy regarding confidentiality.
- Look for opportunities to explain the system. Do so proactively (e.g., faculty meetings, in-service programs, distributive materials).

REFERRALS FROM STUDENTS

Much of the preceding discussion of referrals from professionals and parents also holds true for students. They, too, have misperceptions and unrealistic expectations, and sometimes they are apathetic. They seldom refer a peer, although occasionally they do. Among those students who refer peers are those trained to be peer helpers. Ingredients of the counselor-initiated referrals described at the beginning of this chapter can be part of the training programs for peer helpers.

In most instances, referrals from students are self-referrals, and counselors are challenged to present themselves to students clearly while also living up to realistic expectations. In their efforts to enhance the probability of student self-referrals, counselors face several difficult challenges. Park and Williams (1986) list the following negative expectations that make reaching some students more difficult:

- Adults are persons who give information to students, talking *to* them rather than *with* them.
- Adults give advice, and students view their own role as captive listeners who are forced to accept adult solutions.
- Adults respond critically and tell students how they should feel when students try to express feelings, leading to the conclusion that disclosing feelings is a risky business.
- Adults can be punitive; they have the power to make students feel shame or guilt over mistakes.
- Adults do not treat information about students confidentially. Often, they share it with other people, which sometimes leads to punitive responses.

Obviously, faced with these unflattering perspectives, counselors are truly challenged to prove that they are special adults who are dedicated to helping students and who are different from other adults.

Revisiting Wagner's (1976) study provides further food for thought about student self-referrals. It is less likely that boys who hypothetically might have been referred by teachers will refer themselves. It is also more likely that girls who hypothetically might have been referred by teachers will refer themselves for help. This indicates that boys who need help may be the least likely students to refer themselves. Elementary school boys and girls, however, refer themselves at about an equal ratio, evidence that not all boys are reticent about referring themselves.

What to do? Realize that not all students need to refer themselves for counseling services. They wish to be able to avail themselves of these services if needed. When school counseling is not perceived positively and accurately by students, there are insufficient self-referrals. Insufficient student self-referrals diminish the impact of a counseling program or at least result in an unbalanced program. A proactive stance leads to counselors providing information about their programs to students in a manner that is simple, truthful, and in the students' vernacular. Park and Williams (1986) offer an interesting suggestion for implementing this idea. Applying the principles of social modeling, they exposed elementary school students to live or filmed performances of children modeling behaviors they wanted the students to learn. The targeted behaviors included social skills needed to initiate contacts with adults. Demonstrated were situations in which initiating contacts would be appropriate, showing how the models coped with the anxiety and reluctance associated with approaching adults.

Another idea is offered by LaFountain (1983), who asked elementary school children to complete information-gathering graphic checklists during her weekly classroom visits. One of the checklists is the Smiley-Frowney Face Sheet, on which children in kindergarten and first and second grades are asked to make an X on the face that best depicts their feelings about school, friends, and family. Six faces, ranging from teary-eyed to openly smiling, are presented for each of the three categories. The reverse side of the paper is used for writing news to the counselor. A second graphic checklist is the Feelometer, which LaFountain used in third through sixth grades. Thermometers with scales ranging from *Very Unhappy* to *Very Happy* are located beside each of three questions asking how students are feeling about school, friends, and family. The Feelometer also contains boxes that can be checked by children who wish to see the counselor. In a space on the reverse side, children can write messages to the counselor. The information is used for reaching out to children proactively and as a resource when referrals are made to the counselor.

Student self-referrals occur more often if they are easy to make. Students desire to know that their counselors maintain confidentiality. Counselors who are visible and appear to students as adults who talk with them, participate in the decision-making process as equals, empathize with feelings, and accept individual differences are more likely to receive student self-referrals. To repeat the admonition made earlier in this chapter: Ignoring the importance of devoting the necessary thought and effort to this task is flirting with the danger of reducing the effectiveness of the counseling program.

COMPREHENSIVE SCHOOL COUNSELING PROGRAM COMPONENT

1. Create a presentation to the faculty and administrators of a hypothetical school in which one is presenting a detailed overview of the preferred process for making referrals to the school counselor.

2. Create a school-community collaboration plan for a hypothetical school system or for a system with which you are familiar.

REFLECTION POINT

1. Using the criteria suggested in this chapter, evaluate the referral services in the institution where you are employed and/or where you attended school for counselor-initiated referrals and for referrals to counselors.

2. Using the results of the previous activity, develop a proposal for improving the referral services.

3. List the referral sources you use. Check those with which you have reciprocal relationships. Make a different mark by those about which you have adequate knowledge. What do the results tell you? Are these sources appropriate for serving a multiculturally diverse population?

4. Add possible referral sources to your list.

5. Brainstorm ideas for enhancing the image of counseling among children and adolescents and suggest ways to implement them. What are the underlying principles for your ideas?

6. Cooperatively generate a list of referral sources that can be used to enhance student client development.

APPLICATION TO TECHNOLOGY

1. Create an asset map for a real or imagined school in a setting (e.g., school district or community) that is familiar to you.

2. Consider how school counselors might use social media (Facebook, Twitter in particular) to help in the process of coordinating school counseling services and in locating sources for counseling referrals.

3. How might social media (Facebook in particular) be misused in the process of coordinating school services and locating sources for counseling referrals?

4. Discuss the importance of community agencies keeping their Internet sites up-to-date.

REFERENCES

Adelman, H. S., & Taylor, L. (2002). School counselors and school reform: New directions. *Professional School Counseling, 5,* 235–248.

Amatea, E. S., & Fabrick, F. (1984). Moving a family into therapy: Critical referral issues for the school counselor. *School Counselor, 31,* 285–294.

American Counseling Association. (2014). *ACA code of ethics.* Alexandria, VA: Author.

American School Counselor Association. (1989). American School Counselor Association statement: Cross/multicultural counseling. *Elementary School Guidance and Counseling, 23,* 322–323.

American School Counselor Association. (2010). *Ethical standards for school counselors.* Alexandria, VA: Author.

American School Counselor Association. (2012). *The ASCA National Model: A framework for school counseling programs* (3rd ed.). Alexandria, VA: Author.

Atkinson, D. R., & Juntunen, C. L. (1994). School counselors and school psychologists as school—home–community liaisons in ethnically diverse schools. In P. Pedersen & J. C. Carey (Eds.), *Multicultural counseling in schools* (pp. 103–120). Boston: Allyn & Bacon.

Bobele, M., & Conran, T. J. (1988). Referrals for family therapy: Pitfalls and guidelines. *Elementary School Guidance and Counseling, 22,* 192–198.

Borris, A. F. (1988). Organizational models. *Student Assistance Journal, 1,* 31–33.

Brammer, L. M., Abrego, P. J., & Shostrom, E. L. (1993). *Therapeutic counseling and psychotherapy* (6th ed.). Upper Saddle River, NJ: Prentice Hall.

Bryan, J., & Holcomb-McCoy, C. (2004). School counselors' perceptions of their involvement in school-family-community partnerships. *Professional School Counseling, 7,* 219–227.

Carey, A. R., Black, K. J., & Neider, G. G. (1978). Upping the odds on the referral gamble. *School Counselor, 25,* 186–190.

DeVoe, M. W., & McClam, T. (1982). Service coordination: The school counselor. *School Counselor, 35,* 95–101.

Downing, C. J. (1985). Referrals that work. *School Counselor, 32,* 242–246.

Downing, J., Pierce, K. A., & Woodruff, P. (1993). A community network for helping families. *School Counselor, 41,* 102–108.

Griffin, D., & Farris, A. (2010). School counselors and collaboration: Finding resources through community asset mapping. *Professional School Counseling, 13*(5), 248–256.

Hobbs, B. B., & Collison, B. B. (1995). School-community agency collaboration: Implications for school counselors. *School Counselor, 43,* 58–65.

Hollis, J. W., & Hollis, L. U. (1965). *Organizing for effective guidance.* Chicago: Science Research Associates.

Ivey, A. E., Ivey, M. B., & Zalaquett, C. P. (2014). *Intentional interviewing and counseling: Facilitating client development in a multicultural society* (8th ed.). Belmont, CA: Brooks/Cole Cengage Learning.

Jackson, S. A., & White, J. (2000). Referrals to the school counselor: A qualitative study. *Professional School Counseling, 3,* 277–286.

Keys, S. G., & Bemak, F. (1997). School-family-community linked services: A school counseling role for changing times. *School Counselor, 44,* 255–263.

Kimmerling, G. F. (1993). When saying no is the right thing to do. *American Counselor, 2,* 5–6.

LaFountain, R. (1983). Referrals. *Elementary School Guidance and Counseling, 17,* 226–230.

Park, W. D., & Williams, G. T. (1986). Encouraging elementary children to refer themselves for counseling. *Elementary School Guidance and Counseling, 21,* 8–14.

Ritchie, M. H., & Partin, R. L. (1994). Referral practices of school counselors. *School Counselor, 41,* 263–272.

Roman, P. M. (1989). Perils, payoffs of technology transfer. *Employee Assistance, 1,* 16–17.

Shertzer, B., & Stone, S. C. (1981). *Fundamentals of guidance* (4th ed.). Boston: Houghton Mifflin.

Wagner, C. A. (1976). Referral patterns of children and teachers for group counseling. *Personnel and Guidance Journal, 55,* 90–93.

Weinrach, S. G. (1984). Toward improved referral making: Mutuality between the counselor and the psychologist. *School Counselor, 32,* 89–96.

Zimman, R. N., & Cox, V. (1989). The role of guidance counselors. *Student Assistance Journal, 1,* 22–24.

Zubrod, A. R. (1992). The influence of group social skills development on attitudes and behaviors of at-risk adolescents. *Dissertation Abstracts International, 53–11A,* 3856. (University Microfilms No. AA19236928).

SCHOOL COUNSELOR CONSULTATION: A BRIDGE BETWEEN PREVENTION AND INTERVENTION

10

RELATED STANDARDS OF PRACTICE

CACREP CORE	2.F.5.c.f.g.
CACREP SCHOOL COUNSELING	5.C.2.b.

Goal: To introduce a specific consultation role for school counselors and to cite the similarities and differences between consultation and other school counseling functions while proposing basic competencies and training recommendations.

Here is how a school counselor described how he began consulting with a parent:

> Sondra, a 14-year-old, was experiencing difficulties at school and elsewhere. She was disruptive in class and disturbed other students while they worked. She often returned to class late following lunch breaks. She also used profanity and vulgar language to intimidate teachers and students. Outside school, Sondra was caught vandalizing vending machines and defacing public property.
>
> Sondra's mother—a single parent, divorced for about 2 years—requested help to resolve Sondra's difficulties. She was concerned about raising Sondra without a father. The mother planned to remarry within a few months. Sondra disliked the prospect of having a stepfather.

As shown in the case of Sondra, students often exhibit behaviors and describe feelings that require the school counselor to consult with parents and teachers as a way of alleviating the presenting problems and of preventing the occurrence of future problems. This chapter presents the school counselor as a consultant.

DEMAND FOR CONSULTING IN SCHOOL COUNSELING

Definitions of *consultation* abound in the professional literature; a perusal of them leads to the conclusion that the differences are largely varying degrees of comprehensiveness. When consultation is treated as a topic or process, the definitions are quite comprehensive. When consultation is treated as a competency, the definition is more narrow and compact. Dougherty (1990) offers a useful, comprehensive definition that may appear dated, however, it remains apropos for school counseling in the 21st century: "Consultation is a process in which a human services professional assists a consultee with a work-related (or caretaking-related) problem with a client system, with the goal of helping both the consultee and the client system in some specified way" (p. 8).

SCHOOL COUNSELOR CONSULTING

Dougherty's (1990) definition introduces three terms that are important to a discussion of consulting: *human services professional, consultee,* and *client system.* In this chapter, the human services professional is referred to as a *consultant,* and the client system is referred to as a *student client.* Consultation involves three parties, two of whom are working together to serve a third. The two working together are a consultant and a consultee; the recipient of their efforts is the client. At times, multiple consultants, consultees, or clients may be involved in the consultation process. For example, a school counselor (consultant) is approached by two parents (consultees) for consultation about helping their child (client) be more successful in school. When the school counselor and the parents agree to work together, a consulting relationship takes place in which the school counselor (consultant) works with the parents (consultees) to find ways to help their child (client). The school counselor's interactions with the child are most likely to be indirect. That is, the school counselor directly assists and interacts with others (e.g., parents and teachers) who are working directly with the child. Therefore, the school counselor might be depicted as working behind the scenes. The circumstances just depicted describe *school counselor consulting.*

In most consulting relationships, consultants will help consultees by sharing their expertise in some way. Consultees, in turn, will use that help in their work with clients who receive the help. Therefore, a prime feature of school counselor consulting is that the school counselor participates in the helping process as a helper whose influence on the student client is indirect, and the consultee's influence is direct.

AN EXAMPLE OF SCHOOL COUNSELOR CONSULTING

Students in our training program engage in consulting relationships while enrolled in their school counseling internships, and they are required to report and analyze one of those consultation experiences. The following excerpt of school counseling consultation is taken from one of those reports (Coleman, 2006). References are made within parentheses to the different consultation modes that are presented later in this chapter.

The school counselor intern formed a close relationship with a first-year English teacher. Like many first-year teachers, she was given exceptionally tough classes, and she struggled with classroom management and discipline. Having once been in the teacher's shoes as a classroom teacher who struggled with the same challenges, the intern quickly formed a close bond with the teacher, and they met often to discuss students and strategies the teacher could use in her classroom (initiation mode).

One case involved two girls who were involved in an extremely disruptive dispute. The case first came to the intern's attention when the teacher became worried about the content of an intercepted note from one girl to the other while in class. The teacher asked the intern to talk to the girls (provision mode). After talking to the girls and resolving part of the problem (mediation mode), the intern realized that the hostilities were likely to resurface in the class. Shortly thereafter, continued whispering and name-calling occurred, and the intern met with the teacher to brainstorm solutions (collaboration mode).

Although the dispute originally involved only two girls, the entire classroom was now involved and causing a disruption in the teacher's instruction time. The intern met with the teacher to plan an intervention (collaboration mode). One goal that resulted was to find ways the teacher could deal with the problem without further disrupting class time. The strategy to reach this goal was for the teacher to periodically contact the girls' parents to update them on the undesirable behaviors, and the students knew of this plan. As a result, some of the disruptive behaviors decreased.

Another goal was to get the girls to peacefully coexist while in the class for 90 minutes. The intern recommended that the teacher give the girls ground rules for their classroom behavior (prescription mode). The intern worked with the teacher to determine the rules and consequences for breaking them (collaboration mode). The teacher felt that her meeting with the girls to discuss the ground rules had a positive impact on how they interacted outwardly.

A goal the teacher established was to avoid singling the girls out in class and making them feel she was picking on them. A zero tolerance policy was established for all instances of talking, whispering, and note passing regardless of whom the culprits were. Through being able to consistently enforce this policy in her classroom, the teacher began to feel more confident. The goal and strategy were the teacher's ideas, and the intern provided support through positive verbal reinforcement.

By the end of the grading period, the two girls seemed to have put their differences aside, and classroom disruptions were minimal. The intern, when reflecting on this consultation experience shared the following observations:

> The main thing I learned from this particular consultation relationship was how little I had to do to be helpful. I did offer some suggestions and insight, but mainly I served as a person who the teacher felt comfortable coming to in order to discuss her concerns and frustrations as well as someone who could provide an outsider's perspective. Additionally, I learned that the real expert in many consultation relationships is the classroom teacher; after all, they are the ones who are in the classrooms day after day, and the ones who observe the students regularly and are the ones who ultimately have to employ the strategies.
>
> (Coleman, 2006, p. 3)

A BRIEF HISTORICAL OVERVIEW

Counselors have probably provided consultation as long as there have been counselors; however, a formalized consulting function has been an important part of the school counselor's repertoire only since the late 1970s. Earlier, the proposal that professionals branch out from one-to-one relationships to work with caretakers who, in turn, work with clients was popularized in the mental health field (Caplan, 1959). School counseling was one helping profession that incorporated the idea because the large student-to-counselor ratios in virtually every school district made more effective use of counselor time appealing. Consultation allows counselors to use their skills to influence as many people as possible (Gerler, 1992). That consultation is considered an important function in counseling today and for the future is borne out in the appearance of special issues of counseling journals devoted to consultation (Dougherty, 1992; Kurpius & Fuqua, 1993a, 1993b) and in the specific attention devoted to it as an *indirect student services strategy* by the American School Counselor Association (ASCA, 2012): "School counselors share strategies that support student achievement with parents, teachers, other educators, and community organizations through consultation" (p. 87).

Although the idea has gained momentum and acceptance, the meaning of consultation has been less clear. There is no universal definition of consultation (Scott, Royal, & Kissinger, 2015). Various helping fields have differing versions of what the ingredients of consulting are, and consulting behaviors are based more on trial-and-error activities than on theory. The lack of theory need not be as unsettling for school counselors as it is for counselor educators because the environment in which school counselors work creates a relatively specific consultation role for school counselor consulting.

School counselors work in the schools, where the natural recipients of consulting services are students, teachers, administrators, parents, and occasionally others in the school district. For example, school counselors might consult with civic leaders who want to establish a scholarship program for local students or with members of a local service club. Natural circumstances related to daily activities in school systems create situations in which individuals need consultation, and counselors often can provide the needed assistance. Counselors respond to teachers working with challenging students and/or planning curriculum units about which counselors have topical knowledge or implementation ideas. School counselors do not need to create a consulting service—one exists. Counselors who understand what exists can improve on and manage it.

EVIDENCE OF SCHOOL COUNSELOR CONSULTING

Because consultation is important in both the counseling interventions and prevention programming, it is a vital ingredient in the comprehensive balanced program concept introduced in Chapter 2. Our position is supported by the ASCA (2012) National Model in which consultation is presented as one of indirect student services within the delivery system. Excerpts from the professional literature indicate that school counselors are, in fact, engaging in consulting activities; the activities most often reported involve consulting with teachers as consultees and students as the indirect recipients of the counselors' consulting services.

The most common reports of school counselors consulting with teachers involve teachers receiving assistance with students who exhibit challenging behaviors. Through excerpts of a consultation dialogue between an elementary school counselor and a teacher, Keat (1974) demonstrated that assistance provided by the counselor included empathy, additional ideas, support, confirmation, and recommendations. Dowd and Moerings (1975) reported a case in which an eighth grader's underachievement and social isolation were alleviated when a counselor consulted with three of the student's teachers and developed a treatment strategy. Off-task behaviors having a detrimental effect on the academic performance of six male and female sixth graders were reduced by modifications in the encouraging behaviors of teachers in consulting relationships (Rathvon, 1990). In a case in which the extent of the teacher's presented problem was unclear, Osterweil (1987) offered suggestions for achieving clarity and eventually suggested a treatment plan. Viewing teachers as information gatherers and hypothesis formers, Bauer and Sapona (1988) recommended that counselors have the expertise to help with students who exhibit challenging behaviors. Offering support for school counselor consulting, Bundy and Poppen (1986) reported that significant improvements in student behavior, adjustment, or achievement were found in 77% of consultation studies they reviewed.

Strein and French (1984) pointed out that counselors are also an important consultation source for teachers in helping them foster affective growth in students. Therefore, counselors as consultants are seen as people who can not only help solve or treat existing problems but also offer assistance with proactive prevention program planning. Taking the prevention concept a step farther, Robinson and Wilson (1987) believe that counselor involvement in human relations training groups can be conceived as a form of consultation. Teachers of second and fifth graders in 13 elementary schools received 25 hours of human relations training that led to overall improvements in their skills. Robinson and Wilson also reported evidence suggesting that teachers who learn to be more effective communicators may enhance the academic achievements and self-concepts of their students.

Parents may also find value in the consultation services of school counselors. Purkey and Schmidt (1982) suggested that school counselors help parents enhance their children's growth by adopting an invitational approach to family living. Purkey and Schmidt's (1982) ideas are practical and easily adopted and can be conveyed to parents in several relatively easy ways. Myrick (1977) also stated that parent consultation is a potentially important function for school counselors, especially elementary school counselors, because of the important role of parents in child development. He also noted, however, debate among various writers about the cost-effectiveness of taking time away from other functions to engage in consultations with parents. Mullis and Edwards (2001) suggested that, if school counselors view concerns expressed by parents through a family systems lens, they can help parents to plan interventions that may be successful in a time-efficient manner. We present more about this consulting approach later in the chapter.

Smaby, Peterson, Bergmann, Bacig, and Swearingen (1990) may have identified an approach to parental consultation that is cost-effective. They describe school-based, comprehensive, community suicide prevention and intervention programs in northeastern Minnesota in which school counselors serve as members of community intervention teams. Including teachers, social workers, community mental health workers, law enforcement officials, members of the clergy, and students, the teams develop and present workshops and train personnel from participating schools who, in turn, train others in their respective schools, agencies, and communities. Most of the consultation offered to parents by these school counselors is indirect, allowing them to help more people than direct service consultation could accomplish in this instance.

Mathias (1992) believes that "there is a myriad of interventions available to the [school counselor] consultant" (p. 191). She provided several examples, including listening to parent and teacher concerns about children and adolescents and helping them explore alternative ways to address those concerns, developing and locating helpful printed materials that can be distributed to parents and teachers, working with school librarians to develop bibliotherapy sections in the school library, participating in child study teams with other school professionals, and serving on committees designed to improve the school as a system. Baker, Robichaud, Dietrich, Wells, and Schreck (2009) found that consultation can also be a pathway to providing advocacy, engaging in collaboration, and demonstrating leadership.

BASIC INGREDIENTS OF SCHOOL COUNSELOR CONSULTING

Although less voluminous, the consultation literature, like the counseling literature, offers several recommendations about how consulting may be conducted. As is the case with the basic counseling skills, the competencies of consulting are atheoretical; they can be learned, developed, and incorporated into the behavioral repertoire, and they can be applied according to one's own theoretical persuasion. Two major themes stand out in these positions: modes and steps or stages. *Consulting modes* are the methods that individuals use or the ways they behave when engaging in consulting services. *Consulting steps* or stages are the sequential behaviors in which individuals engage when carrying out any of the consulting modes. Because steps and stages depend on modes, modes are discussed first here.

SCHOOL COUNSELOR CONSULTING MODES

Kurpius (1978) suggested four modes that school counselors might use, each of which leads to different attitudes and behaviors and, therefore, requires different competencies. The following material extends Kurpius's ideas and also reflects thoughts expressed by Gallessich (1985).

We have added a fifth mode (mediation) to the four modes identified by Kurpius (1978). All five consulting modes are available to school counselors, and they are not mutually exclusive. It is very likely that some modes are more prevalent among practicing counselors and in counselor education training programs. It is also likely that some are preferred by counselors or are recommended by counselor educators more than others. When reading this section, reflect on how the modes were used in the example presented earlier in this chapter from Coleman (2006).

Prescription Mode

As consultants, school counselors may provide intervention plans or aid in the selection of intervention strategies for predetermined problems. When doing so, consultants investigate and diagnose the circumstances, negotiating strategies and people to implement them. This is an indirect service. An example of the prescription mode is a case in which an elementary school counselor (consultant) helps a frustrated teacher (consultee) establish a plan for a token economy program designed to enhance students' (clients') on-task behaviors and to reduce their acting-out behaviors. One-to-one consultation sessions with the teacher are accompanied by classroom observations by the counselor, who then analyzes students' behaviors prior to suggesting an intervention plan that the teacher may implement in the classroom. In this mode, the counselor suggests (i.e., prescribes) a plan for the teacher.

Provision Mode

At times, school counselors as consultants provide direct services to clients because consultees lack time, interest, or competence. When doing so, counselors draw on competencies used in responsive counseling and proactive prevention programming. This differs from basic counseling or prevention programming because the assistance is initiated by a consulting relationship. An example of the provision mode might occur from the same concerns that led to the prescription consultation example in the preceding section. In an alternate scenario, the teacher may feel unable to initiate the recommended (i.e., prescribed) plan or may have tried unsuccessfully to do so. As a provision-mode consultant, the counselor could enter the classroom as a substitute or collaborator and implement the proposed token economy program to the students (clients). In this example, the counselor (consultant) serves as a model for the teacher (consultee), who will still have to become involved eventually because the program will take time to complete. If the program necessitates only one class session and the counselor replaces the teacher, the provided consultation services completely eliminate active participation by the teacher.

Initiation Mode

School counselors as consultants may contact prospective consultees proactively after having recognized and studied a problem, offering their consulting services. Depending on the nature of the problem, the consulting services may be either direct or indirect. An example of the initiation mode is a case in which a high school counselor responds to a first-year teacher who makes many disciplinary referrals to the assistant principal's office, appears unhappy when with colleagues, and is heard making comments about leaving the school district or the profession. The counselor (consultant) responds by inviting the teacher (consultee) to meet and talk, taking the opportunity to mention the events and offering to help the teacher resolve the problem. In this example, the consultation mode then becomes prescriptive, provisional, collaborative, or a combination thereof. A happier, more confident teacher may make fewer disciplinary referrals and serve the students (clients) better. The Coleman (2006) example from earlier began as initiation and expanded to provision, mediation, collaboration, and prescription.

Collaboration Mode

As consultants, school counselors may respond to requests from consultees by engaging in mutual efforts to understand the problem, devise an action plan, and implement it. The services are usually indirect. A case of collaborative consulting will occur if the high school teacher (consultee) who has classroom management problems agrees that help is needed and engages in a joint problem-solving relationship with the counselor (consultant). They might engage in such collaborative activities as defining the problem clearly, identifying alternative solutions, selecting mutually agreeable strategies, and figuring out ways to implement them. Their ultimate goal is to discover ideas that, when implemented, will help the teacher be more effective with the students (clients). This stepped counseling process is similar to the one used in the decision-making counseling strategy presented in Chapter 8.

Mediation Mode

As consultants, school counselors may respond to requests from two or more consultees to help them accomplish an agreement or a reconciliation by serving as facilitators for the consultees. The resultant consultation services are direct. Mediation consulting may occur whenever two people or groups become locked in mutual disagreements and seemingly unresolvable differences of opinion. Antagonists may be teacher versus student, student versus parent, student versus student, or administrator versus student. If all sides agree, counselors can mediate by serving as intermediaries. An example is for a counselor (consultant) to help a teacher (consultee) having discipline problems work out differences with a student (client) angered by being sent to the principal's office. The mediating counselor can meet with both parties to help them share their explanations and try to achieve a mutual understanding and an improved relationship leading to a settlement of their differences. In so doing, the counselor might make suggestions but will never dictate resolutions to the disputing parties. It is also important that both the teacher and student believe that the counselor is a fair, impartial mediator. That mediation has become an important consulting mode is seen in the attention paid to conflict resolution in the counseling literature (Messing, 1993).

Several scholars have attempted to provide steps or stages for counselors to use when delivering consulting services and the recommendations, have more commonalities than differences. Essentially, their ideas fit into the five stages of Ivey, Ivey, and Zalaquett's (2014) helping paradigm presented in Table 8.1 in Chapter 8 of this textbook. The following stages are based on those in Chapter 8 with the consulting function replacing the counseling function. Briefly, those stages are (a) building an empathic consulting relationship; (b) listening to the consultees' stories and searching for positive assets; (c) setting goals with consultees mutually; (d) working with consultees to explore alternatives, confront incongruities and conflicts, and decide on constructive action plans; and (e) helping consultees generalize and act on their action plans. The same five stages were previously presented for organizing and implementing responsive counseling services and are also advocated in conjunction with organizing and implementing consulting interventions. Therefore, the task of implementing the systems for both counseling and consulting services is easier because the systems are alike. An example follows:

> Reflect on the two parents (consultees) who approached a counselor (consultant) for consultation about ways to help their child (the student client) become more successful in school (as described in the opening section of this chapter). The mode for this consulting relationship is collaboration. Implementing the first two of Ivey et al.'s (2014) stages (build an empathic relationship, listen to the consultees'stories, and search for positive assets), the counselor/consultant uses basic interviewing skills to help the parents (consultees) tell their story, identify related affect, and discover resources available to them. Next, the counselor/consultant helps the consultees set goals based on a mutual understanding of the problem (Ivey et al.'s third stage). Having agreed on what seemingly needs to be done, the consultant works with the consultees to identify strategies that can be employed to try to reach the goals that were established and to devise plans for implementing the strategies (Ivey et al.'s fourth and fifth stages).

BASIC COMPETENCIES FOR SCHOOL COUNSELOR CONSULTING

The nature of school counseling itself places counselors in a position as prospective consultants. Because opportunities for consulting may present themselves from at least five modes, the school counselor is challenged to be a versatile consultant, able to be the provider, the mediator, or the initiator. The five modes can be further categorized as representing either direct or indirect services. The basic skills of a comprehensive consulting model are presented here in the context of Ivey et al.'s (2014) five stages. Fortunately, consulting does not require a completely independent set of competencies. Instead, many of the counseling and some of the prevention programming competencies are simply applied in a different context. Research by Lin, Kelly, and Nelson (1996) indicates that many verbal behaviors are common to counseling and consulting interactions. The importance of being multiculturally competent—sensitive to the worldviews of consultees and their clients—remains as important as it is in counseling interventions and prevention programming. Because counseling and consulting competencies are similar, we find that school counseling students sometimes get confused and cannot tell the differences. So we challenge you to peruse this information carefully in order to be able to discern the different nuances clearly.

BUILDING EMPATHIC RELATIONSHIPS, LISTENING TO CONSULTEES' STORIES, AND SEARCHING FOR POSITIVE ASSETS

Building Empathic Consulting Relationships

Consultation relationships are often initiated by prospective consultees. In such cases, counselors draw on the same skills used when opening responsive counseling relationships initiated by student clients—open invitations that encourage consultee sharing, identifying, and clarifying. When counselors initiate consulting relationships, clear explanations of the invitation and proposal are necessary, just as they are in counseling interviews initiated by counselors. For example, a counselor will respond with an open invitation to talk with a consultee as the elementary school teacher did who approached a counselor for help out of frustration with students' acting-out behaviors. Horton and Brown's (1990) review of research on the importance of interpersonal skills led them to conclude that successful clinical consultants establish facilitative relationships with their consultees. Therefore, the counselor's initial consulting goal is to establish an empathic relationship.

Listening to the Consultees' Stories and Searching for Positive Assets

After opening the consulting interview successfully, counselors will invite prospective consultees to share their presenting or targeted (initiation mode) problems and establish a facilitative working alliance in the process. In this process, consultees can be encouraged to share pertinent information about themselves (e.g., experiences, feelings, perceived level of competence to resolve the current problem, motives, initial goals), student clients (e.g., culture, age, gender, maturity, behaviors), interactions between clients and consultees (e.g., communications, behaviors, affect, attitudes, antecedents, reactions), and the context in which the interactions occurred (e.g., physical setting, contemporaries, peers, relationships, expectations, distractions, challenges). This process is similar to counseling interviews. Therefore, providing the core facilitative conditions, attending physically, and using the basic verbal counseling responses are as important to consulting as they are to counseling interventions.

The counselor who approached the high school teacher having disciplinary difficulties in the "Initiation Mode" section of this chapter is an example of a prospective consulting relationship that needs to begin with an explanation. Having initiated the meeting, the counselor provides the teacher with an explanation of what appears to be happening and how the counselor as a consultant might help the teacher. In this mode, the consultant tells the story that led to initiating the session in order to encourage the teacher to tell her story.

While prospective consultees respond to invitations to share pertinent information about presenting problems, consulting counselors determine which mode is suggested by the circumstances and whether the consultees are ready and willing to proceed, and the counselor is able to provide consultation assistance. Then counselors are in a position to negotiate their roles and explain their own understanding of the presenting problems and the consultees' motives. Being clear with consultees about one's role as a consultant is important at the outset and remains important throughout the consultation process. Consequently, when providing consulting services, counselors make sure they and their consultees agree about expectations. It is recommended that, early in the consulting process, counselors periodically assess whether the expectations of all parties match and that counselors renegotiate and reiterate those expectations as necessary. One of the many reasons for doing this is that consultees sometimes have hidden agendas. For example, the teacher who expressed a desire for help in coping with a misbehaving student may also harbor a desire to punish that student. Another reason for assessing the consulting relationship periodically is that consultees sometimes misunderstand or misinterpret initial explanations. For example, in cases where consultants perceive their roles as mediators and the consultees expect arbitration, the consultees may be disappointed that the consultants do not dictate a solution.

SETTING GOALS MUTUALLY WITH CONSULTEES

As it is in counseling, goal setting is the heart of consulting, for consulting, like counseling, is a participatory helping relationship. Counselors as consultants help consultees find a sense of direction and share the responsibility of achieving their own goals. The same counseling skills that are important for goal setting in counseling relationships remain important in consulting relationships. Helping consultees set goals focuses their attention on acting constructively, involves them in the helping process either directly or indirectly, makes them aware of what needs to be accomplished, encourages them to act on their own behalf or on behalf of their student clients, and informs them that school counselors are capable partners in the consulting process. For example, the counselor and the parents in the continuing hypothetical case, after having perused the data from observations and records, decide to collaborate with the school counselor as a consultant in order to attempt to help their child become more successful in school.

WORKING WITH CONSULTEES TO EXPLORE ALTERNATIVES, CONFRONT INCONGRUITIES AND CONFLICTS, AND DECIDE ON CONSTRUCTIVE ACTION PLANS

Once the decision to mutually engage in a consulting relationship has been made, the parties engage in further definition of the problem and exploration of possible solutions. Basic challenging skills (e.g., information sharing, immediacy, logical consequences) and the basic counseling competencies will be as useful at this time as they are in counseling relationships. This step in the consulting relationship is similar to identifying alternative response options in the decision-making counseling strategy presented in Chapter 8. Consultants and consultees can brainstorm hypotheses about the problem and possible solutions. This is especially appropriate when counselors are using the initiation and collaboration consulting modes. In brainstorming, the idea is to identify as many solutions or hypotheses as possible without initially engaging in analyses of the ideas—a follow-up task. In the prescription mode, consultants explain the details of their treatment plans and brainstorm or negotiate who will implement them. In the provision and mediation modes, consultants may either brainstorm ideas about possible strategies or inform consultees about what they will do as they carry out their consulting services.

Exploring possible solutions leads to evaluating alternatives once they have been identified. Osterweil (1987) recommends using reasonability, workability, and motivation as criteria for evaluating potential solutions. Additional information about problem antecedents, consequences, and participant responses may be required before conclusions can be made and may require research by consultants and consultees. One important skill in this instance is to observe students in natural settings unobtrusively and concurrently collect relevant data. After that has been done, the stage is set for action plans.

For example, after perusing several alternatives with the assistance of the school counselor/consultant, the parents and counselor in the continuing hypothetical case decide that two strategies will suffice for the time being. They will remain open to reviewing the strategies, revising them, and possibly changing them. The two strategies are to invite the child's teacher to help by employing some strategies designed to keep the child on task when attention deficits occur and to have the parents set aside time each evening to discuss schoolwork with the child and to provide encouragement and, if necessary, appropriate assistance. The counselor agrees to approach the teacher, seek cooperation, and provide instruction. The counselor also helps the parents carefully define and, if necessary, rehearse their interactions with their child. Systems for monitoring the child's progress are determined, and a plan for meeting again to discuss the case is established.

HELPING CONSULTEES GENERALIZE AND IMPLEMENT THEIR ACTION PLANS

Next, the counselor suggests that the goals be considered tentative until there is an opportunity to collect baseline data about how well the child is currently doing in school. An important means of collecting data will be for the counselor (consultant) to observe the child in classroom settings and/or ask the child's teacher to provide information based on observations. Observations are supplemented by data from standardized tests and performance on tasks and assignments in the classroom. After data are collected, the parents and counselor meet to continue solidifying goals and determining constructive action strategies. As was the case in the presentation about individual and small group counseling in Chapter 8, there is a variety of potential strategies that may be employed by consultants and consultees in order to achieve the mutually set goals for the action plans. The next section addresses this topic.

BASIC ACTION STRATEGIES FOR SCHOOL COUNSELOR CONSULTING

The strategies presented here are those that seem most appropriate for school counselors in the majority of their consulting cases. Additions may occur with experience and in response to the peculiarities of one's professional setting.

Action Plan Strategies for Achieving Consulting Goals

Most action plan strategies important for achieving counseling goals presented in Chapter 8 are also important in achieving consulting goals. Settings and applications may differ, but the importance of the skills remains constant. Building empathy will prove useful when engaging in all the consulting modes because of the importance of the basic counseling skills throughout the consulting process.

In all five consulting modes, consultees may need help making decisions. Consequently, decision-making counseling is another action stage strategy applicable to both counseling and consulting services. All the modes may also be approached via the brief counseling model. Other basic counseling service action strategies vary in their applicability to the five consulting modes. All the strategies seem applicable in the provision mode. Table 10.1 provides a summary of this discussion.

TABLE 10.1 *Applicability of Counseling Strategies to Consultation Mode*

Consultation Mode					
Counseling Strategies	**Prescription**	**Provision**	**Initiation**	**Collaboration**	**Mediation**
Empathy and support	Yes	Yes	Yes	Yes	Yes
Decision making	Yes	Yes	Yes	Yes	Yes
Brief counseling	Yes	Yes	Yes	Yes	Yes
Competence enhancement	Yes	Yes	Yes	Yes	
Self-management	Yes	Yes	Yes	Yes	
Nonverbal	Yes	Yes	Yes	Yes	
Rational thinking		Yes			Yes
Assertiveness		Yes			
Group		Yes			
Crisis		Yes			

Assertiveness, group, and crisis counseling seem applicable only in the provision mode, whereas counseling for rational thinking seems applicable in the provision and mediation modes. Competence enhancement counseling seems applicable in the prescription, provision, initiation, and collaboration modes. Self-management and nonverbal counseling seem appropriate for the prescription, provision, initiation, and collaboration modes. The foregoing categorizations are logical but arbitrary, and it may be that the applications are broader or more limited than indicated here. Much depends on the individual counselor providing the consulting. The most important theme is that the basic action strategies are applicable to both counseling and consulting services.

Consulting to Enhance Child and Adolescent Development

In the prescription, initiation, and collaboration modes, school counselors may find themselves trying to help consultees understand and use knowledge about human development to intervene appropriately. Parents, teachers, and administrators are sometimes at a loss to match expectations with maturational differences. Counselors who are knowledgeable about developmental expectations at various age levels and about individual differences within all age levels are in a position to help colleagues and parents understand the behaviors of their students and children more intelligently and make decisions about whether to respond accordingly. When the decision to respond is made in consultation with counselors, helpful interventions can be developed. The key assumption here is that school counselors who offer consultation to enhance child and adolescent development are indeed knowledgeable about the topic. The hypothetical case running through this chapter of the parents who want to help their child become more successful in school is an example of child development consulting.

Consulting With Teachers to Enhance Classroom Management

It is not unusual for counselors working in the prescription, initiation, or collaboration consulting modes to be assisting with management of student classroom behaviors, especially at the elementary and perhaps middle school levels. In these cases, specific undesirable behaviors such as acting out, aggressiveness, and withdrawal can be targeted through teacher/consultee reports and consultant observations. Counselors can introduce teacher/consultees to the importance of recognizing and collecting baseline data to have benchmarks about the presenting behaviors against which efforts to induce changes can be compared.

In general, classroom management consulting involves implementing behavior modification principles. Therefore, counselors responding to requests for such consultation are challenged to be well versed in these basic principles. The principles are summarized in the following list and can be shared with teacher/consultees (Keat, 1974):

- Behavior is learned when it is reinforced consistently;
- Specific behaviors that require acceleration or deceleration can be identified and the child's strengths emphasized;

- When engaging in behavior modification activities, small gains are to be anticipated initially;
- Consequences of behavior must be meaningful to the student;
- Consequences, rewards, or punishments are more meaningful if they follow the behavior immediately;
- Reinforcement may be physical or social;
- Purposes and goals should be clear;
- The target behavior should be the best one for the particular student;
- The aim of behavior control should be self-control.

These principles are applied to changing targeted behaviors. To help teacher/consultees achieve desired behavior changes, counselors may select from among several available behavior modification strategies. The most applicable strategies are response differentiation, fading, shaping, chaining, token systems, contingency management, and time-out procedures. Finally, counselors help teacher/consultees keep sufficient records for evaluating progress toward achieving desired objectives. (Evaluation involves assessment skills, a topic covered more comprehensively in Chapter 3.) That part of the hypothetical case in this chapter in which the teacher is being asked to enhance the student client's on-task behavior in class is an example of classroom management consultation. For instance, one strategy the teacher may use is shaping (e.g., gently reminding the student to pay attention to the desired task when off task, reinforcing on-task behavior with praise when noticed, and generally paying attention to on-task and off-task behavior).

Consulting With Individuals to Enhance Their Understanding of Schools as Organizations

Schools operate according to organizational principles. Sometimes this is manifested pathologically, or individual applications of and responses to these principles are pathological. Similar circumstances occur in organizations outside the school, and the effects may be manifested in the school. Organizational pathologies and pathological responses to organizations may lead to situations in which counselors engage in prescription, initiation, or collaboration consulting services. For example, students, parents, or teachers need assistance determining how to respond to school regulations they perceive as being repressive or unreasonable, such as dress codes and tardiness criteria. As with classroom management consulting, this form of consultation often takes the form of sharing knowledge with consultees that will empower them to behave more effectively.

To be effective at helping individuals in this way, it behooves counselors to understand the schools as organizations. An example of information that may help counselors in this role is knowledge of how well educated staff members are and how liberal or conservative they are regarding new ideas and innovations. Better-educated and secure professionals are more open to innovations. It is also useful to know whether the school's decision-making structure is centralized or decentralized, because centralized power tends to retard innovation, whereas distribution of decision making among groups seems to encourage it. It follows that counselors who are familiar with the balance of power in the school system are more likely to know how to influence it positively. Identifying the most influential stakeholders inside and outside the organization helps a counselor understand the sources of authority and influence. All others have little or no authority or influence unless they find ways to influence the decision makers. Under these circumstances, most counselors, teachers, and students find that diplomacy and subtlety are the best avenues to effect influence.

In summary, counselors engaging in organizational consultation help consultees translate noble dreams into achievable goals that will increase the probability of success and decrease the probability of failure and abandonment (Ponzo, 1974). Acting as consultants, counselors can help consultees understand how the system works and establish action plans that seem to have the best chances of succeeding. At times, consulting counselors are proactive and serve as advocates for their consultees (e.g., representing student consultees or joining them in meetings with administrators) (Baker et al., 2009). At other times, the assistance will be indirect (e.g., preparing student consultees for meetings with administrators through structured behavior rehearsals). Of course, the prospect of redesigning the strategy for additional follow-up efforts is necessary because no plan can be a guaranteed success. An understanding of the organization also helps counselors when offering consultation through in-service programs and when helping colleagues plan curriculum programs. A hypothetical example of organizational consultation follows:

> In a high school setting, the administration (principal and assistants) arbitrarily dictated a student dress code to which some have strong objections. Several students ask to meet with a counselor to air their complaints about the new code and to ask for help. The counselor believes that the administrators have the right to determine policies; she also thinks that the students seem to have some legitimate complaints about the code. These beliefs lead to the counselor offering to serve as a consultant (collaborative mode) to the students to help them try to achieve their goals. Initially, the counselor helps the students identify and clarify their position and the affect associated with it. Next, using knowledge of the school as a system, the counselor helps the students devise a strategy that demonstrates respect for the office of the principal, awareness of the lines of authority in the school system, and conformity with their goals. Having agreed on a strategy, the counselor helps the students prepare to implement it and develops a follow-up strategy for dealing with the range of possible responses from the school's administrators. For example, the counselor may help the students prepare to deliver to the principal an inventory of their objections to the dress code in a manner that is respectful yet appropriately assertive, after advising them on behaviors that seem to have the best potential for success. Follow-up activities will depend on the administration's response. Whether the administrators are conciliatory and willing to negotiate or steadfast in defending their position, the counselor remains available to consult with the students about the process, the outcomes, and the appropriate next step.

Consulting to Achieve Successful Mediation

In the mediation mode, counselors respond directly to requests from two or more consultees to facilitate a mutual agreement or reconciliation. For example, two students who have been feuding and fighting over issues they are unable to resolve agree to meet with a counselor to work out an amicable settlement. Initially, the consultees must understand the assumptions on which mediation is founded: The mediator is not expected to dictate a resolution, the consultees agree to declare a truce during mediation, the mediator facilitates communications between the disputing parties, the disputing parties listen to each other's views, the disputing parties agree that their goal is to achieve a mutually agreeable resolution, and mediation is completed successfully when the disputing parties achieve a mutually agreeable solution.

Counselors who understand and accept the assumptions on which mediation is founded will be quite capable of serving as mediation consultants. The basic counseling and influencing skills coupled with knowledge about interpersonal communications are the requisite skills for mediation consultation. Beyond that, counselors can draw on experience, previous formal knowledge, and familiarity with the schools to help mediation consultees. The following example introduces the use of mediation as a consulting strategy in conflict resolution. In a hypothetical case of conflict resolution, the counselor acts as a mediator in a student-teacher dispute with cultural diversity overtones:

The participants in the simulation are an African American male counselor (the consultant), a White female teacher (the consultee), and a 13-year-old African American female student (the client). Their middle school is located in a middle-class area of a predominantly White community. The student is a client of the counselor whom he has counseled previously regarding school adjustment and academic performance. One class (English) that has been discussed in their counseling sessions is taught by the consultee, and the student has mentioned disliking the teacher as a reason for not performing well in the class, without specifically elaborating on reasons. After about 40% of the school year passes, the teacher approaches the counselor for consultation about getting the student, who appears to be stubbornly refusing to complete assignments, to complete her schoolwork. The consultation relationship opens in the collaboration mode.

Counselor (consultant)-teacher (consultee) discussions lead to defining the problem as student stubbornness, and they agree that the first step is that the counselor meet with the student to share the teacher's concern and position and try to determine whether the student can be persuaded to do her schoolwork. Before proceeding, the counselor makes sure that both the student and the teacher know of his previous relationships with each of them to avoid complications associated with having dual professional relationships. During the interview with the counselor, the student refuses to do any more homework than she is doing because she is passing the course; she also accuses the teacher of being racist, without providing specific examples of racist behaviors.

The counselor suggests a meeting between the student and the teacher, with him present to serve as a mediator. They agree, although the student is not very hopeful in her comments when doing so. The counselor, as a consultant, has introduced the mediation mode. During the meeting, both the student and the teacher, despite the counselor's best efforts to explain how mediation works, behave as if the purpose of the meeting is to have the counselor take their side against the adversary. The student openly accuses the teacher of being racist and refuses to change her study behaviors, again citing her impression that she is passing. The teacher, while recognizing that the student is passing, tries to point out the folly of the student's actions and encourages her to try harder. Surprised by the accusation of racism, she denies it and defends herself as anything but a racist while also saying things that indicate her potential cultural insensitivity. The counselor, acting as a mediator, lets the interactions occur while trying to help both parties clarify their positions and understand each other's. In addition, the counselor attempts to keep the parties focused on trying to resolve the conflict.

Within a week, the counselor, who believes that the mediation session went quite badly, checks with the teacher and the student to find out how things are progressing. To his surprise, he learns from the teacher that the student is turning in assignments and is not behaving belligerently in class. He learns from the student that the teacher's attitude has changed and is more acceptable. There are several possible explanations for why the conflict seems to be resolved. Perhaps the most important observation is that the counselor, using his mediation skills, provided an atmosphere in which the adversaries could find ways to communicate that worked best for them.

Responding to Consultee Reluctance and Resistance

When attempting to initiate consulting, counselors may encounter reluctance from prospective consultees. The same competencies used for coping with reluctance when initiating responsive counseling relationships are important when initiating consulting relationships. Because prescription, provision, collaboration, and mediation consulting relationships are usually initiated by consultees, resistance is more common than reluctance in consulting relationships.

Resistance to consulting is similar to resistance to counseling. Therefore, the requisite competencies are similar. As with counseling, consulting relationships include such variables as individual personalities, different settings, and previous experiences that influence the counselor's responses to resistance and whether those responses work. In summary, when consulting, counselors may encounter reluctance and resistance just as they do when counseling, and the repertoire of possible responses is the same.

Closing Consulting Relationships

The similarity between counseling and consulting relationships includes the closing phase. The same competencies are important in both. Evaluating consulting relationships is as important as evaluating responsive counseling interventions and proactive prevention programming. You are referred to the section of Chapter 8 in which a strategy for evaluating counseling interventions is presented (i.e., "Evaluating Individual and Group Counseling"). We believe the same strategy can be applied to consulting interventions.

EXAMPLES OF CONSULTING IN SCHOOL COUNSELING

Planned Periodic Consulting in an Elementary School Setting

This example and those that follow are paraphrased from reports about consultation activities of school counselors that appeared in the professional literature or are derived from our professional experience. In the first example, Fall (1995) describes a *periodic planned consultation* idea between school counselors and teachers. With the knowledge and support of the principal, the counselor schedules 1-hour meetings with each teacher to whom the counselor is responsible to take place every 10 weeks (three times a year). Each consultation meeting may have its own topics. For example, determining the accuracy of student placement, assessing whether students' needs are being met, and asking how well the entire classroom is functioning may be topics for the first meeting.

Fall (1995) recommends a set of five steps that may be followed in each of the planned consultations. In the first step, the counselor observes the classroom for 30 minutes prior to the consultation meeting. Goals of the observation are acquiring background for understanding concerns the teacher may have; identifying classroom and teacher strengths; and noticing student behavior, particularly potential problem behaviors (e.g., appear withdrawn and unfocused). The second step consists of beginning the consultation session with positive comments from the observation step (e.g., "Your class worked well in groups. I was impressed by the way you let the students express themselves."). The goal of this interaction is to pave the way for accurate, nondefensive communication by being nonjudgmental and respectful.

During the third step, the counselor (consultant) employs reflective listening skills while the teacher is invited to share information about the entire classroom and specific students, including problems. Thereafter, the counselor helps the teacher explore possible solutions. An excerpt from a hypothetical interaction follows:

Counselor: It sounds like Ivy's behaviors are distracting the class and keeping her from being successful academically.
Teacher: Some days are better than others. Mondays seem to be the worst.
Counselor: That may be important. How does she do in subject areas?

Teacher: She's OK when she pays attention. I've tried many things, and nothing seems to work unless I keep on her. I don't have time to do that.

Counselor: Unquestionably, this has exasperated you. It appears as if attention from you works.

Teacher: I hadn't thought of that, but I think you're right.

(Fall, 1995)

The fourth step consists of exploring possible interventions for identified problems. Fall (1995) recommends doing this jointly, similar to the mutual counselor-consultee interaction presented in the collaboration mode described earlier in this chapter. This approach increases potential for identifying a host of possible solutions and for creating a good working alliance between the counselor (consultant) and teacher (consultee). The fifth step finds the counselor summing up what has been accomplished and making plans, jointly with the teacher, to follow up on plans for action that have been generated.

Mediation with Gangs in a Middle School

Tabish and Orell (1996) describe a middle school gang intervention program for which the goal is to allow gang-involved youths to confront issues with rivals in a safe area where respect is maintained. To achieve this goal, Washington Middle School in Albuquerque, New Mexico, initiated peer and formal mediation in 1990. Peer mediation is for two rival gang members; formal mediation is for two or more rival gangs. Trained student mediators provide the peer mediation. The school's gang interventionist or selected outside mediators perform the formal mediations between rival gangs. An overview of the formal mediation process is provided here.

> Initially, the interventionist meets with the rival gangs in a small assembly to explain the purpose, roles, and process. Participation is voluntary; however, it should be noted that the school's administration has made it known that negative gang behaviors will not be tolerated in the school. Each gang selects two representatives and an alternate to negotiate on their behalf. One to 3 hours per day for 3 to 5 days are devoted to the process. They meet in a room selected to provide a formal, serious atmosphere. The following rules are posted in the room: All parties must (a) try to solve the problem; (b) refrain from name calling and putting others down; (c) show respect by not interrupting each other; (d) be honest; (e) avoid using weapons, threats, and intimidating behaviors; and (f) maintain confidentiality. There is an agenda, and a list of gang members is distributed. The formalities are seen as indicating to the participants that the atmosphere is mature and serious. The mediation process itself is a form of social modeling that will help the participants generalize the process to other problems.

The process consists of four meetings. The introductory events just described occur during the first meeting. Establishing an atmosphere of mutual trust and understanding while allowing all parties to share their feelings and views is the focus of the second meeting. Witnesses may be called in to clarify the problem. Solutions to the problem are identified during the third meeting, using a brainstorming approach. Adjournment occurs only after an agreement is reached among all parties. The fourth meeting is devoted to reviewing and confirming the agreement. Follow-up meetings with representatives of both gangs in attendance or with each gang separately are held to evaluate the agreement and acquire signatures missed earlier.

The preceding information describes mediation provided by a trained professional consultant who could be a school counselor using the collaborative mode. An atmosphere of respect for each student was promoted.

Supervising Peer Counselors in a Secondary School Setting

A high school counselor trained student volunteers to help their peers meet with the peer counselors on a regular basis to provide them with support and supervision. The following scenario represents a hypothetical supervisory relationship. The counselor supervisor is the consultant, the student peer counselor is the consultee, and the students whom she is helping are the clients:

The counselor-supervisor opens a supervision meeting with an open-ended question or open invitation to the peer counselor to share whatever concerns her most. The peer counselor describes the circumstances of a case that is particularly challenging for her. The client is a student who sought out the peer counselor for help because she is failing her mathematics course, having relationship problems with a boyfriend, and experiencing pressure from her parents about her schoolwork and the relationship. She believes that her parents have unrealistic academic expectations and should not try to influence her choice of boyfriends.

After helping the peer counselor tell her story and clarify the facts, the counselor consultant invites her to share her feelings about the case. The peer counselor wonders aloud whether she is competent enough to deal with the issues the student client has presented. The counselor/consultant agrees that this may be a genuine concern and asks the peer helper what options she has considered, offering to help brainstorm them (collaboration mode). The brainstorming session leads the counselor/supervisor (consultant) to conclude that the peer helper (consultee) may be able to help the student client in some ways but is not the appropriate person to respond to all the issues that were presented. The supervisor-consultant then offers suggestions for the peer helper to consider (initiation mode).

The consultant offers the following recommendations for the consultee to consider (prescription mode). Meet with the student client again and ask whether she is interested in receiving tutoring for her mathematics difficulties. If she is, the peer helper can then make the necessary arrangements for her to receive that help. Inform the student client that she (the peer counselor) discussed the case with the consultant/supervisor who, in turn, recommends that the student client see one of the school's professional counselors about the relationship and parental issues, indicating that the counselor/supervisor is willing to receive the referral. Following discussion of the merits of the recommendations, the peer counselor agrees to the plan. After attempting to carry out the agreed-on strategy, the consultee will report what transpired with the student client to the supervisor/consultant, and together they will determine what to do next.

The hypothetical consulting relationship transpired across the five stages described earlier in the chapter, and the consultant used several consulting modes in the process. Switching modes is not uncommon. As presented herein, the modes are primarily means of classifying, studying, and understanding different ways to engage in consultation.

Solution-Focused School Consultation

Kahn (2000) uses a middle school setting to provide an example of solution-focused school consultation. Kahn emphasizes that school counselor (consultants) should help consultees (e.g., teachers or parents) to set goals that they can control rather than assessing their success in terms of student client change. Kahn's approach is for the school counselor as consultant to begin with an orientation to solution-focused consulting and help the consultee to identify strengths and resources and set initial goals. In a case illustration, the school counselor (consultant) begins with an invitation to the teacher (consultee) to share what she hoped to accomplish in the first consulting session. The teacher reveals her frustration with a literature/language class. The counselor's response focuses on the teacher's recent accomplishments (e.g., started an after-school study hall and tailored her curriculum to students). After the teacher remembers that she has experienced success, the counselor restates the problem positively ("Let's see what we can do to help you feel like you are staying afloat"; p. 252). The counselor follows with a request for a survey of what's been happening in the teacher's class.

The teacher then describes a class out of her control and a specific student who takes over the class, sabotaging her lesson plans. The (counselor) consultant's brief response is to ask how the teacher will know when things are better for the most troublesome student in her classroom. When the teacher responds, the counselor attempts to help her be specific and use concrete terms (i.e., "When he's tuned in" becomes "He wouldn't disrupt my class"; p. 252). Next, the counselor asks the teacher how she will feel when the student is "tuned in." The teacher lists several positive outcomes. At this point, the goals have been established.

Having established goals early in the consultation process, the counselor proceeds to seek solutions that will be acceptable to the consultee. The process begins with the counselor helping the teacher to remember occasions when the troublesome student was not troublesome. This is followed by an analysis of the circumstances that led to his not being troublesome (e.g., "shorten his task . . . ask him what he needs during breaks between tasks"; p. 252). The counselor then asks: "What do you need to do to make it happen again?" (p. 253). When the teacher states that she should initiate again the procedures that once worked, the counselor/consultant gives her immediate positive verbal reinforcement. The counselor follows this with a recommendation to the teacher for evaluating the effects of her efforts ("So if Jon is a four this week, what will have to happen for him to be a five by our next meeting?" p. 253 [principle: incremental changes will cause a rippling effect]). The counselor closes the session by recommending that the teacher think about how she can react differently to the troublesome student and perhaps change their relationship before the next consultation session.

Kahn (2000) stresses that the solution-focused approach can be conducted in one or a few sessions, focuses on the future, uses the consultee's strengths as resources, and is collaborative in nature. The primary steps in the process, as just demonstrated, are (a) perform initial structuring, (b) establish goals for consultation, (c) examine previously attempted solutions and exceptions, (d) help the consultee find a solution, and (e) summarize goals and praise the consultant for past successes. As presented, the model seems user friendly for school counselors as consultants and their consultees.

A School Counselor as Consultee

There are circumstances that lead to school counselors seeking consultation and consequently serving their student clients from a consultee's perspective. An example is found in Baker et al. (2009). A high school counseling intern realized that she needed assistance from others whose expertise was beyond her own when working with an 18-year-old student who had moved out of her home and was worried about being pregnant. In order to adequately serve the student, the intern approached the school nurse to learn what options the student had about addressing the potential pregnancy concern. The nurse informed the intern that a pregnancy test could be performed at the school because the student was 18 (provision mode). The intern accompanied the student to a decision-making meeting with the nurse. The pregnancy results were inconclusive and the nurse provided information about available services covering several options to both the student and the intern (provision mode).

The intern had also consulted with the county school counseling program coordinator in order to identify an appropriate course of action. The coordinator informed the intern that she did not have to inform the parents about the pregnancy test results and needed to monitor the student's health closely (prescription mode). The intern shared the following observations about her experience as a consultee:

> Being able to consult with other professionals who had expertise beyond my own was enlightening and allowed me to be a more effective advocate for the student. In turn, my relationship with the student served to make the consultations with the nurse, who was a stranger to the student, more effective.
>
> (Baker et al., 2009, p. 204)

CONSULTATION: A NATURAL FUNCTION FOR SCHOOL COUNSELORS

Consulting is a widely accepted counseling function. It is not as clearly understood as responsive counseling interventions and proactive prevention programming and varies across settings. Natural circumstances in the schools provide school counselors with a relatively specific consultation role that can manifest itself in several modes. Many students, teachers, administrators, and parents view counselors as being in a relatively neutral position in the schools and as possessing competencies that can be shared in consulting relationships. Therefore, being available for, and sought out by, others for consultation assistance are natural functions for school counselors. They are strategically located in the schools as people who might be trusted to serve as consultants via the various consulting modes introduced in this chapter. School counselors who recognize the interrelationships between consulting and other important school counseling functions can appreciate the unique qualities of consultation activities and recognize opportunities to consult in an organized fashion.

COMPREHENSIVE SCHOOL COUNSELING PROGRAM COMPONENT

1. List ways that consulting assignments can be incorporated into your field internship or practicum.
2. Develop a framework for informing administrators, teachers, students, and parents/guardians about the school counselor consulting functions available at your prospective school setting. Attempt to include the five modes in the presentation while keeping it sufficiently brief yet informative.

REFLECTION POINT

1. Debate the position taken in this chapter that school settings naturally determine the parameters of school counselor consulting.

2. Take an inventory of the competencies taught in your core counseling methods course that are applicable to consultation.

3. Review the five consulting modes presented in this chapter; determine which ones you would be comfortable providing and which do not appeal to you.

4. Analyze, discuss, and/or debate the following statement: "Courses in school counselor training programs devoted only to consultation are unnecessary because there is so much in common between counseling and consulting."

5. Debate the merits of the basic consulting action strategies mentioned in this chapter. Which ones seem appropriate to you and which do not? What are the reasons for your decisions?

6. Analyze the conflict resolution mediation consulting simulation (the simulation in which a female student thought her teacher was a racist) in this chapter from the perspective of critiquing the (counselor) consultant's actions and trying to hypothesize possible explanations for the outcomes.

7. After having read the section "Examples of Consulting in School Counseling," what new thoughts about consultation occurred to you?

8. Discuss or debate how the modes and stages of consultation presented in this chapter fit into a multicultural perspective of helping diverse consultees and clients with varied worldviews. Are they sufficient, or do they need to be altered in some way?

APPLICATION TO TECHNOLOGY

1. How might counselors use their school Internet sites to assist them with their consulting activities?

2. How might school counselors use the resources on the ASCA website to improve the effectiveness of their consultation with students, parents, and fellow professionals? (www.schoolcounselor.org/)

3. Do a Google search for online resources that address school counselor consultation. What did you find?

REFERENCES

American School Counselor Association. (2012). *The ASCA National Model: A framework for school counseling programs* (3rd ed.). Alexandria, VA: Author.

Baker, S. B., Robichaud, T. A., Dietrich, V.C.W., Wells, S. C., & Schreck, R. E. (2009). School counselor consultation: A pathway to advocacy, collaboration, and leadership. *Professional School Counseling, 12,* 200–206.

Bauer, A. M., & Sapona, R. H. (1988). Facilitation and problem solving: A framework for collaboration between counselors and teachers. *Elementary School Guidance and Counseling, 23,* 5–9.

Bundy, M. L., & Poppen, W. A. (1986). School counselors' effectiveness as consultants: A research review. *Elementary School Guidance and Counseling, 29,* 215–222.

Caplan, G. (1959). *Concepts of mental health and consultation.* Washington, DC: U.S. Department of Health, Education and Welfare, Children's Bureau.

Coleman, S. (2006). *Consultation reflection.* Unpublished manuscript. Raleigh: North Carolina State University.

Dougherty, A. M. (1990). *Consultation: Practice and perspectives.* Pacific Grove, CA: Brooks/Cole.

Dougherty, A. M. (1992). School consultation in the 1990s. *Elementary School Guidance and Counseling, 26,* 163–164.

Dowd, E. T., & Moerings, B. J. (1975). The underachiever and teacher consultation: A case study. *School Counselor, 22,* 263–266.

Fall, M. (1995). Planning for consultation: An aid for the elementary school counselor. *School Counselor, 43,* 151–156.

Gallessich, J. (1985). Toward a meta-theory of consultation. *Counseling Psychologist, 13*(3), 336–354.

Gerler, E. R., Jr. (1992). Consultation and school counseling. *Elementary School Guidance and Counseling, 26,* 162.

Horton, G. E., & Brown, D. (1990). The importance of interpersonal skills in consultee-centered consultation. *Journal of Counseling & Development, 68,* 423–426.

Ivey, A. E., Ivey, M. B., & Zalaquett, C. P. (2014). *Intentional interviewing and counseling: Facilitating client development in a multicultural society* (8th ed.). Belmont, CA: Brooks/Cole Cengage Learning.

Kahn, B. B. (2000). A model of solution-focused consultation for school counselors. *Professional School Counseling, 3,* 248–254.

Keat, D. B. (1974). *Fundamentals of child counseling.* Boston: Houghton Mifflin.

Kurpius, D. J. (1978). Consultation theory and process: An integrated model. *Personnel and Guidance Journal, 56,* 335–338.

Kurpius, D. J., & Fuqua, D. R. (1993a). Consultation I: Conceptual, structural, and operational dimensions. *Journal of Counseling & Development, 71,* 596–708.

Kurpius, D. J., & Fuqua, D. R. (1993b). Consultation II: Prevention, preparation, and key issues. *Journal of Counseling & Development, 72,* 115–198.

Lin, M., Kelly, K. R., & Nelson, R. C. (1996). A comparative analysis of the interpersonal process in school-based counseling and consultation. *Journal of Counseling Psychology, 43,* 389–393.

Mathias, C. E. (1992). Touching the lives of children: Consultative interventions that work. *Elementary School Guidance and Counseling, 26,* 190–201.

Messing, J. K. (1993). Mediation: An intervention strategy for counselors. *Journal of Counseling & Development, 72,* 67–72.

Mullis, F., & Edwards, D. (2001). Consulting with parents: Applying family systems concepts and techniques. *Professional School Counseling, 5,* 116–123.

Myrick, R. D. (1977). *Consultation as a counselor intervention.* Washington, DC: American School Counselor Association.

Osterweil, Z. O. (1987). A structured process of problem definition in school consultation. *School Counselor, 34,* 245–252.

Ponzo, Z. (1974). A counselor and change: Reminiscence and resolutions. *Personnel and Guidance Journal, 53,* 27–32.

Purkey, W. W., & Schmidt, J. J. (1982). Ways to be an inviting parent: Suggestions for the counselor-consultant. *Elementary School Guidance and Counseling, 17,* 94–99.

Rathvon, N. W. (1990). The effects of encouragement on off-task behavior and academic productivity. *Elementary School Guidance and Counseling, 24,* 189–199.

Robinson, E. H., & Wilson, E. S. (1987). Counselor-led human relations training as a consultation strategy. *Elementary School Guidance and Counseling, 22,* 124–131.

Scott, D. A., Royal, C. W., & Kissinger, D. B. (2015). *Counselor as consultant.* Thousand Oaks, CA: Sage.

Smaby, M. H., Peterson, T. L., Bergmann, P. E., Bacig, K.L.Z., & Swearingen, S. (1990). School-based community intervention: The school counselor as lead consultant for suicide prevention and intervention programs. *Elementary School Guidance and Counseling, 37,* 370–377.

Strein, W., & French, J. L. (1984). Teacher consultation in the affective domain: A survey of expert opinion. *School Counselor, 31,* 339–344.

Tabish, K. R., & Orell, L. H. (1996). RESPECT: Gang mediation at Albuquerque, New Mexico's Washington Middle School. *School Counselor, 44,* 65–70.

PARTNERS IN BUILDING A POSTSECONDARY EDUCATION–GOING CULTURE

11

RELATED STANDARDS OF PRACTICE

CACREP CORE	2.F.5.a.b.c.d.e.f.g.h.i.j.
CACREP SCHOOL COUNSELING	5.G.1.b.c.2.a.c.3.b.d.e.g.i.k.l.o.

Goal: To introduce a specific proactive career and college readiness enhancement role for school counselors.

Here are the comments of a student who decided that college is not for him:

> My sister has just graduated from college. She cannot find a job and has moved back home with us. I had freedom until she moved back in. My mom and dad are constantly complaining that she did not apply herself at college and that she is not grateful for all the money they have spent to send her to college. My parents had to borrow money to send my sister to college, and they don't know how they are going to save for retirement and pay back these loans.
>
> I will never go to college. It is a waste of time. I'm already earning more money than my sister, and I don't have to sit in boring classes and take tests. I will graduate from high school, but I will not be graduating from any other place.
>
> My parents are glad not to have to spend money on my education. My counselor at school wants to visit with my parents about my situation, but I want the counselor to back off. I know what I want. My parents know what they want. We don't need any help from a counselor who knows nothing about how my sister wasted her time and my parents' money.
>
> I will be just fine!

In an era when some are questioning the value of postsecondary education, how can school counselors exercise advocacy and leadership to support collaboration among all professional school personnel, families, and communities in exploring ways to enhance the postsecondary education–going culture?

POSTSECONDARY EDUCATION–GOING CULTURE

The value of a high school diploma has gradually diminished in recent years for a number of reasons, including the emergence of a global economy and the ever-increasing importance of possessing requisite technological skills for employment in the 21st century. Twentieth-century career goals for youths such as education for life and employment security have been challenged by changing circumstance, including (a) the emergence of numerous postsecondary education pathways to career readiness, (b) the increasing importance of acquiring a sophisticated knowledge base and related skills, (c) the necessity of engaging in lifelong learning to upgrade one's skills continuously, and (d) the potential for having to work beyond the traditional retirement age (Feller, 2014).

We believe that an appropriate way to respond to these challenges is to create a postsecondary education–going culture in K–12 education that involves collaboration among all professional school personnel, families, and communities. If all of these entities can agree on the broad goal and then collaborate by contributing in their own important ways, the potential for children and adolescents to be better prepared for constantly changing and increasingly sophisticated 21st-century careers will be enhanced. Children and adolescents will benefit from an environment that encourages them to understand the importance of continuing education beyond high school and preparation for continued learning while engaged in K–12 education endeavors. Consequently, achieving this goal will require collaboration among a number of adults, including professional school counselors who have their own unique and significant contributions to offer.

CAREER AND COLLEGE READINESS

Creating a postsecondary education–going culture is a broad goal. Preparing children and adolescents to engage in postsecondary education successfully requires appropriate preparation and a conducive educational environment. Various entities have been engaged in attempting to achieve these goals over the past decade, and the efforts have been housed under a broad concept referred to as career and college readiness.

Considerable attention has been devoted to enhancing career and college readiness by institutions such as Achieve, Inc., ACT, Inc., the American Association of Colleges for Teacher Education, the Bill and Melinda Gates Foundation, the Center for Mental Health in Schools, the College Board, the National Governors Association, and U.S. Department of Education. Each of these entities has its own definition of readiness and emphases for achieving readiness goals. For example, the ACT (2010) College Readiness Assessment tool emphasizes acquisition of English, mathematics, reading, science, and writing competence as important pathways to readiness. A somewhat broader definition of career readiness is possession of the content knowledge and key learning skills and techniques sufficient to begin studies in a career pathway (Conley, 2010). College readiness was defined as being prepared to succeed in entry-level postsecondary general education courses by Conley (2010).

A common underlying element in these definitions is an emphasis on achievement, that is, academic competence, including acquisition of requisite knowledge, skills, and behaviors. These are very important readiness components, however, attitudes are equally important, and it is in the attitude domain that we believe professional school counselors can make their own unique contribution while continuing to support the academic achievement efforts of their professional education colleagues.

Our position then is that professional school counselors can make important contributions toward achieving the broad postsecondary education–going goal and also make a unique contribution to the career and college readiness goal. That unique contribution is to understand and enhance the career and college readiness self-efficacy of children and adolescent through specifically designed classroom guidance and individual and small group counseling interventions.

CAREER AND COLLEGE READINESS SELF-EFFICACY

Readiness

Our view of the readiness concept is based on the classic work of Super (1990) in the 20th century and the more recent contributions of Savickas (2011). Super's research led him to believe that individuals experienced stages of career development and that success associated with coping with the intraindividual and environmental demands of each stage depended upon readiness to cope with the demands. Degree of readiness indicated one's level of career maturity. That is, the more ready one was to cope with career development demands, the more career mature they were.

Savickas's (2011) career construction theory builds on the work of Super (1990). Savickas's approach is to help individuals take possession of their lives and connect insights about themselves to what they will do in the future, including work and careers. The goal is to be ready to design one's life and decide how to use work in that life.

Self-Efficacy

The self-efficacy construct is a component of Bandura's (1997) social-cognitive theory. A broader social-cognitive theory component is human agency, that is, "through cognitive self-regulation, humans can create visualized futures that act on the present; construct, evaluate, and modify alternative courses of action to secure valued outcomes; and override environmental influences" (Bandura, 2006, p. 164). The core properties of human agency are (a) intentionality (i.e., forming intentions that include plans and strategies for realizing them), (b) forethought (i.e., setting goals and anticipating likely outcomes), (c) self-reactiveness (i.e., constructing appropriate course of action), and (d) self-reflectiveness (i.e., reflecting on one's personal efficacy and soundness of thoughts and actions). According to Bandura (2001), "Efficacy beliefs are the foundation of human agency. Unless people believe they can produce desired results and forestall detrimental ones by their actions, they have little incentive to act or to persevere in the face of difficulties" (p. 10).

If the self-efficacy tenant of Bandura's (1997) social-cognitive theory is accurate, then concentrating career and college readiness strategies solely on enhancing acquisition of knowledge and skills of children and adolescents will be insufficient if their self-efficacy beliefs are deficient. Unfortunately, the importance of the self-efficacy construct is often unfamiliar to or overlooked by those who are focused on acquisition of knowledge and skills. Consequently, because self-efficacy is potentially more familiar to school counselors, they are in a position to focus on enhancing this important ingredient of the total career and college readiness concept in support of efforts by others to enhance the knowledge and skills domains.

Assessing Career and College Readiness Self-Efficacy

Previous educational service fieldwork devoted to promoting postsecondary education–going knowledge and behaviors of ninth-grade students included developing a Career and College Readiness Self-Efficacy Inventory (CCRSI; Baker & Parikh Foxx, 2012) for assessing the effects of classroom guidance interventions. An exploratory factor analysis identified four factors that accounted for 58% of the variance across a 14-item scale, and a confirmatory factor analysis supported the four-factor instrument (Baker et al., 2015). The four factors are (1) procedural and financial challenges (aka college knowledge), (2) positive personal characteristics, (3) academic competence, and (4) potential to achieve future goals.

Enhancing Career and College Readiness Self-Efficacy

We believe that the content of the CCRSI factors can be the foundation for developing classroom guidance and individual student planning interventions designed to enhance career and college readiness self-efficacy. The CCRSI items associated with each of the factors provide recommendations for goals, objectives, and presentation strategies that school counselors might employ. All of the items represent Bandura's (2006) self-reflectiveness human agency property. Examples of interventions based on the CCRSI components are presented later in this chapter.

Procedural and Financial Challenges

Interventions focusing on helping participants understand the postsecondary education application process, acquire requisite information, gain access to financial aid, learn about different ways to pay for postsecondary education, and locate accurate information about wages needed to make a good living are recommended. These recommendations also focus on Bandura's (2006) forethought human agency property.

Possessing Positive Personal Characteristics That Will Enhance Readiness

Participants will also benefit from learning how to set personal goals, developing confidence in their ability to live a good life in the future, identifying persons who believe in them, and identifying persons who can help them achieve their goals. These recommendations also respond to the intentionality, forethought, and self-reflectiveness properties of Bandura's (2006) human agency concept.

Believing That One Possesses the Academic Competencies Needed to Be Successful in the Future

Confidence in one's academic competence is highlighted in this factor. Examples are reading a textbook, taking class notes, and preparing for tests successfully. These CCRSI ingredients also reflect Bandura's (2006) intentionality human agency property.

Believing One Has the Potential to Set and Achieve Future Goals

Understanding how post–high school education can help one achieve life and career goals and belief in one's potential to succeed in postsecondary education settings are important ingredients of this factor. Bandura's (2006) intentionality, forethought, and self-reactiveness human agency properties are also associated with these challenges.

COMPLEMENTARY STRATEGIES

Other authors identified concepts and strategies that complement our career and college readiness self-efficacy ideas. We present them here as additional resources for you to consider when attempting to create or enhance a postsecondary education–going culture in their settings. They are not as fully developed as our career and college readiness self-efficacy presentation, yet they may provide useful complementary ideas for a more comprehensive approach to the challenge.

School Bonding

When students feel connected to or have strong bonds with their schools they are more likely to experience academic success (Bryant et al., 2012). School bonding is a multidimensional construct consisting of (a) attachment to the school, (b) attachment to teachers and school personnel, (c) school commitment, and (d) school involvement. All of these components affect achievement in some way. Bryant et al. (2012) recommend focusing on creating and strengthening all four aspects of school bonding, beginning as early as possible.

School counselors cannot accomplish these objectives alone. Bryant et al. (2012) recommend creating a multisystemic focus that is comprehensive and school-wide, and we support this recommendation. A multisystemic focus includes teachers, administrators, parents, and other stakeholders collectively, each contributing to the creation of a postsecondary education–going culture in the schools.

Bryant et al. (2012) recommend interventions that connect students to caring adults in and out of the schools that are focused on improving school attachment and climate. Among their more specific recommendations are attention to enhancing achievement and involvement of 9th and 10th graders and providing extra support for underserved students.

School Connectedness

This idea seems to be related to school bonding. School connectedness occurs when students believe that adults and peers in their schools care about them as individuals as much as their acquisition of knowledge (Centers for Disease Control and Prevention, 2009). Lapan, Wells, Peterson, and McCann (2014) found that school connectedness can be strengthened by increasing protective factors for students. They noted that responsive services delivered by school counselors reduced the effects of risk factors. The counseling interventions provided protection from the risk factors, and reduction of risk factors enhanced school connectedness, positively affecting success in academic and nonacademic areas.

Transition-to-Adulthood

Tat and Toporek (2014) believe that career and college readiness is a component of a broader transition-to-adulthood concept. These transitions require academic preparation and relief from emotional barriers. They also promote collaboratively working for systems-level solutions and promoting a "college-going" culture. Their more specific ideas include the importance of parental engagement and creating career and college centers in all schools.

Relatedly, Campos-Krumholz (2014) also promotes creating a career and college readiness culture with students, staff, and parents while beginning career exploration in early elementary school. There are many ways to promote the desired culture, and finding community partners is essential.

Preventing Dropouts

Negative events occurring early in a student's academic career can set the stage for dropping out. Signs are available in elementary school. White and Kelly (2010) recommend a multifaceted dropout prevention program. They believe that school counselors can play an important role in these prevention efforts.

American School Counselor Association Position

College readiness is a part of many school improvement plans, and the American School Counselor Association National Model (ASCA, 2012) prioritizes college and career readiness as a goal and career preparation as a part of the school counselor's role (Patterson, 2014). Sparks (2014) recommends checking the ASCA mindsets for student success. There are 35 mindset and behavior standards that are aligned with the Common Core State Standards with an emphasis on grade-level competencies. K–12 college and career readiness for every student is a theme. The mindsets and behavior standards can help school counselors align programming directly with ongoing academic instruction in their respective schools.

NOSCA Goals

The National Office for School Counselor Advocacy (NOSCA; College Board Advocacy & Policy Center, n.d.) offers eight components or goals for career and college readiness counseling. The NOSCA's recommendations complement those that have been presented previously and provide additional suggestions. As was stated earlier, they recommend including the entire community in the process and working systemically, as well as being equitable and using data to inform the process. The eight NOSCA goals are as follows:

Goal 1: College Aspirations

Attempt to build a college-going culture. Enhance college awareness early by nurturing confidence to aspire to engage in postsecondary education and the resilience to overcome challenges. Maintain high expectations. Provide adequate support for building social capital. Convey a belief that all students can succeed in college.

Goal 2: Academic Planning for College and Career Readiness

Aspire to promote student planning and preparation for potential participation in rigorous academic programs that are connected to related college and career aspirations and goals.

Goal 3: Enrichment and Extracurricular Engagement

Present opportunities for exposure to and engagement in a wide range of extracurricular and enrichment activities. These opportunities should be presented in a manner that is equitable across all student populations. Desired outcomes are building leadership potential, nurturing talents, and enhancing interests.

Goal 4: College and Career Exploration and Selection Processes

Provide access to information and experiences that help students make informed decisions related to postsecondary education options and their career development. Begin the process early and make it continuous and ongoing. Connect the process to students' academic preparation and future aspirations.

Goal 5: College and Career Assessments

Help all students prepare for postsecondary education and career development assessments. Focus efforts on preparation, participation, and performance.

Goal 6: College Affordability Planning

Help all students plan for affording postsecondary education options. School counselors can assist in this process by providing comprehensive information about costs, options for making payments, ways of acquiring financial aid, and eligibility requirements.

Goal 7: College and Career Admission Processes

Help all students and their families to understand the postsecondary education admissions application processes. Help them as well to match postsecondary admissions decisions with their aspirations and interests.

Goal 8: Transition From High School Graduation to College Enrollment

Help students to overcome the barriers they may encounter when transitioning from high school to postsecondary education institutions. Gaining access to helpful community resources may be important for accomplishing this goal.

Recommendations for Achieving the NOSCA Goals

The NOSCA recommends goals 1 through 6 for elementary and middle school counselors and goals 1 through 8 for high school counselors. All are considered equally important and, when used collectively, the most comprehensive way for school counselors to enhance the career and college readiness of their students.

There also seems to be a relationship between the eight NOSCA goals and the four CCRSI factors presented earlier. Goals 4, 6, 7, and 8 seem to be related to the postsecondary education–going knowledge self-efficacy factor. Goals 1 and 3 appear to be related to the possession of requisite positive personal characteristic self-efficacy factor. Goals 2, 3, and 5 mirror the academic competence self-efficacy factor. Goals 1, 4, and 7 speak to the potential to achieve future goals self-efficacy factor.

HISTORICAL PERSPECTIVE

The recent emphasis on career and college readiness in the school counseling literature and elsewhere has roots in earlier related emphases. The vocational guidance movement in the early part of the 20th century included an emphasis on vocational guidance devoted to helping youths find meaningful work by having access to dependable information about vocations. This emphasis on vocational guidance blended with components of the psychometric movement. By the mid-20th century, a popular vocational guidance approach was to use standardized test data, especially from aptitude tests, diagnostically to attempt to match individuals with the jobs on the basis of the test scores (i.e., trait and factor approach). Goldman's (1972) *marriage that failed* analogy challenged the trait and factor approach severely enough to cause a trend toward using assessment data developmentally, especially interest inventory assessments. Rather that attempting to predict future success in specific training programs and jobs, counselors attempted to help individuals acquire information about their interests and abilities and use the information to explore options in advance of making their own decisions.

Helping students make transitions from school to school and from school to work has been an important role for school counselors since the early days of the profession. An important contribution was the focus on *career education* in the early 1970s. The basic career education principle was integrating school counseling programs as well as vocational education and general instruction around a career development theme from kindergarten through 12th grade. This comprehensive emphasis on career development across all components of the basic education enterprise seems to be a forerunner of the current emphasis on enhancing career and college readiness by creating a postsecondary education–going culture in the schools. It also seems to mirror the emphasis on collaboration with numerous stakeholders such as families and communities.

An additional foundation to the current emphasis on career and college readiness is a focus on equity. As spokespersons for the Transforming School Counseling Initiative, House and Hayes (2002) highlighted the strategic role that school counselors can play in achieving equity for all students. They believed that school counselors should be inclined to promote access to academic achievement opportunities for all students and positioned to assess their schools for barriers while advocating for those students affected by the barriers. The ASCA and the American Counseling Association have supported this position, and the current focus on career and college readiness across a variety of entities in and out of the education domain seems to indicate universal agreement.

Therefore, our current attention to promoting a postsecondary education–going culture has historical roots and is aligned with very current concerns about the welfare of individual students and about the national and world economies. The big picture includes many potential contributors, and comprehensive collaboration is indeed important. Within this broad context, professional school counselors have an important role to play. In the next section, we offer some specific suggestions for engaging in individual student planning and classroom guidance activities that may be effective.

RECOMMENDATIONS FOR SCHOOL COUNSELING PRACTICE

INDIVIDUAL STUDENT PLANNING

All individual and group counseling interventions can potentially enhance the college and career readiness of recipients of those services in some way. These interventions are provided in response to specific concerns presented by students, and successful responding by school counselors can affect individual development positively in some way.

On the other hand, individual student planning tends to be proactive in nature. That is, school counselors engage in individual planning with students on the basis of predetermined assumptions about their needs and proactively determined plans for responding to those assumptions. The professional literature is replete with recommendations for engaging in individual student planning successfully, and we support efforts to learn about and use those recommendations in one's counseling practice. Our emphasis here is on using the information provided by CCRSI data and based on the content of the four CCRSI factors to engage in individual student planning proactively.

One approach is to assume that each of the four factors is important for all students and plan accordingly. Consequently, individual student planning efforts for all students will be designed to enhance students' beliefs that they (a) know how to meet procedural and financial challenges associated with postsecondary education and future careers, (b) possess the positive personal characteristics that will enhance their readiness, (c) possess the competencies required for success in the future, and (d) have the potential to set and achieve future goals.

An alternative option is to use CCRSI data to customize individual student planning on the basis of the factors that seem to need the most attention. For example, CCRSI data for one student may indicate that knowing how to meet postsecondary education financial challenges seems to be on the front of her or his mind, and the first meeting thereafter might be devoted to finding out what the student knows and needs to know and helping the student acquire the information. In another scenario, the CCRSI data might indicate that a student lacks confidence in her or his ability to succeed in a postsecondary education program. In the next session for that student, the counselor might inquire about the specifics of that concern and help the student consider the accuracy of those concerns and develop strategies for attempting to address them successfully. Note that in the first example the counselor was focusing on helping the student acquire useful information, whereas in the second example the counselor was focusing on helping the student address what might be self-defeating attitudes. Other scenarios might be more complex with more than one of the factors being addressed concurrently and possibly all factors needing to be addressed concurrently or eventually. The basic premise of our recommendation is to encourage school counselors to use the CCRSI data to design customized individual planning for their students.

We close this section with an inventory of possible strategies that school counselors might use to engage in customized individual student planning based on the CCRSI factors. The inventory is suggestive and by no means exhaustive. Note that some intervention strategies are common across factor categories and that the focus of the strategies is what varies. There are probably developmental stages below which these recommendations are not useful; however, they may be more related to individual differences than across-the-board human development stages. Classroom guidance may be more a more appropriate vehicle in these instances, and that topic is covered next.

Knowledge About Procedural and Financial Challenges

Provide students with an inventory of important information they should know. Inquire about how much they know about each category. Note the information that needs to be corrected or needs to be enhanced. Help students plan how they will acquire needed information. Help students understand and process the information they currently have and the information they acquire later. Keep as up-to-date about this information as one can be.

Possessing the Positive Personal Characteristics That Will Enhance Readiness

Provide students with a comprehensive inventory of important personal characteristics for career and college readiness. Encourage students to rate themselves on each characteristic and identify others that may have been overlooked. Help students process the findings. Help them to recognize and develop their strengths further. Recommend developing plans to address areas that need further enhancement.

Possessing Competence Needed to Be Successful in the Future

Again, provide students with a comprehensive inventory of competencies needed to be successful academically and in one's career.

Encourage students to rate themselves on each competency and identify others that may have been overlooked. Help students process the findings. Help them to recognize and develop their strengths further. Recommend developing plans to address areas that need further enhancement.

Having the Potential to Set and Achieve Future Goals

Inquire about the students' understanding of the meaning of setting goals and why they are important. Attempt to achieve mutual understanding of the goals and goal-setting concepts before inquiring about specific goals. Once mutual understanding is accomplished, help students to consider important immediate and long-range goals for themselves. Thereafter, help them rate levels of confidence in achieving the goals. Help students to determine ways to achieve the goals about which they feel confident. In addition, help students to understand the underlying reasons for goals they feel less confident about and help them to discover pathways to greater resilience.

CLASSROOM GUIDANCE

The following classroom guidance strategies are aligned with the findings from the CCRSI factors. We encourage you to think developmentally about the topics. That is, consider what could be useful and relevant knowledge at the elementary, middle, and high school levels. Some of these topics may transcend the levels and can easily be adapted for the right age group. Also keep in mind that these strategies are not exhaustive of all the topics that can align to each factor. However, we have offered a starting point to help you in developing postsecondary advising skills, and we encourage continued efforts to identify and develop your own skills.

Knowledge About Procedural and Financial Challenges

- Educate students about the Free Application for Federal Student Aid (FAFSA). Consider explaining the process, timeline, and types of funding.
- Provide example of the types of scholarships that are available for students (athletic, academic, private, etc.).

- Consider the top universities in your state. Locate the costs associated with each institution and provide examples of how students might fund their education.
- Have students practice college applications and writing college essays.
- Bring in guest speakers (current college students who are graduates of that school) and have them share how they prepared for the college admissions process.

Possessing the Positive Personal Characteristics That Will Enhance Readiness

- Work with students to explore their career aspirations.
- Create case studies in which students analyze the differences between positive and negative study habits, organizations skills, and time management. Have students explore how their decisions can have an impact on their future choices.

Possessing Competence Needed to Be Successful in the Future

- Teach students the importance of effective study habits.
- Have students develop methods of keeping organized and teach the importance of time management.
- Have students develop an academic plan that will align with their postsecondary goals. Within that plan, explain the importance of rigorous coursework and how that relates to admission to four-year institutions.
- Discuss the connection between careers and wages. Have students connect their beliefs about their future ways to their future choices. Have students calculate their grade point averages on the basis of their most current report card and help make the connection between grade point averages and postsecondary admissions.
- Explain to students the difference among advanced placement, dual enrollment, honors, and regular education course and the connection to postsecondary options.

Having the Potential to Set and Achieve Future Goals

- Have students connect their future career choices to postsecondary options.
- Have students examine their own personal qualities that are positive and useful in helping them achieve their future goals.
- Have students identify adults (parents, guardians, teachers) in their lives who are positive roles models and who believe in them.
- Work with students to set short-term goals that will help them get closer to achieving their future goals.

FINAL THOUGHT

In July 2014, First Lady Michelle Obama spoke at the Annual ASCA conference in Orlando, Florida. During her speech, she noted the important role school counselors play in the postsecondary attainment of all students. Although the national attention was good promotion for the profession, those who live this work daily know the weight of those words. School counselors have always had a responsibility in the career development of students. It has been one of the three domains identified in the ASCA National Model (ASCA, 2012). As previously noted, school counselors have historically served this role although the national goals have been different. For example, the vocational guidance movement in the early part of the 20th century focused on assisting young people to find meaningful employment and access to information about various vocations. So although the call today is different, it is the same in essence and responsibility. School counselors are tasked to be leaders and advocates for students to have the widest array of postsecondary education choices and career options. Although the task may seem tall, remember that by 2020, 65% of the jobs in the United States will require some sort of postsecondary education (Carnevale, Smith, & Strohl, 2013).

COMPREHENSIVE SCHOOL COUNSELING PROGRAM COMPONENT

1. Discuss why it is important for school counselors to think in terms of postsecondary education readiness rather that college readiness? Our position is that many students who are more likely to benefit from military service, associate degree programs and advanced technical training will view programming referred to as "college readiness" from a narrow perspective (i.e., college and university degrees) and think it is not for them.

2. Discuss the importance of enhancing students' self-efficacy both generally (multifaceted self-efficacy components) and specifically (e.g., career and college readiness self-efficacy).

3. Discuss how realistic the recommendations for customized individual planning based on the content of the four factors of the CCRSI are for professional school counselors. Are they too complicated or amenable to your view of school counselor skills, attitudes, and behaviors?

4. Discuss the importance of the idea that the career and college readiness goals will be easier to meet if a variety of stakeholders, including school counselors, collaborate to attempt to create postsecondary education–going cultures in K–12 schools.

5. Choose a grade level and create postsecondary education readiness lesson plans and align them to the standards to the ASCA Mindsets & Behaviors.

6. Establish a plan for working with parents and families and sharing information about college affordability, FAFSA, college requirements, and so forth.

REFLECTION POINT

1. Request a copy of the CCRSI from us and analyze the face validity of the items and the four factors they represent. How convincing are the supportive validity and reliability data in our manual? How useful does it appear to be as a diagnostic tool for customized individual planning with students? If it does seem

useful, what age levels seem most appropriate for using it? How useful does it appear to be as a preassessment and postassessment measure for related classroom guidance programs?

2. Think back to your decision to attend college. Who supported you with factors such as deciding to apply and attend, completing college applications, and understanding how to finance a college education?

3. What are your beliefs about the role of school counselors creating postsecondary education access for all students? Are there some populations that would be more difficult to support than others? If so, who and why?

4. What are your thoughts about the concept of self-efficacy and its relationship to postsecondary education–going readiness?

APPLICATION TO TECHNOLOGY

1. Search for National Office for School Counselor Advocacy online and check out the results (recommended readings are "Resources for School Counselors," "Eight Components of College and Career Readiness," "High School Counselor's Guide," "Middle School Counselor's Guide," and "Elementary School Counselor's Guide."

2. Go to www.schoolcounselor.org and review the ASCA "Mindsets & Behaviors" for resources that can be applied to developing career and college readiness interventions.

3. Create a PowerPoint presentation designed for students and/or parents on college affordability and financial aid.

4. Search the Internet for free resources and websites that you can use to create a postsecondary education–going culture.

REFERENCES

American College Testing, Inc. (ACT). (2010). *Mind the gaps: How college readiness narrows the gaps in college success.* Iowa City, IA: Author.

American School Counselor Association. (2012). *The ASCA National Model: A framework for school counseling programs* (3rd ed.). Alexandria, VA: Author.

Baker, S. B., & Parikh Foxx, S. (2012). *Career and college readiness self-efficacy inventory.* Unpublished scale, Counselor Education Program. Raleigh, NC: North Carolina State University.

Baker, S. B., Parikh Foxx, S., Akcan Aydin, P., Gavin Williams, R., Ashraf, A., & Martinez, R. R. (2015). *Psychometric properties of the career and college readiness self-efficacy inventory.* Unpublished manuscript. Raleigh, NC: Counselor Education Program, North Carolina State University.

Bandura, A. (1997). *Self-efficacy: The exercise of control.* New York: Freeman.

Bandura, A. (2001). Social cognitive theory: An agentic perspective. *Annual Review of Psychology, 52*(1), 1–26.

Bandura, A. (2006). Toward a psychology of human agency. *Perspectives on Psychological Science, 1*(2), 164–190.

Bryant, J., Moore-Thomas, C. Gaenzle, S., Kim, S., Lin, C-H., & Na, G. (2012). The effects of school bonding on high school seniors' academic achievement. *Journal of Counseling & Development, 90,* 467–480.

Campos-Krumholz, C. (2014). Dreams into plans. *ASCA School Counselor, 52*(2), 24–29.

Carnevale, A. P., Smith, N., & Strohl, J. (2013). *Recovery: Job growth and education requirements through 2020.* Report issued by the Center on Education and the Workforce, Georgetown Public Policy Institute. Washington, DC: Georgetown University. Retrieved from https://cew.georgetown.edu/report/recovery-job-growth-and-education requirements-through-2020/

Centers for Disease Control and Prevention. (2009). *School connectedness: Strategies for Increasing protective factors among youth.* Atlanta: U.S. Department of Health and Human Services.

College Board Advocacy and Policy Center: National Office for School Counselor Advocacy. (n.d.). *Eight components of college and career readiness counseling.* New York: Author.

Conley, D. T. (2010). *College and career ready.* San Francisco: Jossey-Bass.

Feller, R. (2014). College and career readiness for learners of all ages. *Career Developments, 30*(3), 5–9.

Goldman, L. (1972). Tests and counseling: The marriage that failed. *Measurement and Evaluation in Guidance, 4,* 213–220.

House, R. M., & Hayes, R. L. (2002). School counselors: Becoming key players in school reform. *Professional School Counseling, 5,* 249–256.

Lapan, R. T., Wells, R., Peterson, J., & McCann, L. A. (2014). Stand tall to protect students: School counselors strengthening school connectedness. *Journal of Counseling & Development, 92*(3), 304–315.

Patterson, J. (2014). Solution-focused college and career planning. *ASCA School Counselor, 52*(2), 18–22.

Savickas, M. L. (2011). *Career counseling.* Washington, DC: American Psychological Association.

Sparks, E. (2014). Change behaviors by changing mindsets. *ASCA School Counselor, 52*(2), 45–49.

Super, D. E. (1990). A life-span, life-space approach to career development. In D. Brown & L. Brooks (Eds.), *Career choice and development: Applying contemporary theories to practice* (2nd ed., pp. 197–261). San Francisco: Jossey-Bass.

Tat, A., & Toporek, R. L. (2014). Partnership and urban youth. *Counseling Today, 57*(1), 44–50.

White, S. W., & Kelly, F. D. (2010). The school counselor's role in school dropout prevention. *Journal of Counseling & Development, 88,* 227–235.

BEYOND THE TRAINING PROGRAM: A SCHOOL COUNSELING CAREER

12

Goal: To offer suggestions for enhancing the professional identity and well-being of school counselors and discuss future prospects for school counselors.

Here is a testimonial from professional school counselor and doctoral candidate Jacob Olsen:

> The more experience I get as a school counselor, the more I find myself needing to remember why I became a school counselor. While I honestly believe school counseling is one of the most exciting and impactful careers in education, my experience as a school counselor reminds me that being a school counselors is as challenging as it is rewarding. It has become cliché, but the days can be very long, and the energy you expend to support students can make your eyes heavy and your feet sore. I can think of dozens of examples of being in my office, after a full day of school, and just looking at my surroundings. I can see myself hunched over in my chair, the color of markers on my pants from some time I spent in a class that day, my coffee cup half full of cold coffee, and my e-mail and phone inboxes full of unread and unheard messages. Although tiring, those days are the best days I can remember. Those are the days I got to school early to plan an engaging classroom lesson, met with a student eating breakfast in the cafeteria to review her or his academic or behavioral goals for the day, or met a parent in the parking lot to try and get their anxious child to build up the courage to enter the school building. Those are the days that I taught multiple classroom lessons, facilitated group interventions, and met with teachers to strategize about engaging their class and getting their most challenging student to complete academic work during class time. Some of these days I felt more accomplished because I was being proactive, reaching many of the students in my school, and implementing key components of the school

counseling program. On other days, however, the plans on my calendar had to wait. Those days were spent patiently working with students who refused to stay in class, refused to leave class, tore up the hallway, refused to work, or were so angry that they yelled, punched, or kicked anything or anyone that was around. As I think about my experiences as a school counselor, I feel so many different emotions. I feel excitement, I feel honored, I feel inspired, and I feel thankful. To be able to walk into a school building and lead the work of creating a school climate where the adults and students feel safe and respected and where systems were in place to support all students' academic achievement and personal growth is a privilege.

Reflecting on my experience also reminds me of the importance of being intentional about my own well-being and professional development. Collaboration with colleagues in my school and other schools within my district was essential. I also carved out time each year to attend state-level conferences and trainings to learn effective strategies to support students. I clearly saw the benefit of these efforts because students were positively impacted. Collaborating also became a tremendous support system essential for my own well-being and growth as a school counselor. Continuing to learn and improve has been essential to my effectiveness as a school counselor and to keeping me motivated and excited to continue in the profession. A challenge for all of us in the field of school counseling is to never forget why we became school counselors. Whether we are in our first year or thirtieth year, we always have to tap into the passion, excitement, and energy that brought us to the profession. I think we can benefit by remembering two things to stay driven to do the work we do. First, we need to periodically check in with ourselves and remember why we became school counselors in the first place. This will help us to tap into the passion, excitement, and energy that brought us to the profession. Second, we have to remember that students' success and well-being should be at the forefront of every decision we make. Among all the school systems, policies, programs, and practices we are involved in, students matter the most. There is no better time to be a school counselor.

BEYOND THE TRAINING PROGRAM

Jacob's experiences clearly demonstrate the complexities of this work. The complexities are in direct relation to the diverse needs of our students. Our theme in this section of the chapter is that upon completing their training, graduates are challenged to keep motivated and current as professional school counselors. Several studies published by the American School Counselor Association (ASCA) and Association for Counselor Education and Supervision (ACES) journals in 2005 and 2006 support this theme. All of the five studies employed multiple-regression statistical analyses that provided information about how strong relationships between predictors and estimated outcomes (i.e., criteria) seem to be. Four studies had national samples, and the one with the largest sample had participants from the state of Florida. In all, the five studies sampled 2,851 school counselors. The estimated outcomes or criteria included role incongruence and ambiguity (Culbreth, Scarborough, Banks-Johnson, & Solomon, 2005), emotional exhaustion and personal accomplishment (Butler & Constantine, 2005), overall job satisfaction and stress (Rayle, 2006), career satisfaction and commitment (Baggerly & Osborn, 2006), and job and life satisfaction (Bryant & Constantine, 2006).

The important predictors of these criteria were perceiving high self-efficacy, experiencing high levels of personal accomplishment, mattering to others, being positively perceived by others, having appropriate job duties, possessing the ability to manage multiple life roles in their lives effectively, experiencing low levels of emotional exhaustion, and receiving district and peer supervision. Negative predictors were role conflict and stress. The research teams conducted their investigations independently, so the terminology used is peculiar to the measures they employed. It appears as if the best summary of the overall findings is that school counselors are more likely to feel good about themselves and their work if their job duties conform with their training, they are regarded highly for their professional competence, they can manage all of their professional and personal responsibilities effectively, they are able to keep current professionally, and they believe they can be competent and effective professionally.

Thus, we now turn to recommendations for achieving these outcomes. They are presented as ideas about keeping motivated and keeping current.

KEEPING MOTIVATED

Burnout is a widely used label for a broad range of symptoms leading to losing the interest or competence to perform one's job effectively. It is something to be avoided. No one wishes to be burned out. Yet many professionals receive the label. Without getting overly diagnostic, several challenges cause school counselors to experience burnout. One may be the stress associated with trying to be all things to all people while having too little control over their professional identity. Principals who treat counselors like administrative assistants, teachers who are unhappy with class enrollments, parents who blame counselors because their children fail to get accepted to a preferred college, students who cannot be successfully helped, student-to-counselor ratios that are too large to manage, and insufficient secretarial and clerical support are but a few additional examples. Low status in the professional hierarchy, insufficient budgetary support and resources, low pay, professional isolation, loss of competence and confidence, and personal problems are also examples of stressors school counselors face that may take their toll and lead to burnout. Using the Counselor Occupational Stress Inventory, Moracco, Butcke, and McEwen (1984) documented the causes of stress among a sample of 361 ASCA members. Their analysis led to an observation that occupational stress seems to be a multidimensional concept. The dimensions they identify in their factor analysis are lack of decision-making authority, financial stress (small rewards), nonprofessional duties, job overload, and dissatisfying professional relationships with teachers and principals. Behannon (1996) assembled comments from several counseling professionals that, in summary, pointed out that the nature of their work makes school counselors at high risk of burning out.

The purpose of this discourse is not to lament these problems, for school counselors are not the only individuals who experience such stressors and suffer from burnout. Rather, they are presented as challenges. Individually and collectively, school counselors are challenged to accept stressors as a fact of life and do everything within their power to prevent themselves from burning out, treating the symptoms quickly and appropriately when they occur. As can be determined from the sampling of causes listed earlier, school counselors have many stressors with which to cope. Some can be managed individually or in cooperation with colleagues, and support from larger bodies, such as professional organizations and legislatures, and from enlightened individuals with sufficient influence to cause change is also needed. What can individual counselors do to prevent burnout? Our belief is that keeping motivated and current are strategies within the control of each counselor that have promise for self-enhancement and burnout prevention.

The theme of this presentation on keeping motivated is "Be proactive." We are challenged to take the responsibility for motivating ourselves. Many strategies for implementing this idea exist. Following is a presentation of goals, not to be considered a listing of strategies. Strategies are varied and numerous and do not work universally. You can more easily respond to suggested goals, determining whether they are personally appropriate and deciding on your own strategies for implementing them. In a book aptly entitled *A Survival Guide for the Secondary School Counselor,* Hitchner and Tifft-Hitchner (1987) suggest establishing consulting alliances with colleagues to find sanity in numbers and leaving the emotions associated with problems at work so that they do not interfere with one's home life. Both are commendable goals that may be accomplished differently by individual counselors.

Cognitive Health

One arena over which individuals have potential control is their own thoughts. Self-acceptance is an important goal. Self-acceptance is founded on the belief that one is doing her or his best and making decisions in good faith. A belief in having acted in good faith allows individuals to accept constructive criticism as challenging rather than as damning. Recognizing irrational and self-defeating thoughts may prevent corresponding irrational ideation and self-defeating behaviors. The same tactics that counselors use to recognize and treat irrational ideation experienced by student clients can be applied to themselves. The investigations by Butler and Constantine (2005) and Rayle (2006) point out the perceived importance of self-esteem and mattering to others in the workplace respectively.

Dollarhide and Saginak (2003) highlight the importance of achieving personal mental health through balancing external reality and internal needs. They also stress the importance of finding one's spiritual or moral center, that is, awareness of our own morals and values, and by extension, those of our student clients. They challenge school counselors to understand when they have done their best, realizing that student clients are empowered to choose their own responses to efforts to help them, and to be able to let them make their decisions while taking responsibility for the consequences.

Physical Health

A second arena over which individuals have potential control is their physical health. Some symptoms of stress can be treated and prevented physically. Relaxed individuals with healthful diets are less likely to experience burnout. The health sciences offer numerous suggestions for achieving and maintaining good physical health. Physical health will make individuals better able to cope with stress while also causing them to think about themselves more positively. Some symptoms of stress can be treated successfully by such physical responses as deep diaphragmatic breathing and progressive muscle relaxation. These treatments may be even more effective if used in conjunction with cognitive strategies for coping with irrational and self-defeating ideation (Cormier, Nurius, & Osborn, 2013).

Social Health

A third arena over which control can be achieved is interactions with others. The environment includes other people. Achieving appropriate assertiveness is an important goal for coping with others. Individuals are challenged to achieve direct or open, honest, and appropriate expressions of their affectionate or oppositional feelings, preferences, needs, and opinions (Fitch, Newby, Ballestero, & Marshall, 2001; Galassi & Galassi, 1977). Appropriate assertiveness means that one is able to give and receive compliments; make requests; express liking, love, and affection; initiate and maintain conversations; express one's legitimate rights; refuse requests; and express justified annoyance, displeasure, and anger. Performing all these behaviors successfully will improve the working environment of school counselors. A pleasant, sufficiently spacious, private, and appropriately heated and ventilated physical environment can also work wonders. Counselors can achieve some of these goals on their own, whereas other goals may require assertive action.

Rayle's (2006) investigation points out the importance that school counselors hold for believing that what they do professionally matters to others. Counselors who understand the goals and expectations of other individuals in their environment are better able to develop ways to cope with them successfully. For example, teachers may expect counselors, as coprofessionals, to take their side in disputes with students, rather than approach disputes as student advocates; principals, who have broad definitions of their own jobs, may define counselors' jobs similarly; and parents may view counselors as individuals who will readily share information with them about their children regardless of whether the information is confidential. Some combination of creative thinking, appropriate assertiveness, and diplomacy is required to cope with these and other misperceived expectations and to keep from being worn down by them. Having confidence in one's ability to be a successful professional school counselor is related to career satisfaction (Baggerly & Osborn, 2006). These feelings of self-efficacy are important ingredients in the process of achieving healthy interactions with others and demonstrate the relationship between good cognitive health and healthy interactions with stakeholders.

Reasonable Workload

Student-to-counselor ratios are determined predominantly by the financial condition of the school district and secondarily by the perceived worth of the guidance program (Shaw, 1973). Universal ratios are very difficult to dictate because of individual differences associated with the severity of student problems, amount of available secretarial and clerical assistance, curriculum options, and referral support. In a time of a generally perceived need for good counseling, when the United States was threatened by Soviet technological advances, Conant (1959) recommended 250 to 300 students to each counselor. This was probably a compromise between providing high-quality counseling services and what was economically feasible for school districts. As reported by Peters (1978), the Education Task Force of the 1971 White House Conference on Youth recommended a ratio of 50 to 1 throughout elementary and secondary schools. Peters himself recommended 200 to 1, again as a compromise.

In *A Nation at Risk: The Imperative for Educational Reform,* reported by the National Commission on Excellence in Education in 1983, no mention was made of school counseling (Hitchner & Tifft-Hitchner, 1987). That report and others like it emphasize the importance of improving the knowledge and work habits of Americans to cope with the economic challenges from political allies in the Far East and Western Europe. Consequently, attention was devoted to the cognitive domain. The theme is to produce better educated and disciplined citizens. Although the report was useful, with important goals, it fell short because it did not recognize the affective needs of students, too.

These affective needs are likely to grow. Figures from the 1980 census led to projections that one third of the population in the United States would be either African American or Hispanic by 2020. Historically, children of poverty have come primarily from minority groups. Women are increasingly entering the labor force, and 50% of the labor force in 1985 was women. The number of single-parent homes and latchkey children increased dramatically, and drop-out rates, already significant in some areas of the country, became even more problematic. Poverty, minority status, having a working mother, and coming from a single-parent family are highly correlated with school failure (William T. Grant Foundation Commission on Work, Family and Citizenship, 1988). School failure leads to dropping out or to floundering within the system. The Grant Commission viewed these individuals, "the forgotten half," as being in danger of not finding places for themselves in the economic system.

All the preceding findings lead one to conclude that an emphasis placed solely on improving the environment for cognitive development is insufficient for the United States to meet the economic challenges of the 21st century. This was highlighted in earlier chapters by referring to the work of Adelman and Taylor (2002). Counseling programs with better proactive and responsive counseling responses, in conjunction with improved instruction, are crucial, and they go hand in hand (Dahir, 2001; Gysbers & Henderson, 2001). Better counseling programs are linked to lower student-to-counselor ratios, especially where the most vulnerable students are attending the schools. Exactly what the ratios should be is a moot question. They must be decreased for counselors to be more effective and to perceive themselves as such. The challenge probably has to be met collectively through efforts of national professional organizations. As we go to press, the current American Counseling Association (ACA) and ASCA recommendation is 250 to 1.

Enhanced Competence

Becoming a licensed professional counselor (LPC) is an opportunity available to counselors in all states. Being an LPC is not a requisite for certification/licensure as a school counselor. Therefore, many counselors have this option as a way of keeping current and motivated. Although LPC requirements may vary from state to state, becoming an LPC usually requires having one's credentials reviewed, passing an examination (e.g., the National Counseling Examination), and providing evidence of postgraduate course work and/or clinical supervision. These are activities that help one become and remain current. They may also lead to a sense of personal accomplishment, add to one's perceived professional stature, and provide an opportunity for economic enhancement (e.g., private counseling practice or consultation services).

In a survey of 267 members of the ASCA who were school counselors, Page, Pietrzak, and Sutton (2001) found that 29% were receiving peer clinical supervision, and 57% wanted to receive it. Those expressing a preference for peer clinical supervision expressed a desire that it be provided by school counselors who were trained to provide supervision. Data from the investigations by Baggely and Osborn (2006) and Culbreth et al. (2005) also express the perceived importance of supervision to school counselors.

Sutton and Page (1994) and Agnew, Vaught, Getz, and Fortune (2000) reported on the advantages of peer supervision activities as a way to keep motivated. Working school counselors form peer supervision groups similar in nature to those they experienced in counseling and internship practicums while graduate students. Agnew et al. (2000) found that counselors who participated in a peer group clinical supervision program experienced improved professional relationships, believed they had increased the opportunities to learn counseling skills and techniques, and experienced an increased sense of professionalism. The report also stressed the importance of administrative support, training in clinical supervision, adequate funding, and adequate time in making the activity successful.

In the 21st century, it appears as if most professional school counselors feel comfortable using computer technology such as electronic mail and the Internet (Carlson, Portman, & Bartlett, 2006). Yet most have probably only scratched the surface of enhancing their competence in this and in the labyrinth of challenges associated with social media. Continued exposure and experience will increase usage and the prospects for using various forms of useful software.

KEEPING CURRENT

At mid-20th century, one axiom stated in counselor training programs was that there will be future jobs that do not exist today. That turned out to be true, accurately depicting the rapid changes in the second half of the 20th century and indicating a continuation of the same circumstances into the 21st century. Rapidly changing times feature increasing educational and technological developments. Consequently, matriculating from the most up-to-date and comprehensive counselor training program may still leave a graduate's preparation dated within a decade unless an effort is made to keep current with new developments—an effort to seek self-renewal. Walz and Benjamin (1978) suggested that self-renewal be viewed from two perspectives. The first perspective defines self-renewal as updating and streamlining previously acquired skills and knowledge to ensure that one knows what has been learned and adds new ideas to old approaches. From the second perspective, counselors can use self-renewal to acquire techniques, ideas, and skills they never had before, making them even more versatile. Thus, whether keeping current involves refurbishing the old model or developing a new hybrid, the need for self-renewal is a real and constant issue confronting school counselors.

As so eloquently stated by the reflection from Jacob at the beginning of this chapter, counselors are challenged to keep current and to achieve continuous self-renewal. This can be done in many ways, some creative and some traditional. Among the traditional ways to keep current are attending workshops; enrolling in university and college courses via on-site or distance learning; reading professional journals, books, and reports; listening to audio and observing visual media; attending professional conferences and conventions; participating in webinars and similar online options; and teaching, that is, sharing one's knowledge and skills with others. Creative responses are determined by the ideas each counselor generates individually. For instance, those who have access to the information highway provided by the Internet found exploring it an opportunity to gain useful information and mastering the Internet an interesting challenge (e.g., "Google it").

When self-renewal activities require time away from work or travel and tuition expenses, school counselors are encouraged to demonstrate to their administrators that what they are doing meets the school's goals and objectives (Hatch, 2001). In this way, the efforts are more likely to receive moral and perhaps financial support.

The National Board for Certified Counselors (NBCC) provides an opportunity for counselors to keep current while engaging in a certification process. The NBCC certifies counselors who pass NBCC examinations, referring to them as National Certified Counselors. Among the certificates is that for National Certified School Counselor. Preparation for the examinations and involvement in NBCC-approved workshops and continuing education programs are examples of ways to keep current that have been sponsored by professional counseling associations such as the ACA and ASCA. They are designed to meet the needs of practicing counselors.

Membership in professional associations such as the ACA and ASCA and their regional and state affiliates provides a number of avenues for keeping current. Those opportunities include published newsletters and professional journals, electronic news-letters, comprehensive Internet websites, webinars, and professional conferences/conventions. A visit to one or more of these websites can be quite illuminating to individuals motivated to self-renewal through keeping current.

Of all the challenges to the professional identity of school counselors, keeping current may be the one most within the power of individual counselors to achieve. No less important than the others, it is a goal that can be achieved at any time. Perhaps it should be the first goal set by graduates of counselor training programs. The trainers, having done their best to make students up-to-date when they complete training, pass to their students the responsibility for keeping the torch of knowledge lit. Students, in turn, by keeping the flame burning, make themselves valuable to their stakeholders throughout their years of service.

BEYOND THE PRESENT: WHAT DOES THE FUTURE HOLD FOR SCHOOL COUNSELORS?

Clearly, the profession has changed considerably since the beginnings of the 20th century. School counselors have continued to advocate for their professional identity and roles in schools. Although there is still some debate, First Lady Michelle Obama's Reach Higher Initiative has served as yet another impetus for profession. What is evident is that the focus still remains on the use of data, advocacy, leadership, collaboration, and a commitment to serving all students to ensure they have access to a wide range of postsecondary choices. Although we have a current model to help guide our practice, you may find yourselves in a position where your colleagues may have been trained under a different model. The following will help you understand some of the disconnects.

Unfortunately a point/counterpoint presentation in the June 2006 issue of *Counseling Today* depicted the role-seeking process for school counselors in an either-or light. Anderson and Perryman (2006) were presented as spokespersons for mental health expert role:

> The school counselor is quite possibly the only mental health professional in the school and perhaps the community uniquely equipped to recognize and refer students for specialized needs. . . . This ultimately enhances the academic success rates because problems are treated.
>
> (p. 14)

Presenting the other perspective, Tejada (2006) stated, "The first word in our job title is 'school.' Often, the best way for school counselors to help children succeed academically and socially is to address the academic and social needs of large groups of children" (p. 14).

One of the characteristics of this form of print debate is that the proponents of each point of view are not interacting face to face. And we are uncertain about whether they read each other's point of view before stating their own. One consequence of this form of debate is that the differing proponents are unable to locate and negotiate points of agreement and separate them from their major differences. Thus, a careful reading of the presentations may lead one to conclude that the supposed differences are a mirage because of differing terminology or focusing on small, albeit disparate, parts of the big picture.

Our belief is that both points of view presented in that debate are valid, yet limited, and represent components within a larger comprehensive balanced school counseling program such as that described and promoted in the present textbook. Evidence of stakeholder regard is presented in studies reported by Amatea and Clark (2005) and by Zalaquett (2005). The former study was qualitative in nature with a small sample ($N = 26$ school administrators) yet yielding *richer data*. Amatea and Clark reported that four distinctive role emphases for school counselors were preferred: (1) innovative school leader, (2) collaborative case consultant, (3) responsive direct service provider, and (4) administrative team player. Three of the role emphases fit within the roles promoted in this textbook and the ASCA (2012) National Model. The administrative team player data provides evidence that there is still work to achieve with stakeholders.

The participants in Zalaquett's (2005) survey study were 500 principals in Florida. These stakeholders had high regard for their school counselors and expressed confidence in their positive impact on student academic, behavioral, and mental health development. Zalaquett noted that expressions of confidence in academic, behavioral, and mental health domains were a confirmation of the ASCA National Model.

In the remainder of this chapter, we will offer our evidence of what we perceive are the initiatives that have the best potential for responding school counselor role confusion and enhancing the profession's development. They are (a) meeting the need for leadership, (b) meeting the need for collaboration, (c) achieving licensure portability, and (d) promoting the utility of the ASCA National Model for School Counseling Programs.

MEETING THE NEED FOR LEADERSHIP

In Chapter 6, we explored the role of leadership in school counseling and cited what seem to be important competencies school counselors should develop and acquire as leaders. This challenge for leadership seems pervasive, that is, it is needed at all levels of the profession—from the schoolhouse to the national level. The school counseling profession appears to be redefining its identity in the early years of the 21st century (Kaffenberger, Murphy, & Bemak, 2006). Challenges causing this redefinition process include school reform emphases on closing the achievement gap and financial challenges leading to budget cuts in some school systems. We agree with the conclusion stated by Kaffenberger et al. (2006) that "It is essential that the leaders of the school counseling field shape the discussion which involves a number of critical issues that will define the future direction of school counseling" (p. 288).

In our opinion, although the challenges may change with time, a leadership structure for meeting the challenges is needed. Such a structure needs grassroots support and coordination at various levels such as local school districts, county and state professional organizations, and regional and state organizations. Currently, existing professional organizations such as the ASCA, the ACA, and ACES and their local, state, and regional affiliates seem to be the best vehicles for accomplishing this goal. If a structure is in place and ongoing, challenges requiring professional leadership can be better addressed as they occur.

Kaffenberger et al. (2006) described an apparently successful example of achieving leadership structure in the northern Virginia area. The collaboration included professional school counselors and counselor educators and was influenced by national professional organizations. The accomplishments of the northern Virginia School Counseling Leadership Team (SCLT) were quite impressive (e.g., reinstatement of a permanent school counseling position in the Virginia State Department of Education, revision of the Virginia school counselor standards, and a series of workshops and summit meetings for school counselors and guidance directors). Kaffenberger et al. (2006) provide information about how the SCLT was formed that should be instructive to others seeking ideas for achieving leadership structure. Highlights of the recommendations for forming collaborative leadership teams are (a) including a comprehensive range of stakeholders among the team members; (b) identifying leaders of the team who can manage logistical details, lead meetings, mediate individual differences, balance the interests of all participants, and serve as spokespersons for the team; (c) identifying short-term and long-term goals; (d) spreading the influence of the team via a variety of training formats; and (e) achieving accountability through regular and consistent evaluations.

Accepting the importance of a leadership role at all levels of the school counseling profession and working to achieve leadership structure is one of our recommendations for you. This goal can be achieved both individually through your behaviors as a professional school counselor and collectively in cooperation with other school counselors and by supporting professional associations that work to advance the school counseling profession and serve students better.

MEETING THE NEED FOR COLLABORATION

Also a component of Chapter 6, collaboration is closely associated with leadership. Therefore, the content of this section is presented and interactive with that of the previous section on leadership. The same circumstances that demand leadership currently and in the future will promote the need for collaboration from the grass roots to the national levels of the school counseling profession. Recognition of the value of collaboration is especially important in the personal/social development domain of students directly. As was pointed out earlier in the text, many students are unable to take advantage of opportunities for achieving academic success, if opportunities are available, because of mitigating circumstances that interfere with their being successful in school (e.g., poverty, mental health challenges, substance abuse, broken homes, and truancy). The school-community collaboration (SCC) model was introduced as a vehicle for attempting to address this challenge. An underlying principle is that academic achievement/development cannot be achieved for some students until personal/social obstacles in their lives are addressed successfully and that most school systems do not have the sufficient resources to achieve this goal from within the system. The SCC model stresses the importance of forming collaborations between schools and their communities in order to better address these challenges. The SCC literature suggests a number of ways that the collaboration model can be implemented and what the outcomes have been where such collaborations have occurred (Adelman & Taylor, 2002).

We believe that collaboration thrust, particularly between schools and community support services, is an important goal for the future enhancement of the school counseling profession and those whom we serve. A very basic part of the challenge is to convince local administrators that the concept is viable, that school counselors can be leaders and players in the collaboration process, and that turf issues that may occur between school and community personnel will need to be resolved (Brown, Dahlbeck, & Sparkman-Barnes, 2006). The various parties who need to cooperate in order to achieve collaboration goals may be more likely to engage in a mutually cooperative manner if they concurrently accept the principle of focusing on the development of the whole child in order to deal with the complicated process students who have in-school and out-of-school lives (Walsh & Galassi, 2002).

Working to build a foundation for collaboration in one's local school system that will make it acceptable to stakeholders is one way that beginning school counselors can work to achieve this goal. Obviously, there is much to do beyond this first step, and successful collaborative relationships will probably result from a series of steps taken by those who are trying to achieve this goal. And success may require going back to the drawing board and retracing one's steps at times. Although the need for collaboration may be national in nature, in our opinion the foundation for achieving this goal successfully is located in each local school district where collaborations unique to those schools and communities will have to be forged.

ACHIEVING LICENSURE PORTABILITY

Professional school counselors (PSCs) and LPCs usually have met the licensure/certification requirements for a specific state upon finishing their training programs, passing requisite examinations and submitting various documents attesting to their legitimacy of their preparation. Unfortunately, there are no reciprocity agreements among the states. Therefore, PSCs and LPCs are often limited in their ability to move beyond the state of original licensure without engaging in a time-consuming, frustrating, and expensive process of being licensed in another state. At first glance, this seems to be a problem associated with the counselors who need or want to move elsewhere and prospective employers in some locales who are facing professional personnel shortages. Events associated with the massive destruction caused by Hurricane Katrina in 2005 pointed out that another class of victims of the delays caused by lack of the portability of counselor credentials is those prospective clients who are in great need of help immediately. Yet that help cannot be made readily available until the credentials of individuals who may be willing to travel across state lines to respond to an emergency have been approved.

We are believers in a national registry for PSCs and LPCs that would be the ultimate portability plan. And there are national standards in place that could be adopted by all states if the parties involved were willing to do so. Unfortunately, this is a domain rife with concerns about turf issues and influenced by local and state politics. So the national registry is currently a goal unlikely to be achieved very soon.

THE UTILITY OF THE ASCA NATIONAL MODEL

The ASCA National Model (ASCA, 2012) was introduced early in this text and has been mentioned in relation to a variety of topics throughout the succeeding chapters. Because the ASCA National Model is so well developed, comprehensively presented, and thoroughly supported in the school counseling profession and beyond, we believe that it is currently the best idea for enhancing the school counseling profession. Important reasons for our support are as follows:

- It attempts to define the role of school counselors;
- There is a comprehensive emphasis on meeting the developmental needs of students across academic, career, and personal/social domains;
- The standards-based focus emphasizes the importance of school counselors being accountable for setting and achieving goals and objectives and having a positive influence on students;
- The Model has a historical connection to the existing knowledge base in counseling and education and was developed in cooperation with individuals who have been important contributors to the profession's development for decades;
- Although there seems to be a greater emphasis on proactive prevention and large group guidance–related curricular programming than on responsive services and individual and small group counseling in the Model, it still has the elements of a balanced program within the framework;
- Important concepts such as leadership, advocacy, and collaboration are emphasized;
- There is an emphasis on working within school systems for constructive change;
- There is advocacy of a system for managing and delivering services within school counseling programs;
- There is some empirical evidence that school counselors across the United States support the model (Foster, Young, & Hermann, 2005);
- The ASCA has a system in place for promoting and recognizing implementation of the Model (Sparks, Johnson, & Lewis, 2005);

- The ASCA is establishing a National School Counseling Research Center (Sabella, 2006);
- The model provides school counselors a measure of accountability for their position in schools.

Although lauding the potential influence the ASCA National Model may have on enhancing the school counseling profession, we also believe that it is probably an imperfect paradigm. You are encouraged to view the Model as analogous to a theory. In this analogy, the ASCA National Model seems to be a presentation of principles that appear to be plausible to the presenters (e.g., preventive in design, developmental in nature, and an integral part of the total educational program). The principles are based on both scientific knowledge and informed ideals or plausible hypotheses. For example, although the ASCA National Standards Students that are part of the National Model appear to be plausible, they have not been supported empirically to any great extent as far as we know. And, as Galassi and Akos (2004) pointed out, the ASCA National Standards

> Do not explicitly draw on current developmental theory and research. As such, these standards propose outcomes for academic, personal/social, and career development, but they do not address development by level; rather, they only articulate content areas that should be addressed.
>
> (p. 148)

As well, Keys, Bemak, and Lockhart (1998), point out that the Model's "primary prevention focus may be too broad, causing programs to be less sensitive to the differences in needs presented by at-risk youth" (p. 382). They believe that many primary prevention programs (i.e., the National Model focus) do not meet the needs of at-risk students sufficiently. Keys et al. (1998) promote an additional focus on secondary and tertiary prevention programs that does not seem to be a part of the current ASCA National Model. They believe that these secondary and tertiary prevention programs should emphasize responsive services that have greater depth than the Model recommends, recognize that individual change is a function of school-based strategies *and* changes in the environments of at-risk youths, realize that individual school systems cannot themselves provide the broad range of services at-risk students need, and recognize that needs assessments should focus on what is the situation in the schools rather than what should be the needs. It appears as if the expectations offered by Keys et al. suggest that the National Model may need to be expanded in order to incorporate ideas from or similar to the SCC model.

If you accept our theory analogy, what should you do next? We believe that theories are to be tested rather than accepted as presented without debate. Therefore, you are encouraged to familiarize yourselves thoroughly with the ASCA National Model and all of activities being generated in conjunction with it. Some school counselors will have to become participants in the implementation process because their school districts have adopted it. Others will be able to decide whether to promote the National Model in their school systems, wait and watch what develops, or reject it.

On the basis of the ASCA's professed interest in evaluation leading to accountability, those who participate in the process of implementing the National Model will have opportunities to test it in real-world settings. We believe that testing the National Model is a good idea. And if some of the principles appear to be invalid, a purpose of the evaluation/accountability process is to use the evaluation data to reconsider and revise ideas, goals, and practices if necessary.

The ASCA National Model has the support of some individuals whose promotion of the paradigm may appear similar to selling a product. These behaviors are probably necessary in order to get the attention of grassroots school counseling professionals and provide opportunities for the Model to be adopted and tested. We believe that widespread adoption and testing of the Model is the best thing that can happen. And we believe that the findings from cumulative attempts to test the Model will lead to further attempts to improve it. As the process of testing, analyzing, and improving the Model grows, we believe the outcomes will be the most productive efforts to enhance the school counseling profession and corresponding services to students that will occur in the foreseeable future.

FINAL THOUGHT

Clearly, the school counseling profession has continued to evolve to meet the ever-changing needs of a diverse and global society. From changes in the educational landscape to advances in technology, the profession must continue to develop appropriate and relevant responses. We believe this book has provided a thorough outline of the important competencies and skills required to successfully carry out this important work. Although we do not foresee that the work will get any easier, we do believe that through important skills of leadership, advocacy, collaboration, and use of data will ensure that all students receive every opportunity to earn a high-quality education that will prepare them for the widest range of postsecondary choices. Above all, we must be flexible, seek out opportunities for professional development, and continue to value the decision to enter into this profession.

COMPREHENSIVE SCHOOL COUNSELING PROGRAM COMPONENT

1.   Create a brochure that you can share with stakeholders about your role and responsibilities as a professional school counselor.

REFLECTION POINT

In this chapter, we discuss a career in school counseling. As counselor educators, we have many opportunities to listen to our students' ideas about a career in school counseling. Students who are enrolled in internships often have the idealism they held early in their graduate study challenged by the realities of everyday life in schools. One school counseling intern recently wrote:

> I want to do so much when I work with students at my internship site; however, I don't seem to have the time to do what I want to do. I guess I hoped to change the world when I started my counselor education program. Now, I'm not so sure about how much I'll be able to accomplish. My supervisor, a terrific counselor, encourages me to be optimistic—and I really am trying. BUT, the question I face every afternoon when I leave my internship school is: How am I going to have a positive influence on students' lives?

How are you going to have a positive influence on students' lives through a career in school counseling? Tell us what you think.

1.   Examine your views about school counseling when you decided to enter into this profession. How does that view compare and contrast to what you have learned thus far?

2.   Reflect upon the importance of advocating for your role. How might you accomplish this when you interview for your first school counseling position?

APPLICATION TO TECHNOLOGY

1.   If you have been building the components of your professional website, go live and continue to add content as you move through your preparation program.

2.   Create a business card that includes a link to your professional website. Be sure to share this business card when you interview for potential jobs or are searching for an internship site.

REFERENCES

Adelman, H. S., & Taylor, L. (2002). School counselors and school reform: New directions. *Professional School Counseling, 5,* 235–248.

Agnew, T., Vaught, C. C., Getz, H. G., & Fortune, J. (2000). Peer group clinical supervision program fosters confidence and professionalism. *Professional School Counseling, 4*(1), 6–12.

Amatea, E. S., & Clark, M. A. (2005). Changing schools, changing counselors: A qualitative study of school administrators' conceptions of the school counselor role. *Professional School Counseling, 9,* 16–27.

American School Counselor Association. (2012). *The ASCA National Model: A framework for school counseling programs* (3rd ed.). Alexandria, VA: Author.

Anderson, L., & Perryman, K. (2006). School counselors are uniquely qualified as mental health experts. *Counseling Today, 42*(8), 14.

Baggerly, J, & Osborn, D. (2006). School counselors' career satisfaction and commitment: Correlates and predictors. *Professional School Counseling, 9,* 197–205.

Behannon, M. (1996). Overworked and under stress. *Counseling Today, 39*(2), 17.

Brown, C., Dahlbeck, D. T., & Sparkman-Barnes, L. (2006). Collaborative relationships: School counselors and non-school mental health professionals working together to improve the mental health needs of students. *Professional School Counseling, 9,* 332–335.

Bryant, R. M., & Constantine, M. G. (2006). Multiple role balance, job satisfaction, and life satisfaction in women school counselors. *Professional School Counseling, 9,* 265–271.

Butler, S. K., & Constantine, M. G. (2005). Collective self-esteem and burnout in professional school counselors. *Professional School Counseling, 9,* 55–62.

Carlson, L. A., Portman, T.A.A., & Bartlett, J. R. (2006). Professional school counselors' approaches to technology. *Professional School Counseling, 9,* 252–256.

Conant, J. B. (1959). *The American high school today.* New York: McGraw-Hill.

Cormier, S., Nurius, P. S., & Osborn, C. (2013). *Interviewing strategies for helpers: Fundamental skills and cognitive behavioral interventions* (7th ed.). Pacific Grove, CA: Brooks/Cole.

Culbreth, J. R., Scarborough, J. L., Banks-Johnson, A., & Solomon, S. (2005). Role stress among practicing school counselors. *Counselor Education and Supervision, 45,* 58–71.

Dahir, C. (2001). The national standards for school counseling programs: Development and implementation. *Professional School Counseling, 4,* 320–327.

Dollarhide, C. T., & Saginak, K. A. (2003). *School counseling in the secondary school: A comprehensive process and program.* Boston: Allyn & Bacon.

Fitch, T., Newby, E., Ballestero, V., & Marshall, J. L. (2001). Future school administrators' perceptions of the school counselors' role. *Counselor Education and Supervision, 41,* 89–99.

Foster, L. H., Young, J. S., & Hermann, M. (2005). The work activities of professional school counselors: Are the national standards being addressed? *Professional School Counseling, 8,* 313–321.

Galassi, J. P., & Akos, P. (2004). Developmental advocacy: Twenty-first century school counseling. *Journal of Counseling and Development, 82,* 146–157.

Galassi, M. D., & Galassi, J. P. (1977). *Assert yourself! How to be your own person.* New York: Human Sciences Press.

Gysbers, N. C., & Henderson, P. (2001). Comprehensive guidance and counseling programs: A rich history and a bright future. *Personnel and Guidance Journal, 53,* 647–652.

Hatch, T. (2001). The power of professional development. *ASCA School Counselor, 39*(1), 8–12.

Hitchner, K. W., & Tifft-Hitchner, A. (1987). *A survival guide for the secondary school counselor.* West Nyack, NY: Center for Applied Research in Education.

Kaffenberger, C. J., Murphy, S., & Bemak, F. (2006). School Counseling Leadership Team: A statewide collaborative model to transform school counseling. *Professional School Counseling, 9,* 288–294.

Keys, S. G., Bemak, F., & Lockhart, E. J. (1998). Transforming school counseling to serve the mental health needs of at-risk youth. *Journal of Counseling and Development, 76,* 381–388.

Moracco, J. C., Butcke, P. G., & McEwen, M. K. (1984). Measuring stress in school counselors: Some research findings and implications. *School Counselor, 32,* 110–118.

Page, B. J., Pietrzak, D. R., & Sutton, J. W., Jr. (2001). National survey of school counselor supervision. *Counselor Education and Supervision, 41,* 142–150.

Peters, D. (1978). The practice of counseling in the secondary school. In *The status of guidance and counseling in the nation's schools: A series of issue papers* (pp. 81–100). Washington, DC: American Personnel and Guidance Association.

Rayle, A. D. (2006). Do school counselors matter? Mattering as a moderator between job stress and job satisfaction. *Professional School Counseling, 9,* 223–230.

Sabella, R. A. (2006). The ASCA National Counseling Research Center: A brief history and agenda. *Professional School Counseling, 9,* 412–415.

Shaw, M. C. (1973). *School guidance systems: Objectives, functions, evaluation, and change.* Boston: Houghton Mifflin.

Sparks, E., Johnson, J., & Lewis, R. (2005). Re-forming the role of school counselor. *ASCA School Counselor, 42*(5), 10–15.

Sutton, J. M., Jr., & Page, B. J. (1994). Post-degree clinical supervision of counselors. *School Counselor, 42,* 32–39.

Tejada, L. (2006). The first word in our job description is 'school.' *Counseling Today, 48*(8), 14–15.

Walsh, M. E., & Galassi, J. P. (2002). An introduction: Counseling psychologists and schools. *The Counseling Psychologist, 30*(5), 675–681.

Walz, G. R., & Benjamin, L. (1978). Professional development and competency. In *The status of guidance and counseling in the nation's schools: A series of issue papers* (pp. 127–136). Washington, DC: American Personnel and Guidance Association.

William T. Grant Foundation Commission on Work, Family and Citizenship. (1988). *The forgotten half: Non-college youth in America: An interim report on the school-to-work transition.* Washington, DC: Author.

Zalaquett, C. P. (2005). Principals' perceptions of elementary school counselors' role and functions. *Professional School Counseling, 8,* 451–457.

Appendix A

CACREP STANDARDS FOR SCHOOL COUNSELING PROGRAMS

SECTION 5: ENTRY-LEVEL SPECIALTY AREAS—SCHOOL COUNSELING

G. SCHOOL COUNSELING

Students who are preparing to specialize as school counselors will demonstrate the professional knowledge and skills necessary to promote the academic, career, and personal/social development of all P-12 students through data-informed school counseling programs. Counselor education programs with a specialty area in school counseling must document where each of the lettered standards listed below is covered in the curriculum.

1. FOUNDATIONS
   a. history and development of school counseling
   b. models of school counseling programs
   c. models of P-12 comprehensive career development
   d. models of school-based collaboration and consultation
   e. assessments specific to P-12 education

2. CONTEXTUAL DIMENSIONS
   a. school counselor roles as leaders, advocates, and systems change agents in P-12 schools
   b. school counselor roles in consultation with families, P-12 and postsecondary school personnel, and community agencies
   c. school counselor roles in relation to college and career readiness
   d. school counselor roles in school leadership and multidisciplinary teams
   e. school counselor roles and responsibilities in relation to the school emergency management plans, and crises, disasters, and trauma
   f. competencies to advocate for school counseling roles
   g. characteristics, risk factors, and warning signs of students at risk for mental health and behavioral disorders
   h. common medications that affect learning, behavior, and mood in children and adolescents

      i.   signs and symptoms of substance abuse in children and adolescents as well as the signs and symptoms of living in a home where substance use occurs

      j.   qualities and styles of effective leadership in schools

      k.   community resources and referral sources

      l.   professional organizations, preparation standards, and credentials relevant to the practice of school counseling

      m.   legislation and government policy relevant to school counseling

      n.   legal and ethical considerations specific to school counseling

3.   PRACTICE

      a.   development of school counseling program mission statements and objectives

      b.   design and evaluation of school counseling programs

      c.   core curriculum design, lesson plan development, classroom management strategies, and differentiated instructional strategies

      d.   interventions to promote academic development

      e.   use of developmentally appropriate career counseling interventions and assessments

      f.   techniques of personal/social counseling in school settings

      g.   strategies to facilitate school and postsecondary transitions

      h.   skills to critically examine the connections between social, familial, emotional, and behavior problems and academic achievement

      i.   approaches to increase promotion and graduation rates

      j.   interventions to promote college and career readiness

      k.   strategies to promote equity in student achievement and college access

      l.   techniques to foster collaboration and teamwork within schools

      m.   strategies for implementing and coordinating peer intervention programs

      n.   use of accountability data to inform decision making

      o.   use of data to advocate for programs and students

Appendix B

Reprinted with permission from ASCA/Kathleen Rakestraw

ASCA Mindsets & Behaviors for Student Success:
K-12 College- and Career-Readiness Standards for Every Student

The ASCA Mindsets & Behaviors for Student Success: K-12 College- and Career Readiness for Every Student describe the knowledge, skills and attitudes students need to achieve academic success, college and career readiness and social/emotional development. The standards are based on a survey of research and best practices in student achievement from a wide array of educational standards and efforts. These standards are the next generation of the ASCA National Standards for Students, which were first published in 1997.

The 35 mindset and behavior standards identify and prioritize the specific attitudes, knowledge and skills students should be able to demonstrate as a result of a school counseling program. School counselors use the standards to assess student growth and development, guide the development of strategies and activities and create a program that helps students achieve their highest potential. The ASCA Mindsets & Behaviors can be aligned with initiatives at the district, state and national to reflect the district's local priorities.

To operationalize the standards, school counselors select competencies that align with the specific standards and become the foundation for classroom lessons, small groups and activities addressing student developmental needs. The competencies directly reflect the vision, mission and goals of the comprehensive school counseling program and align with the school's academic mission.

Research-Based Standards
The ASCA Mindsets & Behaviors are based on a review of research and college- and career-readiness documents created by a variety of organizations that have identified strategies making an impact on student achievement and academic performance. The ASCA Mindsets & Behaviors are organized based on the framework of noncognitive factors presented in the critical literature review "Teaching Adolescents to Become Learners" conducted by the University of Chicago Consortium on Chicago School Research (2012).

This literature review recognizes that content knowledge and academic skills are only part of the equation for student success. "School performance is a complex phenomenon, shaped by a wide variety of factors intrinsic to students and the external environment" (University of Chicago, 2012, p. 2). The ASCA Mindsets & Behaviors are based on the evidence of the importance of these factors.

Organization of the ASCA Mindsets & Behaviors
The ASCA Mindsets & Behaviors are organized by domains, standards arranged within categories and subcategories and grade-level competencies. Each is described below.

Domains
The ASCA Mindsets & Behaviors are organized in three broad domains: academic, career and social/emotional development. These domains promote mindsets and behaviors that enhance the learning process and create a culture of college and career readiness for all students. The definitions of each domain are as follows:

Academic Development – Standards guiding school counseling programs to implement strategies and activities to support and maximize each student's ability to learn.

Career Development – Standards guiding school counseling programs to help students 1) understand the connection between school and the world of work and 2) plan for and make a successful transition from school to postsecondary education and/or the world of work and from job to job across the life span.

Social/Emotional Development – Standards guiding school counseling programs to help students manage emotions and learn and apply interpersonal skills.

Standards
All 35 standards can be applied to any of the three domains, and the school counselor selects a domain and standard based on the needs of the school, classroom, small group or individual. The standards are arranged within categories and subcategories based on five general categories of noncognitive factors related to academic performance as identified in the 2012 literature review published by the University of Chicago Consortium on Chicago School Research. These categories synthesize the "vast array of research literature" (p. 8) on noncognitive factors including persistence, resilience, grit, goal-setting, help-seeking, cooperation, conscientiousness, self-efficacy, self-regulation, self-control, self-discipline, motivation, mindsets, effort, work habits, organization, homework completion, learning strategies and study skills, among others.

Category 1: Mindset Standards – Includes standards related to the psycho-social attitudes or beliefs students have about themselves in relation to academic work. These make up the students' belief system as exhibited in behaviors.

Category 2: Behavior Standards – These standards include behaviors commonly associated with being a successful student. These behaviors are visible, outward signs that a student is engaged and putting forth effort to learn. The behaviors are grouped into three subcategories.

a. Learning Strategies: Processes and tactics students employ to aid in the cognitive work of thinking, remembering or learning.

b. Self-management Skills: Continued focus on a goal despite obstacles (grit or persistence) and avoidance of distractions or temptations to prioritize higher pursuits over lower pleasures (delayed gratification, self-discipline, self-control).

c. Social Skills: Acceptable behaviors that improve social interactions, such as those between peers or between students and adults.

The ASCA Mindsets & Behaviors for Student Success: K-12 College- and Career-Readiness Standards for Every Student

Each of the following standards can be applied to the academic, career and social/emotional domains.

Category 1: Mindset Standards
School counselors encourage the following mindsets for all students.

1. Belief in development of whole self, including a healthy balance of mental, social/emotional and physical well-being
2. Self-confidence in ability to succeed
3. Sense of belonging in the school environment
4. Understanding that postsecondary education and life-long learning are necessary for long-term career success
5. Belief in using abilities to their fullest to achieve high-quality results and outcomes
6. Positive attitude toward work and learning

Category 2: Behavior Standards
Students will demonstrate the following standards through classroom lessons, activities and/or individual/small-group counseling.

Learning Strategies	Self-Management Skills	Social Skills
1. Demonstrate critical-thinking skills to make informed decisions	1. Demonstrate ability to assume responsibility	1. Use effective oral and written communication skills and listening skills
2. Demonstrate creativity	2. Demonstrate self-discipline and self-control	2. Create positive and supportive relationships with other students
3. Use time-management, organizational and study skills	3. Demonstrate ability to work independently	3. Create relationships with adults that support success
4. Apply self-motivation and self-direction to learning	4. Demonstrate ability to delay immediate gratification for long-term rewards	4. Demonstrate empathy
5. Apply media and technology skills	5. Demonstrate perseverance to achieve long- and short-term goals	5. Demonstrate ethical decision-making and social responsibility
6. Set high standards of quality	6. Demonstrate ability to overcome barriers to learning	6. Use effective collaboration and cooperation skills
7. Identify long- and short-term academic, career and social/emotional goals	7. Demonstrate effective coping skills when faced with a problem	7. Use leadership and teamwork skills to work effectively in diverse teams
8. Actively engage in challenging coursework	8. Demonstrate the ability to balance school, home and community activities	8. Demonstrate advocacy skills and ability to assert self, when necessary
9. Gather evidence and consider multiple perspectives to make informed decisions	9. Demonstrate personal safety skills	9. Demonstrate social maturity and behaviors appropriate to the situation and environment
10. Participate in enrichment and extracurricular activities	10. Demonstrate ability to manage transitions and ability to adapt to changing situations and responsibilities	

Grade-Level Competencies

Grade-level competencies are specific, measurable expectations that students attain as they make progress toward the standards. As the school counseling program's vision, mission and program goals are aligned with the school's academic mission, school counseling standards and competencies are also aligned with academic content standards at the state and district level.

ASCA Mindsets & Behaviors align with specific standards from the Common Core State Standards through connections at the competency level. This alignment allows school counselors the opportunity to help students meet these college- and career-readiness standards in collaboration with academic content taught in core areas in the classroom. It also helps school counselors directly align with academic instruction when providing individual and small-group counseling by focusing on standards and competencies addressing a student's developmental needs. School counselors working in states that have not adopted the Common Core State Standards are encouraged to align competencies with their state's academic standards and can use the competencies from the ASCA Mindsets & Behaviors as examples of alignment.

ASCA Mindsets & Behaviors Database

The grade-level competencies are housed in the ASCA Mindsets & Behaviors database at *www.schoolcounselor.org/studentcompetencies*. School counselors can search the database by keyword to quickly and easily identify competencies that will meet student developmental needs and align with academic content as appropriate. The database also allows school counselors to contribute to the competencies by sharing other ways to meet or align with a specific standard.

Citation Guide

When citing from this publication, use the following reference:

American School Counselor Association (2014). *Mindsets and Behaviors for Student Success: K-12 College- and Career-Readiness Standards for Every Student*. Alexandria, VA: Author.

Resources Used in Development of ASCA Mindsets & Behaviors

The following documents were the primary resources that informed ASCA Mindsets & Behaviors.

Document	Organization	Description
ACT National Career Readiness Certificate	ACT	Offers a portable credential that demonstrates achievement and a certain level of workplace employability skills in applied mathematics, locating information and reading for information.
ASCA National Standards for Students	American School Counselor Association	Describes the knowledge, attitudes and skills students should be able to demonstrate as a result of the school counseling program.
AVID Essentials at a Glance	AVID	Promotes a college readiness system for elementary through higher education that is designed to increase schoolwide learning and performance.
Building Blocks For Change: What it Means to be Career Ready	Career Readiness Partner Council	Defines what it means to be career-ready, and highlights the outcome of collaborative efforts of the Career Readiness Partner Council to help inform policy and practice in states and communities.
Career and Technical Education Standards	National Board of Professional Teaching Standards	Defines the standards that lay the foundation for the Career and Technical Education Certificate.
Collaborative Counselor Training Initiative	SREB	Offers online training modules for middle grades and high school counselors that can improve their effectiveness in preparing all students for college, especially those from low-income families who would be first-generation college students.
Cross Disciplinary Proficiencies in the American Diploma Project	Achieve	Describes four cross disciplinary proficiencies that will enable high school graduates to meet new and unfamiliar tasks and challenges in college, the workplace and life.
Eight Components of College and Career Readiness Counseling	College Board	Presents a comprehensive, systemic approach for school counselors to use to inspire and prepare all students for college success and opportunity, especially students from underrepresented populations.
English Language Arts Standards	National Board of Professional Teaching Standards	Defines the standards that lay the foundation for the English Language Arts Certificate.
Framework for 21st Century Learning	Partnership for 21st Century Skills	Describes the skills, knowledge and expertise students must master to succeed in work and life; it is a blend of content knowledge, specific skills, expertise and literacies.
NETS for Students 2007	International Society for Technology in Education	Describes the standards for evaluating the skills and knowledge students need to learn effectively and live productively in an increasingly global and digital world.
Ramp-Up to Readiness	University of Minnesota	Provides a schoolwide guidance program designed to increase the number and diversity of students who graduate from high school with the knowledge, skills and habits necessary for success in a high-quality college program.
Social and Emotional Learning Core Competencies	CASEL	Identifies five interrelated sets of cognitive, affective and behavioral competencies through which children and adults acquire and effectively apply the knowledge, attitudes and skills necessary to understand and manage emotions, set and achieve positive goals, feel and show empathy for others, establish and maintain positive relationships and make responsible decisions.
Teaching Adolescents to Become Learners: The Role of Non-Cognitive Factors in Shaping School Performance	The University of Chicago Consortium on Chicago School Research	Presents a critical literature review of the role of noncognitive factors in shaping school performance.
What is "Career Ready"?	ACTE	Defines what it means to be career-ready, involving three major skill areas: core academic skills, employability skills, and technical and job-specific skills.

Appendix C

MULTICULTURAL AND SOCIAL JUSTICE COUNSELING COMPETENCIES

Developed by
The Multicultural Counseling Competencies Revisions Committee:
Dr. Manivong J. Ratts, chair (Seattle University)
Dr. Anneliese A. Singh (University of Georgia)
Dr. Sylvia Nassar-McMillan (North Carolina State University),
Dr. S. Kent Butler (University of Central Florida)
Julian Rafferty McCullough (Georgia State University)

Appointed by
Dr. Carlos Hipolito-Delgado
President, Association for Multicultural Counseling and Development (2014–2015)

Endorsed on June 29, 2015 by
Association for Multicultural Counseling and Development Executive Council
A Division of the American Counseling Association

Endorsed on July 20, 2015 by
American Counseling Association Governing Council

MULTICULTURAL AND SOCIAL JUSTICE COUNSELING COMPETENCIES

The Multicultural and Social Justice Counseling Competencies (MSJCC), which revises the Multicultural Counseling Competencies and Standards developed by Sue, Arredondo, and McDavis (1992) offers counselors a framework to implement multicultural and social justice competencies into counseling theories, practices, and research. A conceptual framework (see Figure 1 on routledge.com/foxx for the MSJCC framework) of the MSJCC is provided to illustrate a visual map of the relationship between the constructs and competencies being articulated within the MSJCC. Moreover, quadrants are used to highlight the intersection of identities and the dynamics of power, privilege, and oppression that influence the counseling relationship. Developmental domains reflect the different layers that lead to multicultural and social justice competence: (1) counselor self-awareness, (2) client worldview, (3) counseling relationship, and (d) counseling and advocacy interventions. Embedded within the first three developmental domains of the MSJCC are the following aspirational competencies: attitudes and beliefs, knowledge, skills, and action. The socioecological model is incorporated within the counseling and advocacy interventions domain to provide counselors a multilevel framework for individual counseling and social justice advocacy.

MULTICULTURAL AND SOCIAL JUSTICE COUNSELING COMPETENCIES

I. COUNSELOR SELF-AWARENESS

Privileged and marginalized counselors develop self-awareness, so that they may explore their attitudes and beliefs, develop knowledge, skills, and action relative to their self-awareness and worldview.

1. *Attitudes and beliefs*: Privileged and marginalized counselors are aware of their social identities, social group statuses, power, privilege, oppression, strengths, limitations, assumptions, attitudes, values, beliefs, and biases.

   Multicultural and social justice competent counselors:
   - Acknowledge their assumptions, worldviews, values, beliefs, and biases as members of privileged and marginalized groups;
   - Acknowledge their privileged and marginalized status in society;
   - Acknowledge their privileged and marginalized status influences their worldview;
   - Acknowledge their privileged and marginalized status provides advantages and disadvantages in society;
   - Acknowledge openness to learning about their cultural background as well as their privileged and marginalized status.

2. *Knowledge*: Privileged and marginalized counselors possess an understanding of their social identities, social group statuses, power, privilege, oppression, strengths, limitations, assumptions, attitudes, values, beliefs, and biases.

Multicultural and social justice competent counselors:

- Develop knowledge of resources to become aware of their assumptions, worldviews, values, beliefs, biases, and privileged and marginalized status;
- Develop knowledge about the history and events that shape their privileged and marginalized status;
- Develop knowledge of theories that explain how their privileged and marginalized status influences their experiences and worldview;
- Develop knowledge of how their privileged and marginalized status leads to advantages and disadvantages in society.

3. *Skills*: Privileged and marginalized counselors possess skills that enrich their understanding of their social identities, social group statuses, power, privilege, oppression, limitations, assumptions, attitudes, values, beliefs, and biases.

Multicultural and social justice competent counselors:

- Acquire reflective and critical thinking skills to gain insight into their assumptions, worldviews, values, beliefs, biases, and privileged and marginalized status;
- Acquire communication skills to explain how their privileged and marginalized status influences their worldview and experiences;
- Acquire application skills to interpret knowledge of their privileged and marginalized status in personal and professional settings;
- Acquire analytical skills to compare and contrast their privileged and marginalized status and experiences to others;
- Acquire evaluation skills to assess the degree to which their privileged and marginalized status influences their personal and professional experiences.

4. *Action*: Privileged and marginalized counselors take action to increase self-awareness of their social identities, social group statuses, power, privilege, oppression, strengths, limitations, assumptions, attitudes, values, beliefs, and biases.

Multicultural and social justice competent counselors:

- Take action to learn about their assumptions, worldviews, values, beliefs, biases, and culture as a member of a privileged and marginalized group;
- Take action to seek out professional development opportunities to learn more about themselves as a member of a privileged or marginalized group;

- Take action to immerse themselves in their community to learn about how power, privilege, and oppression influence their privileged and marginalized experiences;
- Take action to learn about how their communication style is influenced by their privileged and marginalized status.

II. CLIENT WORLDVIEW

Privileged and marginalized counselors are aware, knowledgeable, skilled, and action oriented in understanding clients' worldview.

1. *Attitudes and beliefs*: Privileged and marginalized counselors are aware of clients' worldview, assumptions, attitudes, values, beliefs, biases, social identities, social group statuses, and experiences with power, privilege, and oppression.

    Multicultural and social justice competent counselors:
    - Acknowledge a need to possess a curiosity for privileged and marginalized clients' history, worldview, cultural background, values, beliefs, biases, and experiences;
    - Acknowledge that identity development influences the worldviews and lived experiences of privileged and marginalized clients;
    - Acknowledge their strengths and limitations in working with clients from privileged and marginalized groups;
    - Acknowledge that learning about privileged and marginalized clients may sometimes be an uncomfortable or unfamiliar experience;
    - Acknowledge that learning about clients' privileged and marginalized status is a lifelong endeavor;
    - Acknowledge the importance of reflecting on the attitudes, beliefs, prejudices, and biases they hold about privileged and marginalized clients;
    - Acknowledge that there are within-group differences and between-group similarities and differences among privileged and marginalized clients;
    - Acknowledge clients' communication style is influenced by their privileged and marginalized status.

2. *Knowledge*: Privileged and marginalized counselors possess knowledge of clients' worldview, assumptions, attitudes, values, beliefs, biases, social identities, social group statuses, and experiences with power, privilege, and oppression.

    Multicultural and social justice competent counselors:
    - Develop knowledge of historical events and current issues that shape the worldview, cultural background, values, beliefs, biases, and experiences of privileged and marginalized clients;

- Develop knowledge of how stereotypes, discrimination, power, privilege, and oppression influence privileged and marginalized clients;
- Develop knowledge of multicultural and social justice theories, identity development models, and research pertaining to the worldview, culture, and life experiences of privileged and marginalized clients;
- Develop knowledge of their strengths and limitations in working with clients from privileged and marginalized groups;
- Develop knowledge of how to work through the discomfort that comes with learning about privileged and marginalized clients;
- Develop a lifelong plan to acquire knowledge of clients' privileged and marginalized status;
- Develop knowledge of the attitudes, beliefs, prejudices, and biases they hold about privileged and marginalized clients;
- Develop knowledge of the individual, group, and universal dimensions of human existence of their privileged and marginalized clients;
- Develop knowledge of the communication style of their privileged and marginalized client (e.g., high context vs. low context communication, eye contact, orientation to time and space).

3. *Skills*: Privileged and marginalized counselors possess skills that enrich their understanding of clients' worldview, assumptions, attitudes, values, beliefs, biases, social identities, social group statuses, and experiences with power, privilege, and oppression.

    Multicultural and social justice competent counselors:
    - Acquire culturally responsive evaluation skills to analyze how historical events and current issues shape the worldview, cultural background, values, beliefs, biases, and experiences of privileged and marginalized clients;
    - Acquire culturally responsive critical thinking skills to gain insight into how stereotypes, discrimination, power, privilege, and oppression influence privileged and marginalized clients;
    - Acquire culturally responsive application skills to apply knowledge of multicultural and social justice theories, identity development models, and research to one's work with privileged and marginalized clients;
    - Acquire culturally responsive assessment skills to identify limitations and strengths when working with privileged and marginalized clients;
    - Acquire culturally responsive reflection skills needed to work through the discomfort that comes with learning about privileged and marginalized clients;
    - Acquire culturally responsive conceptualization skills to explain how clients' privileged and marginalized status influence their culture, worldview, experiences, and presenting problem;

- Acquire culturally responsive analytical skills to interpret the attitudes, beliefs, prejudices, and biases they hold about privileged and marginalized clients;
- Acquire culturally responsive conceptualization skills to identify the individual, group, and universal dimensions of human existence of privileged and marginalized clients;
- Acquire culturally responsive cross-cultural communication skills to interact with privileged and marginalized clients.

4.   *Action*: Privileged and marginalized counselors take action to increase self-awareness of clients' worldview, assumptions, attitudes, values, beliefs, biases, social identities, social group statuses, and experiences with power, privilege, and oppression.

Multicultural and social justice competent counselors:

- Take action by seeking out formal and informal opportunities to engage in discourse about historical events and current issues that shape the worldview, cultural background, values, beliefs, biases, and experiences of privileged and marginalized clients;
- Take action by attending professional development trainings to learn how stereotypes, discrimination, power, privilege, and oppression influence privileged and marginalized clients;
- Take action by applying multicultural and social justice theories, identity development models, and research to one's work with privileged and marginalized clients;
- Take action by assessing one's limitations and strengths when working with privileged and marginalized clients on a consistent basis;
- Take action by immersing oneself in the communities in which privileged and marginalized clients reside to work through the discomfort that comes with learning about privileged and marginalized clients;
- Take action by using language to explain how clients' privileged and marginalized status influence their culture, worldview, experiences, and presenting problem;
- Take action by pursuing culturally responsive counseling to explore the attitudes, beliefs, prejudices, and biases they hold about privileged and marginalized clients;
- Take action by collaborating with clients to identify the individual, group, and universal dimensions of human existence that shape the identities of privileged and marginalized clients;
- Take action by consistently demonstrating cross-cultural communication skills required to effectively interact with privileged and marginalized clients.

III. COUNSELING RELATIONSHIP

Privileged and marginalized counselors are aware, knowledgeable, skilled, and action oriented in understanding how client and counselor privileged and marginalized statuses influence the counseling relationship.

1. *Attitudes and beliefs*: Privileged and marginalized counselors are aware of how client and counselor worldviews, assumptions, attitudes, values, beliefs, biases, social identities, social group statuses, and experiences with power, privilege, and oppression influence the counseling relationship.

    Multicultural and social justice competent counselors:
    - Acknowledge that the worldviews, values, beliefs and biases held by privileged and marginalized counselors and clients will positively or negatively influence the counseling relationship;
    - Acknowledge that counselor and client identity development shapes the counseling relationship to varying degrees for privileged and marginalized clients;
    - Acknowledge that the privileged and marginalized status of counselors and clients will influence the counseling relationship to varying degrees;
    - Acknowledge that culture, stereotypes, discrimination, power, privilege, and oppression influence the counseling relationship with privileged and marginalized group clients;
    - Acknowledge that the counseling relationship may extend beyond the traditional office setting and into the community;
    - Acknowledge that cross-cultural communication is key to connecting with privileged and marginalized clients.

2. *Knowledge*: Privileged and marginalized counselors possess knowledge of how client and counselor worldviews, assumptions, attitudes, values, beliefs, biases, social identities, social group statuses, and experiences with power, privilege, and oppression influence the counseling relationship.

    Multicultural and social justice competent counselors:
    - Develop knowledge of the worldviews, values, beliefs and biases held by privileged and marginalized counselors and clients and its influence on the counseling relationship;
    - Develop knowledge of identity development theories and how they influence the counseling relationship with privileged and marginalized clients;
    - Develop knowledge of theories explaining how counselor and clients' privileged and marginalized statuses influence the counseling relationship;

- Develop knowledge of how culture, stereotypes, discrimination, power, privilege, and oppression strengthen and hinder the counseling relationship with privileged and marginalized clients;
- Develop knowledge of when to use individual counseling and when to use systems advocacy with privileged and marginalized clients;
- Develop knowledge of cross-cultural communication theories when working with privileged and marginalized clients.

3. *Skills*: Privileged and marginalized counselors possess skills to engage in discussions with clients about how client and counselor worldviews, assumptions, attitudes, values, beliefs, biases, social identities, social group statuses, power, privilege, and oppression influence the counseling relationship.

Multicultural and social justice competent counselors:
- Acquire assessment skills to determine how the worldviews, values, beliefs and biases held by privileged and marginalized counselors and clients influence the counseling relationship;
- Acquire analytical skills to identify how the identity development of counselors and clients influence the counseling relationship;
- Acquire application skills to apply knowledge of theories explaining how counselor and clients' privileged and marginalized statuses influence the counseling relationship;
- Acquire assessment skills regarding how culture, stereotypes, prejudice, discrimination, power, privilege, and oppression influence the counseling relationship with privileged and marginalized clients;
- Acquire evaluation skills to determine when individual counseling or systems advocacy is needed with privileged and marginalized clients;
- Acquire cross-cultural communication skills to connect with privileged and marginalized clients.

4. *Action*: Privileged and marginalized counselors take action to increase their understanding of how client and counselor worldviews, assumptions, attitudes, values, beliefs, biases, social identities, social group statuses, and experiences with power, privilege, and oppression influence the counseling relationship.

Multicultural and social justice competent counselors:
- Take action by initiating conversations to determine how the worldviews, values, beliefs and biases held by privileged and marginalized counselors and clients influence the counseling relationship;
- Take action by collaborating with clients to identify the ways that privileged and marginalized counselor and client identity development influence the counseling relationship;

- Take action by exploring how counselor and clients' privileged and marginalized statuses influence the counseling relationship;
- Take action by inviting conversations about how culture, stereotypes, prejudice, discrimination, power, privilege, and oppression influence the counseling relationship with privileged and marginalized clients;
- Take action by collaborating with clients to determine whether individual counseling or systems advocacy is needed with privileged and marginalized clients;
- Take action by using cross-communication skills to connect with privileged and marginalized clients.

IV. COUNSELING AND ADVOCACY INTERVENTIONS

Privileged and marginalized counselors intervene with, and on behalf of, clients at the intrapersonal, interpersonal, institutional, community, public policy, and international/global levels.

A.   Intrapersonal: The individual characteristics of a person such as knowledge, attitudes, behavior, self-concept, skills, and developmental history.

Intrapersonal Interventions: Privileged and marginalized counselors address the intrapersonal processes that impact privileged and marginalized clients.

Multicultural and social justice competent counselors:
- Employ empowerment-based theories to address internalized privilege experienced by privileged clients and internalized oppression experienced by marginalized clients;
- Assist privileged and marginalized clients develop critical consciousness by understanding their situation in context of living in an oppressive society;
- Assist privileged and marginalized clients in unlearning their privilege and oppression;
- Assess the degree to which historical events, current issues, and power, privilege and oppression contribute to the presenting problems expressed by privileged and marginalized clients;
- Work in communities to better understand the attitudes, beliefs, prejudices, and biases held by privileged and marginalized clients;
- Assist privileged and marginalized clients with developing self-advocacy skills that promote multiculturalism and social justice;
- Employ quantitative and qualitative research to highlight inequities present in current counseling literature and practices in order to advocate for systemic changes to the profession.

B.   Interpersonal: The interpersonal processes and/or groups that provide individuals with identity and support (i.e., family, friends, and peers).

Interpersonal Interventions: Privileged and marginalized counselors address the interpersonal processes that affect privileged and marginalized clients.

Multicultural and social justice competent counselors:

- Employ advocacy to address the historical events and persons that shape and influence privileged and marginalized client's developmental history;

- Examine the relationships privileged and marginalized clients have with family, friends, and peers that may be sources of support or nonsupport;

- Assist privileged and marginalized clients understand that the relationships they have with others may be influenced by their privileged and marginalized status;

- Assist privileged and marginalized clients with fostering relationships with family, friends, and peers from the same privileged and marginalized group;

- Reach out to collaborate with family, friends, and peers who will be a source of support for privileged and marginalized clients;

- Assist privileged and marginalized clients in developing communication skills to discuss issues of power, privilege, and oppression with family, friends, peers, and colleagues;

- Employ evidenced-based interventions that align with the cultural background and worldview of privileged and marginalized clients.

C.   Institutional: Represents the social institutions in society such as schools, churches, and community organizations.

Institutional Interventions: Privileged and marginalized counselors address inequities at the institutional level.

Multicultural and social justice competent counselors:

- Explore with privileged and marginalized clients the extent to which social institutions are supportive;

- Connect privileged and marginalized clients with supportive individuals within social institutions (e.g., schools, businesses, church) who are able to help alter inequities influencing marginalized clients;

- Collaborate with social institutions to address issues of power, privilege, and oppression impacting privilege and marginalized clients;

- Employ social advocacy to remove systemic barriers experienced by marginalized clients within social institutions;

- Employ social advocacy to remove systemic barriers that promote privilege that benefit privileged clients;

- Balance individual counseling with systems-level social advocacy to address inequities that social institutions create that impede on human growth and development;

- Conduct multicultural and social justice–based research to highlight the inequities that social institutions have on marginalized clients and that benefit privileged clients.

D. Community: The community as a whole represents the spoken and unspoken norms, value, and regulations that are embedded in society. The norms, values, and regulations of a community may either be empowering or oppressive to human growth and development.

Community Interventions: Privileged and marginalized address community norms, values, and regulations that impede on the development of individuals, groups, and communities.

Multicultural and social justice competent counselors:

- Take initiative to explore with privileged and marginalized clients regarding how community norms, values, and regulations embedded in society that hinder and contribute to their growth and development;

- Conduct qualitative and quantitative research to evaluate the degree to which community norms, values, and regulations influence privileged and marginalized clients;

- Employ social advocacy to address community norms, values, and regulations embedded in society that hinder the growth and development of privileged and marginalized clients;

- Use the norms, values, and regulations of the marginalized client to shape the community norms, values, and regulations of the privileged client.

E. Public Policy: Public policy reflects the local, state, and federal laws and policies that regulate or influence client human growth and development.

Public Policy Interventions: Privileged and marginalized counselors address public policy issues that impede on client development with, and on behalf of, clients.

Multicultural and social justice competent counselors:

- Initiate discussions with privileged and marginalized clients regarding how they shape and are shaped by local, state, and federal laws and policies;

- Conduct research to examine how local, state, and federal laws and policies contribute to or hinder the growth and development of privileged and marginalized clients;

- Engage in social action to alter the local, state, and federal laws and policies that benefit privileged clients at the expense of marginalized clients;

- Employ social advocacy to ensure that local, state, and federal laws and policies are equitable toward privileged and marginalized clients;
- Employ social advocacy outside the office setting to address local, state, and federal laws and policies that hinder equitable access to employment, health care, and education for privileged and marginalized clients;
- Assist with creating local, state, and federal laws and policies that promote multiculturalism and social justice;
- Seek out opportunities to collaborate with privileged and marginalized clients to shape local, state, and federal laws and policies.

F.   International and Global Affairs: International and global concerns reflect the events, affairs, and policies that influence psychological health and well-being.

International and Global Affairs Interventions: Privileged and marginalized counselors address international and global events, affairs, and polices that impede on client development with, and on behalf of, clients.

Multicultural and social justice competent counselors:

- Stay current on international and world politics and events;
- Seek out professional development to learn about how privileged and marginalized clients influence, and are influenced by, international and global affairs;
- Acquire knowledge of historical and current international and global affairs that are supportive and unsupportive of privileged and marginalized clients;
- Learn about the global politics, policies, laws, and theories that influence privileged and marginalized clients;
- Use technology to interact and collaborate with international and global leaders on issues influencing privileged and marginalized clients;
- Take initiative to address international and global affairs to promote multicultural and social justice issues;
- Use research to examine how international and global affairs impact privileged and marginalized clients.

REFERENCES

APPENDIX A

Council for Accreditation of Counseling & Related Educational Programs. (2015). *2016 CACREP Standards: Section 5-G: Entry-level specialty areas—School counseling*. Retrieved from http://www.cacrep.org/section-5-entry-level-specialty-areas-school-counseling/

APPENDIX B

American School Counselor Association. (2014). *Mindsets & behaviors for student success: K-12 college- and career-readiness standards for every student*. Alexandria, VA: Author.

APPENDIX C

Ratts, M. J., Singh, A. A., Nassar-McMillan, S., Butler, K. S., & McCullough, J. R. (2015). *Multicultural and social justice counseling competencies*. Retrieved from http://www.counseling.org/docs/default-source/competencies/multicultural-and-social-justice-counseling-competencies.pdf?sfvrsn=20

Sue, D. W., Arredondo, P., & McDavis, R. J. (1992). Multicultural counseling competencies and standards: A call to the profession. *Journal of Counseling & Development, 70,* 477–486.

AUTHOR INDEX

SUBJECT INDEX